The Law of International Trade

The Law of International Trade

by

Ademuni-Odeke

BLACKSTONE
PRESS LIMITED

First published in Great Britain 1999 by Blackstone Press Limited, Aldine Place, London W12 8AA. Telephone: (020) 8740 2277
www.blackstonepress.com

© Ademuni-Odeke, 1999

ISBN: 1 85431 937 X

British Library Cataloguing in Publication Data
A CIP catalogue record for this book is available from the British Library

Typeset by Montage Studios Limited, Horsmonden, Kent
Printed by Ashford Colour Press, Gosport, Hants

Contents

1.1 Introduction   1.2 Mercantilism and international trade   1.3 Why international trade? The theory of comparative advantage   1.4 Patterns of international trade   1.5 State participation and intervention in international trade   1.6 Countertrade   1.7 Commodity and futures   1.8 Preshipment inspection   1.9 Sources and development of the law   1.10 Development of the main terms and principles   1.11 Panoramic view of international sales

2.1 A contract of sale   2.2 Conditions and warranties   2.3 Implied terms   2.4 Exclusion clauses   2.5 The passing of property   2.6 The *'nemo dat quod non habet'* rule   2.7 Initial impossibility, risk and

freight   7.8 Rights of the unpaid shipowner   7.9 Guarantee of payments for freights

8   The Hague-Visby and Hamburg Rules

8.1 Common law liability of the carrier   8.2 The Hague-Visby Rules   8.3 Application of the COGSA 1971 and the Hague-Visby Rules   8.4 The stage when the rules begin to apply   8.5 Seaworthiness: Art. III r. 1   8.6 The second obligation: Art. III r. 2   8.7 The exemptions   8.8 The duty of the carrier to issue a bill of lading: Art. III r. 3   8.9 Contracts of indemnity   8.10 Time limit: Art. III r. 6   8.11 Availability of an action in tort   8.12 Limitation of liability   8.13 The contract of carriage and third parties   8.14 Countries applying the Hague-Visby Rules   8.15 Countries applying the Hague Rules   8.16 The Merchant Shipping Acts   8.17 The Hamburg Rules   8.18 Limit of liability for maritime claims

9   Carriage of Goods by Air, Land and Multimodal Transport

9.1 Introduction   9.2 Carriage of goods by air   9.3 Carriage of goods by road   9.4 Carriage of goods by railway   9.5 Carriage of goods by combined transport

Further reading for Part III

Part IV   Payments and Finance in International Trade

10   Payments in International Trade

10.1 Introduction   *Part 1 Direct Methods of Payment*   10.2 Cash and direct means of payment   10.3 Novation   10.4 Assignment of the debt   *Part 2 Bills of Exchange*   10.5 Introduction   10.6 The statutory definition   10.7 Computation of time in bills of exchange   10.8 The date of the bill   10.9 The fictitious or non-existing payee   10.10 Transfer   10.11 Acceptance   10.12 Liabilities of the parties   10.13 Exclusion of liability   10.14 The holder   10.15 The rights of a holder   10.16 The forged signature   10.17 Prerequisites for enforcement   10.18 Remedies for dishonour and the form of action   10.19 Cheques

11   Finance in International Trade

11.1 Introduction   11.2 The Uniform Customs and Practice for Documentary Credits (UCP)   11.3 The parties   11.4 Types of credit   11.5 The mandate   11.6 Taking up the seller's documents   11.7 The autonomy of

16   Arbitration and Dispute Settlement

16.1 Introduction   16.2 Types of arbitration   16.3 The law governing the arbitration   16.4 The jurisdiction of the arbitrator   16.5 History of arbitration legislation   16.6 The Arbitration Act 1996   16.7 Stay of proceedings   16.8 Enforcement of the award

Further reading for Part VI

Preface

This book deals with export or international trade: goods and services supplied for reward to persons in other countries for which payment is generally due in the currency of the supplier. The contract obliges the seller to supply the goods and the ship and sometimes to insure them and the contract obliges the purchaser to make arrangements in that currency to the immediate benefit of the vendor and the immediate benefit of both countries. The book does not, however, deal with the wider public aspects of international trade which includes international economic laws. International trade is also classified as visible or invisible, the former being goods and the latter being services such as banking, shipping, insurance. The book concentrates on the former. To perform their obligations in international trade, the seller and buyer will between them have entered into five principal contracts, i.e., of sale, insurance, carriage, financing and dispute settlement (arbitration). There will be numerous ancillary contracts involving, e.g., agents, brokers, guarantors, forwarders, etc. The book deals directly with the five principal contracts and only indirectly with the ancillary ones.

There are three aims to this book. The first is to make the reader aware that international trade is a living, practical and growing subject. Whenever we purchase or consume a foreign product, little do we appreciate the intricacies of the process that has brought it to our market, living room or table. A long chain which made it possible will have involved, e.g., farmers, factory workers, industrialists, merchants, insurers, shippers, carriers, bankers, financiers, lawyers, brokers, forwarding agents, etc. Because of the global nature of international trade and the time difference between different nations, even as the reader is opening the pages of this book cargo ships, lorries, trains, aircraft, telephone messages, faxes, telexes, mail and e-mails are criss-crossing the world's oceans, borders, landmasses, airways, airwaves and seas in an effort to win orders and/or perform contracts of international sales.

The second aim is to provide literature on the subject, but with a particular focus. Until the last few decades, international trade in the UK was not taught formally in law schools. Rather it was learnt by experience through work in legal practice, banking, insurance, shipping and commercial practice. However, the subject is now an established part of undergraduate and graduate teaching and research syllabuses. It is also in the last few decades that increasing numbers of academic and professional guides and text books have been published which have helped to popularise the subject for, especially, law and business studies. Moreover, the earlier publications such as Schmitthoff's *Export Trade*, Benjamin's *Sale of Goods* and Sassoon's *CIF and FOB Contracts* have tended to be rather specialised, expensive and beyond the financial reach of many readers. At the other end of the spectrum there have been lower quality books which did this important subject a disservice.

The third aim of this book is, therefore, to fill that yawning gap between the two extremes by providing an affordable, yet respectable, source of literature. The book is aimed at both students and practitioners, insurers, bankers, merchants, carriers, agents, brokers and managers. The book aims to put international trade in perspective and emphasises the links between the contract of sale and related contracts.

In writing the book I have drawn on my own practical work experience in legal practice, merchant banking, merchant shipping, port administration and export trade, as well as in nearly two decades of teaching and research, acting as a consultant to governments and the United Nations, and a long association with the Institute of Export in London, the Southampton Chamber of Commerce and the UK National Committee of the International Chamber of Commerce in London. I hope the reader finds it as rewarding to read the book as I did to write it.

Ademuni-Odeke
Southampton, UK
Vienna, Austria
Summer 1999

Acknowledgements

I am indebted to John and Helen Spelman for full secretarial and initial editing services; Rosemary Mountjoy for typing; Carlos Bueno-Guzman and Sita Weinrich of the UNCITRAL Library in Vienna; and my family for the sacrifice and deprivation of quality family time during the preparation of this and my previous books.

Dedication

To Helmy, Zinzile and Ateker

Table of Cases

Table of Statutes

Table of Statutory Instruments

Table of Conventions

Table of Abbreviations

AB	Advising Bank
BEA	Bills of Exchange Act 1882
BLA	Bills of Lading Act
CB	Confirming Bank
c.fr.	Cost and Freight
c.i.f.	Cost, Insurance and Freight
CIM	Règles Uniformes Concernant le Transport International Ferroviaire des Merchandises
c.i.p.	Carriage and Insurance Paid To
CIV	Règles Uniformes Concernant le Contrat de Transport International Ferroviaire des Voyageurs et des Bagages
CJJA	Civil Jurisdiction and Judgments Act 1982
CMI	Convention on International Carriage of Goods by Rail
CMR	Convention on International Carriage of Goods by Road
COGSA	Carriage of Goods by Sea Act
COTIF	Convention Concerning International Carriage by Rail
CPR	Civil Procedure Rules
c.p.t.	Carriage Paid To
CRF	Clean Report of Findings
CSC	International Convention on Safe Containers
CST	Constructional Short Term (Guarantee)
CT	Combined Transport
CTD	Combined Transport Document
CTO	Combined Transport Operator
d.a.f.	Delivered At Frontier
d.d.p.	Delivered Duty Paid
d.d.u.	Delivered Duty Unpaid
d.e.q.	Delivered Ex Quay
d.e.s.	Delivered Ex Ship
EC	European Community
ECGD	Export Credits Guarantee Department
EDI	Electronic Data Interchange

EDT	Electronic Data Transmission
EEC	European Economic Community
ETA	Estimated Time of Arrival
EU	European Union
EXFINCO	Export Finance Company Limited
exw.	Ex Works/Ex Warehouse
FA	Factors Act 1889
f.a.s.	Free Alongside Ship
f.ca.	Free Carrier
f.o.b.	Free On Board
f.o.r.	Free On Rail (now f.ca.)
f.o.t.	Free On Truck (now f.ca.)
GAFTA	Grain and Feed Trade Association
GOSCO	Sugar Trading Association
HSSC	Heat, Sweat and Spontaneous Combustion
IATA	International Air Transport Association
IB	Issuing Bank
ICC	International Chamber of Commerce
ICCA	International Council for Commercial Arbitration
IFIA	International Federation of Inspection Agencies
IMF	International Monetary Fund
INCOTERMS	International Commercial Terms
LCIA	London Court of International Arbitration
LLMC	Limitation of Liability for Maritime Claims [Convention on the]
MMO	Multi-modal Operator
MTD	Multimodal Transport Document
MTO	Multimodal Transport Operator
NI	Northern Ireland
NVOCC	Non-vessel Owning Common Carrier (used in the USA)
OECD	Organisation for Economic Co-operation and Development
P&I	Protection and Indemnity Clubs
PIC	Preshipment Inspection Companies
PPI	Policy Proof of Interest
PSI	Preshipment Inspection
RSC	Rules of the Supreme Court (revoked and replaced by CPR)
SAD	Single Administrative Document
SDR	Special Drawing Rights
SGA	Sale of Goods Act
SGAA	Sale of Goods Amendment Act
SGSA	Supply of Goods and Services Act
SITPRO	Simplification of International Trade Procedures
SSGA	Sale and Supply of Goods Act
TCM	Draft Convention on the Combined Transport of Goods 1971
UCP	Uniform Customs and Practice for Documenting Credits

UCTA	Unfair Contract Terms Act 1977
UN	United Nations
UNCITRAL	United Nations Conference on International Trade Law
UNCTAD	United Nations Conference on Trade and Development
UN(ECE)	United Nations Economic Commission for Europe
VAT	Value Added Tax

PART I

INTERNATIONAL AND DOMESTIC TRADE

1 International Trade in Perspective

1.1 INTRODUCTION

This opening chapter attempts to put international trade into context. To do so it has been necessary to stray into political economy and history. This approach is necessary for a full understanding of the terms, rules and principles contained in the multitude of disciplines that make up international trade law. Although international trade law, as used in this book, refers to private international commercial law, it is nevertheless important to appreciate that states are not the idle participants that we are led to believe. Having said that, discussions of this wider topic are summarised to the extent necessary for the book.

1.2 MERCANTILISM AND INTERNATIONAL TRADE

Accounts of barter of goods or of services among different peoples can be traced back almost as far as the record of human history. International trade, however, is specifically an exchange between members of different nations, and accounts and explanations of such trade begin only with the rise of the modern nation-state at the close of the European Middle Ages. As political thinkers and philosophers began to examine the nature and function of the nation, trade with other nations became a particular sub-topic of their inquiry. It is, accordingly, no surprise to find one of the earliest attempts to describe the function of international trade within that highly nationalistic body of thought now known as 'mercantilism'. Mercantilist analysis, which reached the peak of its influence upon European thought in the sixteenth and seventeenth centuries, focused directly upon the welfare of the nation. It insisted that the acquisition of wealth, particularly wealth in the form of gold, was of paramount importance for national policy. Mercantilists took the virtues of gold almost as an article of faith; consequently, they never undertook to explain adequately why gold deserved such a high priority in their economic plans.

The trade policy dictated by mercantilist philosophy was accordingly simple; encourage exports, discourage imports, and take the proceeds of the resulting export surplus in gold. Because of their nationalistic bent, mercantilist writers either brushed aside the fact, or else did not realise that, from an international viewpoint, this policy would necessarily prove self-defeating. The nation that successfully gains an export surplus must ordinarily do so at the expense of one or more other nations that record a matching import deficit Mercantilists' ideas often were intellectually shallow, and indeed their trade policy may have been little more than a rationalisation of the interests of a rising merchant class that wanted wider markets — hence the emphasis on expanding exports — coupled with protection against competition in the form of imported goods. Yet mercantilist policies, as will be noted later, are by no means completely dead today.

1.3 WHY INTERNATIONAL TRADE? THE THEORY OF COMPARATIVE ADVANTAGE

1.3.1 Developments

The theory of comparative advantage has roots in classical economics. The British school of 'classical economics' began in no small measure as a reaction against the inconsistencies of mercantilist thought. Adam Smith (1723–90) was the founder of this school; his famous work, *The Wealth of Nations*, is in part an anti-mercantilist tract. In *The Wealth of Nations*, Smith emphasised the importance of specialisation as a source of increased output, and he treated international trade as a particular instance of specialisation. In a world where productive resources are scarce and human wants cannot be completely satisfied, each nation should specialise in the production of goods it is particularly well equipped to produce; it should export part of this production, taking in exchange other goods that it cannot so readily turn out. Smith did not expand these ideas at much length; but David Ricardo (1772–1823), the second great classical economist, developed them into the 'principle of comparative advantage', a principle still to be found, much as Ricardo spelled it out, in every international trade text.

1.3.2 Simplified Theory of Comparative Advantage

For clarity of exposition, the theory of comparative advantage is usually first outlined as though only two countries and only two commodities were involved, although it is by no means limited to such cases. Again for clarity, the cost of production is usually measured only in terms of labour time and effort; the cost of a unit of cloth, for example, might be given as two man-days. The two countries will here be A and B, and the two commodities wine and cloth. The labour time required to produce a unit of either commodity in either country is as follows:

1.3.2.1 Cost of Production (Labour Time)

	Country A	Country B
Wine (1 unit)	1 man-day	2 man-days
Cloth (1 unit)	2 man-days	6 man-days

As compared with Country A, Country B is productively inefficient. Its manpower needs more time to turn out a unit of wine or a unit of cloth. This relative inefficiency may result from differences in climate, in worker training or skill, or in the amount of available tools and equipment, or from numerous other possible reasons. Ricardo took it for granted that such differences do exist, and he was not concerned, for purposes of his comparative-advantage analysis, with their origins.

One's first inclination is to conclude that in such circumstances Country B could not possibly compete with Country A, and if trade were to be opened up between them, Country B would be competitively overwhelmed. Ricardo insisted that this conclusion is false. The critical factor is that Country B's disadvantage is less pronounced in wine production, in which its workers require only twice as much time for a single unit as do the workers in A, than it is in cloth production, in which the required time is three times as great. This means, Ricardo pointed out, that Country B will have a *comparative* advantage in wine production. Both countries will profit, in terms of the real income they enjoy, if Country B specialises in wine production, exporting part of its output to Country A, and if Country A specialises in cloth production, exporting part of its output to Country B. Paradoxical though it may seem, it is preferable for Country A to leave wine production to Country B, despite the fact that A's workers can produce wine of equal quality in half the time that B's workers can do so.

1.4 PATTERNS OF INTERNATIONAL TRADE

1.4.1 Degrees of National Participation

Nations vary considerably in the extent of their foreign trade. As a very rough generalisation, it may be said that the larger a country is in physical size and population, the less is its involvement in foreign trade, mainly because of the greater diversity of raw materials available within its borders and the greater size of its internal market. Thus the participation of the United States is relatively low, its export and import totals each being just over 8 per cent of its gross national product, and that of the former USSR even lower. The US gross national product, however, is so immense by world standards that the US still ranks as one of the world's most important trading countries. Some of the smaller countries of western Europe (such as the Netherlands) have export and import totals that exceed 45 per cent of their gross national products.

1.4.2   Trade among Developed Countries

The greatest volume of trade occurs among the developed, capital-rich countries of the world, especially among industrial leaders such as Australia, Belgium, Canada, France, Germany, Italy, Japan, the Netherlands, Spain, Sweden, the United Kingdom and the US. Generally, as a country matures economically its participation in foreign trade grows more rapidly than its gross national product.

The European Community (EC) affords an impressive instance of the gains to be derived from freer trade. In economic terms, the EC is simply a plan for unrestricted movement of goods, labour, and capital across the boundaries of its member countries. A major part of the increases in real income in EC countries is almost certainly attributable to the removal of trade barriers. The EC's formation cannot, however, be interpreted as reflecting an unqualified dedication to the free-trade principle. EC rules require member countries to maintain a common and often substantial tariff against goods from outside the Community. The EC has recently adopted a single currency, the Euro, among eleven of its fifteen member states.

1.4.3   Trade among Developed and Underdeveloped Countries

Difficult problems frequently arise out of trade between developed and underdeveloped countries. Many less-developed countries are tropical, frequently relying heavily for income upon the proceeds from export of one or two crops, such as coffee, cocoa, or sugar. Markets for such goods are highly competitive in the sense in which economists use the term *competitive* — that is, prices are extremely sensitive to every change in demand or in supply. Prices of manufactured goods, the typical exports of developed countries, are commonly much more stable. Hence, as the price of its export commodity fluctuates, the tropical country experiences large fluctuations in its 'terms of trade', the ratio of export prices to import prices, often with painful effects on the domestic economy. With respect to almost all important primary commodities, efforts have been made at establishing price stabilisation and output control. These efforts have met with varied success.

Comparable problems arise when the underdeveloped country exports a mineral, such as petroleum or copper. The initiative in developing such a resource is often taken by a foreign company from a developed country that owns (in part if not in full) the extracting capital facilities. Particularly since the mineral resource is exhaustible, charges of exploitation are common. The matter is a continuing source of political strife and may on occasion lead to expropriation of the mineral properties.

Several underdeveloped countries have joined in creating organisations for the promotion of trade between themselves. Notable examples include the Central American Common Market (1961), Latin-American Free Trade Association (1961), Organisation Commune Africaine et Mauricienne (1965), Association of Southeast Asian Nations (1967), the Caribbean Community and Common Market (1973), the East African Community (1974) and the Economic Community of West African States (1975).

1.5 STATE PARTICIPATION AND INTERVENTION IN INTERNATIONAL TRADE

1.5.1 Methods of Interference

Regardless of what comparative-advantage theory may say about the virtues of unrestricted trade, all nations interfere with international exchanges to at least some degree. Tariffs may be imposed on imports, in some instances making them so costly as to bar completely the entry of the goods involved. Quotas may limit the permissible volume of imports. State subsidies may be offered to encourage exports. Money-capital exports may be restricted or prohibited. Investment by foreigners in domestic plant and equipment may be similarly restrained.

These interferences may be simply the result of special-interest pleading for, as already noted, particular groups suffer as a consequence of import competition; or a government may impose restrictions because it feels impelled to take account of factors that comparative-advantage sets aside. It is of interest to note that in so far as goods and services are concerned, the general pattern of interference follows the old mercantilist dictum of discouraging imports and encouraging exports.

1.5.2 Reasons for Interference

The more important considerations that prompt governmental regulation are summarised below.

1.5.2.1 Revenue
Underdeveloped nations in particular often lack the institutional machinery needed for effective imposition of income or corporation taxes. The governments of such nations may then finance their activity by resort to tariffs on imported goods, since such levies are relatively easy to administer. The amount of tax revenue obtainable through tariffs, however, is always limited. If the government tries to increase its tariff income by imposing higher duty rates this may choke off the flow of imports and so reduce tariff revenue instead of increasing it.

1.5.2.2 Protection of Domestic Industry
Probably the commonest argument for tariff imposition is that particular domestic industries need tariff protection for survival. Comparative-advantage theorists will, of course, argue that the industry in need of such protection ought not to survive and that the resources so employed ought to be transferred to occupations having greater comparative efficiency. The welfare gain of citizens taken as a whole would more than offset the welfare loss of those groups affected by import competition; that is, total real national income would increase. An opposing argument would be, however, that this welfare gain would be widely diffused, so that the individual beneficiaries might not be conscious of any great improvement. The welfare loss, in contrast, would be narrowly and acutely felt. Although resources *can* be transferred

to other occupations, just as comparative-advantage theory says, the transfer process is sometimes slow and painful for those being transferred. For such reasons, comparative-advantage theorists rarely advocate the immediate removal of all existing tariffs. They argue instead against further tariff increases — since increases, if effective, attract still more resources into the wrong occupations — and they press for gradual reduction of import barriers.

1.5.2.3 Unemployment

A variant of the industry-protection argument is that tariffs or quotas are needed to maintain domestic employment, particularly in times of recession. Today, there is near-unanimity among economists that proposals to remedy unemployment by means of tariff increases are misguided. In so far as a higher tariff is effective for this purpose, it simply 'exports unemployment': the rise in domestic employment is matched by a drop in production in some foreign country. That other country, moreover, is likely to impose a retaliatory tariff increase. Finally, the tariff remedy for unemployment is a poor one because it is usually ineffective and because more suitable remedies are now available. Today it is generally recognised that unemployment is far more efficiently dealt with by the implementation of proper fiscal and monetary policies.

1.5.2.4 Economic Development

The comparative-advantage principle supports, as indicated earlier, free-trade and laissez-faire policies. Ordinarily, a mature and developed country, with widely diversified and self-confident industries, has no difficulty in accepting the validity of this principle, with the exception of those producers who are afflicted by import competition.

Considerations are quite different for an underdeveloped country — that is, a country with a low *per capita* income, with limited industry, and typically relying on the export of one or two agricultural or mineral primary products. Today, all such underdeveloped countries are forced to direct their policies toward growth and higher real standards of living. Progress is commonly viewed in terms of industrial growth and diversification. These countries, however, are unlikely to think in laissez-faire terms. The less privileged nations may vary in the extent of their belief that growth and development can and should be fostered by governmental action, but that some such action is needed is almost universally accepted. The leaders of such countries are thus inclined to regard laissez-faire, comparative-advantage theory as an apology for the status quo devised by the more affluent countries. Many underdeveloped nations are thus in a painful position, they depend on their exchanges with richer countries for survival, and yet they suspect that this foreign trade is a form of exploitation, whether so intended or not, that keeps them in a subservient position as 'hewers of wood and drawers of water' and that prevents the development of their domestic industries.

Unfortunately, comparative-advantage theory is deficient on precisely this matter of the growth and expansion of resources. As noted earlier, the concern of this theory is with the best possible use of a given stock of industrial and other resources. It is thus difficult to resolve the issues involved. In general, the poorer nations have had limited success in the attempt to foster the development of their domestic industries by means of restrictions on foreign trade, and most economists are disdainful of the 'infant industry' argument that tariffs and similar protection are effective means of generating industrial growth. A comprehensive evaluation of such attempts at development must await a more complete theory of the sources and effects of international trade.

1.5.2.5   National Defence
A common appeal made by an industry seeking tariff or quota protection is that its survival is essential in the national interest: its product would be needed in wartime, when the supply of imports might well be cut off. The verdict of economists on this argument is fairly clear: the national defence argument is frequently a red herring, an attempt to 'wrap oneself in the flag', and insofar as an industry is essential, the tariff is a dubious means of ensuring its survival. Essential industries ought instead to be given a direct subsidy to enable them to meet foreign competition, with explicit recognition of the fact that the subsidy is a price paid by the nation in order to maintain the industry for defence purposes.

1.5.2.6   Autarky, or Self-sufficiency
Many demands for protection, whatever their surface argument may be, are really appeals to the autarkic feelings that prompted mercantilist reasoning. (Autarky is defined as the state of being self-sufficient at the level of the nation.) A proposal for the restriction of free international trade can be described as 'autarkic' if it appeals to those half-submerged feelings that 'we' (citizens of the nation involved) form a community sharing a common welfare and common interests, whereas 'they' (foreigners) have no regard for such welfare and interests and might even be actively opposed to them. It is quite true that a country that has become heavily involved in international trade has given hostages to fortune: a part of its industry has become dependent upon export markets for income and for employment. Any cut-off of these foreign markets (brought about by recession abroad, by the imposition of new tariffs by some foreign country, or by numerous other possible changes) would be acutely serious; and yet it would be a situation largely beyond the power of the domestic government involved to alter. Similarly, another part of domestic industry may rely on an inflow of imported raw materials, such as oil for fuel and power. Any restriction of this import inflow could have the most serious consequences. The vague threat implicit in such possibilities often results in a yearning for autarky, for national self-sufficiency, for a life free of dependence on the hazards of the outside world.

In point of fact, no nation in today's world, no matter how rich and varied its endowment of resources, could really practise self-sufficiency, and attempts in that direction could produce sharp drops in real income. Nevertheless, protectionist arguments — particularly those made 'in the interests of national defence' — often draw heavily on the strength of such autarkic sentiments.

1.5.2.7   Balance of Payments Difficulties

Governments may interfere with the processes of foreign trade for a reason quite different from those thus far discussed: shortage of foreign exchange. Under the international monetary system established after World War II and in effect until the 1970s, most governments tried to maintain fixed exchange rates between their own currencies and those of other countries. Even if not absolutely fixed, the exchange rate was ordinarily allowed to fluctuate only within a narrow range of values.

Fixed exchange rates are believed to facilitate trade because they eliminate the uncertainty arising out of a fluctuating rate. If the rate fluctuates, either the exporter is uncertain as to the revenue he will earn from his sale, or the importer is uncertain as to what his purchase will cost him in terms of domestic currency. The maintenance of a fixed exchange rate requires a government to keep a foreign-exchange reserve. Historically, this reserve was maintained in gold or in a major currency such as the United States dollar or the pound sterling. This reserve is drawn upon whenever the country's total imports outrun its total exports in value. An import surplus means that the demand for foreign currencies (to pay for imports) outruns the supply of foreign currencies (earned through exports).

If balance of payments difficulties arise and persist, a nation's foreign exchange reserve runs low. In a crisis, this situation may force the government to devalue the nation's currency; that is, to give it a new and lower value in foreign exchange markets. But before being driven to this extremity, it may try to redress the balance by restricting imports or encouraging exports, in much the old mercantilist fashion.

The problem of reserve shortages became acute for many countries during the 1960s. Although the total volume of international transactions had risen steadily, there was not a corresponding increase in the supply of international reserves. In 1971 the United States, largely because of its balance of payments deficits, ended the convertibility of the dollar to gold and, along with the then West Germany and the Netherlands, 'floated' its currency, allowing exchange rates to fluctuate. By 1973 most other major industrial nations were floating their currencies, thus ending the international system of fixed exchange rates. As a replacement for gold and the United States dollar, the system of Special Drawing Rights (SDR), established earlier by the International Monetary Fund (IMF), assumed new importance as the principal foreign reserve asset.

A country that finds itself barred from an attractive foreign market by tariffs or quotas may be able to leapfrog the barrier simply by establishing a manufacturing plant within that foreign country. This policy of foreign plant investment has expanded enormously since the close of World War II. United States companies have taken the lead, investing particularly in western Europe, Canada, and South America. Industry in other developed countries has followed a similar pattern, some foreign companies establishing plants within the United States as well as in other areas of the world.

The governments of countries subject to this new investment find themselves in an ambivalent position. The establishment of new foreign-owned plants may mean more than simply the creation of new employment opportunities and new productive capacity; it may also mean the introduction of new technologies and superior business-control methods. But the government that welcomes such benefits must also expect complaints of 'foreign control', an argument that will inevitably be pressed by domestic owners of older plants who fear a new competition that cannot be blocked by tariffs. Many governments are still wrestling with this problem, particularly in so far as investment by US firms is involved. Countries such as Great Britain and Canada have been liberal in their admissions policy; others, notably Japan, impose tight restriction on foreign-owned plants. The law and practice of international trade should be read against this background.

1.6 COUNTERTRADE

A phenomenon which emerged in the last two decades but did not develop is countertrade. This is a transaction which uses goods as payment instead of money. There are five forms: barter, buy-back, compensation, counter-purchase and switch trading. The most important of them is buy-back, a form of countertrade which involves the delivery of the means of producing goods or services in exchange for manufactured products to be paid at a later date. A buy-back agreement usually has some kind of turnkey plant or equipment associated with it. China and countries in Eastern Europe make substantial use of buy-backs in their countertrade arrangements. After a certain portion of the product is delivered, the entire plant or equipment usually becomes the property of the host country.

Countertrade has its advantages and disadvantages. There are reasons why countries engage in this type of transacting business in international trade. It has been suggested that countertrade distorts the practice of international trade since it does not involve payments in cash or money. For these and other reasons the topic is not covered in this book.

1.7 COMMODITY AND FUTURES

Commodity and Futures, also known as commodity exchange, spot market or futures, is a market where a commodity is bought and sold. It is not necessary for the commodities to be physically exchanged; only rights to ownership need be. The commodity exchanges in London cover a wide variety, such as coffee, cocoa, sugar, cereals, vegetable oils, wool, cotton, rubber and non-ferrous metals.

The old practice of auctioning commodities from warehouses in which samples could be inspected beforehand has become less important. An efficient system of grading and modern systems of communication have enabled the practice of c.i.f. trading to develop. A buyer can buy a commodity in the country of origin for delivery c.i.f. to a specific port at which he can off-load for direct delivery to his own premises.

This method saves warehousing costs and auction charges. The market not only enables commodities to be sold 'spot' or for delivery at some specified time and place, but it also includes a market in futures. This latter market enables merchants to avoid the effect of price fluctuations by buying for forward delivery at an agreed price, which will not be affected by intervening changes in the spot rate.

Futures are contracts made in the future market for the purchase or sale of commodities. Many commodities have established futures markets which permit manufacturers and traders to hedge against changes in price of the raw materials they use, or deal in forward exchange market or speculation, i.e. where contracts are made to supply currencies at fixed dates in the future at fixed prices.

For purposes of the commodities and futures market, currencies can also be bought and sold in the foreign exchange market either spot or forward. In the former case the transaction takes place immediately, and it is in this market that exchange rates are kept at their manageable levels by government intervention. In the forward exchange market, currencies are bought for transaction at some future date, e.g. in three or six months time.

The difference between the spot and forward rate of exchange depends on the rate of interest and the exchange risk, i.e. the possibility of appreciation or depreciation. The size of the premium or discount of forward and spot rate indicates the strength of the market's expectations.

Commodities and Futures represents a highly developed method of transacting international trade especially in large commodity centres like London. Unfortunately most of its concepts lie in the realms of international finance policy. Apart from a mention here, it is therefore not treated fully in a book such as this which is limited to the legal aspects of the subject.

1.8 PRESHIPMENT INSPECTION

A fairly recent development in international trade is preshipment inspection (PSI), a mechanism by which an overseas buyer, normally a government or state entity, requests to have the goods inspected before they are shipped. Its purpose is to eliminate fraud especially against developing countries that suffer from chronic shortages of foreign exchange. It has impacts on the parties' liabilities not yet fully investigated. Detailed discussion on the preshipment inspection is excluded from this book for the reason, among others, that the law and practice in this area is still not fully developed. However, the PSI certificate is covered at 5.7.1.

1.9 SOURCES AND DEVELOPMENT OF THE LAW

International trade is essentially the sale of goods with the addition of an international element. The buyer and seller are in different countries and the goods must travel from the seller's country to the buyer's country. Consequently contracts for the carriage of those goods must be procured. Given the risks that are incidental to such transit, the goods will usually be insured. The goods must also be paid for and various methods for payment have been devised to facilitate international trade. Yet at the heart of this trade are individual contracts for the sale of goods and the rest of this chapter is intended to provide a brief outline of the law relating to the sale of goods.

An international sales contract, like any other contract, is governed by a particular national law. That system of law will govern the contract wherever it is to be performed and has been traditionally referred to as the proper law of the contract. A court will determine which national law is to govern the contract by applying its rules of private international law. The approach of the English courts is to apply whichever law the parties have chosen and in the absence of such choice to apply that system of law with which the contract is most closely connected. This matter is discussed in greater detail in Chapter 14.

Where the proper law of the contract is English law, then the English law relating to the sale of goods, which is to be found primarily in the Sale of Goods Act 1979 (the SGA 1979) is to be applied to the contract of sale. The SGA 1979 is a codifying statute which consolidates with some amendments the Sale of Goods Act 1893 which was a codifying statute. The SGA 1979 has been amended by the Sale and Supply of Goods Act (SSGA) 1994, which came into force in January 1995, and the Sale of Goods Amendment Act 1995 (SGAA 1995). The effects of the amendments have been incorporated into the text where necessary. This chapter and the next one are largely concerned with the SGA 1979 and its interpretation and all references in the text are to the SGA 1979, as amended, unless otherwise stated. It is, however, only an outline of the main provisions and reference should be made to the more specialised texts in the area.

1.10 DEVELOPMENT OF THE MAIN TERMS AND PRINCIPLES

1.10.1 Characteristics of an International Trade Contract

The main characteristic of an international sale is that it will involve a transaction between a buyer in one state and a seller in another, requiring the movement of goods from the seller's state to the buyer's, typically by sea.

A typical export sale contract will involve five elements. First, there will be the underlying contract of sale which sets out the goods, the mode and place of delivery, the way payment is to be made and other incidentals. Secondly, there will be a contract of carriage entered into by either the seller or the buyer depending on their respective obligations as set out in the contract of sale. Thirdly, there will be a contract of insurance for the goods whilst in transit from the seller to the buyer. Again, which party is to make the contract of insurance will depend on the terms of the contract of sale. Fourthly, there will be certain conditions required by the export and import authorities to be fulfilled by either the seller or the buyer. Finally, there will be the particular mechanism of payment to be erected by the buyer: whether simply by cash, or by bill of exchange, or by documentary credit.

Many of the obligations to be performed by the parties to an international sale will involve documents and so the goods may be represented by a bill of lading or some other document purporting to perform the same function as a document of title. The contract of insurance may be contained in a policy or evidenced by a certificate. The financing of the sale will often involve bills of exchange and documentary credits. It is the use of documents which has enabled the practice of selling overseas to develop and, with modern systems of transport and communication, to become more secure and successful.

1.10.2 Elements of an International Sales Contract

Over the years as international sales have become more common, merchants and traders have developed practices around which they make and perform their contracts. The names used for the different types of contracts into which the parties may enter reflect the delivery point of the goods on which the contract price is based, and use a form which is an abbreviation established by trade practice. The two most common are f.o.b. and c.i.f. These terms are principally price terms, indicating what is included in the price, but they also indicate the extent of the respective parties' obligations. Whilst the former function is usually reliable, the latter is only a rule of thumb, and the parties can agree to vary their actual obligations.

The following is a list of the most common price and delivery terms indicating the location to be stated in the contract and the delivery point:

Abbreviation	Full Name	Location Stated
exw.	Ex works	Named place
f.ca.	Free carrier	Named place
f.a.s.	Free alongside ship	Named port of shipment
f.o.b.	Free on board	Named port of shipment
c.fr.	Cost and freight	Named port of destination
c.i.f.	Cost, insurance and freight	Named port of destination
c.p.t.	Carriage paid to	Named place of destination
c.i.p.	Carriage and insurance paid to	Named place of destination
d.a.f.	Delivered at frontier	Named place
d.e.s.	Delivered ex ship	Named port of destination
d.e.q.	Delivered ex quay (duty paid)	Named port of destination
d.d.u.	Delivered duty unpaid	Named place of destination
d.d.p.	Delivered duty paid	Named place of destination

These terms will be dealt with briefly below and some will be dealt with in detail in Chapters 3 and 4.

1.11 PANORAMIC VIEW OF INTERNATIONAL SALES

The thirteen main contract terms in international sales are contained in the International Chamber of Commerce's *Incoterms* 1990 and are described below.:

1.11.1   Ex Works (. . . named place) exw.

'Ex works' means that the seller fulfils his obligations to deliver when he has made the goods available at his premises (i.e. works, factory, warehouse, etc.) to the buyer. In particular, he is not responsible for loading the goods on the vehicle provided by the buyer or for clearing the goods for export, unless otherwise agreed. The buyer bears all costs and risks involved in taking the goods from the seller's premises to the desired destination. This term thus represents the minimum obligation for the seller. This term should not be used when the buyer cannot carry out directly or indirectly the export formalities. In such circumstances, the f.ca. term should be used (see 4.8).

1.11.2   Free Alongside Ship (. . . named port of shipment) f.a.s.

'Free alongside ship' means that the seller fulfils his obligation to deliver when the goods have been placed alongside the vessel on the quay or in lighters at the named port of shipment. This means that the buyer has to bear all costs and risks of loss of or damage to the goods from that moment.

The f.a.s. term requires the buyer to clear the goods for export. It should not be used when the buyer cannot carry out directly or indirectly the export formalities.

This term can only be used for sea or inland waterway transport (see 4.7).

1.11.3   Free Carrier (. . . named place) f.ca.

'Free carrier' means that the seller fulfils his obligation to deliver when he has handed over the goods, cleared for export, into the charge of the carrier named by the buyer at the named place or point. If no precise point is indicated by the buyer, the seller may choose within the place or range stipulated where the carrier is to take the goods into his charge. When, according to commercial practice, the seller's assistance is required in making the contract with the carrier (such as in rail or air transport) the seller may act at the buyer's risk and expense.

This term may be used for any mode of transport, including multimodal transport.

'Carrier' means any person who, in a contract of carriage, undertakes to perform or to procure the performance of carriage by rail, road, sea, air, inland waterway or by a combination of such modes. If the buyer instructs the seller to deliver the cargo to a person, e.g., a freight forwarder who is not a 'carrier', the seller is deemed to have fulfilled his obligation to deliver the goods when they are in the custody of that person (see 4.8).

1.11.4   Free on Board (. . . named port of shipment) f.o.b.

'Free on board' means that the seller fulfils his obligations to deliver when the goods have passed over the ship's rail at the named port of shipment. This means that the buyer has to bear all costs and risks of or damage to the goods from that point.

The f.o.b. term requires the seller to clear the goods for export.

This term can only be used for sea or inland waterway transport. When the ship's rail serves no practical purpose, such as in the case of roll-on/roll-off or container traffic, the f.ca. term is more appropriate to use (see Chapter 4).

1.11.5   Cost and Freight (. . . named port of destination) c.fr.

'Cost and freight' means that the seller must pay the costs and freight necessary to bring the goods to the named port of destination but the risk of loss of or damage to the goods, as well as any additional costs due to events occurring after the time the goods have been delivered on board the vessel, is transferred from the seller to the buyer when the goods pass the ship's rail in the port of shipment.

The c.fr. term requires the seller to clear the goods for export.

This term can only be used for sea and inland waterway transport. When the ship's rail serves no practical purpose, such as in the case of roll-on/roll-off or container traffic, the c.p.t. term is more appropriate to use (see 4.14).

1.11.6   Cost, Insurance and Freight (. . . named port of destination) c.i.f.

'Cost, insurance and freight' means that the seller has the same obligations as under c.fr. but with the addition that he has to procure marine insurance against the buyer's risk of loss of or damage to the goods during the carriage. The seller contracts for insurance and pays the insurance premium.

The buyer should note that under the c.i.f. term the seller is only required to obtain insurance on minimum coverage.

The c.i.f. term requires the seller to clear the goods for export. This term can only be used for sea and inland waterway transport. When the ship's rail serves no practical purpose, such as in the case of roll-on/roll-off or container traffic, the c.p.t. term is more appropriate to use (see Chapter 3).

1.11.7   Carriage Paid To (. . . named place of destination) c.p.t.

'Carriage paid to' means that the seller pays the freight for the carriage of the goods to the named destination. The risk of loss of or damage to the goods, as well as any additional costs due to events occurring after the time the goods have been delivered to the carrier, is transferred from the seller to the buyer when the goods have been delivered into the custody of the carrier.

'Carrier' means any person who, in the contract of carriage, undertakes to perform or to procure the performance of carriage, by rail, road, sea, air, inland waterway or by a combination of such modes. If subsequent carriers are used for the carriage to the agreed destination, the risk passes when the goods have been delivered to the first carrier.

The c.p.t. term requires the seller to clear the goods for export.

This term may be used for any mode of transport including multimodal transport (see 4.14).

1.11.8   Carriage and Insurance Paid To (... named place of destination) c.i.p.

'Carriage and Insurance paid to' means that the seller has the same obligations as under c.p.t. but with the addition that the seller has to procure cargo insurance against the buyer's risk of loss of or damage to the goods during the carriage. The seller contracts for insurance and pays the insurance premium.

The buyer should note that under the c.i.p. term the seller is only required to obtain insurance on minimum coverage.

The c.i.p. term requires the seller to clear the goods for export.

This term may be used for any mode of transport including multimodal transport (see 4.13).

1.11.9   Delivered at Frontier (... named place) d.a.f.

'Delivered at frontier' means that the seller fulfils his obligation to deliver when the goods have been made available, cleared for export, at the named point and place at the frontier, but before the customs border of the adjoining country. The term 'frontier' may be used for any frontier including that of the country of export. Therefore, it is of vital importance that the frontier in question be defined precisely by always naming the point and place in the term.

The term is primarily intended to be used when goods are to be carried by rail or road, but it may be used for any mode of transport (see 4.15).

1.11.10   Delivered Ex Ship (... named port of destination) d.e.s.

'Delivered ex ship' means that the seller fulfils his obligation to deliver when the goods have been made available to the buyer on board the ship uncleared for import at the named port of destination. The seller has to bear all the costs and risks involved in bringing the goods to the named port of destination (see 4.9).

This term can only be used for sea or inland waterway transport.

1.11.11   Delivered Ex Quay (duty paid) (... named port of destination) d.e.q.

'Delivered ex quay (duty paid)' means that the seller fulfils his obligation to deliver when he has made the goods available to the buyer on the quay (wharf) at the named port of destination, cleared for importation. The seller has to bear all risks and costs including duties, taxes and other charges of delivering the goods thereto.

This term should not be used if the seller is unable directly or indirectly to obtain the import licence.

If the parties wish the buyer to clear the goods for importation and pay the duty, the words 'duty unpaid' should be used instead of 'duty paid'.

If the parties wish to exclude from the seller's obligations some of the costs payable upon importation of the goods (such as value added tax (VAT)), this should be made clear by adding words to this effect: 'Delivered ex quay, VAT unpaid (... named port of destination)'.

This term can only be used for sea or inland waterway transport (see 4.10).

1.11.12   Delivered Duty Unpaid (... named place of destination) d.d.u.

'Delivered duty unpaid' means that the seller fulfils his obligation to deliver when the goods have been made available at the named place in the country of importation. The seller has to bear the costs and risks involved in bringing the goods there (excluding duties, taxes, and other official charges payable upon importation as well as the costs and risks of carrying out customs formalities). The buyer has to pay any additional costs and to bear any risks caused by his failure to clear the goods for import in time.

If the parties wish the seller to carry out customs formalities and bear the costs and risks resulting therefrom, this has to be made clear by adding words to this effect.

If the parties wish to include in the seller's obligations some of the costs payable upon importation of the goods (such as VAT), this should be made clear by adding words to this effect: 'Delivered duty unpaid, (... named place of destination)'.

This term may be used irrespective of the mode of transport.

1.11.13   Delivered Duty Paid (... named place of destination) d.d.p.

'Delivered duty paid' means that the seller fulfils his obligation to deliver when the goods have been made available at the named place in the country of importation. The seller has to bear the risks and costs, including duties, taxes and other charges of delivering the goods, cleared for importation. Whilst the exw. term represents the minimum obligation for the seller, d.d.p. represents the maximum obligation.

This term should not be used if the seller is unable directly or indirectly to obtain the import licence.

If the parties wish the buyer to clear the goods for importation and to pay the duty, the term d.d.u. should be used.

If the parties wish to exclude from the seller's obligations some of the costs payable upon importation of the goods (such as VAT), this should be made clear by adding words to this effect: 'Delivered duty paid, VAT unpaid (... named place of destination)'.

This term may be used irrespective of the mode of transport.

2 Domestic Sale of Goods

2.1 A CONTRACT OF SALE

A contract for the sale of goods is defined in s. 2(1), SGA 1979 as:

> ... a contract by which the seller transfers or agrees to transfer the property in goods to the buyer for a money consideration, called the price.

From the buyer's point of view the legal objective of a contract for the sale of goods is to obtain ownership of the goods, and from the seller's to receive the price.

Section 61(1), the definition section, defines 'contract of sale' as including an agreement to sell as well as a sale, and 'sale' itself is defined as including a bargain and sale as well as a sale and delivery. A 'seller' is a person who sells or agrees to sell goods and a 'buyer' is a person who buys or agrees to buy goods. The term 'goods' includes all personal chattels other than things in action and money. Land is, therefore, excluded from the definition unless the part to be sold is to be severed before the sale or under the contract of sale. See *Kursell* v *Timber Operators and Contractors Ltd* [1927] 1 KB 298.

The essence of a contract for the sale of goods is the transfer of property in goods for money consideration. Section 61(1) defines 'property' as the general property in goods, and not merely a special property in the goods. The parties must intend that the general property in the goods should pass to the buyer and not merely some limited interest such as passes under a contract of bailment, pledge or mortgage (s. 62(4)). A hire-purchase contract is not a contract of sale, though closely resembling one, but is a bailment of the goods together with an option to purchase the goods which may or may not be exercised.

Where the goods are supplied in the course of a contract for services one looks to the Supply of Goods and Services Act (SGSA) 1982. This imposes almost identical conditions, in respect of title (s. 2), description (s. 3), quality and fitness (s. 4) and sample (s. 5) as are found in the SGA 1979, to such 'quasi-sales'. The service provided must be carried out with reasonable care and skill (s. 13, SGSA 1982), within a reasonable time of the making of the contract if no time is expressed (s. 14) and for a reasonable charge (s. 15).

Property in the goods must be transferred for 'money consideration'. An exchange of goods for other goods is not, therefore, a contract for the sale of goods but a barter. Likewise a gift for no consideration is not a contract of sale. Where the contract involves a part exchange of goods plus money consideration the position is more difficult. The characterisation of such a contract should depend on the intention of the parties and if the money element is just a makeweight part of the consideration, the contract will not be a contract of sale, see *Chappell & Co. Ltd* v *Nestlé Co. Ltd* [1960] AC 87, *Esso Petroleum Co. Ltd* v *Customs & Excise Commissioners* [1976] 1 WLR 1. If, on the other hand, the seller quotes an exclusive money price but then agrees to purchase goods from the buyer in part exchange, the proper analysis should be that there is a contract of sale in which the seller merely sets off the price of the part exchange goods against the price in the main contract of sale.

2.2   CONDITIONS AND WARRANTIES

Contractual terms may be conditions, warranties or innominate terms. The SGA 1979, however, only divides contractual terms into conditions and warranties. The distinction between conditions and warranties is drawn in s. 11(3) which also indicates that whether a particular term is a condition or warranty depends on the construction of the contract:

> Whether a stipulation in a contract of sale is a condition, the breach of which may give rise to a right to treat the contract as repudiated, or a warranty, the breach of which may give rise to a claim for damages but not to a right to reject the goods and treat the contract as repudiated, depends in each case on the construction of the contract; and a stipulation may be a condition, though called a warranty in the contract.

The terms of a contract which can properly be categorised as conditions are the principal terms of the contract. The non-performance of the obligation imposed by such a condition is regarded as so serious that the innocent party should be relieved from further performance of his obligations under the contract. Breach of a contractual condition goes to the root of the contract and the question of whether a particular term is a condition is to be determined by construing the contract to ascertain the intention of the parties thereto. The label attached by the parties to any particular term is not decisive.

The party who is guilty of failing to perform the obligation imposed upon him by a contractual condition is said to have repudiated the contract. This repudiation may either be accepted or rejected by the innocent party. If the innocent party chooses to accept the guilty party's repudiation the contract comes to an end and both parties are relieved from any further performance of the contract. If the innocent party decides not to accept the guilty party's repudiation of the contract but in fact rejects it, the contract remains alive and both parties must continue to perform their respective obligations under the contract. In such a case the innocent party is, however, entitled to sue for any loss or damage he may have suffered by reason of the guilty party's breach of contract. This option is expressly provided for in s. 11(2):

> Where a contract of sale is subject to a condition to be fulfilled by the seller, the buyer may waive the condition, or may elect to treat the breach of the condition as a breach of warranty and not as a ground for treating the contract as repudiated.

A warranty is a term which is collateral to the main purpose of the contract, the breach of which gives rise to a claim for damages but not to a right to treat the contract as repudiated (s. 61(1)). A breach of warranty does not go to the root of the contract but is a comparatively minor breach when looked at in the context of the contract as a whole.

The classification of contractual terms into conditions and warranties is not exhaustive. There is a third category of contractual term, the 'innominate term'. If the parties were not concerned so much with the nature of the term but with the consequences of its breach, the court will give effect to that intention and treat the term as innominate; see *Hong Kong Fir Shipping Co. Ltd v Kawasaki Kisen Kaisha Ltd* [1962] 2 QB 26. Whether the breach of such a term is repudiatory, entitling the innocent party to bring an end to the contract, or whether the breach is such that it only gives rise to damages, depends on the consequences of the breach. If the consequences are such that the commercial purpose of the contract is frustrated then the breach will be repudiatory; see *The Hansa Nord* [1976] QB 44.

The SGA 1979 implies into contracts for the sale of goods various conditions as to title (s. 12), description (s. 13), quality and fitness for purpose (s. 14) which are examined below but in commercial contracts there will often be other conditions. In commercial contracts time will normally be regarded as of the essence so a term requiring performance of an obligation by a particular date will normally be regarded as a condition; see *Bunge Corporation v Tradax Export SA* [1981] 1 WLR 711. In particular if the contract of sale calls for goods to be shipped by a particular date or within a particular period the time of shipment will be a condition of the contract. In *Bowes v Shand* (1877) 2 App Cas 455 two contracts for the sale of rice called for shipment in March and/or April from Madras. The rice was largely shipped in February and the House of Lords held that the buyers did not have to accept that rice.

> The parties have chosen for reasons best known to themselves to say: We bargain to take rice, shipped in this particular region, at that particular time, on board that particular ship, and before the defendants can be compelled to take anything in fulfilment of that contract, it must be shown not merely that it is equally good, but that it is the same article as they have bargained for otherwise they are not bound to take it . . .

Moreover in international sales contracts there may be terms which relate not to the goods but to their transit from the seller's country to the buyer's country. Such terms, relating to the route and scope for deviation for example, may be conditions. In *Bergerco USA* v *Vegoil* [1984] 1 Lloyd's Rep 440 the contract called for direct shipment of the goods to the destination specified in the contract of sale. The goods were shipped on a vessel which was to call at a number of intermediate ports. Hobhouse J held that the term was not innominate but a condition so that the buyers could reject the goods as soon as they were aware of the breach. Thus if the route is specified in the contract of sale the contract of carriage must be one which covers that route. See *Colin & Shields* v *Weddell & Co.* [1952] 2 All ER 337. If no route is specified the contractual route must be a reasonable one which is either the customary route or, if none, one which is practical and commercial. In *Tsakiroglou & Co. Ltd* v *Noble Thorl GmbH* [1962] AC 93 there was no contractual provision covering the route. The goods were to be transported from Sudan to Hamburg. The normal route was to go through the Suez Canal but this was closed. The only other route was to go via the Cape of Good Hope, considerably increasing the time and expense of the voyage. The seller failed to ship the goods. The House of Lords held that the contract had not been frustrated since there was no express term as to the specific route, notwithstanding that it was reasonable to assume that both the buyer and seller contemplated a voyage through the Canal. The absence of such a term meant objectively that the buyer was not concerned with the route. The extra time required did not radically alter the commercial nature of the contract of sale and the additional cost would have to be borne by the seller. His failure to perform was, therefore, a repudiatory breach of the contract, and the buyer was entitled to damages for a total failure of consideration.

2.3   IMPLIED TERMS

There are a number of contractual terms which are implied into every contract for the sale of goods by the SGA 1979. There are conditions as to title (s. 12), description (s. 13), satisfactory quality (s. 14(2)) and fitness for purpose (s. 14(3)). If the sale is a sale by sample further conditions are implied into the contract (s. 15). The obligations imposed by these conditions must be complied with by the seller otherwise the buyer may be entitled to reject the goods. The SGA 1979 also implies into every contract for the sale of goods certain warranties (s. 12(2)) the breach of which entitles the seller to damages.

These implied conditions and warranties will now be more closely examined.

2.3.1   The Seller's Right to Sell

In a contract of sale there is an implied condition on the part of the seller that in the case of a sale he has a right to sell the goods, and in the case of an agreement to sell he will have such a right at the time when the property is to pass (s. 12(1)).

The words 'right to sell' mean that title need not be in the seller himself, but that the sale is made with the consent of the party in whom title is vested, e.g. an agent selling for an undisclosed principal. Moreover, the seller will be in breach of the implied condition if the sale infringes some patent, trademark, or other proprietary interest which entitles the holder of the patent or other right to stop the sale, either altogether or in the form in which the goods are to be supplied under the contract; see *Niblett* v *Confectioners' Materials Co. Ltd* [1921] 3 KB 387.

As this is a condition of the contract of sale any breach (however minor) is repudiatory and entitles the buyer to reject the goods and claim from the seller damages on the grounds that there has been a total failure of consideration; see *Rowland* v *Divall* [1923] 2 KB 500.

The date on which the seller must have the right to sell is the date property is to pass, which is determined according to the intentions of the parties (s. 17). If the seller has a right of disposal at that time, the fact that a third party subsequently acquires a right to prevent the buyer using or dealing with the goods does not give rise to a breach of the implied condition of title. The condition is not a continuing obligation so that once satisfied the seller's liability under it ceases. The buyer in this situation may have a remedy for a breach of the implied warranty of quiet possession. In s. 12(2) there are implied warranties that:

(a)   the goods are free from any encumbrance or charge known by or disclosed to the buyer before the contract is made; and

(b)   the buyer will enjoy quiet possession of them.

These implied terms are classified as warranties, the breach of which gives rise only to damages. The implied warranty of quiet possession is broken only if the person disturbing the buyer's possession has a legal right to do so. There is, therefore, no breach if a thief or fraudster interferes. There is still a breach if the interference results not from any defect in the seller's title, but from the lawful act of a third party. Hence in *Microbeads AG* v *Vinhurst Road Markings Ltd* [1975] 1 WLR 218 the seller's title was good at the time property passed, but the buyer's quiet enjoyment of the goods was disrupted when a third party registered a patent in a design which the goods in question infringed. The seller was found to have broken the s. 12(2) implied warranty and was liable in damages to the buyer.

The implied warranties do not exist in circumstances where it appears from the contract of sale that the seller was intended to transfer only such title as he had (s. 12(3)), although there is an implied warranty in such cases that the seller has disclosed all existing charges and the buyer will otherwise enjoy quiet possession (s. 12(4) and (5)).

2.3.2   Correspondence with Description

Where there is a contract for the sale of goods by description, there is an implied condition that the goods will correspond with the description (s. 13(1)).

The seller must, therefore, supply goods of the same type as those which he contracted to sell. If the goods supplied do not conform to their contractual description the buyer is entitled to reject the goods and claim from the buyer damages for their non-delivery. Even a minor non-conformity between the goods and their description, unless the non-conformity is *de minimis*, will entitle the buyer to reject the goods; see *Arcos Ltd* v *E A Ronaasen & Son* [1933] AC 470; *Re Moore & Co.* and *Landauer & Co.* [1921] 2 KB 519. However, s. 15A (inserted by SSGA 1994) provides that if the buyer is not dealing as a consumer, he will not be able to reject the goods if the breach is so slight that it would be unreasonable to reject them.

Problems can arise in identifying the words used by the parties which might properly be referred to as descriptive and thus within the scope of s. 13. The first step is to ascertain whether the words in question formed part of the contractual description or whether those words were merely representations made by the seller to induce the buyer into the contract of sale. If the words were mere representations then the implied condition does not apply to those words; see *T & F Harrison* v *Knowles and Foster* [1918] 1 KB 608.

Furthermore a distinction has to be drawn between words which are used to describe the goods and those which merely relate to the quality or condition of the goods. When the words in question relate only to the quality of the goods and not their description, the condition implied by s. 13 has no application; see *Alfred C Toepfer* v *Continental Grain* [1974] 1 Lloyd's Rep 11. Yet in cases of contamination of the goods the contamination might be such that not only is the quality of the goods affected but their very nature may change so that the goods no longer correspond with their contractual description; see *The Bow Cedar* [1980] 2 Lloyd's Rep 601; *Gill & Duffus* v *Berger & Co. Inc* [1981] 2 Lloyd's Rep 233. The yardstick used by the courts was identified by Lord Wilberforce in *Ashington Piggeries Ltd* v *Christopher Hill Ltd* [1972] AC 441 at page 489:

> I do not believe that the Sale of Goods Act was designed to provoke metaphysical discussions as to the nature of what is delivered in comparison with what is sold. The test of description, at least where commodities are concerned, is intended to be a broader, more common sense, test of mercantile character. The question whether that is what the buyer bargained for has to be answered according to such tests as men in the market would apply, leaving more delicate questions of conditions, or quality to be determined under other clauses of the contract or sections of the Act.

Furthermore not all descriptive words used in a contract have legal force as conditions or even contractual terms. In *Reardon Smith Line Ltd* v *Hansen-Tangen* [1976] 1 WLR 989 the contract concerned a particular ship which was to be built to certain specifications at Yard No 354 at Osaka Zosen but the ship was in fact built at another yard. The House of Lords held that the words used to indicate the fact that the ship was to be built at Yard No 354 Osaka Zosen did not form part of the contractual description of the ship. Lord Wilberforce thought that it would be better if s. 13 were confined to descriptive words which constituted a substantial ingredient of the identity of the goods sold. It would, however, be wrong to say that words which identify where goods are located cannot be words of description within s. 13; see *Macpherson Train & Co.* v *Howard Ross & Co.* [1955] 1 WLR 640.

The sale must be one by description but the fact that goods, being exposed for sale or hire, have been selected by the buyer does not prevent the contract from being a sale by description (s. 13(3)). In the Privy Council's decision in *Grant* v *Australian Knitting Mills Ltd* [1936] AC 85 it was said at page 100 that:

> ... there is a sale by description even though the buyer is buying something displayed before him on the counter: the thing is sold by description, though it is specific, so long as it is sold not merely as a specific thing but as a thing corresponding to a description, e.g. woollen undergarments, a hot water bottle, a second-hand reaping machine, to select a few obvious illustrations.

2.3.3 Satisfactory Quality (as amended by SSGA 1994)

The duty to supply goods of satisfactory quality is found in s. 14(2):

> Where the seller sells goods in the course of a business, there is an implied term that the goods supplied under the contract are of satisfactory quality.

The term implied is a condition. Subsection (2C), inserted by s. 1 of the SSGA 1994 provides:

> (2C)   The term implied by subsection (2) ... does not extend to any matter making the quality of goods unsatisfactory—
> (a)   which is specifically drawn to the buyer's attention before the contract is made,
> (b)   where the buyer examines the goods before the contract is made, which that examination ought to reveal, or
> (c)   in the case of a contract for sale by sample, which would have been apparent on a reasonable examination of the sample.

The obligation applies equally to new and second-hand goods, though in the case of the latter the content of the duty is reduced to the standard of quality a reasonable buyer would expect; see *Shine* v *General Guarantee Corporation* [1988] 1 All ER 911; *Business Applications Specialists Ltd* v *Nationwide Credit Corporation Ltd* [1988] RTR 332. These cases and those below were dealing with the old requirement of merchantable quality.

The goods must have been supplied 'in the course of a business' so that private sales do not fall within the scope of s. 14(2). A 'business' includes a profession and the activities of any government department or local or public authority (s. 61(1)). In the context of international sales the sale will normally satisfy this requirement.

The condition extends to all the 'goods supplied under the contract' so as to include the containers in which the goods are stored (see *Gedling* v *Marsh* [1920] 1 KB 668; *Niblett* v *Confectioners' Materials Ltd* [1921] 3 KB 387), other articles supplied with the contractual goods (see *Wilson* v *Rickett, Cockerell & Co. Ltd* [1954] 1 QB 598) as well as information and instructions supplied with the goods (see *Wormell* v *RHM Agriculture* (East) Ltd [1987] 1 WLR 1091). Inadequacy sufficient to breach the condition of satisfactory quality in any of the goods supplied under the contract will be a breach of condition for the whole of the goods and will entitle the buyer to reject the goods and sue the seller for a total failure of consideration subject to s. 15A. 'Satisfactory quality' is defined by s. 14(2A):

> ... goods are of satisfactory quality if they meet the standard that a reasonable man would regard as satisfactory, taking account of any description of the goods, the price (if relevant) and all the other relevant circumstances.

Subsection (2B) further provides that:

> ... the quality of goods includes their state and condition and the following (among others) are in appropriate cases aspects of the quality of goods—
>   (a)   fitness for all the purposes for which goods of the kind in question are commonly supplied;
>   (b)   appearance and finish;
>   (c)   freedom from minor defects;
>   (d)   safety; and
>   (e)   durability.

It is therefore important to identify the purpose or purposes for which the goods in question are commonly bought. If the buyer requires the goods for some purpose for which the goods are not commonly bought, that is a matter which is dealt with by s. 14(3) and the requirement of fitness for purpose. Yet what if the buyer requires the goods for one of their common purposes and the goods delivered, while being fit for some of their common purposes, are not fit for the buyer's particular common purpose? Prior to the SSGA 1994 it seemed that the goods in those circumstances would not be of unmerchantable quality; see *Henry Kendall & Sons* v *William Lillico & Sons Ltd* [1969] 2 AC 31; *Aswan Engineering Establishment Co.* v *Lupdine Ltd* [1987] 1 WLR 1. These cases must now be read subject to s. 14(2B).

What is the standard of fitness for purpose? Will any defect which affects the fitness for the purpose for which the goods are commonly bought breach the condition however minor the defect? In respect of manufactured goods this has occasionally been the case; see *Parsons (Livestock) Ltd* v *Uttley Ingham & Co.* [1978] QB 791; *Rogers* v *Parish (Scarborough) Ltd* [1987] QB 933. The Court of Appeal in *Cehave NV* v *Bremer Handelsgesellcshaft GmbH (The Hansa Nord)* [1976] QB 44 decided, however, that goods will be of merchantable quality if the reasonable commercial man would consider that the proper way of dealing with the matter was not by rejection of the goods but by an allowance of the price. It may be dangerous to read too much into this decision as the facts were peculiar and the merits were with the seller but this may be a suitable approach when dealing with international commercial contracts.

The condition of merchantability (pre SSGA 1994) was not a continuing one and had to be satisfied at the point of delivery. This caused problems in some forms of international sales as the point of delivery may be when the goods are loaded on to the ship ready for carriage to the buyer, and not when the buyer physically receives them. Since there was no obligation of 'durability' the courts circumvented the problem by holding that the condition that the goods be of merchantable quality required the goods to be of such condition that they would remain of merchantable quality from the time of shipment throughout normal transit to the destination and for a reasonable time thereafter for disposal; see *Mash & Murrell Ltd* v *Joseph Emanuel* [1961] 1 WLR 862. Presumably this will apply to 'satisfactory quality', but in appropriate cases, the durability of the goods can be taken into account (s. 14(2B)).

The seller cannot be in breach of the implied condition by reason of defects in the goods which have been specifically drawn to the buyer's attention (s. 14(2C)). The seller need not personally draw the defect to the buyer's attention but the section clearly envisages some positive act.

If the buyer examines the goods, then there is no implied condition as to satisfactory quality as regards defects which that examination ought to have revealed (s. 14(2C)). The buyer is not put under any duty to examine the goods but if he does he must conduct his examination with reasonable care, assessed by reference to the reasonable man. If the buyer is given the opportunity to examine the goods and not only fails to do so (which would have no effect) but positively represents that he waives his right to examine, it seems that the buyer will be deemed to have examined the goods according to the type of examination offered and thus the transaction could fall within s. 14(2C); see *Thornett & Fehr* v *Beers & Son* [1919] 1 KB 486.

2.3.4   Fitness for Purpose

The primary function of this implied condition is to deal with cases where the seller knows that the buyer has a special use for the goods which may or may not fall outside the range of purposes for which the particular goods are commonly bought. Section 14(3) provides:

Where the seller sells goods in the course of business and the buyer expressly or by implication makes it known—
(a)   to the seller ... any particular purpose for which the goods are being bought, there is an implied condition that the goods supplied under the contract are reasonably fit for that purpose, whether or not that is a purpose for which such goods are commonly supplied, except where the circumstances show that the buyer does not rely, or that it is unreasonable for him to rely, on the skill and judgment of the seller ...

There is an overlap between the implied condition of satisfactory quality and that of fitness for purpose. The condition of fitness for purpose requires the goods to be fit for such non-normal purposes specified by the buyer in addition to being fit for their normal purposes. It follows, therefore, that the goods may be fit for the particular purpose known by the buyer and yet be unsatisfactory, failing to conform to the standard required for goods sold under the contractual description.

As with the implied condition as to satisfactory quality the implied condition as to fitness for purpose arises only when the goods are being sold in the course of a business. The important distinction is that for s. 14(3) to operate, the particular purpose for which the goods are being purchased by the buyer must be communicated to the seller. The buyer should, therefore, communicate the particular purpose he has in mind if that purpose is one for which the goods are not normally purchased. Given the flexible interpretation that has been given to the condition as to merchantable quality the buyer, if he intends to use the goods for one particular purpose for which the goods are normally purchased, should communicate that purpose to the seller. In those circumstances the seller may have provided goods which were of satisfactory quality in that they were fit for a number of the purposes for which those goods are commonly bought but the buyer may, nonetheless, be able to invoke s. 14(3).

Section 14(3) is subject to the limitation that there must be actual and reasonable reliance by the buyer on the seller's skill and judgment at the date of the contract. Once knowledge of the buyer's purpose is established, reliance is presumed and the burden is then on the seller to show either that there was in fact no reliance, or that it was unreasonable in the circumstances. Hence in *Teheran-Europe Co. Ltd* v *S T Belton (Tractors) Ltd* [1968] 2 QB 545 it was found it was unreasonable for an Iranian company, which carried on business in Teheran as importers of machinery and other goods, to rely on the seller's skill and judgment. Diplock LJ said that:

> ... where a foreign merchant buys by description goods, not for his own use, but for resale in his own country of which he has no reason to suppose the English seller has any special knowledge, it flies in the face of common sense to suppose that he relies on anything but his own commercial judgment as to what is saleable there.

As with satisfactory quality, the implied condition of fitness for purpose is not a continuing duty, but is a once-and-for-all obligation which has to be satisfied at the time of delivery. However, if the goods cease to function or evince defects within a shorter period than is normal, that is evidence that the condition of fitness was not fulfilled at the date when the goods were delivered; see *Crowther* v *Shannon Motor Co.* [1975] 1 WLR 30; *Lambeth* v *Lewis* [1981] 1 All ER 1185; *Rogers* v *Parish Ltd* [1987] QB 933; *Bernstein* v *Pamson Motors* [1987] 2 All ER 220.

2.3.5   Sales by Sample

A contract of sale is a contract for sale by sample where there is an express or implied term to that effect in the contract. In the case of a contract for sale by sample, there is an implied condition: (1) that the bulk will correspond with the sample in quality; (2) that the buyer will have a reasonable opportunity of comparing the bulk with the sample; and (3) that the goods will be free from any defect, making their quality unsatisfactory, which would not be apparent on reasonable examination of the sample (see s. 15(1) and (2), SGA 1979).

There are, therefore, two elements which must be satisfied before the contract is a contract of sale by sample: first, the buyer must have been shown a small quantity of the goods at or before the time the contract was made; and, secondly, the seller must have undertaken (expressly or impliedly) that the sample represents exactly that which is to be supplied under the contract. In effect the sample replaces or reduces the role of the description. It extends the definition of the goods into precise requirements of quality.

When there is a sale by sample the seller is placed under three conditions by s. 15(2), SGA 1979. First, the bulk must correspond in quality to the sample. What is meant by correspondence in quality is a question of fact and depends on the sophistication of the parties and the contract. The contract may require the correspondence to be at the level of a chemical analysis, or it may simply require a rough visual check. Lord Macnaghten in *James Drummond & Sons* v *E H Van Ingen & Co.* (1887) 12 App Cas 284 described the function of the sample as follows:

> ... the office of a sample is to present to the eye the real meaning and intention of the parties with regard to the subject-matter of the contract which, owing to the imperfection of language, it may be difficult or impossible to express in words. The sample speaks for itself. But it cannot be treated as saying anything more than such a sample would tell a merchant of the class to which the buyer belongs, using due care and diligence, and appealing to it in the ordinary way and with the knowledge possessed by a merchant of that class at the time. No doubt the sample might be made to say a great deal more. Pulled to pieces and examined by unusual tests which curiosity or suspicion might suggest, it would doubtless reveal every secret of its construction. But that is not the way in which business is done in this country. Some confidence there must be between merchant and manufacturer. In matters exclusively within the province of the manufacturer, the merchant relies on the manufacturer's skill, and he does so all the more readily when, as in this case, he has had the benefit of that skill before.

The effect of this implied condition is that the buyer is only entitled to require the bulk to correspond to the sample in respect of those qualities that would be apparent from such examination as is normal in the trade.

Once what is meant by correspondence for the particular contract has been established, the condition is broken by any slight divergence — however easily remedied. Hence in *Ruben* v *Faire Bros* [1949] 1 All ER 215 the buyer purchased vulcanised rubber the sample of which was flat. When the rubber was delivered it was crinkled and only required warming to be made smooth and flat. The buyer was held to be entitled to reject the rubber; he was not under any obligation to do anything to make the goods conform to the sample.

The buyer is also to have a reasonable opportunity to make the comparison of the bulk with the sample. This term is a condition. Hence if the seller does not afford the buyer this opportunity, the buyer is not obliged to accept and pay for the goods and can terminate the contract.

Finally, it is a condition of the sale by sample that the goods in bulk are free from any defects rendering them unmerchantable which would not be apparent on a reasonable inspection of the sample.

By s. 13(2) SGA 1979 if the sale is by sample and description, the goods must conform to both. Hence in *Nichol* v *Godts* (1854) 10 Exch 191 the contract of sale was expressed to be 'of foreign refined rape oil warranted equal to sample'. The oil which was supplied matched the sample. The buyer was, nevertheless, entitled to reject the goods for a breach of the s. 13(2) condition of compliance with description as the oil was not 'foreign refined rape oil'.

2.3.6   Section 15A (inserted by SSGA 1994)

This section provides that in a contract of sale where the buyer does not deal as a consumer, if the seller's breach of a term implied by ss. 13, 14 or 15 is so slight that it would be unreasonable for the buyer to reject the goods, then the breach is to be treated as a breach of warranty. This is subject to a contrary intention appearing in, or being implied from, the contract. It is for the seller to show that the breach is so slight that it would be unreasonable for the buyer to reject the goods.

2.4   EXCLUSION CLAUSES

Often the parties to the contract of sale will attempt to exclude or limit their liability in the event of a breach of contract by the use of clauses inserted in the contract which limit or exclude liability in the event of breach. It is largely up to the parties to regulate their contractual relationship. Parliament has, however, restricted the parties' ability to exclude or limit their liability to a limited extent.

With regard to the implied terms under the SGA 1979 the position is set out in s. 55(1) which provides as follows:

Where a right, duty or liability would arise under a contract of sale of goods by implication of law, it may (subject to the Unfair Contracts Terms Act 1977) be negatived or varied by express agreement, or by course of dealing between the parties, or by such usage as binds both parties to the contract.

Three questions arise when one considers an exclusion or limitation of liability clause. The first is whether the clause has actually been incorporated into, and so forms part of, the contract of sale.

The second is whether the exclusion clause expressly covers the situation in question. The courts take a restrictive interpretation of such clauses; see *Photo Production* v *Securicor* [1980] AC 827; *George Mitchell Ltd* v *Finney Lock Seeds*

Ltd [1983] 2 AC 803; *Ailsa Craig Fishing Ltd* v *Malvern Fishing Co.* [1983] 1 WLR 164.

The third is whether the Unfair Contract Terms Act (UCTA) 1977 applies to the contract and clause in question and, if so, how the statute modifies the parties' obligations.

A typical form of clause in overseas sales is a 'non-rejection' clause, which purports to deprive the buyer of his right to reject if the goods do not comply with the required elements of description or quality, and limits him to a right to damages.

At common law in overseas sales the courts were unwilling to allow the seller to rely upon such a clause, particularly when the seller had not complied with stipulations as to the time, place or method of shipment.

If the proper law of the contract is English law then any clause which purports to limit or exclude the operation of the terms implied by the SGA 1979 must satisfy the requirement of reasonableness found in s. 11, UCTA 1977, if the sale is a non-consumer sale, i.e. one in which the buyer buys or holds himself out as buying in the course of a business; see s. 6(3), UCTA 1977. This test will not apply to a contract where the proper law of the contract is the law of any part of the United Kingdom only by the choice of the parties; see s. 27(1), UCTA 1977. The test will, however, apply where the parties have chosen the law of some country outside the United Kingdom as the proper law of the contract but it appears that the choice was imposed for the purpose of evading the operation of this Act (s. 27(2)(a), UCTA 1997).

Of particular importance with regard to international trade is the special provision that is made for international supply contracts. The limitations imposed by UCTA 1977 do not apply to liability arising under such a contract (s. 26(1), UCTA 1977).

For a contract to be classified as an international supply contract it must have the characteristics set out in s. 26(3) and (4), UCTA 1977 which are in the following terms:

(3)   Subject to subsection (4), that description of contract is one whose characteristics are the following:

(a)   either it is a contract of sale of goods or it is one under or in pursuance of which the possession of ownership of goods passes; and

(b)   it is made by parties whose places of business (or, if they have none, habitual residence) are in territories of different States (the Channel Islands and the Isle of Man being treated for this purpose as different States from the United Kingdom).

(4)   A contract falls within subsection (3) above only if either:

(a)   the goods in question are, at the time of the conclusion of the contract, in the course of carriage, or will be carried, from the territory of one State to the territory of another, or

(b)   the acts constituting the offer and acceptance have been done in the territories of different States, or

(c)   the contract provides for the goods to be delivered to the territory of a State other than that within whose territory those acts were done.

It should be stressed that the contract must be between parties whose place of business, or habitual residence, are in different states. Only then, provided that one of the additional conditions found in s. 26(4) exists, can the contract be classified as an international supply contract and thus fall within the exception found in s. 26, UCTA 1977.

At common law non-rejection clauses, though they do not exclude the right to damages, are treated as exclusion clauses. After *Photo Production* and the rejection of the doctrine of fundamental breach, the operation of the clause is a question of ascertaining the true intentions of the parties. If these are clearly expressed as to adhere to the non-rejection clause in the situation in question, the courts will honour those intentions. This does not prevent strict construction under the *contra proferentem* rule.

In *Montague Mayer Ltd* v *Kivisto* (1930) 142 LT 480 it was held that a clause that 'the buyer shall not reject the goods herein specified' only prevented rejection where goods which conformed exactly with the express and implied terms were delivered. Since these were the only goods 'herein specified', it seems, therefore, that the clause had no effect. If the goods were those specified in the contract, there would be no scope for rejection, because they were conforming. The clause did not affect the buyer's right to reject goods for reasons other than failure to comply with the contractual 'specification', such as carriage on deck or bad stowage; see *Vigers* v *Sanderson Bros* [1901] 1 KB 608.

In *F Aron Ltd* v *Comptoir Wegimont* [1921] 3 KB 435 the non-rejection clause provided that the buyer was 'not entitled to reject whatever the difference the shipment may be in value from grade, type or description'. It was held that the buyer could reject when the goods were shipped out of time. The term as to the time of shipment was held to be an independent condition precedent to the buyer's obligations and not just part of the description.

There are two typical types of limitation of liability clauses. The first is the liquidated damages clause. This specifies the entitlement to damages of the respective parties in the event of specified breaches. The clause should be construed to see which breaches it covers, and then to assess whether it represents a genuine pre-estimate of liability. If it satisfies that test, it will be held not to be a penalty clause and valid. If valid it will be enforceable whether the actual loss is greater or smaller than the liquidated amount. It is not a true limitation of liability clause as it could be to the benefit of either party.

The second type of limitation of liability clause is a clause which either fixes a limit to the amount recoverable or excludes one particular head of damage. This is a true limitation of liability clause and is, therefore, construed in accordance with the intentions of the parties but strictly *contra proferentem*; see *Ailsa Craig Fishing* v *Malvern Fishing* (above).

Conclusive evidence clauses and clauses requiring the seller to obtain a certificate from an independent source as to the quality of the goods are also found in international sale contracts. These are treated akin to exclusion clauses and receive a strict interpretation. In *Gill & Duffus* v *Berger* (see 2.3.2) the contract provided that a certificate of quality procured by the seller from an inspector at the port of discharge was to be final. The House of Lords held:

> ... where the description of the goods agreed to be sold includes a statement as to the quality and provides that a certificate of quality is to be final, then the certificate is in fact final as regards whether the goods correspond to the standard required by the contract description even if it later turns out to be wrong.

2.5 THE PASSING OF PROPERTY

As previously mentioned one of the principal objectives of a contract for the sale of goods is the transfer of property from the seller to the buyer (s. 2(1)) and it may be important, for a variety of reasons, to ascertain when this has occurred.

The availability of the proprietary remedy as between the parties to the contract is determined by the question of whether or not property in the goods has passed. This may be critical where one party to the contract has become insolvent. Where a buyer, for example, has paid the price due under the contract but has not yet received the goods he will only have a contractual claim against the seller, unless property in the goods has passed to him in which case he can claim the goods. Likewise where a seller has parted with property in the goods but has not yet been paid he will only be able to sue for the price and will not be able to recover the goods sold.

If one of the parties to the contract of sale wishes to claim in respect of damage to the goods he will only be able to put forward a claim in tort if he had property in, or possessory title to, those goods at the time when the damage occurred; see *The Aliakmon* [1986] AC 785. Furthermore if the buyer of goods wished to take advantage of s. 1 of the Bills of Lading Act 1855 (as to which see Chapter 7) he had to show that property in the goods had passed to him within the terms of s. 1.

The rules as to the passing of property in goods are fairly simple but the terminology used by the SGA 1979 often hinders rather than helps the process of understanding these rules. The two principal rules are:

(a)   property passes when the parties intend it to pass; but
(b)   property in goods cannot pass until those goods have been clearly identified as the goods which are the subject of the contract in question.

These rules will now be examined in detail but in reverse order for it is a prerequisite to the passing of property that the goods have been identified as the contractual goods.

2.5.1   Identification

Before property can pass, the contractual goods must be clearly identified because the parties must know exactly what is, and what is not, their property. In this respect the SGA 1979 draws a distinction between two types of goods, 'specific goods' and 'unascertained goods'.

Where the parties are dealing with a particular item, such as the seller's motorcar, there will be no problem in identifying the subject matter of the contract. The SGA 1979 refers to such goods as 'specific goods', being goods identified and agreed on at the time of the contract of sale (s. 61(1)).

If the parties are dealing with a commodity such as wheat the position is more difficult. If the buyer agrees to purchase say 100 tons of wheat from a seller who has 500 tons of wheat on board a particular vessel, the particular 100 tons of wheat the property in which is to be transferred from the seller to the buyer must be identified. That 100 tons must be set aside from the other 400 tons and identified as the 100 tons which is the subject matter of the contract. Unless and until there has been this act of identification the goods are 'unascertained goods' within the terms of the SGA 1979. Once the goods have, however, been identified they are not specific goods but ascertained goods.

Where there is a contract for the sale of unascertained goods no property in the goods is transferred to the buyer unless and until the goods are ascertained (s. 16).

Unascertained goods can themselves be divided into two categories. There are 'wholly unascertained' (or 'generic') goods and 'quasi-specific' goods. The latter refers to goods which form part of an identified bulk, the former to all other unascertained goods. Thus, using the example given above, if the contract between the buyer and seller was for 100 tons of the 500 tons of wheat on board the vessel the contract would be for 'quasi-specific' goods. The 100 tons would have to come from an identified source, that is to say the 500 tons on board the vessel. If, on the other hand, the contract was merely for 100 tons of wheat without specifying a particular source then the contract would be for 'wholly unascertained' goods.

If the goods are quasi-specific there are ways other than the actual setting aside of the goods by which the goods may become ascertained so that property can pass. The process of ascertainment may be achieved by exhaustion of the bulk or consolidation of parts of the bulk without any final act by the seller.

Exhaustion is the reduction in the specified or appropriated bulk to a quantity no greater than that stipulated in the contract. This reduction can occur in various ways: by delivery of the rest of the bulk to another buyer or by reduction in the bulk through destruction leaving only that which the seller is obliged to deliver to the buyer under the contract of sale.

Ascertainment by consolidation occurs where the goods in question derive from different contracts of sale but form the totality of a particular and ascertained bulk which becomes destined for delivery to a single buyer. In *Karlshamns Olijefabriker v Eastport Navigation Corporation, The Elafi* [1982] 1 All ER 208 the buyer agreed to purchase part of a quantity of goods on board a vessel. He had five separate contracts, four with one seller and one with another. The remainder of the cargo was delivered to other purchasers. The balance was held to have become ascertained in part by exhaustion but also by consolidation.

2.5.2 Intention

Where there is a contract for the sale of specific or ascertained goods the property in them is transferred to the buyer at such time as the parties to the contract intend it to be transferred (s. 17(1)). In ascertaining the intention of the parties one must have regard to the terms of the contract and the circumstances of the case (s. 17(2)).

The general provisions of s. 17 are supplemented by the more precise 'rules for ascertaining intention' in s. 18, which are presumptive guides to when property will be transferred unless a contrary intention appears.

The rules in s. 18 are further supplemented by the conventions which have developed in respect of particular forms of international sale contracts. Hence in c.i.f. contracts the parties are presumed to have intended that property should pass when the documents are delivered to the buyer or his authorised agent. In f.o.b. contracts property is presumed to pass when the goods cross the ship's rail, but in every case the overriding principle is that property passes when the parties intend it to pass.

The first three of the presumptive rules in s. 18 are concerned with specific goods.

Rule 1

Where there is an unconditional contract for the sale of specific goods in a deliverable state the property in the goods passes to the buyer when the contract is made, and it is immaterial whether the time of payment or the time of delivery, or both, be postponed.

'Unconditional' in rule 1 does not relate to the type of terms used in the contract, but to whether the transfer of property in the goods is subject to some specified contingency. If such a contingency is expressed in the contract, then rule 1 cannot apply.

Goods are in a 'deliverable state' for the purposes of rule 1 when they are in such a condition that the buyer under the contract would be bound to take delivery of them. The requirement has nothing to do with the ability of the seller actually to deliver the goods. Hence if goods are to be delivered 'on rail', then the buyer is not obliged to take them and property will not pass under rule 1 unless the goods have been loaded on rail; see *Underwood Ltd v Burgh Castle Brick and Cement Syndicate* [1922] 1 KB 343. Similarly if the seller has agreed to sell 'fitted carpets' the carpets will not be in a deliverable state and property will not pass until properly fitted in accordance with the terms of the contract. If the carpets are stolen from the house in question before being fitted this is the seller's and not the buyer's loss; see *Head & Sons Ltd v Showfronts Ltd* [1970] 1 Lloyd's Rep 140.

Rule 2

Where there is a contract for the sale of specific goods and the seller is bound to do something to the goods for the purpose of putting them into a deliverable state, the property does not pass until the thing is done and the buyer has notice that it has been done.

The contracts to which rule 2 applies are by definition conditional upon the seller putting the goods into a deliverable state and the buyer having notice that this has been done. If the buyer is obliged to do the things required, rule 2 does not apply. As regards notice, it seems sufficient that the buyer is aware that the things necessary have been done. There is no obligation on the seller to inform the buyer.

Rule 3

Where there is a contract for the sale of specific goods in a deliverable state but the seller is bound to weigh, measure, test, or do some other act or thing with reference to the goods for the purpose of ascertaining the price, the property does not pass until the act or thing is done and the buyer has notice that it has been done.

Again it is only if the seller is obliged to perform the necessary acts in order to ascertain the price that rule 3 will apply. Again the buyer must have notice that the requisite acts or things have been done, but there is no requirement that he be notified.

Where the goods are not specific goods they must be ascertained before property in those goods can pass to the buyer. Once the goods have been ascertained, property in them can pass and it will pass when the parties intend it to pass. Section 18, rules 5(1) and 5(2) are, however, presumptive guides.

Rule 5(1)

Where there is a contract for the sale of unascertained or future goods by description, and goods of that description and in a deliverable state are unconditionally appropriated to the contract, either by the seller with the assent of the buyer, or by the buyer with the assent of the seller, the property in the goods then passes to the buyer; and the assent may be express or implied, and may be given either before or after the appropriation is made.

The goods, therefore, to which rule 5 applies are all forms of unascertained goods as well as future goods, even if these are specific. The rule is confined to sales by description. There are five elements to be satisfied before the rule can apply, bearing in mind that it can be rebutted if a contrary intention appears. First, there must be an appropriation of the goods; secondly, that appropriation must be unconditional and therefore irrevocable; thirdly, the goods appropriated must correspond to the contract description; fourthly, the goods must be in a deliverable state; and, fifthly, the non-appropriating party must give his assent to the appropriation. The assent can be given either before the act of appropriation (see *Aldridge* v *Johnson* (1857) 7 E & B 885), or after.

Goods are unconditionally appropriated to a contract when they have been irrevocably identified by the parties as the goods which are the subject of the contract; that is to say the goods have been earmarked as the contractual goods. The commonest way by which goods are unconditionally appropriated to a contract of sale is by delivery of the goods. It may also be the case that the act of appropriation is the same act as that which ascertains the goods, as for instance, when a motorist fills his car with petrol from a self-service pump. Indeed when one is dealing with quasi-specific goods which have become ascertained by exhaustion, the seller is taken to have made an unconditional appropriation since it is clear that having designated the particular bulk the seller has lost the power to substitute other goods; see *Wait & James* v *Midland Bank* (1926) 31 Com Cas 172.

Rule 5(2) provides an example of an act of unconditional appropriation which has particular relevance in the context of international sales.

Rule 5(2)

Where in pursuance of the contract, the seller delivers the goods to the buyer or to a carrier or other bailee or custodian (whether named by the buyer or not) for the purpose of transmission to the buyer, and does not reserve the right of disposal, he is taken to have unconditionally appropriated the goods to the contract.

It must be remembered that this is not an absolute rule and will be rebutted in the event of a contrary intention. This sub-rule must also be read subject to s. 16 so that if the seller delivers goods to a carrier mixed with other goods, no property can pass as the goods are still unascertained despite what would otherwise be an unconditional appropriation; see *Healey* v *Howlett & Sons* [1917] 1 KB 337.

Furthermore whether there is an unconditional appropriation within rule 5(2) depends on the seller's duty of delivery. If the extent of his obligation is to arrange for goods to be sent to the buyer, the rule will apply, subject to contrary intention. If, on the other hand, the seller's duty is to deliver the goods to a particular place, the seller must ensure the goods get there. The carrier is taken to be the seller's rather than the buyer's agent and until the goods reach the designated place rule 5(2) cannot apply; see *Comptoir d'Achat et de Vente du Boerenbond Belge SA* v *Luis de Ridder Limitada, The Julia* [1949] AC 293.

The question of whether goods had been unconditionally appropriated to a contract was considered in *Carlos Federspiel & Co. SA* v *Charles Twigg & Co. Ltd* [1957] 1 Lloyd's Rep 240 in which the seller had agreed to sell a quantity of bicycles to an overseas buyer on f.o.b. terms (see Chapter 4). The buyer paid the price in advance and the bicycles were packed and marked with the buyer's name at the seller's premises. The seller informed the buyer of the shipping marks and that the goods were ready to load. Before the bicycles were shipped, however, the seller became insolvent. The question was whether property in the bicycles had passed to the buyer prior to the seller's insolvency. The court found that property had not passed as there had been no unconditional and irrevocable act of appropriation of the bicycles with the buyer's name on them to the buyer's contract. Appropriation in this case was taken as being the last decisive act to be performed by the seller. In this case, that act was the shipment of the goods. Until that time the seller was free to change his mind and use other goods in performance of the sale; see also *Hendy Lennox Ltd* v *Grahame Puttick Ltd* [1984] 2 All ER 152; *Mucklow* v *Mangles* (1808) 1 Taunt 318. In international sales parties often agree that a notice of appropriation is to be given within a specified time period for the avoidance of doubt.

One final instance of unconditional appropriation is when a third party with authority from the seller and in possession of ascertained goods as agent or bailee of the seller irrevocably attorns to the buyer. Attornment is an express representation to the buyer by the third party that he holds the goods for and on behalf of the seller. If the third party did not have the actual authority of the seller to make such an attornment the seller may nevertheless be estopped from denying the third party's authority; see *Sterns Ltd* v *Vickers Ltd* [1923] 1 KB 78.

2.5.3   Reservation of Title

As has been stated above the fundamental rule in respect of the passing of property is that property passes when the parties to the contract of sale intend it to pass.

The parties may agree in the contract of sale that property in the goods should not pass until a particular condition has been fulfilled by the buyer, such as the payment of the price. This general principle is set out in s. 19(1). This agreement between buyer and seller may take the form of a reservation of title clause in the contract of sale. Such clauses are common in commercial agreements and are intended to protect the seller in the event of the buyer's insolvency. These clauses have become increasingly sophisticated and may, for example, generate a proprietary right to the proceeds of the sale of the goods by the buyer (see *Aluminium Industrie Vaasen B* v *Romalpa Aluminium Ltd* [1976] 1 WLR 676), or reserve title until all debts due to the supplier have been paid by the buyer (see *Armour* v *Thyssen Edelstahlwerke AG* [1990] 3 All ER 481).

There are, however, other methods aside from agreement by which the seller can retain title to the goods. Section 19(2) provides an example of a situation in which the seller is taken to have reserved title to his goods. Where goods are shipped for delivery to the buyer and the seller takes a bill of lading from the carrier drawn to the order of the seller or his agent, the seller is *prima facie* to be taken to have reserved the right of disposal of those goods. The seller has prevented property from passing as he still retains the bill of lading which is the document of title to the goods (see Chapter 5). Property in the goods will pass to the buyer when the seller endorses and delivers the bill of lading to the buyer.

Similarly the seller will be taken to have prevented property from passing to the buyer when he takes a bill of lading in the buyer's name, but does not deliver it to him; see *The Kronprinsessa Margareta* [1921] AC 515.

Section 19(3) provides another statutory example of when the seller is to be regarded as having reserved the right of disposal of the goods. This is when the seller sends the bill of lading together with a bill of exchange drawn on the buyer for the price of the goods. The buyer must accept or pay the bill of exchange, otherwise he must return the bill of lading which he is deemed to hold on trust for the seller. Even if the buyer wrongfully retains the bill of lading, property in the goods represented by the bill of lading does not pass to him.

2.6 THE *'NEMO DAT QUOD NON HABET'* RULE

The basic rule is that no one can give what he does not have. A person who does not own goods cannot give another property in those goods unless he does so with the authority of the owner. The buyer acquires no better title to the goods than that of the seller (s. 21(1)).

There are, however, exceptions to this basic rule and these are found at common law, in the SGA 1979 and the Factors Act (FA) 1889. The FA 1889 is broadly similar to, though slightly more extensive than the relevant provisions of the SGA 1979. The SGA 1979 has not repealed or replaced the FA 1889. The exceptions to the general rule are found in ss. 21–25 and s. 48(2) which will now be examined in some detail.

2.6.1 Where the Owner is Estopped

There would appear to be two types of cases where the owner is precluded from denying the seller's authority to sell. The first is where the owner has, by his words or his conduct, represented to the buyer that the seller is the true owner, or has the owner's authority to sell. The second case is where the owner, by his negligent failure to act, allows the seller to appear as the owner of the goods or as having the owner's authority to sell.

Two restrictive rules limit the scope of this estoppel. First, the delivery of the goods by the owner to a third party is not a representation by the owner that the third party has the authority to sell. It has no consequence in the context of estoppel; see *Central Newbury Car Auctions Ltd* v *United Finance Ltd* [1957] 1 QB 371. The other restrictive rule is that delivery of the documents of title to the goods does not raise the estoppel against the owner; see *Mercantile Bank of India* v *Central Bank of India* [1938] AC 287.

The estoppel will only operate if there has been an actual sale by the third party in possession. It is not enough that there is an agreement to sell. This is because there must be some detrimental reliance by the representee for the estoppel to stand; see *Sham* v *The Metropolitan Police Commissioner* [1987] 1 WLR 1332.

It seems that whilst an innocent owner is not estopped when he delivers the goods or documents of title to a third party without authority to sell, a negligent owner in the same circumstances may be estopped if the buyer from the third party relies upon the apparent authority or ownership of his seller and the owner's negligence is a proximate cause of the buyer's purchase; see *Mercantile Credit Ltd* v *Hamblin* [1965] 2 QB 252; *Moorgate Mercantile Co.* v *Twitchings* [1977] AC 890.

This exception has particular importance with regard to sales by agents. A sale within the 'ostensible' or 'usual' authority of an agent will bind his principal even though he may have exceeded his actual authority. Since this exception to the *nemo dat* rule is essentially based on equity, the estoppel will not be available to a buyer who was or ought to have been aware of the seller's lack of title and authority to sell on behalf of the owner.

2.6.2   Section 2 of the Factors Act 1889

The next exception to the *nemo dat* rule is found in the FA 1889. Section 21(2), SGA 1979 provides:

Nothing in this Act affects—
(a)   The provisions of the Factors Acts, or any enactment enabling the apparent owner of goods to dispose of them as if he were their true owner.

Section 2, FA 1889 provides:

Where a mercantile agent is in possession of goods with the owner's consent and the mercantile agent sells, pledges, or otherwise disposes of the goods in the ordinary course of a mercantile agent's business to a *bona fide* purchaser without notice at the time of the disposition of any lack of authority, then the sale, pledge or disposition is to be as valid as if expressly authorised by the owner.

The meaning of this subsection requires some consideration. A mercantile agent is defined, by s. 1(1), FA 1889 and s. 26, SGA 1979, as an agent who has, in the customary course of his business, authority either to sell goods or to consign goods for the purpose of sale, or to buy goods, or to raise money on the security of goods. The mercantile agent must have possession of the goods with the consent of the owner and it would seem that it does not matter that the owner's consent was obtained by fraud or deception; see *Pearson* v *Rose & Young Ltd* [1951] 1 KB 275.

If documents of title are used the rule is the same. Documents of title for the purposes of the exceptions to the *nemo dat* principle are the statutory documents of title and not just the shipped bill of lading, which is the only recognised document of title at common law (s. 1(4), FA 1889).

2.6.3   Seller in Possession

Where a person having sold goods retains possession of the goods, or of the documents of title to the goods, the delivery or transfer by that person, or by a mercantile agent acting for him, of the goods or documents of title under any sale, pledge, or other disposition thereof, to any person receiving the same in good faith and without notice of the previous sale, has the same effect as if the person making the delivery or transfer were expressly authorised by the owner of the goods to make the same (s. 24, SGA 1979).

The seller in possession must have sold the goods to the first buyer. An agreement to sell is not enough, as in such a case, no property will have passed to the first buyer and the second sale would not be in breach of the *nemo dat* rule, although the seller would be in breach of the first contract for non-delivery.

The seller will not be able to transfer a better title to the second buyer than the title he transferred to the first, as the sale is one stated as being 'as if authorised by the owner' — the first buyer who is himself bound by the *nemo dat* rule.

Any break in the seller's possession will prevent s. 24 from operating in the second buyer's favour. It does not matter, however, that the character of the seller's possession has changed, e.g., from being owner to bailee. Also it does not matter for the purposes of s. 24 that the seller's possession is without the first buyer's consent.

2.6.4   Seller with a Voidable Title

When the seller of goods has a voidable title to them, but his title has not been avoided at the time of the sale, the buyer acquires a good title to the goods, provided he buys them in good faith and without notice of the seller's defect of title (s. 23). This is a true exception to the *nemo dat* rule in that the buyer's title, if taken in good faith and without notice, is not affected by the fraud, misrepresentation, duress, etc, that flaws the seller's title.

2.6.5   Resale by the Unpaid Seller

The unpaid seller's rights of lien and stoppage in transit are defeated by the buyer's sale to a *bona fide* transferee for value of a document of title to the goods (s. 47(2)(a)). If the buyer does not sell but pledges or otherwise disposes of the goods, the unpaid seller's rights are subordinated to those acquired by the transferee.

Where an unpaid seller who has exercised his right of lien or stoppage resells the goods, the buyer acquires a good title as against the original buyer (s. 48(2)). The section does not require the second buyer to be without notice of the seller's breach of duty to the original buyer. However, the section is limited to resale and does not protect a pledgee or other disponee of the goods.

2.6.6   Buyer in Possession Before Property has Passed

Where a person having bought or agreed to buy goods obtains, with the consent of the seller, possession of the goods or the documents of title to the goods, the delivery or transfer by that person, or by a mercantile agent acting for him, of the goods or documents of title under any sale, pledge, or other disposition thereof, to any person receiving the same in good faith and without notice of any lien or other right of the original seller in respect of the goods, has the same effect as if the person making the delivery or transfer were a mercantile agent in possession of the goods or documents of title with the consent of the owner (s. 25).

The original buyer must be someone bound to the contract even if the contract is executory at the time of the second disposition. If the original buyer has an option to buy, as in hire-purchase agreements, s. 25 does not protect the second transferee. This also excludes the thief of the goods from the seller as he is never someone in possession of the goods or documents of title with the consent of the owner; see *National Employers' General Insurance Mutual Association* v *Jones* [1990] 1 AC 24.

The original buyer must be in possession of the goods; this includes certain forms of constructive possession. In *Four Point Garages* v *Carter* [1985] 3 All ER 12 the original seller delivered a car to a sub-purchaser at the buyer's request and this was held to be sufficient to give the buyer constructive possession of the goods, though of a fleeting nature.

The seller must consent to the buyer's possession, and as in s. 24 it does not matter that this consent has been withdrawn or procured by fraud or misrepresentation.

The buyer's disposition is only effective if made in the guise of a sale by a mercantile agent; see *Newtons of Wembley Ltd* v *Williams* [1965] 1 QB 560.

The documents of title referred to are found in s. 1(4), FA 1889. It seems that for s. 25, SGA 1979 to protect the second transferee, he need not receive the same documents of title as were in the possession of the original buyer with the consent of the owner; see *Mount* v *Jay* [1960] 1 QB 159.

2.6.7   The Meaning of Good Faith and Notice

For the purposes of the exceptions to the *nemo dat* rule, good faith in the transferee denotes honesty in fact, even if unreasonable or negligent. Want of notice, however, is assessed against the yardstick of the reasonable man and so the transferee will be regarded as having notice of his transferor's want of authority if, though acting in good faith, he acquires the goods in such circumstances that no reasonable man would have taken them without further inquiry. Constructive notice does not apply to commercial dealings and, therefore, the transferee will not be fixed with the seller's want of authority merely because he has failed to inquire of the seller's right to sell. In addition, there must be a failure to do that which the reasonable man would have done in the circumstances.

2.7   INITIAL IMPOSSIBILITY, RISK AND FRUSTRATION

These principles arise in sale of goods law as defences or excuses for having delivered damaged goods or not delivering at all. Three issues arise: first, what is the effect of impossibility of performing at the time of the contracting?; secondly, who should bear the loss or damage to the goods caused at the time of performance?; and, thirdly, what happens when something makes the contract impossible to perform subsequent to the making of the contract?

2.7.1   Impossibility

Where there is a contract for the sale of specific goods and the goods without the knowledge of the seller have perished at the time when the contract was made, the contract is void (s. 6, SGA 1979). The section cannot be excluded by the parties and is therefore an absolute rule.

The SGA 1979 does not deal with the case when there is a contract for specific goods which never existed. At common law one of two solutions applies depending upon the construction of the contract: either there was a fundamental assumption in the agreement that the goods existed, in which case the contract would be void on account of the mutual mistake; or one party is found to have warranted that the goods were in existence and, therefore, assumed the risk of the goods not existing. In this case there is a contract, which would be broken if the goods did not exist; see *McRae* v *Commonwealth Disposals Commission* (1951) 84 CLR 377.

If the contract is for unascertained (i.e. generic) goods the question of initial impossibility does not arise unless the whole of the world supply of those goods has been exhausted. The fact that the seller intended using a particular source or particular goods which are no longer available is irrelevant if he has not unconditionally appropriated them to the contract.

If the sale is for an unidentified part of an identified bulk (i.e. for quasi-specific goods) and that bulk is destroyed before the contract is made, then it seems that the contract would be void; see the *obiter dictum* in *Barrow, Lane & Ballard Ltd* v *Phillip Phillips & Co. Ltd* [1929] 1 KB 574.

'Perish' within s. 6 includes the lawful sale of the goods by a bailee (see *Couturier* v *Hastie* (1856) 5 HLC 673); the theft of the goods if there is no possibility of recovery before the date of delivery under the contract (see *Barrow, Lane & Ballard* v *Phillip Phillips & Co.*); and the physical destruction of the goods. There is uncertainty in the authorities as to whether damage to the goods is included within the meaning of 'perish' and, if so, what extent of damage there must be. However, the consensus of opinion seems in favour of a narrow meaning, i.e. that damage, however severe, is not sufficient. Of course, the narrower the meaning of perish, the more readily there would be a contract, but the more easily the seller would be in breach of either s. 13 or s. 14; see *Asfar & Co.* v *Blundell* [1896] 1 QB 123.

2.7.2 Risk

When a person is bound to bear the accidental damage to, or loss of, goods they are said to be at his risk. For example, if goods were damaged or lost while they were at the buyer's risk the buyer is nonetheless liable for the price. Risk has been described by Dr Sealy ([1972] 31 CLJ 226) as:

> ... a derivative, and essentially negative, concept — an elliptical way of saying that either or both the primary obligations of one party shall be enforceable, and that those of the other party will be deemed to have been discharged even though the normally prerequisite conditions have not been satisfied.

The general rule is that risk *prima facie* passes with property in the goods. Section 20(1) provides:

Unless otherwise agreed, the goods remain at the seller's risk until the property in
them is transferred to the buyer, but when the property in them is transferred to the
buyer, the goods are at the buyer's risk whether delivery has been made or not.

The rule is rebuttable by express or implied agreement. In c.i.f. sales there is a
rebuttable principle that risk passes on shipment, thus divorcing risk from the passing
of property; see *The Julia* (2.5.2, Rule 5(2)). This rule has the odd effect that if goods
are shipped before being appropriated to the buyer's contract, once they have been
unconditionally appropriated, risk is deemed to have been on the buyer as from the date
of shipment. If the goods were destroyed before the purported act of appropriation, such
act is void and the seller is required to use other goods in the performance of the sale. If
the goods are damaged before the purported act of appropriation but after shipment,
there is a conflict of academic opinion but no decided authority. Goode suggests that
the seller should be prevented from using such damaged goods — whatever the extent
of the damage. The buyer has contracted to buy goods of the contractual description. By
permitting the seller to appropriate damaged goods the buyer would never be in a
position to receive conforming goods but would be forced to accept the damaged goods
and the possibility of a claim in damages for any loss. Goode further argues the futility
of permitting the seller to use goods which breach s. 13 or 14 as the buyer on delivery
could reject them in any event. Benjamin accepts that the seller should not be capable
of appropriating goods which are a commercial loss (i.e. which breach ss. 13 or 14), but
thinks that the rule should not prevent the seller from using slightly damaged goods
which would amount only to a breach of warranty since this is the approach that most
commercial men would adopt; see the similar reasoning in *The Hansa Nord* at 2.3.3.

The two cases frequently cited in this debate do not actually face the issue. In
Groome Ltd v *Barber* [1915] 1 KB 316 Atkin J was concerned with reiterating the
rule that in c.i.f. contracts documents may be tendered as constructive delivery and
in performance of the contract of sale notwithstanding that at that time the goods had
been lost. He was not, therefore, considering the prior question of whether lost,
destroyed or damaged goods can be appropriated to the contract, the condition
precedent to any transfer of documents in constructive performance of the seller's
delivery obligation. Similarly, in *Mambre Saccharine Co. Ltd* v *Corn Products Ltd*
[1919] 1 KB 198 McCardie J held that the loss of goods did not preclude a
subsequent tender of documents in a c.i.f. sale. He did not discuss the question of
post-loss appropriation and was not, therefore, concerned with the need for an
appropriation to identify the goods represented by the documents.

In f.o.b. contracts, however, the rule in s. 20 is generally adopted and risk passes
when the goods pass over the ship's rail, i.e. the same notional point when property
is deemed to pass; see *Inglis* v *Stock* (1885) 10 App Cas 263.

Therefore, in both c.i.f. and f.o.b. contracts if the loss of specific or ascertained
goods occurs before shipment, the seller bears the risk and will be liable to the buyer
for non-delivery.

In general, risk will not pass in goods whilst they remain unascertained; see *obiter
dicta* of the House of Lords in *The Julia* (2.5.2, Rule 5(2)). Again, however, there is

no absolute rule so that if the seller has done all in his power to deliver the goods to the buyer without actually unconditionally appropriating them to the contract, it is possible for risk to pass if a third party in possession of the goods attorns to the buyer in respect of them and the buyer expressly or impliedly assents to the attornment; see *Sterns Ltd* v *Vickers Ltd* (2.5.2, Rule 5(2)).

There are three statutory qualifications to the *prima facie* rule that risk follows property. First, where delivery has been delayed through the fault of either buyer or seller, the goods are at the risk of the party at fault as regards any loss which might not have occurred but for such delay (s. 20(2)). It seems that the section puts the burden on the guilty party of proving that the loss in question would have occurred in any event, subject to the duty of the innocent party to minimise his loss.

Secondly, nothing in s. 20 affects the duties or liabilities of either seller or buyer as a bailee or custodian of the goods of the other party (s. 20(3)). The duty of a bailee is to exercise reasonable care in looking after the goods of the bailor. However, once the delivery date has passed it seems that if the seller is left in possession of the goods because the buyer has failed to collect the goods, he is in the position of a gratuitous or involuntary bailee. This reduces the seller's duties, although there are *obiter dicta* in *Demby Hamilton & Co. Ltd* v *Barden* [1949] 1 All ER 435 suggesting that his duties remain those of taking reasonable care of the goods.

Thirdly, when the goods are sent by a route involving sea transit under circumstances in which it is usual to insure, the seller must give such notice to the buyer as may enable him to insure them during their sea transit; and if the seller fails to do so, the goods are at his risk during such sea transit (s. 32(3)). This provision is particularly relevant to international sales. Obviously, the section does not apply to c.i.f. contracts as one of the seller's contractual obligations is to insure the goods for the whole of the transit. It has been applied, however, to f.o.b. contracts even when the buyer has the obligation of making the contract of carriage, though in such a case the duty is not an onerous one; see *Wimble & Sons* v *Rosenberg & Sons* [1913] 3 KB 743.

2.7.3 Frustration

Where there is an agreement to sell specific goods and subsequently the goods, without any fault on the part of the seller or buyer, perish before the risk passes to the buyer, the agreement is avoided (s. 7). The statutory rule on frustration merely restates the general rule at common law, whilst remembering that once risk has passed to the buyer frustration is irrelevant. 'Perish' in s. 7 bears the same meaning as in s. 6 (see 2.7.1).

As at common law, the rule in s. 7 will not apply if the parties have made provision in the contract of sale for their rights and liabilities should the particular event in question happen. The common law supplements s. 7. Events which do not result in the goods 'perishing' for the purposes of s. 7 will frustrate the contract if sufficient to do so at common law.

Section 7 is limited to specific goods. If the contract is for a sale of generic goods then, unless the frustrating event in question is supervening illegality, it is inherently unlikely that the contract will be frustrated, as the destruction of any particular source of goods intended by the seller for his performance of the contract is irrelevant. If the goods are quasi-specific (i.e. an unidentified part of an identified bulk), destruction of the bulk can constitute frustration; see *Kursell* v *Timber Operators and Contractors Ltd* [1927] 1 KB 298.

2.8   DELIVERY

The rules for delivery in the SGA 1979 apply equally to international sales as they do to domestic contracts. However, because of the extensive use of documents in the former, the SGA 1979 applies in a modified fashion.

It is the duty of the seller to deliver the goods, and of the buyer to accept and pay for them, in accordance with the terms of the contract of sale (s. 27). A delivery of goods which is not in conformity with the contract of sale will not necessarily be ineffective, as the breach may not be such as to entitle the buyer to reject the goods or, in a case where the buyer is entitled to reject, he may elect not to exercise that right. Also in sales of generic goods, provided that the seller has not unconditionally appropriated the particular goods, a non-conforming delivery may be substituted by a conforming one provided that time has not become of the essence. Finally, the concept of delivery should be distinguished from that of acceptance.

Section 6(1) defines 'delivery' as the '... voluntary transfer of possession from one person to another'. Alone, therefore, it has nothing to do with the transfer of property or risk.

Delivery may be either actual or constructive. Constructive delivery is the most common form of delivery in international sales. It may take one of a variety of forms:

(a)   By the transfer of the document of title. The document of title itself must be in the transferee's possession and must indicate that he is the lawful holder. The only common law document of title is the bill of lading (see *Lickbarrow* v *Mason* (1787) 2 TLR 63), but there are various statutory documents of title (s. 1(4), Factors Act 1889).

(b)   By the delivery of an object giving physical control, such as a key to the warehouse in which the goods are stored.

(c)   By attornment, which is when a party in possession lawfully acknowledges that goods which he previously held for himself or another are now held for the buyer (s. 29(4), SGA 1979).

(d)   Where the buyer, originally in possession of the goods under some limited interest such as bailment, purchases the goods and then continues to hold them in his own right.

(e)   By delivery to a carrier in pursuance of the contract of sale. This is provided for in s. 32(1), SGA 1979:

Where, in pursuance of a contract of sale, the seller is authorised or required to send the goods to the buyer, delivery of the goods to a carrier (whether named by the buyer or not) for the purpose of transmission to the buyer is *prima facie* deemed to be a delivery of the goods to the buyer.

Section 32(1), therefore, makes the carrier agent for the buyer. If the circumstances are such that the carrier is clearly the seller's agent, then the *prima facie* rule will not apply. This would typically be the case when the seller's obligation is not 'to send the goods' but actually to ensure delivery to the buyer. In both c.i.f. and f.o.b. contracts, the seller's duty is at most 'to send' and not to ensure actual delivery.

If the seller's duty is to send the goods then, unless otherwise authorised by the buyer, the seller must make such contract with the carrier on behalf of the buyer as may be reasonable having regard to the nature of the goods and the other circumstances of the case; and if the seller omits to do so, and the goods are lost or damaged in course of transit, the buyer may decline to treat the delivery to the carrier as a delivery to himself or may hold the seller responsible in damages (s. 32(2)).

The place of delivery and whether it is for the buyer to collect or for the seller to send for the goods depends in each case on the contract (s. 29(1)). The *prima facie* rule is that it is for the buyer to collect the goods. Of course, this is rarely the case in international sales.

The seller must tender delivery at the time stipulated in the contract. The buyer can reject the tender if it is late only if time is of the essence, as is frequently the case in international sales. Where under the contract of sale the seller is bound to send the goods to the buyer, but no time for sending them is fixed, the seller is bound to send them within a reasonable time (s. 29(3)). Demand or tender of delivery may be treated as ineffectual unless made at a reasonable hour; and what is a reasonable hour is a question of fact (s. 29(5)).

In international sales the expense of delivery is clearly outlined in the contract: in c.i.f. it is the seller's burden; in f.o.b. it is the buyer's.

2.8.1 Instalment Deliveries

This section considers when the seller is entitled to perform by delivery of the goods in instalments and what is the effect of defective performance by the respective parties. Unless otherwise agreed, the buyer of goods is not bound to accept delivery of them by instalments (s. 31(1)). One consequence of this rule is that if the buyer in such a case accepts delivery of a quantity less than the contractual amount, he does not have to accept a subsequent tender of the balance; see *Behrend & Co. Ltd* v *Produce Brokers & Co. Ltd* [1920] 3 KB 530.

The parties' contractual relationship will either be governed by a series of separate contracts or a single contract. If the proper construction of the parties' legal relationship is not a single contract but several contracts, then the SGA 1979 rules on delivery apply to each contract independently, but not to the relationship as a whole. There are several guides to the difference between several or single contracts:

(a)   If there is a single order form for a number of items, this is a clear indication that a single contract was intended.

(b)   If there are separate order forms for delivery of differing goods at different times, this is an indication of separate contracts.

(c)   When the parties agree on a set of standard trading conditions under which goods are to be supplied as and when ordered, the terms do not constitute a contract in themselves, and each order will be a separate contract.

(d)   If the buyer purchases a global amount of goods on one order form, to be delivered as and when he directs, this is an indication of a single contract.

(e)   Provisions in the contract that each shipment or delivery is to be treated as a separate contract will not be construed literally if this would produce an artificial division of what in truth is a single contract with delivery by instalments.

If the relationship is governed by a single contract, the parties' rights and obligations will fall into one of the following three analyses.

2.8.1.1   Single Contract: Seller's Obligation of Delivery is Divisible

A single contract may provide for delivery by instalments in which the seller's obligation of delivery is 'divisible'. This type of obligation will often be inferred when the contract provides for separate deliveries each with a corresponding payment obligation. Section 31(2) makes the effect of such a provision depend on the circumstances of the case.

A divisible delivery obligation will normally have the effect of preventing the buyer from rejecting individual non-conforming tenders unless and until the seller's default is such as to evince an intention to repudiate the contract or an inability to perform. The courts look first at the ratio quantitatively which the breach bears to the whole and, secondly, at the degree of probability or improbability that such a breach will be repeated; see *Maple Flock Co. Ltd* v *Universal Furniture Products (Wembley) Ltd* [1934] 1 KB 148.

The seller is entitled to require the buyer to accept and pay for each instalment tendered in conformity with the contract, and this right is not affected by the seller's breach in relation to other instalments except where *Maple Flock* is satisfied. Also, the buyer's acceptance of one instalment does not debar him from rejecting subsequent non-conforming instalments, because s. 11(4) does not apply to contracts which are severable.

The buyer's improper rejection of instalments does not constitute a repudiation of the contract unless and until it reveals an inability or intention not to perform his obligations. For the purpose of the unpaid seller's rights of lien and withholding delivery, each instalment is treated as a separate contract, so that the buyer's failure to pay for one instalment will not entitle the seller to withhold his performance of subsequent deliveries.

A proper rejection of a single instalment in a situation outside the rule in *Maple Flock* will not enable the buyer to repudiate the contract as a whole under s. 30(1), and he is reduced to a claim in damages for the reduction in the global quantity delivered under the contract.

2.8.1.2 Single Contract: Seller's Obligation of Delivery is Indivisible

The second possibility is where there is a single contract providing for delivery by instalment, but in which the delivery obligation is 'indivisible' or 'entire'. In this case, the seller cannot require the buyer to pay the price of one instalment, but must wait until he has performed the entirety of his obligations. If the buyer, however, accepts one instalment this constitutes an adoption of the contract as a whole and precludes him from rejecting the remainder of the goods even if they do not conform (s. 11(4)).

This raises the question of the interaction of s. 11(4) and the rules as to 'delivery of the wrong quantity' in s. 30. The following propositions may be made:

(a)   If the seller delivers goods which he contracted to sell mixed with goods of a different description not included in the contract, the buyer would be bound to accept the goods which are in accordance with the contract but he may reject the rest (s. 30(4)). Because of the rule in s. 11(4) it would seem that the buyer could not reject the whole as non-conforming.

(b)   If an instalment tendered is excessive in quantity, the buyer can either accept the lot and pay pro rata or he can reject the excess (s. 30(2), (3)). It would seem, however, that the possibility of rejecting the whole in such a situation of over-delivery provided for in s. 30(2) would not be available to the buyer if he had already accepted a prior instalment and thus adopted the contract under s. 11(4). Section 30(2A) (inserted by SSGA 1994) provides that a buyer who does not deal as a consumer may not reject the whole under s. 30(2) if the excess is so slight that it would be unreasonable for him to do so.

(c)   If the contract has been adopted by the buyer within s. 11(4) it would also seem that the buyer must accept future instalments of conforming goods notwithstanding that they are of insufficient quantity. Section 30(1) would not apply. However, if the seller then attempts to deliver the balance, but the effect would be to exceed the global amount provided for in the contract, the buyer may decline the balance.

If the buyer can show that his acceptance of one instalment was conditional on a proper delivery of the remainder, s. 11(4) will not apply and he will only be bound by the contract when the full contract quantity is delivered. In this case, the buyer's improper rejection of one instalment will constitute a repudiation of the entire contract; see the discussion by Rougier J in *Bernstein* v *Pamson Motors* [1987] 2 All ER 220.

Two general points under this type of contract are, first, that the seller's lien and right to withhold delivery for non-payment extends to the whole of the undelivered goods and secures the whole of the price; and, secondly, accidental destruction of part of the goods before the risk has been passed to the buyer may frustrate the entire contract.

2.8.1.3   Single Contract: Delivery by Instalment Prohibited

The third possibility is of a single contract which prohibits delivery by instalment. The delivery obligation in such a contract is *ex hypothesi* indivisible and the rule in s. 11(4) applies. The buyer may reject short delivery under s. 30(1), but acceptance of a short delivery of the goods will constitute an adoption of the contract under s. 11(4) and entitle the seller to claim the price of the goods delivered pro rata with the contract price (s. 30(1)). Section 30(2A) provides that a buyer who does not deal as a consumer may not reject the goods under s. 30(1) if the shortfall is so slight that it would be unreasonable for him to do so. The buyer would not be obliged to accept a tender of the balance of the goods since under s. 31(1) he is not bound to accept delivery by instalments.

Where the seller delivers a quantity of goods in excess of the contract amount, the buyer can accept the contract amount and reject the excess; or he may reject the lot (s. 30(2)) subject to s. 30(2A); or he may accept the lot and pay for the excess pro rata with the contract price (s. 30(3)).

2.9   ACCEPTANCE

The doctrine of acceptance is concerned with assessing when the buyer is barred from rejecting the goods. What constitutes acceptance is governed by s. 35, SGA 1979, as amended by SSGA 1994.

There are three ways in which acceptance may occur. The first is when the buyer intimates, either expressly or impliedly, that he is keeping the goods. The buyer is not deemed to have accepted the goods merely by asking for, or agreeing to, their repair by or under an arrangement with the seller (s. 35(6) as amended).

The second type of acceptance is when the buyer, having had a reasonable opportunity to examine the goods for the purpose of ascertaining whether they correspond to the contract requirements (regardless of whether he has taken the opportunity or not), does an act which is inconsistent with the seller's ownership. By 'ownership' s. 35 means the ability to revest the legal title in the goods back in the seller; see *Kwei Tek Chao* v *British Traders and Shippers Ltd* [1954] 2 QB 459. Dealing with the goods, such as resales, delivery to a sub-buyer and using the goods as security for a loan, are acts which are inconsistent with the seller's right to have the goods restored if not accepted by the buyer. Routine acts, such as unloading, packing and stacking the goods, are not inconsistent acts. Similarly, when the goods comprise equipment or consumer products, then using them is not *per se* an inconsistent act, not least because this would be the only way of exercising the s. 34 right of examination.

Section 35, when subject to the right to a reasonable opportunity to examine the goods for the purpose of assessing whether they conform to the contract, treats that right as an overriding condition precedent to acceptance. If the buyer, therefore, does an act in relation to the goods which is inconsistent with the seller's right to have the property in the goods restored to him without having had a reasonable opportunity to examine the goods, he is not taken to have accepted them unless and until the opportunity is given to the buyer. There is a *prima facie* rule in s. 34 that any buyer may demand and must then be given an opportunity to inspect the goods. If this is refused, he need not accept the goods notwithstanding their conformity to the contract description.

The place for the inspection under s. 34 will depend upon the intentions of the parties. However, there are some guidelines to be taken from the cases.

(a)   Where the contract is silent, the presumption is that the point for examination is the place where delivery is to take place; see *Perkins* v *Bell* [1893] 1 QB 193.

(b)   If the goods are lawfully diverted during transit, the place for examination may be the place to which the goods are diverted if this constitutes the delivery point.

(c)   However, the circumstances in which the contract is made may indicate that the presumption above should not be applied. If delivery is to a carrier under s. 32(1), it is unlikely that the point of examination will be where the carrier receives the goods. Similarly, if the buyer is to collect pre-packed goods from the seller's premises, it would be unreasonable to require the buyer to inspect the goods there. Also if the seller has agreed to deliver the goods to a sub-buyer on behalf of the buyer, inspection will normally be at the sub-buyer's premises; see *Molling & Co. Ltd* v *Dean & Sons Ltd* (1901) 18 TLR 217.

(d)   The case which has caused the most difficulty is when the buyer has resold the goods and immediately on receiving them he delivers them to his sub-buyer. Prior to the SSGA 1994, if the seller should reasonably have contemplated that there would be such a resale, and that inspection by the buyer would be impracticable by reason of the nature of the goods and the buyer's business, the place for examination for both the buyer and the sub-buyer would be the point of delivery to the latter; see the result in *Manifatture Tessile Laniera Wooltex* v *F B Ashley Ltd* [1972] 2 Lloyd's Rep 28. If the seller cannot reasonably be fixed with that foresight, then the sub-sale and delivery to the sub-buyer will normally be taken to be a waiver by the buyer of his right to inspect and, therefore, as acceptance of the goods. Similarly, if the seller was not bound by the terms of the contract to deliver the goods direct to the sub-buyer, but is subsequently requested to do so, this would be taken as a waiver of the right to examine by the buyer and, therefore, as acceptance of the goods. This would not be the case if the buyer, at the same time as requesting the seller to deliver to the sub-buyer, reserved his rights.

The SSGA 1994 provides a new s. 35(6) which states that the buyer is not deemed to have accepted the goods merely because the goods are delivered to another under a sub-sale or other disposition.

The question of what is a reasonable time to examine the goods depends upon the circumstances of the case. The more complex the goods and the more difficult the examination, the longer the notion of what is reasonable.

The third type of acceptance in s. 35, SGA 1979 is where the buyer retains the goods for a reasonable time without intimating to the seller that he is rejecting them. The lapse of a reasonable time will be subject to the right of examination to ascertain whether the goods are in conformity with the contract. The lapse of a reasonable time is a question of fact (s. 59).

The effect of acceptance is stated in s. 11(4):

Subject to s. 35A, where a contract of sale is not severable and the buyer has accepted the goods or part of them, the breach of a condition to be fulfilled by the seller can only be treated as a breach of warranty, and not as a ground for rejecting the goods and treating the contract as repudiated, unless there is an express or implied term of the contract to that effect.

The buyer is bound to keep the goods and to pay the price subject to the right to sue the seller for damages for a breach of warranty if the goods do not conform. Section 11(4) does not apply to severable contracts (i.e. those in which the delivery obligation is divisible (see 2.8.1.1)).

2.10   THE BUYER'S REMEDIES FOR BREACH BY THE SELLER

If the buyer has not accepted the goods and he finds that they do not conform to the contract, his remedies depend on: (1) whether the disconformity amounts to a breach of a condition of the contract; (2) if so, on whether he elects to treat the breach as repudiatory or as a breach of warranty (s. 11(2)); (3) on whether his conduct estops him from asserting the rights available under the Act and at common law.

The principal remedy for a breach of condition is to reject the goods and to sue the seller for non-delivery. This right is, however, subject to the ability of the seller to retender conforming goods, which he is entitled to do if the non-conforming goods were not specific goods or had not been unconditionally appropriated to the contract, and time is not of the essence; see *Borrowman, Phillips & Co.* v *Free and Hollis* (1878) 4 QBD 500. It is, therefore, wrong to treat rejection of the goods as termination of the contract. Of course if the seller intimates that he is unwilling or unable to retender, this would be an anticipatory repudiatory breach.

If a refusal by a buyer to accept the goods was an offer to treat the contract as at an end, that offer could be accepted by the seller selling the goods elsewhere without prior notification to the defaulting buyer; see *Vitol SA* v *Norelf Ltd, The Santa Clara* [1993] 2 Lloyd's Rep 301.

If the buyer gives no reason or an invalid reason for his rejection of the goods at the time of rejection, he is entitled to rely upon some other valid reason at trial; see *Boston Deep Sea Fishing & Ice Co.* v *Ansell* (1888) 39 Ch D 339. However, the reason must have existed at the time of the rejection; see *British and Benningtons Ltd* v *North Western Cachar Tea Co.* [1923] AC 48. Also, the buyer will be estopped from using such a reason if the seller could have remedied the problem at the relevant time had he been informed of it; see *Panchaud Frères SA* v *Etablissements General Grain Co.* [1970] 1 Lloyd's Rep 53. Further, the seller will be able to reduce the buyer's award of damages if he can show that the buyer himself would have been unable to perform the contract but for his own breach; see *The Mihalis Angelos* [1971] 1 QB 164.

The question of estoppel arose again in *Vitol SA* v *Esso Australia Ltd* [1989] 1 Lloyd's Rep 96. Parties may agree to resolve a dispute on a particular basis. Should they do so and one party alters his conduct on that basis, both parties are bound, and cannot revert to their original contractual rights. In this case the seller informed the buyer at the time of nomination of the contract vessel and again at the time of loading that there would be a shortfall in the amount shipped. En route the ship was hit by an Exocet missile in the Persian Gulf. Consequently the goods had to be transshipped and were delivered late. Buyer and seller agreed to resolve the loss resulting from late delivery on particular terms. The buyer made no mention of the shortfall. Later when the buyer attempted to reject the whole delivery for shortfall, the Court of Appeal held that he was estopped. It was sufficient for the seller to show that the buyer had made a representation by words or course of conduct, and that the seller had acted differently from that which he would have done without the representation. The seller was not required to prove exactly what he would have done without the representation. The agreement resolving the dispute as to late delivery and the buyer's silence throughout on the shortfall amounted to a representation that the buyer would not reject the lot for short delivery.

Rejection of the goods by the buyer must be an unequivocal act. If he keeps his options open, this will amount to a decision to keep the contract afoot, he will lose his right to reject and will be limited to a claim in damages for breach of warranty. In *Graanhandel T Vink BV* v *European Grain & Shipping Ltd* [1989] 2 Lloyd's Rep 531 the seller sold and shipped 'niggerseed expellers' to the buyer. On 2 August the buyer sent a telex rejecting on the basis that the goods did not correspond to the contractual description. He intimated willingness to sell them on account for any interested party. Further telexes were exchanged between 2 and 7 August. On 10 August, the buyer obtained analysis certificates stating that the goods were, in fact, niggerseed expellers. On 13 August the buyer sold the cargo. On 30 August a second analysis certificate was issued stating that the goods were not niggerseed expellers. On 2 November the buyer sought to take the seller to arbitration in an action for return of the price. On appeal to the QBD, the buyer failed. It was clear from the series of events that the telex dated 2 August was not a final rejection. The seller had refused to accept it, and the buyer entertained further thoughts disclosed by his words and conduct. These did not have to be communicated to the seller. The buyer later affirmed the contract and sold the goods. He thereby lost the right to reject. There had been no unequivocal rejection prior to sale on 13 August.

Section 35A (inserted by the SSGA 1994) provides for the right of partial rejection. Under this section, if the buyer has the right to reject the goods by reason of a breach on the part of the seller, but he accepts some of the goods, he does not lose his right to reject the rest.

The measure of the buyer's damages for non-delivery are assessed according to ss. 51 and 54, SGA 1979. The measure of damages for non-delivery is the estimated loss directly and naturally resulting, in the ordinary course of events, from the seller's breach of contract (s. 51(2)).

Where there is an available market for the goods in question the measure of damages is *prima facie* to be ascertained by the difference between the contract price and the market or current price at the time or times when the goods ought to have been delivered, or (if no time was fixed) at the time of the refusal to deliver (s. 51(3)).

Section 51(2) therefore reiterates the first limb of the rule in *Hadley* v *Baxendale* (1854) 9 Exch 341. The measure in s. 51(3) is stated as being a *prima facie* one, though it is the measure which is generally applied. It is based upon the duty to mitigate placed on the innocent party in that the buyer is expected to go into the market place (if available) immediately and buy the same or equivalent goods. The measure is not displaced if the buyer had himself contracted to sell on goods of the same description at a price lower than the market price. If, however, the buyer had agreed to sell on the selfsame goods and this was in the seller's contemplation, then the buyer would be able to recover his loss of profit (if any) on the resale under s. 54 which imports into the SGA 1979 the second limb of the rule in *Hadley* v *Baxendale*; see *Hall Ltd* v *Pym Ltd* (1928) 30 Ll LR 159.

Where the normal measure for damages for non-delivery of goods under s. 51 is unavailable, the only other measure is the cost of cure or replacement. In such a case, courts should presume that the buyer intends curing the fault or replacing the goods; see *The Alecos M* [1990] 1 Lloyd's Rep 82 applying *Tito* v *Waddell (No. 2)* [1977] 1 Ch 106. Consequently, in *The Alecos M* where the seller failed to deliver a spare propeller together with a boat and other accessories, and where there was no market in which to purchase another such propeller, the only measure of the buyer's loss was the replacement cost. The normal market measure, the difference between the contractual value and the market value of the goods, was not available.

The measure for damages for breach of a warranty is found in s. 53(3) which states that if the breach is one of quality then the loss is *prima facie* the difference between the value of the goods at the time of delivery to the buyer and the value they would have had if they had fulfilled the warranty. In addition, the buyer can set off his loss against any claim for the price brought by the seller. Again, therefore, the measure is based upon the market price rule and incorporates the duty to mitigate loss.

Again, as in the case of a breach of a condition of the contract, any loss on the sub-sale of goods of the same description would not normally be recoverable, whereas if the selfsame goods were to be sold on under the contract description, the buyer would be able to recover the lost profit and any other consequential losses under s. 54 provided that the seller was aware of the sub-sale; see *Molling* v *Dean* (2.9). Any actual sub-sale that the buyer succeeds in performing with the defective goods, notwithstanding the defects, is ignored, so even if the sub-sale was at a price above the market price the buyer can still recover the s. 53(3) measure; see *Slater* v *Hoyle Smith Ltd* [1920] 2 KB 11.

The Act does not consider the case of a late delivery of the goods. The measure at law will normally be the difference between the market price at the date delivery should have been made under the contract and the market or current price when the goods are actually delivered. Again, any consequential losses would be recoverable under s. 54 provided they were within the contemplation of the parties at the time the contract was made.

The question whether there is an available market for the goods at the time delivery should have been made is one of fact and subject to what is reasonable in the circumstances. If no market exists, then the courts must assess the value of the goods, to which end any sub-sale by the buyer is a guide.

In addition to the ss. 51, 53 and 54 remedies, the buyer can seek specific performance of a sale for specific goods under s. 52, which places the remedy in the discretion of the court as in equity; see *Behnke* v *Bede Shipping Co. Ltd* [1927] 1 KB 649. The remedy is not available for the sale of unascertained goods.

The buyer will only have a remedy under the Torts (Interference with Goods) Act 1977 for conversion if he has an immediate right to possession, regardless of whether property has passed to him. If he can establish such a right he will be able to recover the full price of the goods from the guilty third party since the buyer will be liable to his seller for that amount.

The buyer will only have a claim in negligence for damage to the goods if he had at the time possession of or the property in the goods; see *Leigh and Sillivan* v *Aliakmon Shipping Co: The Aliakmon* [1986] AC 785.

2.11 THE SELLER'S REMEDIES

The duties of the buyer under a contract of sale are essentially: (1) to hold himself out as willing and able to perform his obligations at the due date; (2) to take delivery of the goods when tendered in conformity with the contract; to accept the goods, i.e. to refrain from conduct signifying rejection; and (3) to pay for the goods in accordance with the contract.

Payment must be in legal tender, though if the contract stipulates a particular mode of payment — such as by way of bill of exchange drawn to the buyer's order or by documentary credit — the buyer will be in breach of his payment obligation if he attempts to adopt some other method.

Unless otherwise agreed, delivery of the goods and payment of the price are concurrent conditions: the seller must be ready and willing to give possession and the buyer must be ready and willing to pay the price in return for possession of the goods (s. 28). This means that each party's primary obligations stand independently of the other's and which party is to perform first depends on the point of delivery. Hence in a c.i.f. contract the seller must ship the goods and tender conforming documents before the buyer is bound to pay; in f.o.b. contracts the seller must put the goods over the ship's rail before the buyer is to pay.

Where, under a contract of sale, the property in the goods has passed to the buyer and he wrongfully neglects the goods or refuses to pay for them according to the terms of the contract, the seller may maintain an action against him for the price of the goods (s. 49(1)).

Where the price is payable on a certain day irrespective of delivery and the buyer wrongfully neglects to pay such price, the seller may maintain an action for the price, even though the property in the goods has not passed and the goods have not been appropriated to the contract (s. 49(2)). The action for the price is a debt action and so no question of mitigation arises.

In a s. 49(1) case, the seller's entitlement to the price does not arise if the property in the goods has not passed to the buyer, and it does not matter that the buyer's fault is the reason why property has not passed; see *Colley* v *Overseas Exporters* [1921] 3 KB 302 in which the buyer prevented property passing by failing to nominate the ship on which the goods were to be carried.

If for some reason the action for the price is not available, the seller can sue the buyer for damages for non-acceptance under s. 50; he can also claim supplementary damages for any loss he has suffered by reason of the buyer's refusal to take delivery under s. 37 and, in addition, he can claim consequential losses if contemplated by the parties at the time the contract was made under s. 54.

Where there is an available market for the goods in question the measure of damages for non-acceptance is *prima facie* to be ascertained by the difference between the contract price and the market price at the time or times when the goods ought to have been accepted or (if no time was fixed for acceptance) at the time of the refusal to accept (s. 50(3)). Where there is no available market for the goods in question (a question of fact), the measure is usually the amount by which the contract price exceeds the value of the goods to which any resale price obtained by the seller is a guide.

When the seller is ready and willing to deliver the goods, and requests the buyer to take delivery, and the buyer does not within a reasonable time after such request take delivery of the goods, he is liable to the seller for any loss occasioned by his neglect or refusal to take delivery, and also for a reasonable charge for the care and custody of the goods (s. 37(1)). Clearly this section refers to loss occasioned by the seller's involuntary custody of the goods and not a loss of bargain situation: s. 37(2) states that nothing in the section affects the rights of the seller where the neglect or refusal of the buyer to take delivery amounts to a repudiation of the contract. The damages under s. 37 are, therefore, in addition and not an alternative to the action for the price or the damages recoverable under s. 50. Section 37 deals with the expenses incurred by the seller when the buyer refuses to take delivery. Section 50 deals with the situation when the buyer refuses to accept the goods — when he rejects them.

Section 50, like s. 51 in respect of the buyer's damages, is an application of the market price rule, although one must look for a market in which the seller can sell rather than a market in which the buyer can buy. The rule assumes that the seller will resell the goods at once. If the seller resells at a price below the prevailing market price his damages are not correspondingly increased. Similarly, if he manages to resell the goods at a price higher than the market price the buyer cannot take the benefit of this. There is no market where the supply of the particular goods exceeds the demand for them and in such a case, the seller will be able to claim the loss of profit on the sale to the buyer, as that sale cannot be replaced; see *Thompson Ltd* v *Robinson (Gunmakers) Ltd* [1955] Ch 177. However, if demand exceeds supply, our particular buyer's repudiation means that the seller has lost nothing, as he will always be able to find another purchaser for the repudiated goods. Although he will be able to claim expenses caused by the buyer's wrongful rejection, the s. 50(3) measure will produce only a nominal amount; see *Charter* v *Sullivan* [1957] 2 QB 117.

The SGA 1979 confers certain real remedies on the unpaid seller. A seller is 'unpaid' for the purposes of these remedies when the whole of the price has not been paid or tendered; or when a bill of exchange or other negotiable instrument has been received as conditional payment, and the condition on which it was received has not been fulfilled by reason of the dishonour of the instrument or otherwise (s. 38(1)). So even if the seller has received a part-payment he is 'unpaid'.

When the unpaid seller is in possession of the goods, he has in certain circumstances and by virtue of s. 41 a lien on the goods. First, the lien is only available if property has passed to the buyer. This is because a lien is a right over another's property. Secondly, either (1) the goods must have been sold without any stipulation as to credit; or (2) if the goods were sold on credit the term of credit must have expired; or (3) the buyer must have become insolvent. The exercise of the lien has no effect on the contract of sale itself, and the seller must remain ready and willing to perform his obligations until the buyer's action becomes repudiatory or the seller is entitled to resell the goods under the Act (s. 48(1)). Possession for the purposes of the lien must be actual possession, unless the seller has passed the goods to a carrier or other bailee for transmission to the buyer and has reserved the right of disposal of the goods. Delivery to the buyer or his agent will obviously destroy the seller's lien. Delivery of part will not do so, but will indicate the seller's intention to waive the lien.

If property has not passed to the buyer, the seller has a co-extensive right to withhold delivery under s. 39(2). The right of stoppage in transit in ss. 39(2) and 44 is more restricted in its availability, and the lien for it can only be exercised when the seller can show that the goods are still in transit and that the buyer has become insolvent either because he is unable to pay his debts as they fall due, or because his current liabilities exceed the value of his assets. Transit for the purposes of the right of stoppage is deemed to be from the time when the goods are delivered to a carrier or other bailee or custodian for the purpose of transmission to the buyer, until the buyer or his agent in that behalf takes delivery of them from the carrier or other bailee or custodian (s. 45). The essence of this is that the carrier must be in lawful possession of the goods, so if the carrier wrongfully refuses to deliver the goods to the buyer or agent, he cannot thereby prolong the buyer's exposure to the seller's right of stoppage.

The carrier is bound to adhere to the seller's exercise of his right of stoppage. This is so even if it transpires that the seller had acted wrongfully. The buyer's remedy in such a case is against the seller for late or non-delivery and not against the carrier.

Like the exercise of the lien, the right of stoppage does not *per se* affect the contract of sale (s. 48(1)). Where the goods are of a perishable nature, or where the unpaid seller gives notice to the buyer of his intention to resell, and the buyer does not within a reasonable time pay or tender the price, the unpaid seller may resell the goods and recover from the original buyer damages for any loss occasioned by his breach of contract (s. 48(3)). Where the unpaid seller has exercised his right of stoppage in transit and resells the goods, the buyer of those goods acquires a good title as against the original buyer (s. 48(2)); see *Ward Ltd* v *Bignall* [1967] 1 QB 534.

FURTHER READING FOR PART I

Ademuni-Odeke, *Shipping in International Trade Relations*, Aldershot: Gower, 1988.

Alexandrides, C.G., *Countertrade: Practices, Strategies and Tactics*, New York: Wiley & Sons, 1987.

Anjaria, S., Igbal, Z. and Kirmani, N., *Developments in International Trade Policy*, Washington: IMF, 1988.

Bewes, W.A., *The Romance of the Law Merchant*, London: Sweet & Maxwell, 1923.

Fisher, B.S. and Harte, K.M. (eds.), *Barter in the World Economy*, New York: Praeger, 1985.

Goode, R., *Commercial Law*, 2nd edn, London: Butterworths, 1995.

Guest, A.G. (ed.), *Chitty on Contracts*, 27th edn, London: Sweet & Maxwell, 1999.

Horden, I., *The Contracting State*, Brackingham, Philadelphia: OUP, 1992.

Inns of Court School of Law, *Law of International Trade In Practice*, London: Blackstone Press, 1999.

Johnson, G.M., *Commodities Regulation and Title*, Boston: Brewer & Company, 1989.

Lafih, L., Gevurtz, F. and Campbell, D. (eds.), *Survey of the International Sale of Goods*, Deventer: Kluwer, 1986.

Law, P., *Pre-shipment Inspection Services*, Washington D.C.: World Bank, 1995.

Ljubljana Research Centre for Co-operation with Developing Countries, *South-South Co-operation and the New International Economic Order*, Ljubljana, 1984.

McGovern, E., *International Trade Regulation* (GATT, US and EEC), Exeter: Globefield Press, 1986.

Mill, J.S., *Principles of Political Economy*, 2 vols, 1848.

Ricardo, D., *On the Principles of Political Economy and Taxation*, 1817.

Schmitthoff, C.M., 'The unification of the law of international trade' (1968) 105 JEL 113.

Schmitthoff, C.M., *Export Trade*, 10th edn, London: Sweet & Maxwell, 1998.

Smith, A., *An Inquiry Into the Nature and Causes of the Wealth of Nations*, 2 vols, 1776.

Surrey, W.S. and Wallace, D., *A Lawyer's Guide to International Business Transactions*, 2nd edn, Philadelphia: IBA.

Trakman, L.E., 'The evolution of the law merchant: our commercial heritage' (1980) JML&C 1.

Treitel, G.H., *The Law of Contract*, 10th edn, London: Sweet & Maxwell, 1999.

PART II
INTERNATIONAL SALES

3 C.I.F. CONTRACTS

3.1 DEFINITION

When goods are purchased on a c.i.f. basis, the obligation of the seller is to ship the goods at the port of shipment specified in the contract at his own expense and to insure the goods under a policy of marine insurance for the sea voyage as is usual in the trade for the type of goods and voyage involved, or to buy insured goods already afloat on a ship which sailed with its cargo from the designated port of shipment.

The seller completes performance by delivering to the buyer or his authorised agent (often his bank) all the documents required under the c.i.f. contract, namely, a shipped bill of lading (see 5.2.1) covering the contract goods and no others, or some other document permitted by the contract itself; a commercial invoice representing the contract goods; a policy of insurance for the goods for the duration of the sea voyage, or a certificate of insurance if permitted by the contract. In addition, the buyer may require other documents, such as a certificate of inspection and a certificate of quality from designated authorities. Such additional requirements must be stated in the contract. Lord Porter in *Comptoir d'Achat* v *Luis de Ridder, The Julia* [1949] AC 293 described the characteristics of a c.i.f. contract in the following passage:

> The obligations imposed on a seller under a c.i.f. contract are well known, and in the ordinary case, include the tender of a bill of lading covering the goods contracted to be sold and no others, coupled with an insurance policy in the normal form and accompanied by an invoice which shows the price and, as in this case, usually contains a deduction of the freight which the buyer pays before delivery at the port of discharge. Against tender of these documents the purchaser must pay the price. In such case the property may pass either on shipment or on tender, the risk generally passes on shipment or as from shipment, but possession does not pass until the documents which represent the goods are handed over in exchange for the price. In the result, the buyer, after receipt of the documents, can claim

against the ship for breach of the contract of carriage and against the underwriters for any loss covered by the policy.

The letters 'c.i.f.' represent the three contracts involved: the cost (the sale contract), insurance (the contract of insurance) and freight (the contract of carriage).

The seller does not undertake that the goods will arrive, but merely that the buyer will have possession of documents conferring on him the benefit of contractual claims against the carrier and insurers together with the property in the goods and the right to immediate possession from the carrier on arrival at the port of destination. If the seller presents the buyer or his authorised agent with conforming documents, the buyer is bound to pay the price even if, at the time the documents are tendered, the goods have been lost, provided that the act appropriating the goods themselves to the contract of sale occurred before the loss; see 3.3 and *Gill & Duffus* v *Berger* [1984] AC 382.

Although the parties to the contract may state that it is on c.i.f. terms, the true nature of the contract can only be ascertained by an examination of all the terms. Indeed, the contract may take on a different form depending upon how the parties exercise any options they might have under the contract. Therefore, whilst the description as c.i.f. will not be overlooked, neither will it be taken as conclusive. In *The Julia* Lord Porter said:

The true effect of all its terms must be taken into account, though, of course, the description c.i.f. must not be ignored entirely.

The facts of *The Julia* were that the parties contracted on c.i.f. Antwerp terms for the export sale of grain. They agreed, however, that the seller could demand payment against either a bill of lading and insurance policy or a delivery order and insurance certificate. The seller was in any event to pay for any deficiency in weight delivered. The seller used part of a bulk cargo of grain covered by a single bill of lading and policy of insurance. As he was selling to the buyer a proportion of the bulk, the bill of lading and policy of insurance did not conform to the contract as they referred to goods not included in the sale. He was, therefore, bound to perform by using a delivery order and insurance certificate. The buyer paid the price against the tender of those documents. However, when Germany invaded Belgium, the seller, without the buyer's consent, discharged the goods and sold elsewhere hoping that the buyer could recover on the policy of insurance evidenced by the certificate. The buyer instead brought an action for the money paid.

It was held that the contract was not a c.i.f. contract, but an ex ship contract (see 1.11.10 and 4.11) for the delivery of goods at Antwerp. As the goods were not so delivered, there was a total failure of consideration. This was so even though the contract provided for payment in exchange of documents. The House of Lords stressed the facts that the seller had an option as to the way in which he would perform, and that he purported to perform by tendering a delivery order and certificate of insurance. If the seller had chosen to tender a bill of lading and policy of insurance he would, it seems, have been held to have completed his obligations as if under a c.i.f. contract. The contract was, therefore, either a c.i.f. or ex ship contract at the option of the seller, and its true nature could not be determined until that option had been exercised.

Since c.i.f. and f.o.b. are price and not necessarily delivery or obligation terms, there may be some variation of the normal rules in a c.i.f. contract as to the cost of freight and insurance which would not necessarily destroy the character of the contract as a c.i.f. contract. In *D I Henry* v *Clasen* [1973] 1 Lloyd's Rep 159, the c.i.f. contract included that a surcharge was to be paid by the buyer for any ordinary increases in the cost of freight. In a normal c.i.f. contract, the cost of freight is the seller's expense, even though it may be the buyer who actually tenders the money to the carrier. In such a case, the buyer would invoice the seller for the amount. The responsibility for the cost of freight, therefore, remains that of the seller. It was held, however, that provision for the buyer to bear the responsibility for ordinary increases in the cost of freight did not destroy the nature of the contract as a c.i.f. contract as this was something frequently done in the trade.

If the variations from the normal rules are sufficiently far-reaching, they may have the effect of destroying the c.i.f. nature of the contract. In *The Parchim* [1918] AC 157, the price quoted by the seller was stated to be c.i.f. but included the following provisions: that the cost of insurance was for the buyer; that any variations in the cost of freight were the buyer's responsibility; if the ship were lost after part of the goods had been loaded, the contract was to be cancelled as to the balance. In view of these provisions, it was held that the contract was not an ordinary c.i.f. contract, but that it had far more of the characteristics of a f.o.b. contract.

3.2 CHARACTERISTICS OF DOCUMENTARY SALE

It should be noted that in the first passage of Lord Porter cited in 3.1 there is little mention of the goods but much about documents. Indeed the c.i.f. contract has been described as 'a contract for the sale of goods to be performed by the delivery of documents' (per Bankes LJ in *Arnold Karberg* v *Blythe, Green, Jordan & Co)* [1916] 1 KB 495, at p. 510. In *Sharpe* v *Nosawa* [1917] 2 KB 814, Atkin J said that a c.i.f. contract is performed:

> ... by the seller taking reasonable steps to deliver as soon as possible after shipment, the shipping documents including the bill of lading and policy of insurance and the buyer paying the price.

Documents play a central role in the c.i.f. contract and the goods are in one sense secondary. The seller does not undertake that the goods will arrive, but merely that the buyer will have possession of documents conferring on the buyer (1) the right to immediate possession of the goods from the carrier at the port of destination and the benefit of a contractual claim against the carrier; and (2) the benefit of a contractual claim against the insurers.

The term 'c.i.f.' also indicates the three documents central to such a sale and these are:

(a)   a commercial invoice, representing the cost element (sales contract);
(b)   an insurance policy or insurance certificate, representing the insurance element (insurance contract);
(c)   a bill of lading, representing the freight element (contract of carriage).

It therefore does not matter that at the time the documents are tendered in conformity with the contract the goods themselves have been lost or destroyed, provided that they had properly and unconditionally been appropriated to the contract with the assent of the buyer before their loss or destruction. If the buyer fails to accept properly tendered and conforming documents, he is in breach of his fundamental obligations under the contract which, if accepted by the seller as a repudiation of the contract, relieves the seller of any further obligation to deliver the goods and enables him to sue the buyer for non-acceptance; see *Gill & Duffus* v *Berger* (3.1).

3.2.1   Two Rights of Rejection

The fact that documents are central to a c.i.f. sale means that the buyer has two rights of rejection for non-conformity: (1) the right to reject the documents; and (2) the right to reject the goods. In *Kwei Tek Chao* v *British Traders and Shippers Ltd* [1954] 2 QB 459, Devlin J explained the position under a c.i.f. contract in the following terms:

> There is a right to reject the documents and a right to reject the goods and the two things are quite distinct. A c.i.f. contract puts a number of obligations on the seller some of which are in relation to the goods and some of which are in relation to the documents. So far as the goods are concerned he must put on board at the port of shipment goods in conformity with the contract description, but he must also forward documents and those documents must comply with the contract. If he commits a breach, the breaches may in one sense overlap in that they flow from the same act. Thus the same act can cause two breaches of two independent obligations. A right to reject is merely a particular form of the right to rescind, which involves the rejection of a tender of goods or of documents.

The buyer need not reject the goods but may accept them and sue as for breach of warranty. Indeed, if he is deemed to have accepted the goods within s. 35, SGA 1979, he will automatically be reduced to this remedy. The normal measure of damages will apply, namely, the difference between the value of the goods as warranted and their actual value at the date of delivery.

The right to reject the documents arises when the documents are tendered and the right to reject the goods arises when they are landed and after the buyer has had a reasonable opportunity to examine the goods.

3.2.2 Documents

The seller must tender to the buyer the documents stipulated by the contract. If the documents are not contractual then the buyer is entitled to reject those documents and the seller will be in repudiatory breach of contract, subject to the seller's ability to re-tender conforming documents within the time allowed by the contract (*Borrowman, Phillips & Co.* v *Free & Hollis* (1878) 4 QBD 500). The relevant documents must be tendered by the seller within the time stipulated by the contract or, if no time is stipulated, within a reasonable time (*Toepfer* v *Lenersan-Poortman* [1980] 1 Lloyd's Rep 143). So long as these requirements are satisfied it does not matter that the goods arrive before the documents (*Sanders Bros* v *McLean & Co.* (1883) 11 QBD 327).

If the goods are not shipped then the c.i.f. buyer will be able to bring an action for damages for non-delivery. Those damages will *prima facie* be assessed as the difference between the market price at the date when the documents ought to have been delivered and the contract price; see *Sharpe* v *Nosawa* [1917] 2 KB 814.

A buyer will lose his right to reject the documents once they have been accepted by him or his bank and payment has been made against them without protest. By accepting the documents the buyer is not, however, to be taken to have accepted the goods. Indeed, handling the bill of lading and indorsing it to a sub-buyer does not prevent the buyer subsequently rejecting the goods for such an action is not inconsistent with the seller's ownership of the goods; see s. 35. This is because all the buyer deals with is his conditional property in the goods; see *Kwei Tek Chao* v *British Traders & Shippers Ltd* (3.2.1) *per* Devlin J at p. 487.

A buyer may nonetheless lose his right to reject the goods. Thus if a buyer accepts the documents he will only be able to reject the goods for such non-conformity as would entitle a buyer to reject the goods that was not apparent on the face of the documents. If the defect is apparent on the face of the documents then the buyer will be taken to have waived his right to reject the goods because of that defect or will be estopped from asserting his right to reject the goods for that defect. The documents must be read together in this respect; see *Panchaud Frères* v *Etablissements General Grain Co.* [1970] 1 Lloyd's Rep 53.

Upon lawfully rejecting the documents or the goods the buyer can recover from the seller damages for non-delivery of the goods; see ss. 51 and 54.

If the documents conceal a defect in the goods which would have entitled the buyer to reject those goods and the buyer has accepted both the documents and the goods, he might still claim damages for the loss of his right to reject the documents or goods; see *Kwei Tek Chao* v *British Traders and Shippers Ltd.*

There are circumstances in which a conforming tender of documents can be made even though the seller is in breach for shipping non-conforming goods. If the defect in the goods is not noted on the bill of lading and it is not a defect which should have been noted on the bill of lading (i.e. something that the carrier could not be expected to detect and did not detect), the bill of lading is genuine, reasonable and usual in the trade.

3.3 NOTICE OF APPROPRIATION

3.3.1 What a Notice of Appropriation is

A notice of appropriation is not part of the shipping documents. It is a communication from the seller to the buyer (sometimes by telephone, but usually by telex or fax) informing the buyer that the goods have been shipped. It is a preliminary communication that the buyer will receive before the actual shipping documents. This advance statement gives particulars of the shipment, when and on what vessel the goods have been shipped, so that the buyer can enter into sub-contracts knowing that he can perform those c.i.f. contracts as the goods have been appropriated to him. Such a notice of appropriation is not required under common law; but under modern contracts of the Grain and Feed Trade Association (GAFTA), the Federation of Oils, Seeds and Fats Association (FOSFA), and other trade associations, they have frequently been requested.

3.3.2 The Legal Effect of Giving a Notice of Appropriation

3.3.2.1 The Legal Effect
Section 16 of the SGA 1979 states that where there is a contract for the sale of unascertained goods, no property in the goods is transferred to the buyer unless and until the goods are ascertained. This therefore means that at the time of contracting all goods are either specific (ascertainable) or unascertainable (unidentifiable). For the property in the goods to be passed, the goods must first be ascertainable. A notice of appropriation can ascertain goods and permit property to pass thereafter.

For example, if there is a c.i.f. contract for 5000 tonnes of wheat and this has been shipped to the buyer in a ship that can only hold 5000 tonnes, the giving of a notice of appropriation will ascertain the goods, thereby overcoming the preliminary hurdle of passing property in those goods. If, however, the 5000 tonnes contract is being performed with other contracts, e.g. the ship is also carrying another 20,000 tonnes of goods to the c.i.f. destination, the giving of a notice of appropriation will not enable the goods to be ascertained because, with such bulk, the goods cannot be ascertained until physically separated from the other goods on arrival. So here s. 16 cannot be fulfilled by giving a notice of appropriation.

3.3.2.2 Revocation
The giving of a notice of appropriation cannot, unless the contract otherwise provides, be revoked by the seller, even if the seller has declared the wrong ship by mistake. In *Grain Union SA Antwerp v Hans Larsen* [1933] All ER Rep 342, one of the conditions of the contract was that a notice of appropriation with the ship's name, date of the bill of lading and approximate quantity loaded was to be posted to the buyer within three days or telegraphed within seven days from the date of the bill of lading and a valid notice of appropriation once given was not to be withdrawn. The seller received information that a cargo to fulfil the contract had been loaded onto the '*Triton*' but a clerk employed by the seller sent a notice of appropriation to the buyer

saying that the goods had been shipped on the '*Iris*'. The seller later corrected the notice of appropriation but the buyer refused to accept the cargo on the ground that the notice giving the name of the '*Iris*' was a valid notice of appropriation within the meaning of the contract and could not be withdrawn. Branson J held in the case that the buyer could reject. He stated that, '... unless it can be shown that it is not a valid notice of appropriation then it cannot be withdrawn ... it seems to me that a notice of appropriation which contains all the essentials, the ship's name, the date of the bill of lading and the approximate quantity of the goods on board, if all these three elements are in conformity with the contract, is a valid notice of appropriation.'.

Here the contract was for ascertainable goods by description but the notice of appropriation changed the terms of the contract, making it for goods shipped on board the '*Iris*', i.e. specific. The notice of appropriation was valid and so the seller could not amend or withdraw otherwise the seller would be in breach of his obligations.

3.3.2.3   Unconditional Appropriation

Appropriation is not to be confused with s. 18(5), which relates to unconditional appropriation, which is one of the rules that relate to the passing of property. Under s. 18(5)(1), where there is a contract for the sale of unascertained or future goods by description and the goods of that description are in a deliverable state and are unconditionally appropriated to the contract, either by the seller with the assent of the buyer or vice versa, the property in the goods then passes to the buyer. The assent may be expressed or implied and may be given either before or after the appropriation is made.

Section 18(5)(2) goes on to state '... does not reserve the right of disposal, he is to be taken to have unconditionally appropriated the goods to the contract ...' Section 18(5)(2) has been interpreted to mean loss of the power of disposal over the goods. However, the giving of a notice of appropriation does not take away the power to dispose of the goods once the shipping documents are retained. In *Krohn* v *Toepfer* [1978] 2 Lloyd's Rep 118, there was a contract c.i.f. Hamburg for tapioca pellets to be sold on the basis of Grain and Feed Trade Association form 100. Clause 10 in the contract stated that a notice of appropriation was to be given. On 1 February the seller sent the buyer a telex saying that the goods were shipped on 19 January on a ship called the '*Vladamir*' (or better name). On 1 February the buyer replied and said that he rejected the notice of appropriation as no ship by that name had been loaded on 19 January. The seller then amended the notice of appropriation and said that a ship called the '*Vladamir Ilych*' was carrying the goods. The buyer still rejected and said 'or better name' probably referred to mistakes or errors. It was held, with Donaldson J giving the main judgment, that:

Accordingly, validity depends on form and timing and not upon substance or factual accuracy. The appropriation was made within the proper time and was not defective in form. At first sight it might be thought that to specify the '*Vladamir*' (or better name) deprived the appropriation of its essential certainty, but it appears that the addition of these words (or better name) had been accepted in that trade for over forty years.... They have been held to have no further effect than the limited right to correct errors in transmission and accordingly, the appropriation was valid.

The buyer was also unsuccessful in his alternative argument that he could accept the notice of appropriation as an anticipatory breach on the grounds that the seller could not perform as contracted as the goods had been shipped on the '*Vladamir Ilych*' and not on the '*Vladamir*'. In this case, trade practice was introduced to cover the shortcomings and to correct the notice of appropriation. In this area, the law does follow trade practice quite strictly.

A notice of appropriation has elements of contract, not performance and so the notice of appropriation is a matter of contractual completion, rather than one of performance.

3.3.2.4   Completion and Performance

If a notice of appropriation is required but is not given or if it is not given in time, then the contract will be breached. In such circumstances, should litigation arise, then the notice of appropriation will be a matter of performance. In this respect, therefore, a notice of appropriation can be seen as a matter of contractual completion as well as one of performance. In *Tradax* v *André* [1977] 2 Lloyd's Rep 484, Tradax sold soya bean meal to André c.i.f. Rotterdam. The shipment period was April 1973 on a Grain and Feed Trade Association form 100. The bill of lading was dated 6 April. On 6 May, the seller (not the original shippers) received a notice of appropriation that was passed on to the buyer on 17 May. The buyer rejected it. On 18 May, the seller replied, asking the buyer to receive but the buyer said that the notice of appropriation was 42 days late and so the seller would have to prove that he was part of a chain (or string) contract, but he could not and so he was in default. In the Grain and Feed Trade Association form 100 there is a clause that says that a notice of appropriation is to be given within 10 days of the shipment of the goods. However, if the seller is in a string and receives the notice of appropriation before X date and then gives notice on the same day it will be deemed that he has complied with the clause. Even if the notice of appropriation is received after X date and notice is given the following day, the seller will still be deemed to be in compliance with the 10-day rule.

In this case, however, the notice of appropriation was given 42 days after the shipment date and so the seller could only establish that it was a valid notice of appropriation by proving the string. In the litigation that arose, Donaldson J held that unless the provisions of Clause 10 of form 100 were strictly complied with, a notice of appropriation given outside the 10-day period would be invalid. He further held that this strict compliance included the shipper or subsequent sellers. Thus the seller has to prove that not only he but also every other party in the string had dispatched the notice of appropriation within the 10-day provision. This is very difficult because, although he may be able to show this for himself, a string may include as many as 40 to 50 parties and so for him to establish that they were *all* within the 10-day rule is almost impossible. Here the seller was in breach, the date of default being 10 May when the 10-day rule ended.

In *Krohn* v *Toepfer* [1978] 2 Lloyd's Rep 118, failure to give a valid notice of appropriation was a breach of contract, but in *Tradax* v *André*, it was a breach of performance. A seller cannot therefore validate a late notice *vis-à-vis* his buyer by dispatching it promptly.

A valid notice of appropriation cannot be withdrawn except with the buyer's consent, and, if the buyer rejects the first notice as being invalid and stale, then the seller is free to make a new notice of appropriation and tender different goods within the time permitted by the contract. In *Getreide* v *Itoh* [1975] 1 Lloyd's Rep 592, there was a contract for soya beans, based on a Federation of Oils, Seeds and Fats Association form 24, c.i.f. Rotterdam. The Federation of Oils, Seeds and Fats Association form 24 contains a clause to the effect that a notice of appropriation is to be dispatched by the first seller not later than seven days after shipment and that subsequent sellers are to dispatch notices within a reasonable period. The seller, who was not the original shipper, received notice of dispatch on 10 June. On 15 June they tendered notice to the buyer, but the buyer rejected the notice as being outside the time limit. On 23 June, the seller tendered a new notice of appropriation that related to different goods, which were shipped on 17 June. The buyer also rejected this second notice of appropriation, saying that the seller's first notice was valid, although out of time, and so it could not be withdrawn for a new one without the buyer's consent. It was held in the case that the notice of appropriation only served to appropriate goods to the contract and so modified the rights of the parties. Therefore the seller was free to make a new notice of appropriation because the first notice of appropriation was out of time and so invalid and ineffective, and the new notice of appropriation avoided any breach.

It can be concluded that if a seller gives a valid notice of appropriation that is inaccurate, he will be stuck with it *unless* the contract entitles any amendment of such inaccuracies. However, if a new one is issued, then it will avoid any breach. Once a valid, in time, notice of appropriation is given, the seller cannot withdraw or amend it, even if he cannot perform the contract.

3.3.2.5   Time Limits

The Post Chaser [1982] 1 All ER 19 illustrates what the position is when no time limit has been set for giving a notice of appropriation. Here, the seller sold the buyer some palm oil c.i.f. Rotterdam and the contract of sale provided that the notice of appropriation be made to the buyer as soon as possible after the vessel had set sail. On 16 December 1974, the seller received a notice of appropriation in respect of palm oil shipped on 6 December. The seller did not re-tender the notice of appropriation to the buyer until 10 January 1975, which was late. In the meantime, the buyer had concluded a sub-sale and further sub-sales after this. On 13 January a notice of appropriation was passed along the string that was later rejected by a sub-buyer on 14 January. On 20 January the original buyer telexed the seller, asking for documents to be tendered to the sub-buyer and this was done on the same day. On 21 January, the sub-buyer rejected the notice. Then, on 22 January, the seller resold the palm oil for £460 per ton when the original contract between the seller and the buyer was for £792 per ton. The seller sued the buyer for the difference between the market price and contract price. The court held that the buyer's communication to the seller on 20 January asking for tender of documents was an unequivocal representation for the purpose of waiver but it was impossible to say that the seller had acted to his detriment by relying on it.

Robert Goff J stated that the seller had presented the documents on the same day that the buyer made the request. The seller had acted on this representation and conducted his affairs by relying on it and although most of the elements of waiver were present in the instruction on 20 January, these elements were not operative.

Precise compliance is, therefore, required in mercantile contracts as speedy declarations are regarded as being important, even though no time limit may be given to send a notice of appropriation.

3.4   PASSING OF PROPERTY

The paramount rule is that property passes according to the intention of the parties. The presumption in the case of c.i.f. contracts is that property will only pass with the delivery and acceptance of the shipping documents. The seller may not be obliged to actually ship the goods, he may purchase them afloat so that the parties are unlikely to have intended property to pass on shipment as shipment would not necessarily be an act of appropriation.

It is important to remember that the c.i.f. seller in the absence of a term in the contract of sale need not actually ship goods but may, for instance, purchase goods afloat. Donaldson J in *PJ van der Wildhandel NV* v *Tucker & Cross Ltd* [1975] 2 Lloyd's Rep 240 gave the following example:

> The contract called for Chinese rabbits c.i.f. Their obligation was, therefore, to tender documents, not to ship the rabbits themselves. If there were Chinese rabbits afloat, they could have bought them.

Furthermore, the bill of lading will normally be to the order of the seller so that there is a presumption that the seller has reserved the right of disposal; see s. 19(3).

In a c.i.f. contract the intention of the parties will be that passing of property is conditional. If the buyer rejects them upon examination, property in the goods reverts to the seller (*Kwei Tek Chao* v *British Traders & Shippers Ltd* (3.2.1).

When selling unascertained goods the seller must make an effective and unconditional appropriation of the goods to the contract (see 2.5.2). Often in international sales this obligation is augmented by a contractual requirement that the seller furnish the buyer with a 'notice of appropriation'. The object of the notice of appropriation is to give the buyer advance notice of shipment so that he knows exactly what are the contract goods. This would enable him to sub-sell, or he could assess the time of arrival of the ship and could organise collection.

In such a situation the seller's obligations as to the notice are strict. He must furnish the buyer with a notice in the contract form containing the specified particulars and within or at the time specified. It seems that 'furnish' requires that the buyer actually receive the notice and, therefore, there is no scope for the posting rule; see *Compagnie Continentale d'Importation USSR* v *Handelsvertretung in Deutschland* (1928) Ll LR 140.

If the seller complies with the contractual requirements as to the notice, then in the absence of terms to the contrary, the notice is deemed to be irrevocable. If the seller, therefore, tenders a notice relating to shipment 'A' but furnishes the buyer with shipping documents relating to goods on shipment 'B', he would be in breach of his obligations and, if the possibility of re-tendering the correct documents is not available, the seller would be in repudiatory breach of contract; see *Kleinjan & Holst NV Rotterdam* v *Bremer Handelsgesellschaft GmbH Hamburg* [1972] 2 Lloyd's Rep 11.

Normally the notice of appropriation merely identifies the cargo and does not refer to the condition of the goods, so the buyer's acceptance of the notice does not estop him from rejecting either the documents or the goods if they breach the conditions as to quality and description, though if the notice refers to the quantity appropriated, his acceptance might estop him from disputing that quantity.

Breach of the contractual requirements for the notice is repudiatory and entitles the buyer to reject; see *The Post Chaser* (3.3.2.5) in which Goff J held that the requirement that the seller declare the ship by a notice of appropriation in a c.i.f. contract was an essential step in the seller's performance. Once the declaration had been made, the buyer could then perform his obligations to any sub-buyer he might have. Precise compliance with the terms and the time of the notice of appropriation is for that reason necessary. In the decision itself, Goff J held that a requirement that the notice be tendered 'as soon as possible' after appropriation did not derogate from the provision being a condition.

In *Bremer Handelsgesellschaft GmbH* v *Deutsche Conti-Handelsgesellschaft GmbH* [1983] 2 Lloyd's Rep 45, it was found that the c.i.f. buyer must decide promptly whether to accept the tendered notice of appropriation, though if it does not conform to the contractual requirements he is given a reasonable time to decide or to check whether any sub-buyer wishes to accept it. In the circumstances of the case, it was found that a two-day delay amounted to a tacit affirmation, and the buyer was held to have waived the non-conformity.

3.5 RISK

Under a c.i.f. contract the presumption is that risk passes as from shipment of the goods. This means that risk will generally pass to the c.i.f. buyer before property in the goods. The separation of risk and the passing of property may cause problems in that the c.i.f. buyer may not be able to bring an action in tort for damage done to the goods prior to his obtaining property or a right of possession in those goods; see *Leigh & Sillivan Ltd* v *Aliakmon Shipping, The Aliakmon* [1986] AC 75. The c.i.f. seller may, nevertheless, be able to bring an action for damage to the goods while in the custody of the carrier at the time when property remained with him. This is so even if the c.i.f. buyer is liable for the full price because risk has passed to him (*The Sanix Ace* [1987] 1 Lloyd's Rep 465).

The risk which passes is the risk of accidental damage to, or abnormal (but not inevitable) deterioration of, the goods; see *Mash & Murrell Ltd* v *Joseph I Emmanuel Ltd* [1961] 1 WLR 862. It follows that, if the goods are shipped and lost during ocean transit the seller is still entitled to tender the proper shipping documents to the buyer and to claim the purchase price (*Manbré Saccharine Co.* v *Corn Products Co.* [1919] 1 KB 198).

If there has not been an appropriation of unascertained goods the position may, however, be different. It has been held that where there has not been an 'appropriation' the seller may still tender shipping documents; see *C Groome Ltd* v *Barber* [1915] 1 KB 316. In this case the buyer contended that it was the seller's duty to pass property to the buyer before the loss of the goods so that if the goods have been lost and property has not passed and could not pass with the tender of documents, the seller was precluded from tendering the shipping documents in exchange for the price. Atkin J thought that 'business operations would be very seriously embarrassed' if this was the case. This is true considering how often parts of a bulk cargo are sold. Atkin J was not, therefore, concerned with 'appropriation' in the contractual sense, i.e. the unconditional and irrevocable setting aside of goods for delivery under the contract, but with the question of whether the seller must be able to pass property in goods either before or with the tender of documents.

In the absence of clear authority to the contrary, it is suggested that a c.i.f. seller of unascertained generic goods cannot claim the price if the goods have been lost, unless at the time of loss he has appropriated them to the contract in the sense of binding himself contractually to deliver, or tender documents relating to, the particular goods which have been lost, or the particular bulk of which they form a part.

3.6   C.I.F. — SALE OF DOCUMENTS OR SALE OF GOODS?

3.6.1   Introduction

The essential feature of an ordinary c.i.f. contract as compared with an ordinary contract for the sale of goods rests in the fact that performance of the bargain is to be fulfilled by delivery of documents and not by the actual physical delivery of the goods by the vendor. All that the buyer can call for is delivery of the customary documents. This represents the measure of the buyer's right and the extent of the vendor's duty. The buyer cannot refuse the documents and ask for the actual goods; nor can the vendor withhold the documents and tender the goods they represent. (McCardie J in *Manbré Saccharin Co.* v *Corn Products Co.* [1919] 1 KB 198.)

These remarks of McCardie J typify the confusion still surrounding the c.i.f. contract despite several years of its existence. There are two main contracts employed in international trade, namely c.i.f. and f.o.b. There are differences and similarities between these two contracts, notably in their performances, with more emphasis on the physical delivery of goods in the f.o.b. contract. The nature and characteristics of the latter were enshrined by Devlin J in *Pyrene Co. Ltd v Scindia Navigation Co. Ltd* [1954] 2 QB 402; considered in *Renton (GH) & Co. v Palmyra Trading Corporation of Panama* [1957] AC 149; applied in *Thermo Engineers v Ferrymasters Ltd* [1981] 1 All ER 1142. They are that the price paid to the seller includes all costs up to the loading of the goods and onto an overseas vessel nominated by the buyer, property and risk normally passing to the buyer at this point and all subsequent expenses being borne by the buyer. In its original sense the f.o.b. has always been a cash on delivery contract and there has never been a suggestion that the f.o.b. is anything other than a sale of goods. There have not been any controversies surrounding the f.o.b. contract, at least in this aspect.

In contrast, in the c.i.f. emphasis is on the symbolic delivery of goods, using the documents which embody the title to those goods. It is a cash against documents contract. The essence of the c.i.f. contract was enunciated by Lord Porter in *Comptoir d'Achat et de Vente du Boerenbond v Luis de Ridder Limitada, The Julia* [1949] AC 293:

> The obligations imposed on a seller under a c.i.f. contract are well known and in the ordinary case include the tender of a bill of lading, covering the goods contracted to be sold and no others, coupled with an insurance policy in the normal form, and accompanied by an invoice which shows the price — against tender of these documents the purchaser must pay the price. In such a case the property may pass, either on shipment or on tender, the risk generally passes on shipment or as from shipment, but possession does not pass until the documents which represent the goods are handed over in exchange for the price. In the result, the buyer after receipt of the documents can claim against the ship for breach of the contract of carriage and against the underwriter for any loss covered by the policy.

This was considered in *Margarine Union GmbH v Cambay Prince Co. Ltd (The Wear Breeze)* [1967] 3 All ER 775; for 'price' see an editorial by the late Professor Clive M. Schmitthoff in [1958] *JBL* 78 at p. 79; and for passing of property see an editorial by Raoul P. Colinvaux in [1966] *JBL* 277 at p. 278 and 350 at p. 351.

Because of the nature of its performance, especially the emphasis on tender of documents, some authors and judges have assumed c.i.f. to be a sale of documents rather than goods. This has caused some confusion. At first this may appear esoteric but the fact that it has exercised the minds of some eminent jurists and prominent scholars means it cannot be dismissed offhand or treated lightly as a philosophical or academic exercise.

3.6.2   Nature and Root of the Problem

It was Hamilton J who seemed to define most clearly the obligations of a c.i.f. vendor; see *Biddell Brothers* v *E Clemens Horst Co.* [1911] 1 KB 214 at 220:

> ... firstly to ship at the port of shipment the goods contained in the contract, to procure a contract of affreightment, under which the goods will be delivered at the agreed destination, to arrange for an insurance which will be available for the benefit of the buyer and to make out an invoice as described by Blackburn J in *Ireland* v *Livingstone* (1872) LR 5 HL 395 and finally tender these documents to the buyer. It follows that against tender of these documents the buyer must be ready and willing to pay the price.

Yet despite the fact that this was 'well understood in practice', Lord Porter in *The Julia* [1949] AC 293 at p. 312 still believed that a vital question remained unanswered, that is, whether the buyers pay for the documents as representing the goods or for the delivery of the goods themselves. It was not Scrutton J who first proposed the view that c.i.f. contracts are for the sale of documents rather than goods, yet nevertheless it is his judgment in *Karberg (Arnhold) & Co.* v *Blythe Green, Jourdain & Co.* [1915] 2 KB 379 at p. 388 which became famous:

> I am strongly of opinion that the key to many of the difficulties arising in c.i.f. contracts is to keep in mind the cardinal distinction that *a c.i.f. sale is not a sale of goods, but a sale of documents relating to goods. It is not a contract that goods shall arrive, but a contract to ship goods complying with the contract of sale and to tender those documents against payments of the contract price.* The buyer then has the right to claim the fulfilment of the contract of carriage, or, if the goods are lost or damaged, such indemnity for the loss as he can claim under the contract of insurance. *He buys the documents, not the goods*, and it may be that under the terms of the contracts of insurance and affreightment he buys no indemnity for the damage that has happened to the goods. This depends on what documents he is entitled to under the contract of sale. In my view, therefore, the relevant question will generally be not 'what at the time of the declaration of tender of the documents is the condition of the goods?' ... but 'what, at the time of the tender of documents, was the condition of the documents as to compliance with the contract of sale?'. [emphasis supplied]

This ruling has been observed in later cases. Indeed, in 1975 Donaldson J in *Van der Zijden Wildlandel (PJ) NV* v *Tucker and Cross Ltd* [1975] 2 Lloyd's Rep 240 observed that:

> The contract called for Chinese rabbits, c.i.f. Their (the sellers') obligation was therefore, to tender documents, *not to ship the rabbits themselves. If there were*

any Chinese rabbits afloat, they could have bought them, and it is for the
show that no such rabbits were available. [emphasis supplied]

It would seem from these cases that the essence of c.i.f. is erroneously placed in
documents involved: a bill of lading which contains no qualification of the statemen
that the goods are shipped in apparent good order and condition, a marine insurance
policy covering the usual or agreed risks and the invoice strictly as provided for in
the contract. Sight has been lost of the fact that it is as a result of the rights these
documents give to the buyer that c.i.f. contracts are considered contracts for the sale
of documents. Whatever happens to the goods in transit, the bill of lading and the
insurance policy provide an almost complete, continuous cover from the port of
shipment to the port of destination. It is in this context that Roskill J in *Margarine
Union GmbH* v *Cambay Prince Steamship Co. Ltd (The Wear Breeze)* [1969] 1 QB
219 at p. 245 said 'the c.i.f. buyer ... will have either a cause of action against the
shippers or a cause of action against the underwriters on the policy'.

3.6.3   Sale of Documents?

Case law, in particular the older cases taken at their face value, would seem to point
unequivocally to the presumption that c.i.f. contracts are those for the sale of
documents. There are, however, more specific arguments relating to the idea that
Donaldson J appeared to put forward, that the goods themselves are of an almost
peripheral nature in the contract. The first of these, and perhaps the strongest, is that
when goods are lost at sea the documents remain valid and can be tendered as normal
for the full purchase price to be paid. Donaldson J restated in *Golodetz (M) & Co. Ltd*
v *Czarnikow-Rionda Inc, The Galatia* [1980] 1 All ER 501 that the fact that the ship
and the goods have been lost after shipment or that a liability to contribute in general
average or salvage expenses (see 13.8) has arisen is no reason for refusing to accept
and pay for the documents. It has further been held in some cases that it is irrelevant
even though both buyer and seller knew of the loss of the ship before the latter
tendered the documents. Thus in both *Manbré* v *Corn Products* (3.5) and *Groom (C)
Ltd* v *Barber* [1915] 1 KB 316, despite arguments that the goods tendered were
non-existent and consequently that the documents were not in order, it was
nevertheless held that the performance of the contract is fulfilled by delivery of the
documents and not by the actual delivery of goods by the vendor. McCardie J
maintained that ([1919] 1 KB 198 at p. 204):

> In my opinion it is also clear that he (the seller) can make an effective tender even
> though he possesses at the time of tender actual knowledge of the loss of the ship
> or goods.

Indeed, he affirms that in the case of loss the purchaser will receive not the goods but
the documents for which he bargained. It may happen that goods are lost or damaged
in transit and the buyer for some reason is not in a position to make a claim against

'ers. Nevertheless, though it may seem unequitable, the
ver documents and expect payment and if the buyer has
:e he is in no position to demand its return. Thus, a
r the sale of goods who has shipped the appropriate
...act of carriage and obtained the proper documents, can
...ose documents to the purchaser notwithstanding that he knows
. such tender of the loss of the goods.

...ther equally important argument stems from the frequent attempts to alter or
complement the basic c.i.f. contract. Although it has already been stated that
payment is dependent upon the proper documents being delivered, it is nevertheless
possible for a provision to be inserted that payment is to be against documents 'on
arrival of the goods'. This type of clause on first examination would tend to suggest
that arrival of goods is a strict condition of payment and thus that c.i.f. can be in
certain cases a sale of goods. Sassoon puts forward the view, however, that unless the
contract clearly requires otherwise, provisions of that type can either be struck out as
repugnant to the spirit of c.i.f. contracts or only serve to define a time at which
payment is to be made and not making payment conditional on arrival: 'This is to
say, if the goods shipped do not arrive, but for the loss the goods would have arrived'
(D. M. Sassoon, *CIF and FOB Contracts*, 4th edn, London: Sweet and Maxwell,
1998).

Case law supports the view that if such alterations are made to the contract then it
will cease to be a c.i.f. contract. *The Julia* provided the House of Lords with an
opportunity to state that, despite the designation of the contract in question as a c.i.f.
contract by the parties, the true effect of all its terms must be taken into account and
in the light of these the contract was not c.i.f. but a contract to deliver at Antwerp
([1949] AC 293 at p. 312). As a result the sellers' inability to deliver the goods to the
agreed destination led to a total failure of consideration for the payment of the
purchase price. Although the courts will try their best to effect the intention of the
parties, they nevertheless feel bound to uphold the so-called essentials of c.i.f.
contracts — their reliance on documents.

There are many examples of the supposed absolute importance of documents and
their correct tendering which suggest that they seem to be the essence of the contract;
see e.g. *Colombo Trading Society Ltd* v *Segu Mohamed Khaja Alawdeen* [1954] 2
Lloyd's Rep 45. In *Continental Imes Ltd* v *Dibble* [1952] 1 Lloyd's Rep 220, no
documents were tendered though the contract did purport to be of a c.i.f. nature.
Byrne J held that the buyers had an absolute right to terminate the contract as they
had been denied their rights to c.i.f. facilities. Even if no specific time is stipulated
in the contract, it was stated by Hamilton J in *Biddell Brothers* v *Clemens Horst*
[1911] 1 KB 214 at p. 220 that the seller should at least procure the documents within
a reasonable time.

These decisions can only result in the strengthening of the position of the
documents in a c.i.f. contract; they explicitly lay down the notion that the documents
in themselves do not simply represent the goods but, in a manner of speaking, are the
goods. Without the documents properly tendered there can be no c.i.f. contract and

if examination of the physical goods of the contract is made a condition of payment on the contract, then that contract ceases to be a c.i.f. contract in its true sense. But in *Gill & Duffus SA* v *Berger & Co. Inc* [1983] 1 Lloyd's Rep 622, a contract providing for tender of the specified inspection certificate to be conclusive as to quality caused confusion, in the lower courts, over the nature and essence of documents in c.i.f. contracts. The position was only remedied by the House of Lords holding that under the c.i.f. contract the seller was not bound to tender a certificate of quality. Finally, according to *Oriente Co. Ltd* v *Brekke and Howlid* [1913] 1 KB 531, non-existence of an insurance policy is a ground for rejection of the documents. Thus, when goods are sold under a c.i.f. contract, but the seller does not effect insurance upon them for the transit, they are not delivered in accordance with the contract although they arrive safely at their destination, and the buyer is not bound to accept them or to pay the price.

3.6.4 Sale of Goods?

It is by no means a unanimous belief that documents can rightly be termed the real goods of the contract and not all authorities are of that view. An important dissension was made, ironically, in the appeal against Scrutton J's decision in *Karberg* (Arnhold) v *Blythe* (3.6.2). Although overall the appeal was disallowed, both Warrington and Bankes LJJ disagreed with Scrutton J's famous statement concerning the nature of c.i.f. as a sale of documents. Warrington LJ said ([1916] 1 KB at p. 510):

It seems to me that it is not in accordance with the facts relating to these contracts. The contracts are contracts for the sale and purchase of goods, but they are contracts which may be performed ... by first placing [the goods] on board ship, and secondly by transferring to the purchaser the shipping documents.

This author believes that this view of the c.i.f. is the correct one and this is borne out by Bankes LJ who added in the same case (at p. 514), concurring with Warrington LJ, that:

I am not able to agree with that view of the contract, that it is a sale of documents relating to goods. I prefer to look upon it as a contract for the sale of goods to be performed by the delivery of documents.

The emphasis on documents, according to their Lordships, was due simply to the terms and nature of the contract and the manner of its performance, rather than its essence. This was mentioned in *Smyth (Ross T) & Co. Ltd* v *Bailey (TD), Son & Co.* [1940] 3 All ER 60 at p. 70 where Lord Wright, in concurring with Bankes and Warrington LJJ, opined that, although a c.i.f. sale can be completed after the loss of the goods concerned by the transfer of documents, it does not necessarily follow that a c.i.f. contract is a sale of documents. It contemplates the transfer of actual goods in the normal course but, if the goods are lost, 'the insurance policy and bill of lading contract — that is the rights under them — are taken to be, in a business sense, the equivalent protection of the goods'. This important rationale highlights that, until then, the rights conferred by insurance had always been used to mystify the fact that c.i.f. is a sale of goods rather than documents or any other rights contained in those documents.

Scrutton on Charterparties, 20th edn, London: Sweet & Maxwell, 1996 suggests that the difference between the two views is in essence one of language rather than substance. McCardie J also attempted to clarify the problem by stating in *Manbré* v *Corn Products* (3.5) that the documents, although vital in that they must be delivered to the buyer, were vital only because they *represented* the goods; that they were in fact *symbols* for the goods. Possession of the bill of lading places the goods at the disposal of the buyer, because, as Lord Heatherly LC said in *Barber* v *Meyerstein* (1870) LR 4 HL 317:

> In the case of goods which are at sea being transmitted from one country to another, you cannot deliver actual possession of them, therefore the bill of lading is considered to be a symbol of the goods, and its delivery to be a delivery of them.

In *Sanders Brothers* v *Maclean* (1883) 11 QBD 327, Bowen LJ said:

> A cargo at sea while in the hands of the carrier is necessarily incapable of physical delivery. During this period of transit and voyage, the bill of lading by the law merchant is universally recognised as its symbol, and the endorsement and delivery of the bill of lading, operates as a symbolic delivery of cargo. Property in the goods passes by such endorsements and delivery of the bill of lading, whenever it is the intention of the parties that the property should pass, just as under similar circumstances the property would pass by an actual delivery of goods and completing the title of the endorsee to full possession thereof, the bill of lading, until complete delivery of the cargo has been made on shore to someone rightfully claiming under it, remains in force as a symbol and carries with it not only the full ownership of the goods, but also all rights created by the contract of carriage between the shipper and the shipowner. *It is a key which in the hands of a rightful owner is intended to unlock the door of the warehouse, floating or fixed, in which the goods may chance to be.* [emphasis supplied]

His Lordship's observation is another landmark in that it seeks to separate the symbols from the essence. Hitherto the customs and usages (symbolic delivery) had been lumped together and used to observe the essence of the contract. The symbolic delivery is merely for convenience and nothing more, while the insurance documents are merely to provide cover.

At this stage of case law the arguments tend to become somewhat confused. Even Scrutton LJ who had previously defined c.i.f. so clearly in *Karberg (Arnhold)* v *Blythe* (3.6.2), was now reduced to stating, following his elevation to the Court of Appeal, that:

I need not discuss, what perhaps is merely a question of words, whether that sale is a sale of goods or of documents. One of the features of a sale c.i.f. is that, in the absence of special terms, the seller claims payment against presentation of shipping documents.

The decision in the case of *Hindley & Co.* v *East India Produce Co. Ltd* [1973] 2 Lloyd's Rep 575 further supports the view that, despite the apparent preoccupation with the significance of documents, the goods are quite plainly the underlying subject of the contract. In this case the buyers paid the purchase price for jute from Bangkok on the tendering of the documents, but upon arrival of the ship at Bremen there were found to be no goods answering to the description in the contract. The sellers contended, first, that they were not liable for the return of the purchase price since the contract was one for the sale of documents, or to be performed by the delivery of the documents, and at the time of their tendering they were on proper documents. Secondly, they maintained that they were not the shippers of the goods but were merely parties in a string who were unconnected with the circumstances giving rise to the issuing of the bill of lading. It was, however, correctly held that: (1) the sellers were in breach of the obligation under a c. & f. (now c.f.r) (a variation of c.i.f.) contract to ship or procure the shipment of goods of the contractual description, for no goods had in fact been shipped; (2) it was an implied term in a c. & f. contract that the bill of lading should not only appear to be true and accurate in the material statements which it contained, but that such statements should in fact be true and accurate, and that in this case the bill of lading which was tendered was not a proper one and, therefore, the sellers were also in breach on that ground; and (3) it was immaterial whether the buyers had a right of action against the carriers or that the sellers were not the shippers. *Hindley* also destroys the 'right of action' argument provided by insurance in support of the documents view.

It would appear, therefore, that the consideration for the contract rests undoubtedly in the goods themselves and not in the documents representing these goods, although those documents are important. *Hindley* also raises the common-sense argument that one cannot tender documents relating to goods which either never existed in the first place or were never shipped. This is in fact supported by the case of *Johnson* v *Taylor Brothers Co. Ltd* [1920] AC 144 at 155, where a Swedish seller was unable to tender documents to an English buyer because he never shipped goods in the first place; so it would appear, outside fraud, one cannot fabricate and tender documents. Goods must exist in the first place and must have been shipped before tender of documents relating to them.

Thus it would appear reasonable for a businessman involved in such contracts to expect that he is buying goods, not mere papers. According to *Couturier* v *Hastie* (1856) 5 HL Cas 673, one cannot tender documents relating to lost or damaged *specific goods*. *Couturier* could arguably limit the scope of *Manbré, Biddell Brothers* (see 3.6.3) and related cases which allow for tender of documents relating to lost or damaged goods. In *Couturier* v *Hastie* a cargo of corn was shipped by A of Salonica in February 1848, for delivery in London. On 15 May it was sold by H, a factor, who made the sale on a *del credere* commission. (A *del credere* agent is an agent of trust who receives a higher rate of commission in return for a guarantee that his principal will receive due payment for goods sold; see, e.g., *Harburg India Rubber Comb Co.* v *Martin* [1902] 1 KB 778.) The contract described the corn as 'of average quality when shipped', and the sale was made at '27s per quarter free on board, and including freight and insurance to a safe port in the United Kingdom, payment at, etc., upon handling shipping documents'. In fact the corn had, a short time before the date of the contract, been sold at Tunis, in consequence of getting so heated in the early part of the voyage as to render its being brought into England impossible. The contract in England was entered into in ignorance of this fact. When the English purchaser discovered it, he repudiated the contract. In an action for the price brought against the factor it was held that the contract contemplated that there was *an existing something* to be sold and bought and capable of transfer. As this was not the case at the time of the sale by the factor, he was not liable. This contract could have equally been void for mistake or frustration, but the point here is that it contradicts the presumption in favour of documents. The case for goods *seems* to have been made out but is there any way that the two, apparently contradictory, positions can be reconciled? Can the two views co-exist as complementing each other?

3.6.5 Happy Medium or Question of Semantics?

It may well be that in *Kwei Tek Chao* v *British Traders and Shippers Ltd* [1954] 2 QB 459 there is a happy medium between the two differing views. Devlin J noted (at p. 461) that there existed two distinctly separate sets of both rights and obligations:

> The right to reject the documents arises when the documents are tendered and the right to reject the goods arises when they are landed and when after examination they are not found to be in conformity with the contract.

This was adding to McCardie J's observations in *Manbré* v *Corn Products* [1919] 1 KB 198 at p. 204, that the difference of view is one of language only and that:

> ... the obligation of the vendor is to deliver documents rather than the goods — to transfer symbols rather than the physical property represented thereby.

It might be said that *Kwei Tek Chao* can, in the right circumstances, be used to argue both for and against the c.i.f. contract being a sale of documents and not goods, but equally it might be said that it supports neither. Although the right to reject the goods and the right to reject the documents are separate rights, it appears finally in *Kwei Tek Chao* that the value of the documents and the goods cannot be distinguished. Were it not for the fraud, the buyers would have been entitled to reject both the documents and the goods. Without the documents, or with faulty documents, the contract is worthless. But whether or not this is merely a question of words, it is quite clear that a c.i.f. contract imposes upon the seller two sets of obligations which are quite distinct from each other: the one relates to the goods and the other to the documents. Indeed as Devlin J noted (*Kwei Tek Chao* v *British Traders* [1954] 2 QB 459 at p. 480):

> A c.i.f. contract puts a number of obligations upon the seller, some of which are in relation to the goods and some of which are in relation to the documents. So far as the goods are concerned, he must put on board at the port of shipment goods in conformity with the contract description, but he must also send forward documents and these documents must comply with the contract; if he commits a breach the breaches may in one sense overlap in that they flow from the same act. If there is a late shipment — the seller has not put on board goods which conform to the contract description. He has also made it impossible to send forward a bill of lading which conforms. Thus the same act can cause two breaches of two independent obligations.

Equally, without goods or with non-conforming goods the contract will not be completed. This may appear to be an oversimplification of the position but it perhaps represents a more balanced view from which further points can be made.

Both goods and documents have their value. Those who argued that the goods are of sole importance would often rely on a common-sense notion that ultimately nobody will pay out large sums of money unless they are to receive something tangible (more than mere papers) in return. This is rebuttable with an equally common-sense argument that the nature of contemporary import and export trade, and indeed business in general, demands that the parties involved are prepared to do exactly this. It is the inability to separate these two interlinked but quite distinct commercial realities that had many jurists and academics confusing the argument that the contract remains for a sale of goods. Goods travelling by sea can take up to several months to arrive at their destination. In the modern world it would be unthinkable that a businessman should wait this length of time before being in a position to deal further. The nature of international trade has the effect that most buyers and sellers do so not on their own behalf but at the behest of third parties — hence buying and selling afloat. Consequently, their immediate interest may not be in the goods themselves but in their value; a value which is inherent in the documents tendered in a c.i.f. contract. Obviously the goods must exist and the documents must apply to them. The argument is not that the documents themselves have an intrinsic value, but that the documents, *in representing the goods*, have a value equivalent to the value of the goods. They can be, and in most cases are, bought and sold before the goods ever arrive at their port of discharge. But this is only commercial convenience and should not obscure the essence of the contract.

This is linked to the point that such contracts demand the involvement of more than just two parties. In the words of Sassoon, *CIF and FOB Contracts*:

... the documentary nature of the transaction, for example, lends itself readily to the introduction of bankers and other financing or forwarding agents who may act for either buyer or seller as intermediaries.

And one may add insurers, carriers and their brokers. All these interests can only be accommodated by documents before goods arrive, or if goods do not arrive. As a result the duties and obligations arising from a basic c.i.f. contract are of too great a nature to confine them strictly to dealing with the physical goods. It is without doubt the case that many of the decisions in the relevant case law have been determined by practical as much as legal considerations. It has always been the legal aim to avoid, where possible, the imposition of terms or provisions which were not intended by either party at the outset. Equally, it seems that the courts tend to adapt their decisions in order to facilitate international trade. For example, in *Manbré* v *Corn Products* [1919] 1 KB 198 at p. 204, McCardie J stated that with regard to his decision:

> ... this view will simplify the performance of c.i.f. contracts and prevent delay either through doubts as to the loss of the ship or goods or through difficult questions with regard to the knowledge or suspicion of a vendor as to the actual occurrence of a loss.

3.6.6 Rationale and Function

There are several reasons why c.i.f. is the way it is. Among them are the facilitation of international trade and safeguarding the interests of other parties who may have nothing to do with the actual goods themselves; see e.g. *Owen (Edward) Engineering* v *Barclays Bank* [1978] 2 All ER 100 where Lord Denning gave these as the reasons for maintaining the independence of credits and guarantees. 'Other parties' would include innocent third parties such as purchasers for value without notice and/or holders in due course of bills of exchange and negotiable instruments who deal in documents only. Another reason is the requirements demanded by modern standards and modern communication including the age of paperless transactions.

The separation of rights of rejection of documents and goods cannot be overemphasised. In the final analysis, however, acceptance of documents should not jeopardise the buyer's interests. He can always reject goods which do not conform to the contract and claim his money back: he retains the right to examine the goods when they arrive. The c.i.f. contract has both legal and economic functions (Lord Porter in *The Julia* [1949] AC 293 at p. 310) some of which can only be served by documents, e.g. allowing for sale and purchase afloat of goods transported in bulk.

There is also the need to realign c.i.f. contracts to modern means of payment and finance for international business transactions, notably the letter of credit or bankers' documentary credits. This has been done by transplanting the letter of credit's cardinal principle of the *autonomy of credits* to the c.i.f.'s *autonomy of documents* (from the sale contracts on which they may be based) where the former is used (as is often the case) to finance the latter. This principle is enshrined in the *Uniform Customs and Practice for Documentary Credits* (UCP 500):

Article 3

Credits, by their nature, are separate transactions from the sales or other contract(s) on which they may be based and banks are in no way concerned with or bound by such contract(s), even if any reference whatsoever to such contract(s) is included in the credit.

Article 4

In credit operations all parties concerned deal in documents and not in goods, services and/or other performances to which the documents may relate.

This principle has now become case law, a development noted by Lord Denning MR in *Power Curber International Ltd* v *National Bank of Kuwait* [1981] 1 WLR 1233 when he said (at p. 1241):

It is vital that every bank which issues a letter of credit should honour its obligations. The bank is in no way concerned with any dispute that the buyer may have with the seller. The buyer may say that the goods are not up to contract. Nevertheless the bank must honour its obligations. The buyer may say he has a cross-claim in a large amount. Still the bank must honour its obligations.

The letter of credit's autonomy of credits is therefore the c.i.f.'s equivalent of the autonomy of documents: the corresponding or issuing banks can only reject documents for late tender, non-conformity with the contracts and other deficiencies relating to documents but not due to loss, damage or late arrival of the goods. Most cases on whether c.i.f. is a sale of documents or goods, such as *Manbré* v *Corn Products*, *Biddell Brothers* v *Clemens* and *The Julia*, make this point.

Another important reason for the nature of c.i.f. is the economic function of the c.i.f. contract. It needs to be borne in mind that one of the primary functions of the c.i.f. contract is to enable buyers and sellers to deal with goods afloat and be free to enter into and finance further ventures. In brief, the seller in c.i.f. fulfils his obligations by putting the buyer in one of the following three positions whereby he can either:

(a)   sell the goods afloat if he wishes; or

(b)   take delivery of goods from the carrier on arrival if he intends to resell domestically or distribute them himself; and/or

(c)   claim directly in his own rights from the carrier or insurers or third parties damaging or losing or injuring the goods, were such a misfortune to occur.

Finally, it is presumed, from (c), that if the seller performs satisfactorily and tenders the right documents, the buyer in c.i.f. is provided with adequate and more than ample alternative remedies in the event of a misfortune (for details see Sassoon, *CIF and FOB Contracts*). He can sue and claim from any of the many possibilities available to him: carriers using his bill of lading; insurers using his policy; and tortfeasors or any other third parties, since he will have had title or proprietary rights to the goods whichever the case may be; *Leigh & Sillivan Ltd* v *Aliakmon Shipping Co. Ltd, The Aliakmon* [1986] AC 785. In the event of a misfortune the buyer should seek his remedies elsewhere instead of trying to stop further performance of the c.i.f. contract. The real nature of a c.i.f. contract is a sale of goods contract whose environment gives prominence to tender of or dealing in documents.

3.6.7 Future Prospects

The development, nature and function of c.i.f. has tended to blur the position of goods and documents. At best it is a case of a principle changing to keep up with the demands of modern developments. In attempting to play a dual role, i.e. economic and legal, the c.i.f. has brought upon itself some of these problems. This point leads to the conclusion that if the law has developed to serve the needs of its users, then this development will surely continue with present day advances in the method and practicalities of international trade. The debate now is whether c.i.f. contracts are contracts for the sale of goods or documents, although it seems apparent that documents may well soon be a thing of the past, particularly with the increased use of electronic data transmission (EDT). Eventually the arguments may surround the question of whether c.i.f. contracts are those for sale of goods or those based on an electronic system of transactions. For the present it can be concluded that c.i.f. contracts revolve around both goods and documents and, as the preceding discussion in this chapter has shown, one is probably of very little use without the other. A c.i.f. is a contract for sale of goods to be performed by the delivery of documents rather than simply a contract for a sale of documents and nothing else.

It was established in *Biddell Brothers* v *Clemens Horst*, in conformity with commercial practice (at the expense of strict statutory interpretation), that delivery of the goods themselves into the hands of the buyer is not of primary importance in a c.i.f. sale. Nor is the deficient condition of the goods on arrival, nor any malfunctioning in the final delivery process from ship to buyer against the seller. Its only relevance is as evidence that the goods did not in fact conform when loaded. In c.i.f. contracts the embarkation of the goods and the subsequent tender of the relevant documentation replace physical delivery and the transference of property as the two salient incidents in the contract of sale. The duality of the contract also has an economic function in that it enables further sale and purchase afloat. This facilitates international trade and finance in that the multitude of other parties involved through the letters of credit, for instance, do not have to wait for the eventual arrival of the goods themselves.

The question of the true nature of a c.i.f. contract, which at times can seem to be a theoretical, academic question, does have a more practical implication when historical and economic factors are taken into account.

3.7 THE COMMON LAW OBLIGATIONS OF THE C.I.F. SELLER

3.7.1 Shipment

The seller is not himself obliged to ship the goods unless the contract requires. He may instead purchase goods afloat and appropriate them to the contract, provided that those goods conform with the extended requirements as to description in international sales (see 2.3.2). Alternatively, he may appropriate goods already purchased by him afloat before he entered into the contract. He must, however, furnish to the buyer the requisite shipping documents within the stipulated time or, if not, as soon as possible after the goods have been appropriated.

Shipment is also the reference point by which the seller's performance of his ordinary obligations as to the conformity of the goods to the implied and express terms of the contract is tested. The bill of lading must show shipment of conforming goods and, therefore, is not treated as conclusive for purposes of the sale (different considerations apply when banks are required to accept the documents under a documentary letter of credit) if there is a notation referring to events occurring after shipment; see *Golodetz & Co. Ltd* v *Czarnikow Rionda Co. Inc, The Galatia* [1980] 1 All ER 501.

The seller may be required to nominate the vessel (though the duty to nominate occurs more commonly in f.o.b. contracts). Failure to nominate a vessel which will arrive at the port of loading in time amounts to a repudiatory breach of the contract by the seller. The buyer may accept the repudiation and put an end to the contract. In *Nova Petroleum International Establishment* v *Tricon Trading Ltd* [1989] 1 Lloyd's Rep 312, the seller nominated a vessel out of time, but this breach was waived by the buyer. It became obvious that the ship would not arrive at port in time. Prior to the contractual date for arrival, the seller informed the buyer that he was treating the contract as cancelled. The buyer sued for non-delivery. Evans J rejected the seller's argument that since the contract had been cancelled by his communication, the buyer's claim should be limited to loss arising out of breach of the nomination clause and not for non-delivery. Evans J applied Lord Diplock's analysis in *Lep Air Services Ltd* v *Rolloswin Investments Ltd* [1973] AC 331. Breach of the nomination clause entitled the buyer to rescind the contract. All future primary obligations ceased, but were converted into secondary obligations to compensate the innocent party for loss sustained.

If a notice of appropriation is required, the seller must comply with the contractual provisions and failure to do so is repudiatory; see *The Post Chaser* (3.3.2.5). There follows a list of the more common shipping terms in c.i.f. contracts, but this must be read in the light of the above and the general rule that the buyer's and seller's obligations are governed principally by the terms of the contract.

(a)   The seller must ship or appropriate goods on a ship which departed from the port of shipment on the date(s) or within the period for shipping specified in the contract. If no specific date is mentioned, the choice of date is with the seller. Failure to do so is a repudiatory breach, and if the requirement is treated as a condition precedent to the buyer's obligations, he may treat the contract as at an end without having to show his own willingness and readiness to perform; see *J Aron* v *Comptoir Wegimont* [1921] 3 KB 435. In *Ashmore* v *Cox* [1899] 1 QB 436, failure to ship a cargo of hemp between 1 May and 31 July was treated as a breach of condition precedent to the buyer's obligations. Lord Russell CJ said:

> They have said that the buyers shall not be called upon to accept a shipment which is not made between 1 May and 31 July. I hold these stipulations are conditions precedent.

The same applies if the goods were shipped prior to the shipping date(s) or period; see *Bowes* v *Shand* (1877) 2 App Cas 455.

(b)   If the vessel is specified the seller must use this and this only.

(c)   If a port of loading is specified the seller must ship from that port.

(d)   The seller must ensure that the goods are stowed according to the contract.

(e)   The ship must be bound for the agreed port of destination and following the contractual or, if none, the usual or reasonable route.

(f)   Unless there is a provision for deviation, the seller is in breach if the ship in fact deviates. The buyer could reject the goods on this basis, and the seller's recourse would be against the carrier provided that the contract of carriage had prohibited deviation.

3.8   THE COMMON LAW DUTIES OF THE BUYER

The buyer's duty is to pay on tender of documents. The buyer must pay the price if the documents conform and cannot delay until he has examined the goods. If the buyer knows that the goods are not in accordance with the contract, he must nevertheless pay against documents if they are in accordance with the contract. This is a general rule but is subject to two exceptions.

First, the rule does not apply where the non-conformity of the goods is due to the seller's fraud (see *Gill & Duffus* v *Berger* [1984] AC 382). Secondly, it may not apply where the goods *actually shipped* differ fundamentally from those that have been sold. This is a narrow exception for generally the seller will be guilty of fraud as well, or the buyer can refuse the documents on the grounds that they are not genuine.

The buyer does not have to pay when on their face the documents do not conform with the requirements of the contract. Non-conformity can arise in two ways. First, the documents may indicate on their face that they are not in accordance with the contract, e.g. they are claused, or the shipping date is outside the contract period. Secondly, the documents may contain a latent defect. This would be the case where the terms of the documents are false so as to appear consistent with each other and with the requirements of the contract. The documents in such a case are not 'genuine' and can be rejected for that reason, notwithstanding that they appear to conform on their face, the usual criterion by which the buyer's obligation to pay is assessed.

The buyer must pay the price in the manner specified by the contract. This is usually a strict obligation and his use of another unauthorised mode of payment will enable the seller to reject the buyer's purported performance. Provided that goods have been appropriated to the contract and shipped so that the requisite documents can be tendered to the buyer, the subsequent loss or deterioration of the goods is at the buyer's expense unless the seller has broken his duty not to prevent delivery of the goods themselves. The buyer must, therefore, accept the documents and pay the price. His remedies are not against the seller under the contract of sale, but against the carrier, insurer or guilty third party depending upon the circumstances of the case. The question whether the seller is entitled to appropriate goods to the contract which have been shipped and then lost, and other similar issues, have been discussed at 3.6.

3.8.1 The Buyer Must Take Delivery of the Goods

If the buyer has not rejected the documents, he must take delivery of the goods. He then has the rights under ss. 34 and 35, SGA 1979 to inspect the goods and reject them if he can show that the goods did not conform when the seller shipped them. Similarly, if the buyer can show that the incorrect quantity had been shipped, he can exercise the rights conferred on him under ss. 11(4), 30 and 31. Loss and deterioration caused after the time of shipment is at the buyer's expense and he must look either to the carrier under the contract of carriage, or to his insurance.

3.8.2 Other c.i.f. Duties

A c.i.f. contract may impose other duties on the buyer. If the contract specifies several destinations, for instance, the buyer must notify the seller of his choice of destination. The notice should reach the seller within a reasonable time before the beginning of the shipment period so as to enable the seller to ship the goods on the first day of that period (if he so wishes). If the buyer fails to notify the seller in such time as is considered reasonable, the seller is entitled to treat the contract as terminated and sue for non-acceptance.

3.9 INCOTERMS: C.I.F.

The obligations of the parties to a c.i.f. contract have been listed in a document produced by the International Chamber of Commerce. The list differs slightly from the common law decisions, and will only affect the rights and duties of the parties if expressly incorporated into their contract. The list is known as the *Incoterms*. It does not enjoy statutory force. The 1990 edition of the *Incoterms* is considered here, though a new edition is imminent.

3.9.1 The seller must

(a) Provide the goods and the commercial invoice, or its equivalent electronic message, in conformity with the contract of sale and any other evidence of conformity which may be required by the contract.

(b) Obtain at his own risk and expense any export licence or other official authorisation and carry out all customs formalities necessary for the exportation of the goods.

(c) (i) *Contract of carriage*. Contract on usual terms at his own expense for the carriage of the goods to the named port of destination by the usual route in a seagoing vessel (or inland waterway vessel as appropriate) of the type normally used for the transport of goods of the contract description.

(ii) *Contract of insurance*. Obtain at his own expense cargo insurance as agreed in the contract, that the buyer, or any other person having an insurable interest in the goods, shall be entitled to claim directly from the insurer and provide the buyer with the insurance policy or other evidence of insurance cover.

The insurance shall be contracted with the underwriters or an insurance company of good repute and, failing express agreement to the contrary, be in accordance with minimum cover of the Institute Cargo Clauses (Institute of London Underwriters) or any similar set of clauses. The duration of insurance cover shall be in accordance with (e) and (d). When required by the buyer, the seller shall provide at the buyer's expense war, strikes, riots and civil commotion risk insurances if procurable. The minimum insurance shall cover the price provided in the contract plus 10 per cent (i.e. 110 per cent) and shall be provided in the currency of the contract.

(d) Deliver the goods on board the vessel at the port of shipment on the date or within the period stipulated.

(e) Subject to the provisions of 3.9.2(e), bear all risks of loss of or damage to the goods until such time as they have passed the ship's rail at the port of shipment.

(f) Subject to the provisions of 3.9.2(f), pay all costs relating to the goods until they have been delivered in accordance with (d) (above) as well as the freight and all other costs resulting from (c) (above), including costs of loading the goods on board and any charges for unloading at the port of discharge which may be levied by regular shipping lines when contracting for carriage; pay the costs of customs formalities necessary for exportation as well as all duties, taxes and other official charges payable upon exportation.

(g) Give the buyer sufficient notice that the goods have been delivered on board the vessel as well as any other notice required in order to allow the buyer to take measures which are normally necessary to enable him to take the goods.

(h) Unless otherwise agreed, at his own expense provide the buyer without delay with the usual transport document for the agreed port of destination. This document (e.g. a negotiable bill of lading, a non-negotiable sea waybill or an inland waterway document) must cover the contract goods, be dated within the period agreed for shipment, enable the buyer to claim the goods from the carrier at destination and, unless otherwise agreed, enable the buyer to sell the goods in transit by the transfer of the document to a subsequent buyer (the negotiable bill of lading) or by notification to the carrier.

When such a transport document is issued in several originals, a full set of originals must be presented to the buyer. If the transport document contains a reference to a charterparty, the seller must also provide a copy of this latter document. Where the seller and the buyer have agreed to communicate electronically, the document referred to in the preceding paragraphs may be replaced by an equivalent electronic data interchange (EDI) message.

(i) Pay the costs of those checking operations (such as checking quality, measuring, weighing and counting) which are necessary for the purpose of delivering the goods in accordance with (d) (above). Provide at his own expense packaging (unless it is usual for the particular trade to ship the goods of the contract description unpacked) which is required for the transport of the goods arranged by him. Packaging is to be marked appropriately.

(j) Render the buyer at the latter's request, risk and expense, every assistance in obtaining any documents or equivalent electronic messages (other than those mentioned in (h) (above)) issued or transmitted in the country of shipment and/or of origin which the buyer may require for the importation of the goods and, where necessary, for their transit through another country.

3.9.2 The buyer must:

(a) Pay the price as provided in the contract of sale.

(b) Obtain at his own risk and expense any import licence or other official authorisation and carry out all customs formalities for the importation of the goods and, where necessary, for their transit through another country.

(c) [No obligation for contract of carriage.]

(d) Accept delivery of the goods when they have been delivered in accordance with 3.9.1(d) and receive them from the carrier at the named port of destination.

(e) Bear all risks of loss of or damage to the goods from the time they have passed the ship's rail at the port of shipment. Should he fail to give notice in accordance with (g) (below), bear all risks of loss of or damage to the goods from the agreed date or the expiry date of the period fixed for shipment provided, however, that the goods have been duly appropriated to the contract, that is to say, clearly set aside or otherwise identified as the contract goods.

(f) Subject to the provisions of 3.9.1(c), pay all costs relating to the goods from the time they have been delivered in accordance with 3.9.1(d) and, unless such costs and charges have been levied by regular shipping lines when contracting for carriage, pay all costs and charges relating to the goods whilst in transit until their arrival at the port of destination, as well as unloading costs including lighterage and wharfage charges. Should he fail to give notice in accordance with (g) (below), pay the additional costs thereby incurred for the goods from the agreed date or the expiry date of the period fixed for shipment provided, however, that the goods have been duly appropriated to the contract, that is to say, clearly set aside or otherwise identified as the contract goods. Pay all duties, taxes and other official charges as well as the costs of carrying out customs formalities payable upon importation of the goods and, where necessary, for their transit through another country.

(g) Whenever he is entitled to determine the time for shipping the goods and/or the port of destination, give the seller sufficient notice thereof.

(h) Accept the transport document in accordance with 3.9.1(h) if it is in conformity with the contract.

(i) Pay, unless otherwise agreed, the costs of pre-shipment inspection except when mandated by the authorities of the country of exportation.

(j) Pay all costs and charges incurred in obtaining the documents or equivalent electronic messages mentioned in 3.9.1(j) and reimburse those incurred by the seller in rendering his assistance in accordance therewith. Provide the seller, upon request, with the necessary information for procuring insurance.

4   F.o.b. and Other Contracts

4.1   F.O.B. CONTRACTS

4.1.1   Introduction

The term f.o.b. represents 'free on board' and is normally followed by the name of port of departure. This is first and foremost a price term, though it often relates to the delivery obligations of the parties.

The f.o.b. contract has many variants. However, the basic concepts as to delivery, property and risk are common to them all. The variations appear in the other incidents of the relationship between the parties, which are not subject to rigid rules, but depend upon the intentions of the parties as determined by the express terms of the contract and the surrounding circumstances.

The variants of the f.o.b. contract fall into three classes which were distinguished by Devlin J in *Pyrene* v *Scindia Navigation* [1954] 2 QB 402. He referred to the first type as the 'classic' f.o.b. in which the seller puts the goods on board a ship nominated by the buyer. He said, 'in such a case the seller is directly a party to the contract of carriage at least until he takes out the bill of lading in the buyer's name'. He would, even more so, be a party to the contract of carriage if he takes out the bill of lading in his own name. Typically, the seller will make the contract of carriage as the buyer's agent who is, therefore, the principal contracting party.

The second type of f.o.b. contract distinguished by Devlin J was a contract in which 'the seller is asked to make the necessary arrangements (for shipping); and the contract may then provide for his taking the bill of lading in his own name and obtaining payment against the transfer, as in a c.i.f. contract'. This type of f.o.b. contract has subsequently been called the 'extended' f.o.b. or the f.o.b. 'with additional services'. This, therefore, differs from the classic f.o.b. in two essential ways: first, the seller makes the contract of carriage as principal, the buyer is not a party unless he becomes so by operation of the Carriage of Goods by Sea Act 1992; and, secondly, it is the seller who nominates the ship. The extension of the seller's duties may include an obligation to procure insurance. The difference between this type of f.o.b. contract and the c.i.f. would simply be in the computation of the price. In the f.o.b. the price would not include the cost of insurance. The seller would make the contract of insurance for the buyer's account and would invoice him separately for the cost and any expenses incurred.

The third type of f.o.b. contract is one in which the shipping arrangements are made by the buyer or by the buyer's forwarding agent, who books space on a particular ship and, as Devlin J said, 'the seller discharges his duty by putting the goods on board, getting the mate's receipt and handing it to the forwarding agent to enable him to obtain the bill of lading'. This form of f.o.b. contract has been called the 'strict' f.o.b. The seller has no function in the making of the contract of carriage, whether as agent for the buyer or as principal. The buyer nominates the ship.

Devlin J's division of the f.o.b. contract into the three forms above was approved by the Court of Appeal in *The El Amira and The El Minia* [1982] 2 Lloyd's Rep 28.

4.1.2   Passing of Property

In *Mitsui & Co. Ltd* v *Flota Mercante Grancolombiana SA, the Cuidad De Pasto and Cuidad De Neiva* [1988] 2 Lloyd's Rep 208, Staughton LJ dealt with the question of the passing of property in the context of an f.o.b. contract in the following manner:

> The expression f.o.b. determines how the goods shall be delivered, how much of the expense shall be borne by the sellers, and when risk of loss or damage shall pass to the buyers. It does not necessarily decide when property is to pass.

When property passes depends on the intention of the parties. Nevertheless if the goods are ascertained the parties are quite likely to have intended that property in them passes after the goods have been shipped (*Carlos Federspiel & Co. SA* v *Charles Twigg & Co. Ltd* [1957] 1 Lloyd's Rep 240).

The seller, however, may have reserved the right of disposal of the goods until the contract terms of payment have been performed. Furthermore, where the seller obtains the bill of lading (as in the case of the classic f.o.b. contract or the f.o.b. contract with additional services, see below) the passing of title may be postponed until the seller makes the bill of lading available to the buyer or his agent or until some other condition is satisfied (see s 19(2), SGA 1979).

If property did pass on shipment the seller may be entitled to claim the rights of an unpaid seller, and in particular a lien on the goods or the right of stoppage in transit.

4.1.3   Risk

Risk of damage or loss to the goods will normally pass on shipment of the goods and there may be a term in the contract of sale to that effect (see *Inglis* v *Stock* (1885) 10 App Cas 263). Goods are shipped when they have crossed the ship's rail.

Risk may remain with the seller if the seller does not comply with requirements of s. 32(3), SGA 1979 (see below, and *Wimble & Sons* v *Rosenburg & Sons* [1913] 3 KB 743).

If the parties have failed to provide expressly for risk to pass on shipment, i.e. when the goods cross the ship's rail, what is the position where the goods are damaged in the course of loading? There would appear to be two views. The first is that risk passes when the goods pass the ship's rail and it is irrelevant whether they reach the ship safely on completion of the loading operation. The second is that risk passes only when the seller has fulfilled his obligations under the f.o.b. contract, if the goods are deposited safely on board the vessel and the loading operation is complete.

Devlin J in *Pyrene Co. Ltd* v *Scindia Navigation Co. Ltd* (4.1.1), thought that the division of loading into two parts was outdated. He said:

> ... the division of loading into two parts is suited to more antiquated methods of loading than are now generally adopted and the ship's rail has lost much of its nineteenth century significance. Only the most enthusiastic lawyer could watch with satisfaction the spectacle of liabilities shifting uneasily as the cargo sways at the end of a derrick across a notional perpendicular projecting from the ship's rail.

4.2 THE OBLIGATIONS OF THE PARTIES

The f.o.b. contract is an inherently flexible mechanism and, therefore, it is not possible to follow the format adopted in the explanation of the c.i.f. contract in Chapter 3, segregating the seller's obligations from those of the buyer. Instead, each of the three types of f.o.b. contract will be considered individually, and the obligations of the respective parties discussed.

Common to all three are the general duties imposed by the SGA 1979 subject to the express terms of the contract. Hence the seller must deliver to the buyer at the point of delivery in the contract goods which conform with the contract description and with the implied terms as to quality, fitness and (if relevant) sample. He must make his delivery within the time specified, and must comply with all other obligations imposed by the contract within the time specified or, if none, then generally within a reasonable time. The buyer must accept the goods at the point of delivery and pay the price in the manner required by the contract at the time stated.

4.3 THE STRICT F.O.B.

This is the common law f.o.b. and the one envisaged in Incoterms. In the strict f.o.b. the buyer nominates the ship, procures the shipping space and is the legal shipper from the beginning. Unless the contract states otherwise, it is fair to assume the f.o.b. in question is the strict one.

4.3.1   Identification of the Port of Shipment

The due delivery point is the port of shipment designated in the contract of sale. Where the designation is omitted or ambiguous, three possibilities arise. The choice of nomination can be with the seller; or it can be with the buyer; or the contract is void for uncertainty.

The last of the three possibilities would be where it is unclear on the facts whether the parties intended to enter into a legal relationship at all, i.e. when the terms, if any, are so vague that no sense can be made of them together at all. An example would be if the contract merely provided 'f.o.b.' with no qualification as to the port of shipment (see *Cumming* v *Hasell* (1920) 28 CLR 508). The fact that one party is given a choice is not necessarily repugnant to the existence of a contract and if the party with the obligation to choose fails to do so or does so incorrectly, he will be in breach of his contract and the innocent party can reject. In *David Boyd* v *Louis Louca* [1973] 1 Lloyd's Rep 209, the provision 'f.o.b. stowed good Danish port' in the context of a strict f.o.b. contract was held to have given the buyer the option of any good Danish port of discharge. There is a difference between an option to choose any port in the world and one to choose any good Danish port.

Failure to make such a nomination and to notify the seller by an agreed date may amount to a breach of condition precedent to the seller's obligation to supply the contract goods (see *Gill & Duffus* v *Société pour l'Exportation des Sucres* [1985] 1 Lloyd's Rep 621).

The place specified for delivery is a condition of the contract (see *Petrograde Inc* v *Stinnes Handel GmbH, The Times*, 27 July 1994).

4.3.2   Date of Shipment

A date or period of shipment will normally be specified. In the latter case the option for the actual time of shipment within the period lies with the buyer (see *Ian Stach* v *Baker Bosley* [1958] 2 QB 130). The buyer, therefore, has the option of determining the time for loading and the goods are, in effect, at the buyer's call.

Until the buyer has made an effective nomination of the date of shipment, the seller's obligation to have goods ready to load at port does not arise. Hence a seller who takes goods to port for loading in the absence of an effective nomination by the buyer does so at his own risk. In *Cunningham* v *Munro* (1922) 28 Com Cas 42, grain was sold f.o.b. Rotterdam shipment during October. The seller moved his grain to port on 14 October. The buyer did not make an effective nomination until 28 October, by which time the grain had deteriorated to below the contractual standard. The buyer rejected the defective grain, and the seller was found to have been in repudiatory breach attempting to perform using the sub-standard goods.

4.3.3   Nomination of the Vessel

In the strict f.o.b. where the buyer is the legal shipper, it is usual for him to nominate the vessel to be used, if none is specified in the contract of sale, and he must notify the seller of the ship's readiness to load within a reasonable time before the date for shipment to enable the seller to load the goods. The nomination must be made and communicated to the seller to give the seller sufficient time to complete the loading process by the end of the shipping period using either the customary loading procedures or any contractually specified rate for loading. In *Bunge & Co.* v *Tradax England* [1975] 2 Lloyd's Rep 235, where the buyer's notification of the vessel was ineffective because it came too late for the seller to complete loading by the end of the shipping period, it was held that the seller's attempt at loading did not amount to a rejection of the buyer's repudiatory breach and, therefore, the seller was still entitled to reject and sue for non-acceptance.

Unless the buyer's nomination is required by the contract to be final, he is not confined to it and may replace any effective or ineffective nomination by a later one, provided that it is made in time. In *Agricultores Federados Argentinos* v *Ampro SA* [1965] 2 Lloyd's Rep 157, a seller sold a quantity of maize f.o.b. (stated port) shipment between 20 and 29 September. The buyer nominated ship 'A'. This ship was delayed by bad weather and it became apparent that it would be unable to reach the port of loading within the shipment period. At 4.00 p.m. on 29 September, the seller informed the buyer that they intended to cancel the contract as the nominated vessel had not arrived. At 4.30 p.m. the buyer engaged ship 'B'. The seller nevertheless refused to ship on ship 'B'. The court made a finding of fact that there was sufficient time in which to load ship 'B' before the end of the shipping period. The seller was, therefore, held to have been in anticipatory breach of the contract which the buyer accepted and succeeded in a claim for damages for non-delivery.

Agricultores Federados Argentinos v *Ampro SA* was distinguished by the Court of Appeal in *Cargill UK Ltd* v *Continental Ltd* [1989] 2 Lloyd's Rep 290. Parties may expressly or impliedly preclude substitution. Should the party bound to nominate attempt to use a substitute vessel, the other party may refuse it and terminate the contract for repudiatory breach should the first nominated ship fail to arrive at the port of loading in time. In *Cargill* the contract required the buyer to give provisional notice of the nominated vessel eight days before its estimated time of arrival at the port of loading and then definite notice of the ship six days before the expiry of the shipping period. The buyer complied with both requirements naming vessel 'A'. The buyer then gave a second definite notice in time in respect of vessel 'B' since vessel 'A' was unavailable. The seller refused to load vessel 'B' and cancelled the contract. The Court of Appeal held that he was entitled to do so since the contract on its proper construction had expressly precluded substitution. A court must ask itself two questions: (1) was the substituted nomination in time and in accordance with the contract? and, (2) were there any contractual provisions precluding substitution? (1) is not sufficient if (2) is answered affirmatively.

If the buyer substitutes an early nomination for a later one, the seller's expenses incurred by reason of the substitution, e.g. storage charges at the warehouse at port, would be his own loss in the absence of express or implied contractual stipulation to the contrary.

In anticipation of such eventualities, parties often incorporate into the contract a substitution clause. This may take one of three forms. First, the clause may restrict the parties' ability to substitute nominations to a particular time, e.g. up to ten days before the end of the shipping period. Secondly, the clause may extend the shipping period in the event of a substituted nomination. Thirdly, the clause may deny the right of the parties to make substituted nominations (see *Borthwick* v *Bunge & Co.* [1969] 1 Lloyd's Rep 17 which is an example of the second type of substitution clause).

Depending upon the circumstances of the case, the acceptance of a nomination of ship may include acceptance by third parties. For instance, in *Phibro Energy AG* v *Nissho Imai Corporation, The Honam Jade* [1991] 1 Lloyd's Rep 38, the Court of Appeal considered a case relating to a string of contracts for the sale f.o.b. of a quantity of oil. The important point relating to the acceptance of the buyer's nomination of vessel turned on the physical constraints at the loading terminal in question. It was small in size and subject to strict operating rules, such that the time for loading for each oil tanker was limited to a specified three-day slot. The seller could only effectively accept the buyer's nomination of a vessel if a corresponding slot for loading could be agreed with the operators of the terminal. The Court of Appeal construed the contract, therefore, as requiring not only acceptance of the buyer's nomination of vessel by the seller, as in normal cases, but also by the terminal operators. On the facts of the instant case, the buyer had delayed in communicating its acceptance of the seller's nomination, the seller having obtained a slot for loading at the terminal; the time for acceptance was found to be innominate; the delay was unreasonably long and had fundamentally altered the commercial nature of the contract — since it was the first of a string of sell-on contracts of which the first seller was aware, and the delay had jeopardised the later sale contracts. The buyer was entitled to repudiate the contract; which it had done and the seller was, therefore, liable in damages.

4.3.4   Shipping Space on the Vessel

In the absence of contractual stipulation to the contrary, in the strict f.o.b. contract it is the buyer's duty to procure shipping space on the nominated vessel.

4.3.5   Provisions Giving the Seller Options as to Shipment

If the seller is given any of the options mentioned above, it is his duty to advise the buyer of his choice. So, for instance, if it is agreed that the seller is to have the right to decide the loading date within the shipping period, he must notify the buyer of the date on which loading is expected to commence. Until this information has been communicated to the buyer, his duty to nominate a vessel does not arise (see *Harlow & Jones* v *Panex Ltd* [1967] 2 Lloyd's Rep 509). In this case the seller notified the buyer of the date for loading. The buyer was himself in breach when he failed to make arrangements for the nominated ship to be ready to load by the chosen date.

4.3.6 Notice Enabling the Buyer to Insure

Section 32(3), SGA 1979 requires a seller who sends goods by sea to give such notice to the buyer as may enable him to insure them during their sea transit. This has been held to apply to a strict f.o.b. contract, despite the fact that since it is the buyer's responsibility to fix the loading date and furnish the vessel, he ought normally to possess all the information necessary to enable him to arrange insurance (see *Wimble* v *Rosenberg* [1913] 3 KB 743). The Court of Appeal minimised the effect of the section, however, by ruling that it was satisfied if the buyer already had sufficient information to take out insurance. The effect of breach of s. 32(3) is to put the risk of loss during the sea transit back onto the seller.

4.3.7 The Seller's Duty to Load

It is the seller's duty to put on board the ship nominated or designated by the buyer goods which comply with the contractual description, quality and quantity and which are sufficiently packed to withstand the normal rigours of the voyage. Under s. 32(1) the seller is, by performing this duty, deemed to have delivered the goods to the buyer. The place at which the goods are thus delivered is taken as the place of performance under an f.o.b. contract. The duty to load is generally considered to have been discharged when the goods have passed over the ship's rail, even if the goods were in mid air when they were lost (see *Pyrene* v *Scindia Navigation Ltd* (4.1)).

The method of loading specified in the contract is a strict obligation and the seller is not entitled to load by any other means. Similarly, the buyer cannot require delivery by any other way.

The seller must comply with contractual rates of loading or, if none, he must load within a reasonable time of the ship's readiness to load. If the seller fails to load in accordance with these standards, but still manages to complete the loading process before the end of the shipping period, the buyer cannot reject, but may have a claim in damages (see *Tradax Export* v *Italgrani di Francesco Ambrosio* [1986] 2 Lloyd's Rep 112). If the seller does not complete by the end of the shipping period, the buyer is entitled to reject (see *Yelo* v *Machado* [1952] 1 Lloyd's Rep 183) unless the seller's failure is due to the buyer's own ineffective nomination.

If the seller is bound to load within a stipulated period of time, rather than in accordance with a stated rate of loading, then by virtue of the principle that time is of the essence in the commercial context, his failure to do so may be treated as a repudiatory breach entitling the buyer to reject the goods.

4.3.8 The Duty to Procure Export Licence

Normally the parties agree expressly or impliedly that any export licence that may be required is to be procured by the seller (see *AV Pound & Co. Ltd* v *MW Hardy & Co. Inc* [1956] AC 588). Where the parties have neither expressly nor impliedly agreed that the f.o.b. seller should obtain the licence and where the transaction is an export transaction, the duty to obtain the export licence is on the seller and not the buyer. If the f.o.b. buyer is a UK exporter and the contract is a supply contract, for instance f.o.b. London, the duty to obtain the licence would fall on the buyer. The duty is usually to use his best endeavours, and failure in the absence of breach by the seller will operate as a frustrating event; see the discussion above in 3.9.1(b) and 3.9.2(b) under c.i.f. contracts (see also *Pagnan Spa* v *Tradax Ocean Transportation SA* [1987] 2 Lloyd's Rep 342).

4.3.9 Delivery of the Documents

Unless otherwise agreed the seller must furnish to the buyer the documents necessary for him to obtain possession of the goods from the carrier at the port of destination. In the strict f.o.b. sale, where the buyer is the legal shipper, the seller will perform by obtaining from the master of the ship the mate's receipt and transferring this to the buyer, thus enabling the buyer to exchange the mate's receipt for the bill of lading, which in turn entitles him to possession of the goods from the carrier at the port of destination. If any export or other licences were procured by the seller, then these too must be transferred to the buyer. The seller must furnish the documents to the buyer within a reasonable time of completing to load. Unless otherwise agreed, the seller can demand payment in exchange for the documents since the delivery obligation in s. 28 SGA, 1979 is deemed satisfied by the furnishing of the documents.

This view was reinforced by Evans J in *Concordia Trading BV* v *Richco International Ltd* [1991] 1 Lloyd's Rep 475, which reiterated that there was on the f.o.b. seller, who was obliged by his contract to obtain and tender the shipping documents, a duty to perform that obligation forthwith, i.e. with all reasonable despatch, subject to there being no express provision or time limit to the contrary in the contract. More importantly, this duty, for all practical purposes, was commensurate with that which rested on c.i.f. sellers.

4.3.10 Buyer's Right to Reject Documents and Goods

In all three variants of the f.o.b. sale, the buyer is entitled to expect both the documents and the goods to conform with the contract. If the documents are not in order, he may reject them, leaving the seller the opportunity to cure the defect by a fresh and conforming tender of documents if he has time to do so. Even if the buyer accepts the documents he may reject the goods for any non-conformity not apparent on the face of the documents and which is of a repudiatory nature. The principles are the same in f.o.b. as in c.i.f. contracts.

4.4 THE CLASSIC F.O.B.

The main characteristics of the classic f.o.b. are that the seller will make the contract of carriage either as principal or as the buyer's agent by taking out a bill of lading to the buyer s order and will then transfer the bill of lading to the buyer, enabling the latter to call for possession of the goods on arrival at the port of destination from the actual carrier. It would normally be the buyer's duty to nominate the ship which, therefore, prevents the seller from purchasing afloat as in the c.i.f. (and extended f.o.b.) contract.

The duties as to the identification of the port of shipment, the nomination of the vessel, the date of loading, the procuring of shipping space on the nominated vessel, loading, notifying the buyer so that he can insure the goods for the sea transit and procuring any export licences will apply in like manner to the classic f.o.b. as to the strict f.o.b.

In addition, the seller must make a contract of carriage which complies with the contract of sale in like manner to the obligation on the c.i.f. seller:

(a)   The contract must be with the agreed, nominated or designated ship (see *Bowes* v *Shand* (1877) 2 App Cas 455).

(b)   The goods must be stowed in a manner according with any stipulations in the contract, and in the absence of any in the manner customary for that type of goods (see *Messers* v *Morrison Export* [1939] 1 All ER 92).

(c)   The contract must be such that the ship will sail within the agreed shipping period (see *Bowes* v *Shand*, above).

(d)   The transit must comply with the stipulations as to route in the contract of sale (see *Colin & Shields* v *Weddell* [1952] 2 Lloyd's Rep 1021). If no route is specified, then the carriage must be on the customary or if none the reasonable route.

(e)   Unless deviation is permitted by the terms of the contract of sale, the contract of carriage must be for direct transit to the port of destination (see *Bergerco* v *Vegoil* [1984] I Lloyd's Rep 440).

The seller must tender to the buyer a transferable bill of lading which states that the goods have been shipped, which covers the whole of the agreed transit, which covers only those goods which have been sold, which is genuine, valid and effective and which is clean.

The buyer must pay for the goods on the receipt of conforming documents by the method specified in the contract of sale. The one main distinction between strict and classic f.o.b. is that in the latter the seller is given the option to contract for freight as agent or principal.

4.5   THE EXTENDED F.O.B.

In the case of the extended f.o.b. or f.o.b. 'with additional duties' where the seller is the principal to the contract of carriage and has the duty to nominate the ship and time of shipment within the specified shipping period, any one or more of the other duties on the buyer in the strict and classic f.o.b. contract will be excluded by the express terms of the contract, depending upon the seller's contractual undertaking. The extended duty could be either or both of the insurance and carriage contracts. Where the additional duties include both insurance and freight, this type of f.o.b. is almost the same as a c.i.f. contract. The distinguishing factor is that in the f.o.b. with additional duties the seller has to tender at least two (and sometimes three) commercial invoices, one for the goods and the other(s) for insurance and/or freight. A seller in the extended f.o.b. acts as an agent for the buyer regarding insurance and freight, in which case he can charge commission in addition to the premium and freight. This presentation of more than one commercial invoice serves to acknowledge the legal and customary distinctions between the strict and extended f.o.b. The agency element might, however, involve a conflict of interest between the principal (buyer) and the agent (seller) were the seller to find himself in breach of contract. Be that as it may, the traditional distinctions between the c.i.f. and extended f.o.b. are maintained in this kind of scenario.

4.6 INCOTERMS: F.O.B.

The duties of the parties to a f.o.b. contract expressly subject to the *Incoterms* of the International Chamber of Commerce are as follows:

4.6.1 The Seller Must:

(a)   Provide the goods and the commercial invoice, or its equivalent electronic message, in conformity with the contract of sale and any other evidence of conformity which may be required by the contract.

(b)   Obtain at his own risk and expense any export licence or other official authorisation and carry out all customs formalities necessary for the exportation of the goods.

(c)   (i)   *Contract of carriage.* No obligation.
       (ii) *Contract of insurance.* No obligation.

(d)   Deliver the goods on board the vessel named by the buyer at the named port of shipment on the date or within the period stipulated and in the manner customary at the port.

(e)   Subject to the provisions of 4.6.2(e), bear all risks of loss of or damage to the goods until such time as they have passed the ship's rail at the named port of shipment.

(f)   Subject to the provisions of 4.6.2(f), pay all costs relating to the goods until such time as they have passed the ship's rail at the named port of shipment; pay the costs of customs formalities necessary for exportation as well as all duties, taxes and other official charges payable upon exportation.

(g)   Give the buyer sufficient notice that the goods have been delivered on board.

(h)   Provide the buyer at the seller's expense with the usual document in proof of delivery in accordance with (d) above.

Unless the document referred to in the preceding paragraph is the transport document, render the buyer, at the latter's request, risk and expense, every assistance in obtaining a transport document for the contract of carriage (e.g. a negotiable bill of lading, a non-negotiable sea waybill, an inland waterway document, or a multimodal transport document).

Where the seller and the buyer have agreed to communicate electronically, the document referred to in the preceding paragraph may be replaced by an equivalent electronic data interchange (EDI) message.

(i) Pay the costs of those checking operations (such as checking quality, measuring, weighing, counting) which are necessary for the purpose of delivering the goods in accordance with (d) above.

Provide at his own expense packaging (unless it is usual for the particular trade to ship the goods of the contract description unpacked) which is required for the transport of the goods, to the extent that the circumstances relating to the transport (e.g. modalities, destination) are made known to the seller before the contract of sale is concluded. Packaging is to be marked appropriately.

(j) Render the buyer at the latter's request, risk and expense, every assistance in obtaining any document or equivalent electronic messages (other than those mentioned in (h) above) issued or transmitted in the country of shipment and/or of origin which the buyer may require for the importation of the goods and, where necessary, for their transit through another country.

Provide the buyer, upon request, with the necessary information for procuring insurance.

4.6.2 The Buyer Must:

(a) Pay the price as provided in the contract of sale.

(b) Obtain at his own risk and expense any import licence or other official authorisation and carry out all customs formalities for the importation of the goods and, where necessary, for their transit through another country.

(c) Contract at his own expense for the carriage of the goods from the named port of shipment.

(d) Take delivery of the goods in accordance with 4.6.1(d).

(e) Bear all risks of loss of or damage to the goods from the time they have passed the ship's rail at the named port of shipment. Should he fail to give notice in accordance with (g) below, or should the vessel named by him fail to arrive on time, or be unable to take the goods, or close for cargo earlier than the stipulated time, bear all risks of loss of or damage to the goods from the agreed date or the expiry date of the period stipulated for delivery provided, however, that the goods have been duly appropriated to the contract, that is to say, clearly set aside or otherwise identified as the contract goods.

(f) Pay all costs relating to the goods from the time they have passed the ship's rail at the named port of shipment.

Pay any additional costs incurred, either because the vessel named by him has failed to arrive on time, or is unable to take the goods, or will close for cargo earlier than the stipulated date, or because the buyer has failed to give appropriate notice in accordance with (g) below provided, however, that the goods have been duly appropriated to the contract, that is to say, clearly set aside or otherwise identified as the contract goods.

Pay all duties, taxes and other official charges as well as the costs of carrying out customs formalities payable upon importation of the goods and, where necessary, for their transit through another country.

(g)   Give the seller sufficient notice of the vessel name, loading point and required delivery time.

(h)   Accept the proof of delivery in accordance with 4.6.1(h).

(i)   Pay, unless otherwise agreed, the costs of pre-shipment inspection except when mandated by the authorities of the country of export.

(j)   Pay all costs and charges incurred in obtaining the documents or equivalent electronic messages mentioned in 4.6.1(j) and reimburse those incurred by the seller in rendering his assistance in accordance therewith.

4.7   F.A.S.

In this kind of contract the contract goods must be placed free alongside the vessel whether she has entered port or not. Therefore, if the vessel cannot for any reason enter port, the seller must ensure that the goods are carried alongside her on lighters so that they are within reach of the ship's tackle (see also 1.11.2).

The obligations of the parties to a contract on f.a.s. terms are comprehensively listed in the appropriate *Incoterms*.

4.7.1   The Seller Must:

(a)   Provide the goods and the commercial invoice, or its equivalent electronic message, in conformity with the contract of sale and any other evidence of conformity which may be required by the contract.

(b)   Render the buyer, at the latter's request, risk and expense, every assistance in obtaining any export licence or other official authorisation necessary for the exportation of the goods.

(c)   (i)   *Contract of carriage*. No obligation.
      (ii)   *Contract of insurance*. No obligation.

(d)   Deliver the goods alongside the named vessel at the loading place named by the buyer at the named port of shipment on the date or within the period stipulated and in the manner customary at the port.

(e)   Subject to the provisions of 4.7.2(e), bear all risks of loss of or damage to the goods until such time as they have been delivered in accordance with (d) above.

(f)   Subject to the provisions of 4.7.2(f), pay all costs relating to the goods until such time as they have been delivered in accordance with (d) above.

(g)   Give the buyer sufficient notice that the goods have been delivered alongside the named vessel.

(h)   Provide the buyer at the seller's expense with the usual document in proof of delivery of the goods in accordance with (d) above.

Unless the document referred to in the preceding paragraph is the transport document, render the buyer at the latter's request, risk and expense, every assistance in obtaining a transport document (e.g. a negotiable bill of lading, a non-negotiable sea waybill, an inland waterway document).

When the seller and the buyer have agreed to communicate electronically, the document referred to in the preceding paragraphs may be replaced by an equivalent electronic data interchange (EDI) message.

(i)   Pay the costs of those checking operations (such as checking quality, measuring, weighing, counting) which are necessary for the purpose of placing the goods at the disposal of the buyer.

Provide at his own expense packaging (unless it is usual for the particular trade to ship the goods of the contract description unpacked) which is required for the transport of the goods, to the extent that the circumstances relating to the transport (e.g. modalities, destination) are made known to the seller before the contract of the sale is concluded. Packaging is to be marked appropriately.

(j)   Render the buyer at the latter's request, risk and expense, every assistance in obtaining any documents or equivalent electronic messages (other than those mentioned in (h) above) issued or transmitted in the country of shipment and/or of origin which the buyer may require for the exportation and/or importation of the goods and, where necessary, for their transit through another country.

Provide the buyer, upon request, with the necessary information for procuring insurance.

4.7.2   The Buyer Must:

(a)   Pay the price as provided in the contract of sale.

(b)   Contract at his own expense any export and import licence or other official authorisation and carry out all customs formalities for the exportation and importation of the goods and, where necessary, for their transit through another country.

(c)   Contract at his own expense for the carriage of the goods from the named port of shipment.

(d)   Take delivery of the goods in accordance with 4.7.1(d).

(e)   Bear all risks of or damage to the goods from the time they have been delivered in accordance with 4.7.1(d).

Should he fail to fulfil his obligations in accordance with (b) above, bear all additional risks of loss of or damage to the goods incurred thereby, and should he fail to give notice in accordance with (g) below, or should the vessel named by him fail to arrive on time, or be unable to take the goods, or close for cargo earlier than the stipulated time, bear all risks of loss of or damage to the goods from the agreed date or the expiry date of the period stipulated for delivery provided, however, that the goods have been duly appropriated to the contract, that is to say, clearly set aside or otherwise identified as the contract goods.

(f)   Pay all costs relating to the goods from the time they have been delivered in accordance with 4.7.1(d).

Pay any additional costs incurred, either because the vessel named by him has failed to arrive on time, or will be unable to take the goods, or will close for cargo earlier than the stipulated time, or because the buyer has failed to fulfil his obligations in accordance with (b) above, or to give appropriate notice in accordance with (g) below provided, however, that the goods have been duly appropriated to the contract, that is to say, clearly set aside or otherwise identified as the contract goods.

Pay all duties, taxes and other official charges as well as the costs of carrying out customs formalities payable upon exportation and importation of the goods and, where necessary, for their transit through another country.

Pay all costs and charges incurred by the seller in rendering assistance in accordance with 4.7.1(b).

(g)   Give the seller sufficient notice of the vessel name, loading place and required delivery time.

(h)   Accept the proof of delivery in accordance with 4.7.1(h).

(i)   Pay, unless otherwise agreed, the costs of pre-shipment inspection (including inspection mandated by the authorities of the country of exportation).

(j)   Pay all costs and charges incurred in obtaining the documents or equivalent electronic messages mentioned in 4.7.1(j) and reimburse those incurred by the seller in rendering his assistance in accordance therewith.

Where the parties contract on this basis, then on the face of it property passes at the point of delivery alongside, subject to the expression of a contrary intention. Risk also passes at this point, and it is the buyer who must then load the goods at his expense having satisfied his obligation to pay for them.

4.8   F.CA.

F.ca. means free carrier. When goods are sent f.ca., the seller must ensure that they are placed on the train which is to carry them and assumes all responsibility for them prior to this point. In practice, f.ca. has come to mean that the seller must ensure that the contractual goods are safely placed on a British Rail collecting vehicle to be carried to the railway. The buyer assumes risk and on the face of it property at the time that the goods are actually in the hands of the railway for carriage to their destination. The seller must notify the buyer that the goods are in transit to him once they are received by the railway.

Where the goods are sent f.ca., the seller retains responsibility for the goods up to the time that they are actually loaded on to the railway wagon itself. All costs prior to placing the goods on the wagon are borne by the seller.

The 1990 edition of *Incoterms* changed the nomenclature for both f.o.r. (free on rail) and f.o.t. (free on truck) to f.ca. (see 1.11.3).

4.9   D.E.S.

D.e.s. means delivered ex ship. In *Yangtsze Insurance Association* v *Luckmanjee* [1918] AC 585, the Privy Council defined a d.e.s. contract in the following terms:

The seller has to cause delivery to be made to the buyer from a ship which has arrived at the port of delivery and has reached a place therein which is usual for the delivery of the goods of the kind in question.

In this kind of contract the seller bears all cost associated with and risk involved in the goods until they arrive at their destination. Thus the seller will remain liable for risk of damage during the course of transit.

This is clearly very different from a c.i.f. contract in which the delivery of the documents amounts to constructive delivery of the goods. If the goods arrived damaged under a d.e.s. contract or were lost in transit, then the buyer would be under no obligation to accept them even if correct documents were tendered.

If the buyer of such goods wishes to insure them for himself during their transit, he would be able to do so. His insurable interest being the profits he intends to make on them, he is not, therefore, prevented from taking out insurance by reason of having neither risk nor property in the goods (see *Yangtsze Assurance* v *Luckmanjee* (above) and s. 7, Marine Insurance Act 1906).

In a d.e.s. contract both the ship and the date of arrival are part of the description of the goods, failure to comply with which would amount to a repudiatory breach of contract. A d.e.s. contract may also be referred to as an 'arrival contract'. It is important, however, to distinguish it from contracts where the parties agree that their contract is to be an arrival contract in the sense that if the ship and goods do not arrive safely at the agreed destination, then the whole contract is discharged.

The 1990 edition of *Incoterms* changed the nomenclature from ex ship to d.e.s.

4.10   D.E.Q.

D.e.q. means delivered ex quay. Where goods are to be delivered d.e.q., the seller must ensure that they arrive at the quay at their port of destination, and he will make payment of all necessary import duties and charges levied there. Such duties may either rest with the seller (duty paid) or be borne by the seller for the account of the buyer. In such a contract the seller bears risk in the goods until they are delivered at the port of destination. This is rarely used in export sales from Britain because it requires the seller or his agent to make arrangements in the country of destination, which may prove to be expensive unless he has a permanently appointed representative there.

Once the goods arrive at the quay of the named port of destination, the responsibility for transporting them to their final destination and paying any charges necessarily incurred in doing so lies with the buyer.

The 1990 edition of *Incoterms* changed the nomenclature from ex quay to d.e.q.

4.11   EXW.

Exw. means delivered ex works. In an exw., ex store or ex warehouse contract the obligations imposed on the seller are minimal. He simply has to make the contractual goods available for collection to the buyer or his agent in the seller's country.

Whilst the seller may take it upon himself to pack the goods in such a way as to protect them during their export transit, he is not obliged to do so. He need only provide the goods with packing sufficient for a domestic sale which would, therefore, suffice to enable the buyer to take delivery of the goods, and this at his own expense. There may, of course, be a counter stipulation in the contract of sale, imposing the cost of export packing on the seller (see *Commercial Fibres* (Ireland) Ltd v *Zabaida* [1975] 1 Lloyd's Rep 27).

Where the seller carries on business at several places within a particular locality then he must give the buyer sufficient notice of the premises from which the goods are to be collected (see *Davies* v *McLean* (1873) 21 WR 265).

In an exw. contract the seller bears all the costs related to the goods, and the risk in those goods, up to the time of collection from his premises.

The 1990 edition of *Incoterms* changed the nomenclature from ex works to exw.

4.12   C.FR.

C.fr. means cost and freight. Under a normal c.i.f. contract the seller bears the responsibility for all charges associated with shipment of the goods to their destination. He insures the goods for their contractual journey and is responsible for their freight.

Where the contract is on a c.fr. basis, the seller bears no responsibility for the insurance of the goods. Risk in the goods passes on shipment and so the seller must notify the buyer of all details necessary to enable the buyer to take out insurance. In this respect the seller should heed s. 32(3), SGA 1979, as failure to furnish the buyer with adequate notice of details may prevent risk from passing on shipment where the buyer is prevented from taking out insurance. As with c.i.f., property passes on tender of documents.

Where the contract in addition to being c.fr. specifically states that 'insurance is to be effected or arranged by the buyer' then the buyer is not only expected to take out insurance, he is contractually obliged to do so, on terms upon which it would have been taken out by the seller.

The 1990 edition of *Incoterms* changed the nomenclature from c. and f. to c.fr. After c.i.f. and f.o.b. this is probably the third most important international trade contract. The new edition of *Incoterms* retains the change.

5   Documentation in International Trade

5.1   THE DOCUMENTS GENERALLY

In the absence of stipulations to the contrary the c.i.f. seller is bound to tender to the buyer three documents: a bill of lading; a policy of insurance; and an invoice. Contractual variations of these are quite common. The contract may substitute a delivery order for a bill of lading. More frequently today where a combined transport operator is used by the seller, a combined transport document will be stipulated, which will not be a bill of lading unless the combined operator is himself the actual sea carrier. The contract may substitute a certificate of insurance for the policy of insurance. It may call for additional documents. Such additional requirements are to be interpreted against the background of the obligations *prima facie* relating to a c.i.f. seller; see the leading statements of Lord Porter in *The Julia* and the decision in *The Parchim*, both at 3.1.

5.2   THE TRADITIONAL BILL OF LADING

5.2.1   Definition and Functions

A bill of lading is a document issued by or on behalf of the actual sea-carrier of goods to the person (usually called the shipper) with whom he has contracted to transport the goods. A bill of lading performs three functions:

(a)   it is evidence that the goods described in it have been received by the carrier, and if a shipped bill of lading, that they have been shipped;

(b)   it is evidence of or actually contains the contract of carriage;

(c)   provided that it satisfies certain requirements (see below) it is a document of title to the goods both in the common law and statutory senses.

A bill of lading will normally state to whom the goods represented by it are to be delivered. The manner in which the bill does this classifies the bill either as a 'bearer', 'order' or 'straight consigned' bill of lading.

A *bearer bill* is one that does not name the actual consignee of the goods, but simply makes them deliverable 'to bearer', i.e. the person in actual possession of the bill regardless of how he obtained the bill.

There are two kinds of *order bill*. The first provides for delivery to the named consignee or to his 'order (or assigns)', or contains similar words importing transferability. The second type simply makes the goods deliverable 'to order (or assigns)', or again words importing transferability, without naming a consignee. The bill is said to be to the order of the consignor, and entitles that person, the consignor, to indorse the bill and deliver it to a third party, thereby making the indorsee the person entitled to immediate possession of the goods from the carrier on presentation of the bill. The indorsee may himself transfer the bill by indorsement and delivery until the bill is accomplished, i.e. it has been exchanged for the goods on presentation to the carrier by the named consignee or indorsee. The bill is said to be taken out to the shipper's order, and it is the shipper who is entitled to present or indorse and deliver the bill.

A *straight consigned or non-negotiable bill* is one that makes the goods deliverable to the named consignee, and either contains no words importing transferability, or contains words negativing transferability. As will be seen below and later in the chapters on bills of exchange and documentary credits, the use of the word 'negotiable' is strictly inaccurate, and it is better to use 'transferable' in relation to bills of lading. Under such a bill the consignee has no power to transfer the bill and so to direct the carrier to deliver the goods to another person. Under a straight consigned bill of lading, the carrier is entitled and bound to deliver the goods to the consignee without production of the bill of lading, and so any alteration of the bill itself is ineffective.

There is another division in the types of bills of lading which is not connected with the form of the order of delivery. A 'shipped' bill of lading is one which states that the goods have been shipped, i.e. put on board the carrying ship. Normally, it will state the date on which the goods were shipped and, as seen in the cases above, the buyer can reject a bill which contains a false statement as to the date of shipment.

The correct date for a bill of lading is the date on which loading is completed, i.e. all the cargo has been shipped; see *Mendala III Transport* v *Total Transport Corporation, Total International Ltd and Addax Ltd, The Wilomi Tanana* [1993] 2 Lloyd's Rep 41.

A 'received (for shipment)' bill of lading is one which merely states that the goods have been received by the carrier for shipment and provides no evidence of actual shipment. Such a bill of lading may, therefore, be rejected if tendered under a c.i.f. contract unless the parties agree that such a bill of lading may be tendered. It is doubtful whether a received bill of lading is a document of title at common law If, after a 'received' bill has been issued, the goods are shipped, this fact may be noted by the carrier on the bill, and the document then becomes a shipped bill with effect from the date of shipment noted.

5.2.2 Receipt For The Goods

A bill of lading is evidence of the facts stated in it. Hence a shipped bill of lading is evidence that the goods have in fact been shipped on the date specified. Similarly, a statement that the goods were shipped in apparent order and condition is evidence of that fact. At common law that bill of lading is only *prima facie* evidence of the things stated in it, enabling a contesting party to bring evidence to the contrary. This normally only applies between the carrier and the shipper. When the bill is indorsed, an estoppel arises between the carrier and the indorsee which prevents the former from disputing the truth of the contents of the bill. The statements in the bill must, of course, have been made to the indorsee by someone with authority for or on behalf of the indorser, otherwise no estoppel arises.

The bill of lading should be clean and not claused or fouled. A clean bill of lading is one which bears no superimposed clauses expressly declaring a defective condition of the goods or packaging. The bill of lading relates only to the apparent order and condition of the goods and does not attempt to detail the state of the goods themselves. A bill is foul or claused and, therefore, unacceptable if it states that the apparent order and condition of the goods is in some way defective, e.g. that the goods appear damaged, or that the packaging is inadequate, damaged, stained, wet or has been tampered with.

In *Golodetz* v *Czarnikow Rionda Inc, The Galatia* [1980] 1 WLR 495, it was held that a bill is only claused if the defective notation refers to the apparent order and condition of the goods at the time of shipment. Where the notation referred to a fire damaging the goods after shipment in a c.i.f. contract, the bill of lading was not claused for the purposes of the contract of sale and could not be rejected by the buyer for that reason. This is because in c.i.f. sales the buyer is presumed to bear the risk as from shipment, and so any event occurring after that date is his loss or expense. It was further held that a bill is not rendered unclean by the inclusion of the common provision 'weight, measure, quantity, condition, contents and value unknown' since such a statement does not qualify the acknowledgement of receipt or shipment in apparent good order and condition. It was also held that, whether a bill is clean or not is to be determined by the 'legal' test, that is, the requirement that nothing on the bill should qualify the statement as to apparent good order and condition of the goods at the time of shipment, and not by the 'practical' test of whether the bill has, in fact, proved acceptable to a banker or other party to whom it was presented. For this aspect of the case see Chapter 3. The mere fact that a notation is unusual does not render the bill unclean for the purposes of the contract of sale.

The position is largely the same in this respect under the Hague-Visby Rules, which are considered in Chapter 8.

5.2.3 Evidence of The Contract

A bill of lading is also evidence of the contract of carriage, but at common law does not actually contain the contract of carriage whether in the hands of an original party to the contract, or in those of a transferee of the bill. This means that the existence of a bill of lading does not necessarily mean that a contract of carriage has been made, or that the terms stated in the bill reflect the true contractual position. In *The Ardennes* [1951] 1 KB 55, sellers wished to ship a cargo of oranges from Spain to England. The shipowner orally promised that the ship would arrive in London on a particular date, just before import charges were to be increased. The ship did not arrive until after the date of the increase. The seller/shipper sued the carrier/shipowner for the delay. The latter pleaded a 'liberty to deviate clause' in the bill of lading in defence. It was held that the seller/shipper could give evidence of the terms of the contract of carriage which had been entered into before the bill of lading had been issued. The bill of lading was not conclusive evidence of the terms of that contract. The defence therefore did not avail and the seller/shipper succeeded.

Where the shipment is covered by both a charterparty and a bill of lading, the bill of lading may not even be evidence of the contract of carriage, which is contained in the charterparty. In such a case, the bill of lading is a mere receipt and a document of title. The question of conflicts between the terms of the bill of lading and the charterparty in this situation is discussed at 6.5.

5.2.4   Document of Title

A shipped bearer or order bill is at common law the only recognised document of title relating to those goods. Possession of the bill of lading gives its possessor constructive possession of the goods, and if transferred with the intention of passing the transferor's property in the goods will also give the transferee that property (see *Lickbarrow* v *Mason* (1787) 2 Term Rep 63). The carrier is not bound to deliver the goods except on production of the bill, and is liable to the holder of the bill if he wrongfully delivers the goods to someone else. This is the crucial difference between bearer or order bills on the one hand and straight consigned bills on the other, for in the latter case the carrier is bound to deliver the goods only to the named consignee who need not produce the bill. The carrier's failure so to deliver the goods renders him liable in tort for conversion under the Torts (Interference with Goods) Act 1977 and usually liable for breach of his contract of carriage.

The master should not deliver cargo to someone who does not have the original bill of lading, unless that person has a reasonable explanation for the absence of the original bill of lading (see *Sucre Export SA* v *Northern Shipping Ltd, The Sormovskiy 3068, The Times*, 13 May 1994).

If the shipped bearer or order bill of lading falsely states that the goods have been shipped, when in fact none have been shipped, it is not a document of title, for there are no underlying goods (see *Hindley* v *East Indian Produce Co.* [1973] 2 Lloyd's Rep 515).

The statutory definition of documents of title to goods is broader than the common law recognition (see s. 1(4), Factors Act 1889). It seems, however, that even at common law if a particular trade usage treats a particular document as a document of title, the common law will give recognition to that fact. In *Kum* v *Wah Tat Bank*

Ltd [1971] 1 Lloyd's Rep 439, a custom to the effect that mate's receipts (see 5.3.7) were treated as documents of title in the trade between Sarawak and Singapore was proved so that mate's receipts were in that context documents of title. In the case itself, this did not help the holder of the mate's receipt as it was marked 'non-negotiable'.

A 'straight consigned' bill of lading is not a document of title at common law. Hence if the carriage document is noted 'non-negotiable' it will not be transferable and, therefore, will not be a document of title (see *Henderson & Co.* v *The Comptoir d'Escompte de Paris* (1873) LR 5 PC 253).

A transferable bill of lading possesses in relation to goods most of the features of negotiability accorded to instruments in respect of money. However the transferee of a bill of lading does not, by virtue of the nature of the document, acquire any better title than his transferor; though he may do so by reason of some exception to the *nemo dat* rule (see 2.6). There is, therefore, no equivalent to the 'holder in due course' status enjoyed in respect of instruments. Also negotiability is not presumed as in the case of instruments; it is necessary for the bill to be made transferable by notation.

5.2.5 Timing and Procedures

The time within which the bill of lading is issued is important. In *Hansson* v *Hamel & Horley Ltd* [1922] 2 AC 36, it was held that even though the bill is to be issued on shipment it need not be issued contemporaneously with shipment. The requirement is that the bill be issued within such time as is usual in the course of business and without delay.

The bill of lading should be tendered to the buyer in a reasonable time after shipment in the absence of contractual stipulations to the contrary. If the c.i.f. seller has bought afloat, then the tender must be made as soon as possible after appropriation. Provided that the seller has acted within a reasonable time, it is irrelevant that the goods arrive before the documents are tendered (see *Sanders Bros* v *McLean & Co.* (1883) 11 QBD 327). There is, therefore, no implied condition that the seller will deliver the documents in time for the buyer to meet the ship with the bill of lading.

Late delivery of the bill of lading may have an effect on the contract of sale. If there is an express stipulation as to the time by which the document is to be tendered, failure to comply would be a repudiatory breach such that the buyer could reject. In *Toepfer* v *Lenersan-Poortman NV* [1980] 1 Lloyd's Rep 143, the seller's failure to comply with a stipulation that the documents would be tendered not later than 20 days after the date of the issue of the bill of lading was found to be a breach of condition since in commercial contracts stipulations as to time are generally treated as being of the essence. Where the contractual stipulation permits a degree of flexibility; e.g. 'documents to be tendered as soon as possible' or 'within a reasonable time', it is unclear whether such terms are conditions, breach of which is repudiatory, or whether they are innominate, and the court must look to the effect of the particular breach before classifying the nature of the breach. *Benjamin* considers that the term should be innominate, notwithstanding the presumption that time is of the essence in the commercial context. It should be noted that when banks are involved in the financing of the contract of sale by way of documentary credit transactions, banks will generally refuse documents which are presented to them more than 21 days after the date of issue (see Uniform Customs and Practice for Documentary Credits (UCP) Article 43(a)).

5.2.6 Need For Continued Documentary Cover

The seller must provide the c.i.f. buyer with continuous documentary cover during the transit of the goods. This is because in c.i.f. contracts risk of loss is presumed to be on the buyer as from shipment even when goods have been bought afloat. He, therefore, requires the ability to hold the carrier liable for any loss or damage caused during transit. In *Hansson* v *Hamel & Horley Ltd* [1922] 2 AC 36, a quantity of cod was sold 'c.i.f. Yokohama' to be shipped from Norway in March or April. Goods were indeed shipped in April from a Norwegian port to a German port where they were transshipped. The bill of lading tendered to the buyer stated that the goods had been shipped in the shipping period from a Norwegian port, and had been issued by the owners of the second ship after the transshipment. The buyer rejected the bill of lading. It was held that the bill of lading was improper. The owners of the second ship had not undertaken responsibility for the first stage of the voyage from Norway to Germany. It seems that a bill of lading covering the first stage when tendered with the bill of lading for the second stage would still have been improper as it would not have covered the time of transshipment and, therefore, would not have given the buyer the continuous documentary cover to which he was entitled.

5.3 SUBSTITUTES FOR BILL OF LADING

The other types of document which may be substituted for a shipped bill of lading, provided that the contract so permits, are as follows.

5.3.1 Sea Waybill

A sea waybill is a document which contains or evidences an undertaking by the carrier to the shipper to deliver to the person who is for the time being identified as being entitled to delivery. A sea waybill is a receipt for the goods but is non-transferable and is not a document of title. Section 1(3), Carriage of Goods by Sea (COGSA) 1992 defines the sea waybill in the following terms:

> any document which is not a bill of lading but—
>
> (a)   is such a receipt of the goods as contains or evidences a contract for the carriage of goods by sea; and
>
> (b)   identifies the person to whom delivery of the goods is to be made by the carrier in accordance with that contract.

Using a sea waybill has the advantage that it does not have to be transmitted to the consignee to obtain delivery of the goods from the carrier and the shipper can alter his delivery instructions to the carrier at any time during transit. There is no problem in the vessel arriving before the shipping documents and the ship can discharge at once producing savings in the time and cost of transportation. The sea waybill is, therefore, much in use in the short sea trades and in the container business.

5.3.2 A Ship's Delivery Order

Often it is not possible for the seller to procure a bill of lading, especially when he has shipped a large consignment of goods. If he can identify each consignment before shipment, then he could obtain a set of bills of lading covering each specific consignment. Normally, however, there will be just one bill of lading for the bulk cargo.

A bill of lading cannot be divided up. The seller must use delivery orders as an alternative. A delivery order is usually an order in writing given by an owner of goods to a person in possession of them, e.g. as carrier or warehouseman, directing the latter to deliver the goods to the person named in the order.

If the contract permits the use of a delivery order, then the document will only be satisfactory if it puts the buyer in a position as close as possible to that which he would have been in had a bill of lading been used (see *Khron & Co.* v *Thegra NV* [1975] 1 Lloyd's Rep 146). The essential point is that the document tendered should give the person in whose favour it is issued some rights, preferably of a contractual nature, against the ship carrying the goods. It will have this effect if it is issued by or on behalf of the shipowner, and contains a promise or attornment by him to deliver the goods to the person named.

A ship's delivery order is defined by s. 1(4), COGSA 1992 in the following terms:

any document which is neither a bill of lading nor a sea waybill but contains an undertaking which—

(a) is given under or for the purposes of a contract for the carriage of goods by sea of the goods to which the document relates, or for goods which include those goods; and

(b) is an undertaking by the carrier to a person identified in the document to deliver the goods to which the document relates to that person.

In *Laurie & Morewood* v *Dudin & Sons* [1926] 1 KB 223, an attornment was described as a positive act which is not transferable. If the delivery order is after the attornment further transferred by the person in whose favour it was issued, a fresh attornment by the person in possession of the goods is necessary to transfer constructive possession to the new transferee.

One problem with such documents representing an attornment is that it is often difficult to find the consideration moving from the buyer to the carrier so as to found the basis of a contract between the carrier and the buyer.

5.3.3   A Delivery Warrant

This is an immediate promise by the carrier to deliver the goods to the buyer. It is made direct to the buyer and, therefore, requires no attornment. When in receipt of such a warrant the buyer can demand the goods. If consideration can be found moving from the buyer to the carrier, a contract may be implied.

5.3.4   A Mere Delivery Order

A mere delivery order differs from a ship's delivery order in that the former does not represent an attornment by the carrier to the buyer. It is an order addressed by the seller to someone who is not in possession of the goods (usually the seller's agent at the port of destination) to pass the goods on to the person named in the order when the addressee acquires possession of the goods from the ship. Such a delivery order is not good tender under a c.i.f. contract in the absence of contractual provision to the contrary. Even though the buyer will be named in the order, the order does not give the buyer constructive possession of the goods. The order is not drawn on the carrier who is, therefore, not in a position to attorn to the buyer. The buyer is not, therefore in a position to deal with the goods whilst they are on the high seas. The buyer has no right to demand the goods from the ship. The order only confers on the buyer the right to demand the goods from the addressee, the seller's agent at port. Consequently, the order gives the buyer no contractual rights, nor any possibility of such rights, against the ship. It was this form of delivery order which the seller used in performance of his obligations in *The Julia* [1949] AC 293 in which it was held that notwithstanding that the parties had called their contract c.i.f. it was in reality an *ex ship* contract.

5.3.5   A Container Bill of Lading

This is usually issued by a freight forwarder or combined transport operator who is shipping goods in containers. It is a received for shipment document, although it may be turned into a shipped bill if the operator or freight forwarder is in fact the carrier and there is a notation on the bill that the goods have been shipped.

5.3.6   A Through Bill of Lading

This is when the goods are to be transshipped en route between seller and buyer. The seller must stipulate for this as good tender in the contract of sale. If it is issued under the normal conditions for a shipped bill of lading (see 5.2) and genuinely provides continuous documentary cover, it will be good tender.

5.3.7   A Mate's Receipt

This is a document issued on the receipt or shipment of goods by or on behalf of the shipowner to the shipper. It acknowledges receipt of the goods and states their quality and condition. Normally it is presented to the shipowner or his agent in exchange for bills of lading. A mate's receipt does not usually represent a contract of carriage, nor is it a document of title at common law unless a custom giving it this effect can be proved. In *Kum v Wah Tat Bank Ltd* (see 5.2.3) the general approach was stated as: 'it is not ordinarily anything more than evidence that the goods have been received on board'.

A mate's receipt is written acknowledgement of the receipt of goods delivered to a ship. The mate's receipt is prima facie evidence of such receipt; see *Biddulph v Bingham* (1874) 2 Asp MLC 225. It is not conclusive evidence, and the burden of proving that it is incorrect lies on the shipowner; see *Biddulph v Bingham*. Qualifying words may be inserted describing the condition of the goods at the time of receipt, and in the absence of any qualification, the receipt is known as a 'clean receipt'; see *Armstrong v Allan Bros & Co.* (1892) 7 Asp MLC 293, CA.

Possession of a mate's receipt is *prima facie* evidence of ownership entitling the holder to receive a bill of lading; see *Schuster v McKellar* (1857) 7 E & B 704; *Nippon Yusen Kaisha v Ramjiban Serowgee* [1938] 2 All ER 285, CA.

On the production of the mate's receipt, in the absence of notice that the holder is not the owner, the master or agent of the shipowner is justified in signing a bill of lading and delivering it to the holder in exchange for the mate's receipt; see *Craven v Ryder* (1816) 6 Taunt 433. He is not bound to insist on production of the mate's receipt, and may sign the bill of lading without requiring the mate's receipt to be returned or accounted for (*Craven v Ryder*). It is then his duty to satisfy himself that the goods for which he signs are actually on board the ship, and that the person to whom he delivers the bill of lading was at the time of shipment entitled to the bill of lading as owner of the goods or otherwise (*Schuster v McKellar*, (above). If the bill of lading is delivered to the wrong person, and no mate's receipt is asked for, the shipowner remains responsible to the owner (*Schuster v McKellar*).

A transfer of the mate's receipt does not, of itself, usually pass the property in the goods specified in it; see *Hathesing v Laing: Laing v Zeden* (1873) LR 19 Eq 92; but there may be a usage that the property does pass; see *Kum v Wah Tat Bank Ltd* (5.2.3). As against the true owner, therefore, the holder of a mate's receipt cannot claim the bill of lading or the goods themselves, *Hathesing v Laing: Laing v Zeden*. But a transfer of the goods with the intention of passing the property in them to the transferee entitles the transferee, as against the transferor, to receive the bill of lading, notwithstanding that the mate's receipt is not transferred but is retained by the original owner; see *Cowas-Jee v Thompson* (1845) 5 Moo PCC 165.

5.3.8 A Groupage Bill of Lading

This will be used when the carrier is transporting goods belonging to a number of different consignors in the same hold, container, etc, such that it is neither convenient nor possible to issue individual bills of lading for each consignment. Typically, this occurs when a seller is exporting a quantity of goods insufficient to fill the hold or container. The operator or freight forwarder will load a number of consignments together from different consignors into the same container or hold and take out a bill of lading in his own name. The groupage bill, like any other bill of lading, cannot be split up. In such a situation, the operator will either tender ship's delivery orders to the consignors ordering the carrier to deliver the goods to the designated consignee, or he will tender a house bill of lading.

5.3.9   A House Bill of Lading

The house bill of lading is similar to the delivery warrant (see 5.3.3) in that it enables the holder to demand release of the goods from the operator's agent at the port of delivery. The house bill of lading, therefore, is not issued by a sea carrier and, therefore, is not a true bill of lading in any sense. In addition the holder cannot demand possession of the goods from the carrier by virtue of the document.

5.3.10   A Combined Transport Document

A combined transport operator (CTO) is a person who undertakes to arrange the transport of goods from the seller's warehouse to the buyer's place of delivery. Normally, the CTO is not a carrier at all. The CTO usually undertakes the responsibility for transportation as between himself and the seller or buyer, since he is in fact party to all the contracts of carriage involved. Any document issued by the CTO will not usually be a bill of lading because it is not normally issued by a sea carrier. It consequently will not normally give the addressee constructive possession of the goods. Such documents are not recognised as being negotiable, notwithstanding notation to the contrary on the document itself. However, with the increased use of CTOs banks, when involved in the financing of the contract of sale by way of documentary credit transactions, will pay against combined transport documents if issued by a sea carrier unless prohibited by contract. The UCP 500 uses the preferred term 'multimodal transport document' rather than 'combined transport document' (Art. 26).

5.3.11   Seller's duties: The c.i.f. Bill of Lading

For ease of reference, there follows a list of the c.i.f. seller's duties in respect of the bill of lading unless the contract stipulates otherwise:

(a)   It must be a shipped bill of lading: the buyer is entitled to a document stating that shipment has actually begun.

(b)   It must be a clean, not claused or fouled bill.

(c)   It must not be issued under a charterparty unless tendered with the charterparty itself; for its terms would then be qualified by the charterparty, so adversely affecting the buyer's rights and preventing him from knowing by what terms he is bound.

(d)   It must record a date and place of shipment that indicates compliance with the contract of sale.

(e)   It must cover the whole of the agreed course of transit and not, for example, be a bill of lading issued by an intermediate carrier holding the goods at the time when they are purchased afloat unless that intermediate carrier accepts total responsibility for the entire transit.

(f)   Where transshipment is prohibited, the bill must be one which indicates continuous carriage by the same vessel to the port of destination as opposed to a through bill of lading or a combined transport document.

(g)   It must sufficiently identify the goods. Failure to do this will prevent the bill from being a document of title both at common law and under statute.

(h)   It must be confined to the buyer's goods and must not include goods consigned to another purchaser. In the latter case, the buyer would not be able to deal with the bill of lading without committing a conversion of the other purchaser's goods.

(i)   It must be signed on shipment or within a reasonable period thereafter.

(j)   It must be acceptable to the trade, for otherwise it will lose its free transferability. If the bill is altered or appears to have been tampered with it will be unacceptable.

Statements in the bill of lading are examined in detail in Chapters 6 and 7.

5.4   THE INSURANCE POLICY

For a detailed discussion of the question of insurance see Chapters 12 and 13. Under c.i.f. contracts the seller is required to insure the goods for their sea voyage. Unless otherwise agreed, the buyer is entitled to a policy of marine insurance covering the goods against the usual marine risks and such others as may be specified in the contract.

The buyer is entitled to reject the policy if it covers goods other than those comprised in his bill of lading. In practice, the delivery of the policy itself is impracticable, since the seller will normally have contracted on open cover or floating policy terms (see 12.8.3) under which no specific policy for each consignment is issued. In such cases, the seller ought to stipulate for the delivery of a cover note or insurance certificate. If there is no such provision, the buyer can reject such documents not least because they do not give the holder a direct right of action against the insurer (see *Wilson* v *Belgian Grain & Produce Co.* [1920] 2 KB 1). A policy of marine insurance is assignable by indorsement and delivery or in any other customary manner (s. 50, Marine Insurance Act 1906).

5.4.1   Lloyd's Marine Policy

A Lloyd's marine policy is an insurance policy subscribed to by Underwriting Members of Lloyd's as listed in the policy. It is issued by Lloyd's (The Association of Underwriters) of London. A Lloyd's marine policy serves as a contract of cargo insurance. It also covers hull insurance.

5.4.2   Companies' Marine Policy

A companies' marine policy is an insurance policy subscribed to by insurance companies which are members of the Members of the Institute of London Underwriters. It is issued by the Institute of London Underwriters, 40 Lime Street, London EC3M 5DA, United Kingdom.

A companies marine policy serves as a contract of insurance for cargo. The A clause provides comprehensive insurance for goods on an all-risk basis subject to certain exclusions, while on the other hand the B and C clauses are based on a warned perils approach and the cover is much more limited. Overall, the clauses exist to cater for total loss of the goods.

The companies' marine policy is not valid unless it bears the embossment of the policy department of the Institute of London Underwriters. It is subject to English law and must contain an identical description of the cargo as found on the bill of lading, air waybill and feature the valuation and transportation details.

5.4.3   Certificate of Insurance

A typical cargo insurance certificate includes the following data:

    (a)   name and address of the insurer;
    (b)   name of the assured;
    (c)   the endorsement of the assured where applicable so that the rights to claim may be transferred;
    (d)   a description of the risks covered;
    (e)   a description of the consignment;
    (f)   the sum or sums insured;
    (g)   the place where claims are payable together with the name of the agent to whom claims may be directed.

It is issued by an insurance company, insurance broker or freight forwarder. The certificate of insurance is of paramount importance in providing insurance cover against possible loss or damage to the specified merchandise during shipment. The export sales contract detailing the cargo delivery terms/*Incoterms* 1990 will specify who is responsible for the insurance provision, i.e. seller or buyer. For example, under c.i.f. the seller takes care of all the insurance provision to the named destination, whilst under c.fr. the buyer is responsible for all the insurance when the goods pass the 'ship's rail' at the port of shipment. Insurance cover for the goods should embrace the following:

    (a)   transportation of merchandise to the seaport or airport;
    (b)   period during which the goods are stored awaiting shipment or loading;
    (c)   the time whilst on board the ship, aircraft, or other conveyance such as the international road haulage operation;

(d) the 'off loading' and storage on arrival at destination airport, seaport or other specified place;

(e) transportation to the buyer's premises/address.

An insurance certificate should normally indicate that the goods are covered/ insured from the seller's warehouse to the buyer's warehouse. In situations where the insurance certificate is to be included in a presentation under a documentary letter of credit, the certificate must be dated before the date of the document evidencing dispatch such as found on the bill of lading/sea waybill/air waybill/CMR note etc. and must be completely and precisely compatible with such data contained in such accompanying documents.

The cargo description and valuation must conform to the data found on the bill of lading/air waybill or other carrier's documentation. This includes the valuation of the cargo and details of the consignor and consignee and details of shipment such as date, time of flight/sailing and name of vessel.

5.4.4 Insurance Company's Cover Note

This is a note signed on behalf of the insurers by the agent through whom a proposal for insurance is submitted, and issued by him to the proposer giving interim cover while the proposal is being considered by the insurers.

Where the cover note states that it is to remain in force until the insurers intimate that they have rejected the proposal, it remains in force until the rejection is brought to the knowledge of the proposer; see *Rossiter* v *Trafalgar Life Assurance Association* (1859) 27 Beav 377. Where the cover note expressly states that it is to be in force for a fixed period, it does not follow that it remains in force during the whole of that period, since the insurers reserve the right to determine it at an earlier date by intimating their rejection of the proposal. 'It was competent for the office by return of post to decline the proposal without giving a reason, but until such notice was received, the insurance would continue and if a fire happened in the interval, this office would have been answerable': *Mackie* v *European Assurance Society* (1869) 21 LT 102 at p. 104 (Malins V-C). Where the cover note provides that the insurers are to intimate the rejection of the proposal but also that any deposit paid by the proposer is to be returned to him, subject to a deduction in respect of the days during which the cover note has been operative, the insurers remain liable until they have fully discharged their obligation (*Mackie* v *European Assurance*). Where the cover note expressly provides that the insurers are to intimate their acceptance of the proposal, or that the proposed insurance is not to bind them until a policy is issued, the cover note will cease to have any force at the expiration of the specified period unless such acceptance has been intimated or unless the policy has been issued, as the case may be; see *Levy* v *Scottish Employers' Insurance Co.* (1901) 17 TLR 229.

The cover note is in itself a contract of insurance governing the rights and liabilities of the parties in the event of a loss taking place during its currency; see *Re Coleman's Depositories Ltd and Life and Health Assurance Association* (1907) 2 KB 798, CA. The insured can therefore enforce the contract contained in the cover note provided that he has complied with its conditions, e.g. as to the payment of the premium. The cover note usually incorporates the terms of the insurance company's policies, but may do so indirectly by referring to the proposal form which itself alludes to them; see *Wyndham Rather Ltd* v *Eagle Star and British Dominions Insurance Co.* (1925) 21 Ll L Rep 214, CA. The insurance company may also rely on the terms and conditions of the policy if it can be shown that the insured knew of them, or had an opportunity of knowing them and agreed to be bound by them (*Re Coleman's Depositories Ltd and Life and Health Assurance Association* at p. 805, *per* Vaughan Williams LJ). As against the insurers the cover note is to be construed with reference to the common form of policy issued by them, and they cannot rely on a construction of the cover note inconsistent therewith; see *Browning* v *Provincial Insurance Co. of Canada* (1873) LR 5 PC 263 at p. 273 (*per* Sir Montague Smith). The cover note will usually be replaced by a policy but the insurance company is not bound to issue one unless there is an agreement to that effect. The assured too is not bound to accept the policy. 'During that month it was open to the (company) on further inquiry to refuse to grant the policy and to terminate the contract at the end of the month. It was equally open to the assured to say that he did not like the (company), not thinking the capital sufficient, or for other reasons': *Mackie* v *European Assurance Society* (above) at p. 104 (*per* Malins V-C).

5.4.5 Broker's Cover Note

This is a note issued by a broker pending the preparation of the policy, certifying that the insurance has been effected and setting out its terms. By issuing the cover note the broker does not incur liability on the insurance since he does not purport to be an insurer. He is presumed to warrant to the proposer that his instructions have been properly carried out, and that the insurance has been effected. If there is no insurance in fact, he will be liable to the proposer for breach of warranty. A broker's cover note is not binding on the insurers; see *Broit* v *S. Cohen & Son (NSW) Ltd* (1926) 27 SR NSW 29.

5.4.6 Letter of Insurance

There was a practice where the insured would tender, for claim or letter of credit purposes, a letter of insurance. The letter serves to certify that the insured was covered for the shipment in question under a named policy. There is no legal recourse where an insurance claim is rejected or the documents are rejected when presented for payment under letter of credit. The UCP 500 is silent on letters of insurance in Article 34 dealing with insurance documents. Otherwise, letters of insurance serve the same purpose as certificates of insurance.

5.4.7 Declaration Issued Under An Open Cover

The requirement for tendering an insurance policy or certificate may be substituted for a declaration under an open cover and vice versa. For that reason, Article 34(d) of UCP 500 provides that:

Unless otherwise stipulated in the credit, banks will accept an insurance certificate or a declaration under an open cover presigned by insurance companies or underwriters or their agents. If a credit specifically calls for an insurance certificate or a declaration under an open cover, banks will accept, in lieu thereof, an insurance policy.

For details on the open cover see 12.8.3.

5.4.8   Duties: The c.i.f. Insurance Policy

(a)   The policy must cover only the goods comprised in the bill of lading.

(b)   It must cover the transit stipulated in the contract of sale.

(c)   It must be a marine insurance policy covering the usual risks and any others stipulated in the contract.

5.5   THE COMMERCIAL INVOICE

This is an invoice prepared on shipment of the goods and thus evidences the start of transit. It is, therefore, more than a normal type of invoice which is merely a price quotation and request. A commercial invoice is usually required by the buyer to clear the goods through customs, since it is on the price quoted in the commercial invoice that customs duty is assessed. It may also be needed for other authority requirements. In the context of documentary credits, the commercial invoice is important in that it is this document which records the full description of the goods as set out in the letter of credit and by which the perfect tender rule is assessed.

The commercial invoice should identify the buyer's order and should set out the full details of the parties, the goods, the price and the payment terms, shipping marks and numbers, and the shipment itself including the port of loading, route and port of discharge.

5.6   ADDITIONAL DOCUMENTS REQUIRED BY THE CONTRACT

5.6.1   Introduction

Other documents may be required by the express terms of the contract. The most frequently required are export and import licences and certificates of quality. The incidence of the duty to obtain the licence is in the first place a question of the particular terms of the contract and any relevant legislation. In the absence of express stipulation in a c.i.f. contract, the duty to procure the export licence is on the seller and the duty to procure the import licence is on the buyer. In the absence of an express contractual duty, the standard of duty is one of due diligence or best endeavours (see *Re Anglo-Russian Merchant Traders and John Batt & Co.* [1917] 2 KB 679). The duty to procure the required licence is performed as soon as the licence has been obtained. The party subject to the duty is accordingly not in breach if the licence is later revoked, provided that the revocation is not attributable to any fault on that party's part. He may be under a duty to make all reasonable efforts to secure the restoration of the licence (see *Provimi Hellas AE* v *Warinco AG* [1978] 1 Lloyd's Rep 373).

A contract which is made 'subject to licence' does not (as in the case of 'subject to contract') prevent a binding contract from coming into existence. The effect of such a term was described in *Charles H Windshuegl Ltd* v *Alexander Pickering & Co. Ltd* (1950) 84 Ll LR 89 as:

> ... there is introduced into the contract a condition that a licence must be obtained and that neither party will be liable to perform the duties under the contract unless the licence is procured.

The party subject to the duty must use his best endeavours to procure the licence, but he does not warrant that one will be obtained.

The party under the duty to exercise his best endeavours to procure the licence must show the court that he has actually taken those steps. If he has done nothing, he will be liable unless he can show that any steps he could have taken would have been useless. What are the reasonable steps in each case is a question of fact, though in most cases the application must be made without unreasonable delay and to the correct authorities. The fact that the expense of obtaining the licence would render the contract unprofitable for one party is not good reason for refusing to obtain the licence.

If the parties fail to obtain the necessary licences the contract may then be unenforceable for illegality. If one of the parties was in breach of his contractual duty to obtain a licence the innocent party will be entitled to damages for that breach.

Where the duty is one to make reasonable efforts and these were not made, the position is the same. Where no licence is obtained but the party subject to the duty has shown that he used his best endeavours, he is not liable as he has not broken any of his obligations. If the contract was 'subject to licence', then both parties are released from the contract, and no obligations can accrue. If the contract is not subject to licence, then existing secondary obligations must still be discharged by both parties liable. The most usual construction is that the parties are excused future performance, though this has sometimes been equated with frustration of the contract (see *Pound* v *Hardy* [1956] AC 588).

5.6.2   Certificate of Origin

5.6.2.1   Definition
A certificate of origin is a document confirming the nature, quantity, value, etc. of the goods shipped and their place of manufacture, and includes a declaration stating the country of origin of the goods. It is necessary for statistical purposes, import quotas and fulfilment of trade sanctions or embargo that might be in force at the time where a country permits another country's goods to enter free of duty, or at a

preferential rate of duty, and the question often arises, 'can we be sure that these goods are in fact the products of the country to which we have agreed to extend preferential treatment?'.

Thus, if the UK permits Albanian goods to enter duty free, but finds that an Albanian exporter is sending Yugoslav or Iraq goods (both countries were subject to UN trade embargo in the late 1990s) to the UK at the preferential UK rate and in breach of UN sanctions, the UK will naturally not be pleased. For this reason, it has been necessary to introduce and insist on some sort of certificate of origin to reflect a bilateral trade agreement between two nations.

A certificate of origin is therefore a long established document that accompanies the goods and is required as one of the support documents at the time of export and import. No particular format of the document exists internationally, as different institutions issue their own, but the document enables the seller to export, the customs authorities to clear at both ends and the revenue authorities to calculate appropriate levels of duty. A certificate of origin has been adopted for use in the EU and many other countries world-wide exercising the control over the level and origin of their imports. In the UK, it is issued by Chambers of Commerce, e.g. The Arab-British Chamber of Commerce.

5.6.2.2 *Chambers of Commerce and the Certificate of Origin*
In order to make it easy for customs authorities to verify that a certificate of origin is reliable, the International Convention on the Simplification of Customs Formalities 1923 laid down that a small number of organisations should be designated by governments to issue these certificates. For the United Kingdom the appropriate authorities are the Chambers of Commerce, who are prepared to supply sets of forms to exporters. When these forms are completed and presented, together with a commercial invoice and other evidence of origin if the goods were not manufactured by the exporter, the Chamber of Commerce will duly certify them. The invoice and other documents must contain a declaration by the proprietors, a partner or a suitable official such as the company secretary that the goods are of United Kingdom origin. On the official certificate the term is 'European Communities–United Kingdom'.

Some countries require the certificate to be written onto the actual commercial invoice, in which case the words 'United Kingdom' are not enough and the certificate must read 'European Communities–United Kingdom'.

With the development of aligned documentation, SITPRO (Simplification of International Trade Procedures) negotiated the combination of invoices and certificates of origin and value. This is a continuing process and clearly it is a desirable development. The panels for certification can be combined with the invoice in a variety of ways, either by extending the normal A4 invoice to larger sizes (such as A4 extended or A4 square) or by using the back of the form.

One of the challenges facing international trade is that the certificate has become a tool of nationalistic economic policies. The other problem is that in the modern world, a product might be assembled from components manufactured in different countries.

5.6.3 Certificate of Quality

A certificate of quality confirms that the description and specification of the cargo is as described in the contract of sale, bill of lading, certificate of insurance, the commercial invoice, etc. The certificate of quality is normally issued by the exporter, e.g. A.B. Campbell, and shipper. The actual examination is undertaken by a professional taster, normally registered with a local trade association or local Chamber of Commerce. The purpose of the Certificate of Quality is to confirm for the importer that the quality and formal specification of a particular consignment of goods is in accord with the exporter's sales contract at the time of shipment. For example, it would ensure that a Japanese buyer of Johnnie Walker Scotch Whisky 'blue' label is not supplied with an inferior 'black' or 'red' label. Other examples are to ensure an importer paying for 'Assam' tea or 'Arabica' coffee is not supplied with the inferior 'Darjeeling' tea or 'Robusta' coffee respectively. The Certificate of Quality is usually required for tender by both the contract of sale and under letters of credit terms to accord with the terms of sale. A copy is also normally required by the bank for financial settlement purposes and copies are distributed to the agent and buyer. It is important that cargo distribution conforms to its terms found in the contract, statute, invoice, certificate of insurance, etc.

5.6.4 Certificate of Quantity

A certificate of quality should not be mistaken for a certificate of quantity. The two have almost identical spelling and can be mistaken for each other especially when several documents are checked for conformity under pressure. The certificate of quantity works on the same principle as the certificate of quality, save that the former serves to confirm the quantity either in weight or volume. It has been erroneously suggested that the PSI certificate (see 5.7) renders the quality and quantity certificates redundant. This is not necessarily the case, as the PSI certificate confirms in addition whether the goods have been shipped rather than their quantity or quality. Theoretically, it is still possible for a contract to require the tender of the PSI certificate and one or both of the others.

5.6.5 Certificate of Value

Here, the intentions of nations may vary. Some wish to prevent profiteering by foreign suppliers and call for a breakdown of costs charged to their importers — including the charge for the goods, the value of packing, the freight, insurance and other charges paid. Others wish to restrict imports of goods to those not manufactured in their own country, and therefore require a certificate that goods are properly described and that no alternative invoices are being issued to evade regulations. With others, the intention is to avoid 'dumping' — the sale of goods to a foreign country at a lower price than is paid in the home market by a country's own citizens.

There are innumerable ways of dumping goods — the intention being to earn foreign exchange at any price. Thus, a factory making an article at £100 might achieve profitability by selling half its output at £200 to home consumers and the other half at £50 (a dumping price) to foreign customers paying hard currency. A profit margin of 25 per cent has been earned by selling at the differential prices, the home consumer subsidising the foreign consumer but, in the process, competing unfairly with the industry in the foreign country which can only make the product at a price higher than £50. Certificates of value may call for a clear declaration of the various costs incurred in the manufacture of the goods and a guarantee that, taking freight and other costs into account, the goods are being sold at the 'same' price in the home country as in the foreign country. If this is not established, a tariff may be imposed to bring the price up to a fair level, or to one which will virtually exclude the goods in order to discourage the practice.

5.6.6 Certificate of Weight

Even more confusing can be the distinction between the certificate of quantity and a certificate of weight. Quantity indicates volume, whereas weight is limited to measurement of weight only, e.g. kilograms. A certificate of weight confirms that the goods in question accord with the weight specified in the contract, bill of lading, commercial invoice, certificate of insurance or some other specified document and in so doing confirms for the buyer, seller, insurance company or other specified party that the goods were of a specified weight at the time of shipment.

The certificate of weight is normally issued by the exporter, e.g. A.B. Campbell, and shipper. Usually the certificate of weight is requested by the importer to confirm that the weight of the goods is in accordance with the export sales contract at the time of shipment. The certificate of weight is also usually required under the letter of credit, though often under exporter forwarding arrangements involving a bulk cargo shipment. The cargo weight must accord with the details found in the charterparty and its subservient bill of lading. It may well be that as it gains wider appeal, the PSI certificate might replace the functions of the quality, quantity and weight certificates.

5.6.7 Health Certificate

A health certificate is a document issued when agricultural products are being exported to certify that they comply with the relevant legislation in the exporter's country. The best example would have been the saga of the attempted export of livestock with 'mad cow disease' from the UK in the late 1990s.

The document is issued by the appropriate health authority in the exporter's country, e.g. Environmental Health Department, London Borough of Bexley. To comply with the buyer's request, it is necessary in some countries to provide a health certificate. It certifies that the product was in good condition at the time of inspection — prior to shipment — and fit for human consumption.

The health certificate issued in the UK certifies that all relevant legislation is complied with and the requirements of the Food Hygiene Regulations of the UK are certified. The certificate is used worldwide in the conduct of international trade. No special format or text exists. It simply confirms the goods are fit for human consumption and is basically an approval certificate to export the cargo. It is supplied by the governmental department responsible for environmental health and is required by Customs.

5.6.8 Consular Invoice

5.6.8.1 Consular Invoices
A commercial invoice (5.5) should not be mistaken for a consular invoice. Whereas the former is issued by the exporter, itemising the cost of the export to the buyer, the latter is issued by the overseas consulate. A consular invoice is made on a special form obtained from the importing country's consulate, or sometimes from stocks held by authorised Chambers of Commerce. After completion by the supplier it is legalised by the consulate, e.g. by a commercial attaché, and in certain instances needs to be certified by the Chamber of Commerce prior to presentation to the consulate. For this reason, the consular invoice is sometimes referred to as a legalised invoice. Legislation fees are sometimes based on a percentage of the invoice value and can be considerable.

5.6.8.2 Legalised Invoices
A consular invoice which requires to be, or has been, legalised by a consulate is a legalised invoice, as would be a commercial invoice which has been, or needs to go, through the same process. Countries with strict controls to protect home industries, e.g. through infant industry system, or the use of foreign exchange, and countries with political reasons for excluding goods from a particular country or group of countries, may require the commercial, consular and other invoices to be legalised. The process is intended to conserve foreign exchange and protect domestic industries by closing corrupt loopholes and other malpractices in international trade. A legalised invoice is therefore an invoice (commercial, consular, preliminary, etc) which has been submitted to the consulate of an importing country and certified by it (for a fee) to be a legal transaction sanctioned for implementation. It verifies the legality, price, quality and quantity of the goods. Sometimes referred to as 'visaed invoices', they are analogous (for goods) to a visa in a passport. In that case, the legalised invoice can also serve as a certificate of quantity, weight, value, quality, etc.

5.6.8.3 Certified Invoices
Legalisation of invoices involves certification, in which case they become certified invoices. Certified invoices may involve certification of the origin of the goods (a certificate of origin — see 5.6.2) or of value (certificate of value — see 5.6.5). In that respect, a certified invoice is simply a commercial invoice which has been subsequently certified by an authorised Chamber of Commerce. A fee is payable for

this service and should be taken into account when costing contracts involving countries requiring such certificates. The system first developed with regards to certificates of origin. Legalising and certifying invoices did not achieve their intended goals. They have increasingly been replaced by a single process known as the certificate of inspection (see 5.7).

5.6.9   Pro forma Invoices

A pro forma invoice is sometimes called for, or may be used as a matter of course. It is a quotation made out in the form of a commercial invoice and simply headed 'pro forma'. It is used at a much earlier stage of the sales transaction than any of the other types of invoice and is normally required by the importing authorities in cases where there are restrictions on certain types of goods or in foreign exchange. It is a firm offer to sell at the price quoted (though it may have safeguarding clauses about undue delay in acceptance). Acceptance within the time limit makes a binding contract, so it is essential to include in the quotation every cost that can be envisaged. A pro forma invoice should never be sent off in a light-hearted manner — it is essential to think the offer through to the final completion.

5.6.10   Export and Import Licences

Most goods can be exported without any restrictions, but there are certain exceptions such as arms and military equipment, aircraft, strategic goods, some metals, live horses, cattle, sheep and pigs, eggs, antigens, diamonds, etc. Restrictions vary from country to country. Therefore, to export any items, one would need either an export/import licence or a certificate of exemptions. The contract of sale will provide for the party to obtain the licence. In the absence of agreement by the parties, it is the duty of the buyer to obtain an import licence in ex works contracts. In ex ship contracts, it is for the buyer to obtain an import licence and for the seller to obtain an export licence. The same is only *presumably* the case in f.o.b. and c.i.f. common law contracts (*Pound* v *Hardy* [1956] AC 588; *Brandt* v *Morris* [1917] 2 KB 784).

   Incoterms 1990 provides expressly that the buyer obtains the import licence while the seller obtains the export licence. If the duty to obtain the licence is absolute, a party who fails to obtain it will be in breach of contract, but if the duty is merely to use his best endeavours and his best efforts fail, then the contract is discharged by frustration (*Pagnan SPA* v *Tradax Ocean Transport SA* [1987] 1 All ER 81). Frequently, the matter is covered by a force majeure clause. Otherwise, the licence or certificate is issued by the Board of Trade and is of the essential documentation in export trade. There is no particular format for the documents.

5.6.11   Customs Clearance

All goods exported and imported through seaports, airports, etc. need customs clearance. It is the duty of the exporter to obtain the customs documents and to clear goods for export and sometimes for entry into the buyer's country. Where the goods are exported outside the EU, the seller will use the ordinary customs declaration and clearance forms. The reverse is the case for goods entering the EU from outside. However, for goods transiting through and destined to one EU country from another, the process has been simplified. The exporter/importer within that common market now needs to use the Single Administrative Document (SAD) introduced by the Commission in 1988. Both the ordinary and SAD customs forms are obtained from and issued by Her Majesty's Customs & Excise.

5.7   PRESHIPMENT INSPECTION AND CERTIFICATES

5.7.1   Introduction

Preshipment inspection has already been mentioned in 1.8. This paragraph will concentrate on PSI certificates or the documentation aspects of the PSI. There are two types: government and private mandated. Preshipment certificates can comprise a six-part export declaration document, a five-part inspection report, and a two-part inspection report and clean report of findings. In preshipment inspection procedures, both letters of credit and contracts relevant to the import of goods contain a condition that a clean report of findings covering quality, quantity and price must be presented along with other documents required to negotiate payment. It is, however, not a shipping document and is, therefore, not issued by the carrier. The document is issued by independent PSI agencies.

An inspection company, e.g. SGS Inspection Services Ltd (export declaration and inspection report) or Cotecna International Ltd (inspection report and clean report of findings) issues it directly to the cosignee who is the principal or employer of the agency. The PSI certificate has in a way replaced the certificate of quality and the consular invoice.

Preshipment inspection is implementation of a control system imposed by government regulation in certain countries where the buyer's country requires preshipment inspection to be carried out by an inspection company in the seller's country at the port of departure or other convenient place. Its prime function is to ensure goods at the time of despatch are in a good condition and in requisite quantity. The secondary function is to help eradicate fraud in trade generally and as regards foreign currency in particular. There are still unresolved issues regarding the liabilities of the PSI agency.

Preshipment inspection has to satisfy the requirements of the buyer's country exchange control regulations but has no legal role by convention in international trade documentation. Preshipment inspection is a requirement in some 40 countries and its administration in regard to preshipment inspection code is conducted by the International Federation of Inspection Agencies (IFIA) based in London. Most PSI agencies are also European based.

5.7.2 Procedure and Code of Practice

Preshipment inspection has a Code of Practice for Government Mandated Preshipment Inspection which provides as follows:

(a) Activities of preshipment inspection companies (hereinafter 'PIC') in the country of export may be undertaken on behalf of a foreign government, government agency, central bank, or other appropriate governmental authority and may include:

(i) physical inspection for quantity and quality of goods; verification of export prices, including financial terms of the export transaction and currency exchange rates where appropriate;
. (ii) support services to the customs authorities of the country of importation.

(b) The general procedures for physical inspection of goods and the examination of the price of exports out of any particular country will be the same in all exporting countries and the specific requirements established by the importing country will be administered by the PIC in a consistent and objective manner.

(c) The PIC will provide assistance to exporters by furnishing information and guidelines necessary to enable exporters to comply with the preshipment inspection regulations of the importing country. This assistance on the part of the PIC is not intended to relieve exporters from the responsibility for compliance with the import regulations of the importing country.

(d) Quantity and quality inspections will be performed in accordance with accepted national/international standards.

(e) The conduct of preshipment activities should facilitate legitimate foreign trade and assist bona fide exporters by providing independent evidence of compliance with the laws and regulations of the importing country.

(f) Preshipment activities will be conducted and the Clean Report of Findings, or notice of non-issuance thereof, will be sent to the exporter in a timely and convenient manner.

(g) Confidential business information will not be shared by the PICs with any third party other than the appropriate government authority for which the inspection in question is being performed.

(h) Adequate procedures to safeguard all information submitted by exporters will be maintained by the PIC, together with proper security for any information provided in confidence to them.

(i) The PIC will not request from exporters information regarding manufacturing data related to patents (issued or pending) or licensing agreements. Nor will the PIC attempt to identify the cost of manufacture, level of profit or, except in the case of exports made through a buying agent or a confirming house, the terms of contracts between exporters and their suppliers.

(j)   The PIC will avoid conflicts of interest between the PIC, any related entities of the PIC or entities in which the PIC has a financial interest, and companies whose shipments the PIC is inspecting.

(k)   The PIC will state in writing the reason for any decision declining issuance of a Clean Report of Findings.

(l)   If a rejection occurs at the stage of physical inspection the PIC will, if requested by the exporter, arrange the earliest date for reinspection.

(m)   Whenever so requested by the exporter, and provided no contrary instruction has been issued by the government authority, the PIC will undertake a preliminary price verification prior to receipt of the import licence on the basis of the binding contractual documents, proforma invoice and application for import approval. An invoice price and/or currency exchange rate that has been accepted by the PIC on the basis of such preliminary price verification will not be withdrawn, provided the goods and the previously submitted documentation conform with the information contained in the import licence. The clean report of findings, however, will not be issued until appropriate final documents have been received by the PIC.

(n)   Price verification will be undertaken on the basis of the terms of the sales contract and it will take into consideration any generally applicable and allowable adjusting factors pertaining to the transaction.

(o)   Commissions due to an agent in the country of destination will be treated in strict confidence by the PIC, and will only be reported to the appropriate government authority when so requested.

(p)   Exporters or importers who are unable to resolve differences with the PIC may appeal in writing, stating facts of the specific transaction and the nature of the complaint, directly to a designated appeals official of the PIC. Exporters wishing to appeal the results of a preshipment inspection may also seek review of the decision of the PIC in the importing country.

In cases where a PIC is considered not to have observed any article of this Code of Practice, this may be reported to the Director General of IFIA.

5.7.3   Other Aspects

The Code of Practice for Government Mandated Preshipment Inspection outlined in 5.7.2 will yield the following benefits (if it conforms to the buyer's country exchange control regulations):

(a)   it minimises losses of foreign exchange through over-invoicing, concealed commission payments and illegal money transfers;

(b)   it minimises losses of revenue and duty payments through under-invoicing;

(c)   it reduces evasion of import controls and helps combat smuggling;

(d)   it helps control landed prices and therefore helps control local inflation.

To understand the main reasons for the expanding use of preshipment inspection one must bear in mind the following aspects:

(a)   effective protection can only be taken as a preventative measure before goods are shipped and it must cover contractual aspects as well as the physical aspects;

(b)   preshipment inspection is intended to prevent losses due to the normal commercial risks. The examination of both goods and documents is conducted on the basis of natural standards and normal customs and practices of the trades concerned.

5.7.4   Drawbacks of the System

The inspection companies are required to provide an independent opinion as to whether the price on the proforma invoice represents the normal price charged for those goods to overseas buyers. Many factors can cause prices to vary over time and between different orders. If the evaluation of price, description and/or customs classification differs from that given in the order, then it is assumed that some sort of adjusting factor has been overlooked. The exporter is always invited to discuss this and supply additional justification before a final opinion is given. What the inspection authority has to ensure is that any differences can be explained and justified against normal commercial considerations and the normal custom of that trade.

The inspection company is not asked to give advice on sources of supply, contractual conditions, cost effectiveness or user benefits. These are decisions for the appropriate government or free market to determine.

The preshipment certificate is a document of some controversy in certain export markets, particularly in the area of price verification. Sellers take the view that the price is fixed contractually at the time of negotiation and should not be varied at the time of shipment.

FURTHER READING FOR PART II

Benjamin: Sale of Goods, 5th edn, London: Sweet & Maxwell, 1997.

Halsbury's Laws of England, London: Butterworths.

Campbell, D. and Praksch, R., *International Business Transactions*, 3 vols, The Hague: Kluwer, 1988.

Chuah, J.C.T., *Law of International Trade*, London: Sweet & Maxwell, 1998.

Day, D.M. and Griffin, B., *The Law of International Trade*, 3nd edn, London: Butterworths, 1999.

Debattista, C., *The Sale of Goods Carried By Sea*, 2nd edn, London: Butterworths, 1998.

Delaware, *Transnational Contracts*, 6 vols, New York: Oceana.

ICC Incoterms 1990, Paris: ICC, 1990.

Kadar, A. and Whitehead, G., *Export Law,* 2nd edn, Cambridge: Prentice Woodhead, 1995.

Sassoon, D., *CIF and FOB Contracts*, 4th edn, London: Sweet & Maxwell, 1998.
Schmitthoff, C.M., *Export Trade*, 10th edn, London: Sweet & Maxwell, 1998.
Whitehead, G., *Elements of Export Law*, Cambridge: Prentice Woodhead, 1980.

PART III

TRANSPORTATION IN INTERNATIONAL TRADE

6 Carriage of Goods by Sea

6.1 INTRODUCTION

This and Chapters 7, 8 and 9 on the carriage of goods by sea are concerned with the transit of the goods from the shipping port to the port of destination within the context of either a f.o.b. or c.i.f. contract. The various ways in which the party responsible for shipping the goods (the 'shipper') may perform his obligations will be discussed in this chapter. In Chapter 7 the problems relating to rights of suit between the shipper and carrier will be examined both before and after the Carriage of Goods by Sea Act (COGSA) 1992 which has simplified matters considerably. In Chapter 8 the obligations undertaken by the various parties will be considered, first at common law and then under the Carriage of Goods by Sea Act (COGSA) 1971 and the Hague-Visby Rules. In the final chapter concerning the carriage of goods by sea, Chapter 9, questions concerning freight, the remuneration which is paid to the carrier, will be examined.

6.2 THE LEGAL AND THE ACTUAL CARRIER

At this point it is important to note that there may be a distinction between the legal carrier and the actual carrier. The legal carrier is the person who has contracted with the shipper to transport the goods on their voyage. The legal carrier is the party who is privy to the contract of carriage entered into by the shipper. The actual carrier is the person who takes possession of the goods and carries them on their voyage.

Often the legal carrier and the actual carrier are the same person. There are, however, occasions when the legal carrier and actual carrier are different persons, particularly when the vessel is subject to a charterparty. In the latter situation there will be no privity of contract between the shipper and the actual carrier. Should the shipper wish to proceed against the actual carrier for any loss or damage to the goods while in the possession of the actual carrier the shipper may be limited to a claim in tort but it may, in appropriate cases, be possible for a contract to be implied between the shipper and the actual carrier. This will be examined in further detail in Chapter 7.

6.3   HOW THE CONTRACT OF CARRIAGE MAY BE PERFORMED

The seller can perform his obligation to ship the goods in a number of ways. He might charter (hire) the vessel under a charterparty. Alternatively, he may merely book shipping space without chartering the entire vessel. A further alternative would be for the seller to employ the services of a freight forwarder or a combined transport operator, especially when the goods are to be carried in containers.

6.3.1   Carriage on a General Ship

Figure 6.1

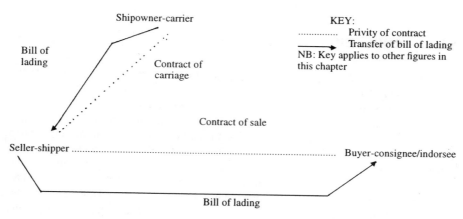

The shipper, usually the seller, may choose to send the goods on a general ship. His goods will be shipped with consignments from other shippers on the same vessel. The seller-shipper would not enter into a charterparty with the shipowner. Once the goods have been shipped, the shipowner, who is both the legal and the actual carrier of the goods, would issue the seller-shipper with a shipped bill of lading covering his goods only. Such a bill of lading in the hands of the seller-shipper performs three functions, namely, it is a receipt for the goods; it is a document of title to the goods; and it evidences the contract of carriage between the shipowner and the seller-shipper. The bill is not the contract so that extrinsic evidence is admissible as to the terms of the contract; see *The Ardennes* [1951] 1 KB 55.

The seller-shipper must then tender the bill of lading and the other documents required by the contract of sale either to the buyer or, if a documentary credit is being used to finance the sale, to the Advising Bank (AB) or the Issuing Bank (IB).

If the buyer or the bank in the documentary credit transaction is actually named on the face of the bill of lading, they are called the 'consignee'. This is rare, since it restricts the seller-shipper's options in the event of some default or damage to the goods in transit. The shipper of the goods will be the 'consignor'.

If the bill of lading is made out to the order of the seller-shipper, the latter will on tendering the documents indorse the bill to the buyer or the bank as is appropriate. The transferee of the bill is then known as the 'indorsee'. Where the indorsee has taken the bill of lading in good faith then he will, by virtue of the COGSA 1992, have transferred to and vested in him all rights of suit under the contract of carriage, contained in or evidenced by the bill of lading, as if he had been a party to that contract. This is a matter which is examined in more detail in Chapter 7.

6.3.2   The Chartered Ship: Time and Voyage Charterparties

Figure 6.2

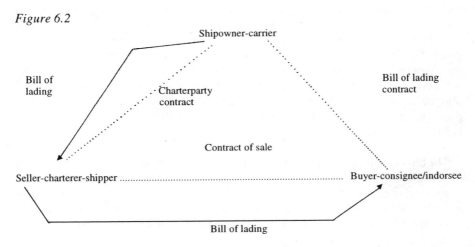

A time charter is when the ship is hired by a charterer, for a definite period of time. A voyage charter is when the ship is hired for a particular voyage or a series of voyages. In both the ship's crew are the servants of the shipowner so that the shipowner is the actual carrier of the goods. In *Omoa Coal v Huntley* (1877) 2 CPD 464 a time or voyage charter was explained as:

> ... one in which the charterers might direct where the vessel is to go and with what she is to be laden, but the shipowner remains in all respects accountable for the manner in which she may be navigated.

Donaldson J described a time charter in *The Berge Tasta* [1975] 1 Lloyd's Rep 422 as a charterparty:

> ... in which the shipowner undertakes to make the vessel available to the charterer within a specified area over a specified period. The shipowner's remuneration is at a fixed rate for a unit of time regardless of how the vessel is used by the charterer.

The shipowner meets the cost of maintaining the vessel and paying the crew's wages but the cost of fuel and port charges fall on the charterer.

Consequently, at the end of the period of hire, the shipowner is entitled to redelivery of the ship in like condition as on hire. Any fuel still on board will normally be purchased by the shipowner from the charterer. As to the time for re-delivery of the vessel, see *Torvald Klaveness A/S* v *Arni Maritime Corporation, The Gregos, The Times*, 28 October 1994.

Similarly, in the voyage charter, the shipowner remains responsible for the navigation and the management of the vessel. Unlike the time charter, the ship is on hire to travel the customary or agreed routes of her specified voyage(s). Again, the shipowner is entitled to delivery of the ship at the end of the voyage, or series of voyages, in like condition to that when the ship went on hire.

In both types of charter, if the shipper-seller-charterer is transporting his own goods, he may request the shipowner to issue a bill of lading for the cargo. When in the charterer's hands, the bill of lading is a receipt for the goods, a document of title, but it does not have any contractual function. The charterparty governs the rights and obligations of the charterer and shipowner in respect of the carriage of the goods. The position was summarised by the then Master of the Rolls in *Temperley* v *Smythe* [1905] 2 KB 791:

> The broad distinction between the position of a charterer who ships and takes a bill of lading and an ordinary holder of a bill is, I think, that in the former case there is the underlying contract of the charterparty which remains till it is cancelled, and taking a bill of lading does not cancel it in whole or in part unless it can be inferred from the inconsistency of the terms of the two documents that it was intended to do so.

Similarly, in *Kruger* v *Moel Tryvan Ship Co.* [1907] AC 272 Lord Halsbury said:

> The bill of lading cannot control what has been agreed upon before between the shipowner and the merchant, and what has been expressed in a written instrument which is the final and concluded contract between the parties.

When the bill is transferred to the consignee/indorsee, at the time when the seller performs the c.i.f. or f.o.b. contract of sale, the bill of lading may become the contract of carriage between the shipowner (the legal and actual carrier) and the consignee/indorsee; see *Leduc* v *Ward* (1888) 20 QBD 475. In *Temperley* v *Smythe* (above) the Master of the Rolls continued:

> On the other hand, in the case where the holder of the bill of lading is not the charterer, there is no presumption that he contracts on any terms other than those in the bill of lading.

Often when the shipowner contracts with the shipper by means of a charterparty, the bill of lading issued may purport to incorporate the terms or part of the terms of the charterparty. Only when certain conditions are satisfied will those terms actually form part of the contract between the shipowner and the consignee/indorsee of the bill (see below).

The principle in *Monarch* v *Karlshamms Olje Fabrike* [1949] AC 196 that the holder of the bill of lading can sue on the contract contained therein for breaches committed by the shipowner prior to the transfer of the bill applies:

> The taking of a bill of lading by the charterer of a ship confers no immediate rights on him under the bill of lading. But it confers an inchoate right which, by indorsing to a third party, makes the bill of lading into an effective contractual document from the start of the voyage and not just from transfer.

It will be seen in Chapter 8 that the Hague-Visby Rules do not apply to charterparties. Hence whilst the bill of lading remains in the shipper-charterer's hands and does not have contractual force, the Hague-Visby Rules are precluded unless expressly incorporated. Once the bill of lading reaches the hands of the consignee/indorsee, the Hague-Visby Rules may apply to the contract of carriage in the bill of lading, provided that the other conditions for application pertain.

Care must be taken to ensure which party to the contract of sale is, in fact, the charterer of the ship. In f.o.b. contracts it is common for the buyer to charter the ship. In such a case, when the seller ships the goods, he receives a bill of lading. The bill will be a receipt for the goods, a document of title to them, but will normally have no contractual function.

When the bill is indorsed and delivered to the buyer to enable him to take possession of the goods from the carrier at the port of destination, it is still the charterparty which is the contract of carriage governing the rights and obligations of the buyer-charterer and the shipowner (the carrier). The bill of lading does not supersede the charterparty merely by virtue of its indorsement and delivery.

Figure 6.3

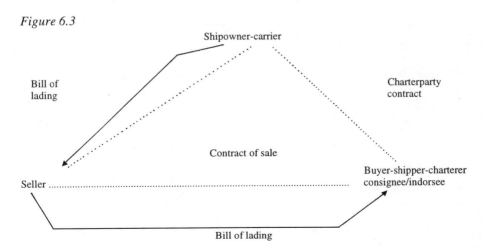

The charterer, instead of shipping his own goods on board the vessel, may choose to ship other people's goods. He may, for example, charter the vessel for a period of time and then use the vessel as a general cargo vessel. Bills of lading will be issued to those persons who ship goods on board the vessel. The question then arises as to who the shipper contracted with on the terms of the bill of lading. That is to say, who is the legal carrier *vis-à-vis* the shipper of the goods?

In such a situation the legal and the actual carrier of the goods will often be different persons. This is answered by considering which party issued the bill of lading as principal.

Figure 6.4

Bill of Lading (1)

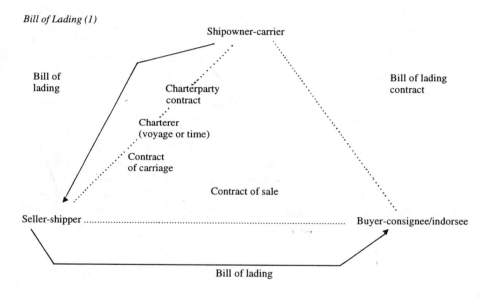

Figure 6.5

Bill of Lading (2)

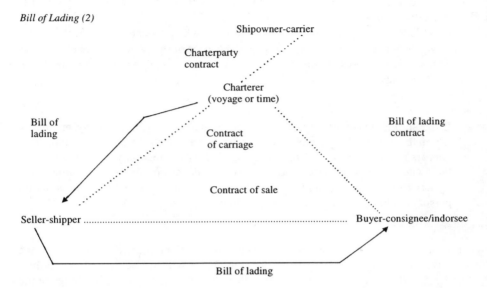

If the bill of lading is issued by or on behalf of the shipowner, the shipowner would be both the legal and the actual carrier; figure 6.4.

If the bill of lading is issued by or on behalf of the charterer, the legal carrier would be the charterer, and in the case of a time or voyage charter the actual carrier would be the shipowner, since the crew remain his servants; figure 6.5.

The following guidelines may assist in determining who is the legal carrier in this situation.

(a)   Where the master signs the bill of lading he will usually be treated as signing under his usual authority as agent of the shipowner or charterer by demise; see *Sanderman* v *Scurr* (1866) LR 2 QB 86. In *The Venezuela* [1980] 1 Lloyd's Rep 393 the master was found on the facts to have contracted on behalf of the charterer, as there was nothing in the bill of lading to indicate that the charterer was not the shipowner.

(b)   Even though the charterparty contains a clause stating that the master is to sign as agent of the charterer, this limitation on the master's usual authority will not affect the shipper or consignee/indorsee unless they have actual notice of the limitation. Constructive notice is not sufficient; see *Manchester Trust* v *Furness* [1895] 2 QB 539.

(c)   Where the bill of lading is signed by the charterer, as authorised agent of the master, since the master is treated as acting as agent of the shipowner or charterer by demise, the legal carrier will be the shipowner or charterer by demise; see *Tillmanns & Co.* v *SS Knutsford* [1908] 1 KB 185.

(d)   Where the bill of lading is signed by the charterer in his own name he will be the legal carrier. However, if in fact the charterer had authority to contract on behalf of the shipowner, it may be that the holder of the bill of lading can sue the shipowner on the bill of lading as undisclosed principal.

(e)   Bills of lading commonly contain a clause which attempts to prevent the time or voyage charterer from becoming the legal carrier of the goods. These clauses are called 'demise' clauses or 'identity of carrier' clauses. Such a clause may be in the following terms:

If the ship is not owned by, or chartered by demise to, the company or line by whom the bill of lading is issued (as may be the case notwithstanding anything that appears to the contrary) this bill of lading shall take effect only as a contract with the owner or demise charterer as the case may be, as principal, made through the agency of the said company or line who act as agents only and shall be under no personal liability whatsoever in respect thereof.

The validity of these clauses should not be in doubt. Even if the contract of carriage is governed by the Hague-Visby Rules, the clause will not be treated as a nullity under Art. III, r. 8 as the Hague-Visby Rules are concerned with the liabilities of the carrier and not the choice of carrier.

The Hague-Visby Rules may govern the relationship between the shipper-seller and the legal carrier, as the bill of lading is evidence of the contract of carriage between the two parties, not the charterparty. The Rules can similarly apply between the buyer as consignee/indorsee of the bill and the legal carrier.

The effect of the legal carrier being a different party from the actual carrier is reflected in the possibility of a claim in tort. In *Tai Hing Cotton Mill* v *Kamsing Knitting Factory* [1979] AC 91 the Privy Council advised that no claim in tort is available where the parties to an action have entered into a contract covering the very situation in dispute and which denies the plaintiff recovery. This principle has more recently been upheld in *Greater Nottingham Co-operative Society* v *Cementation Piling and Foundations Ltd* [1989] QB 71 and *The Maira* [1989] 3 WLR 185. It follows that where the legal and actual carrier are the same person, no claim in tort is available, as the parties' rights will be governed by the contract of carriage.

When the legal carrier and actual carrier are different persons, a claim in tort may be available to the buyer (consignee/indorsee of the bill of lading) as against the shipowner. In such an action it is unclear whether the buyer could rely on the terms in the bill of lading, and in particular on the Hague-Visby Rules and exclusion clauses (see 8.7).

Also, it may be possible for the buyer to establish a contractual relationship with the actual carrier of the goods by virtue of the buyer's taking delivery of the goods on arrival of the ship at the port of destination (see 8.8).

6.3.3 The Charter by Demise

A charter by demise is to be contrasted with the voyage or time charter. In the charter by demise, the charterer takes over the management of the ship. The crew are, therefore, his servants, even if they are members of the shipowner's workforce. The test to be applied in determining whether the charter is by demise or a voyage or time charter is:

Who on construction of the charterparty is intended to have possession of and work the vessel: i.e., which party's servants? (See *Trinity House* v *Clark* (1815) 4 M & S 288.)

Figure 6.6

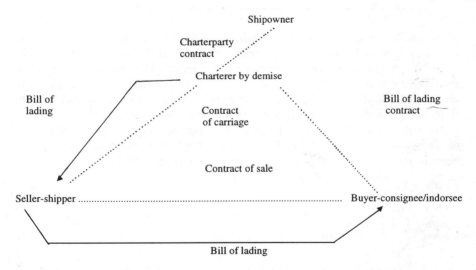

The charterer is, therefore, both the legal and the actual carrier of the goods. The bill of lading issued by the charterer will in the hands of the shipper be a receipt for the goods, a document of title to them and will merely evidence the contract of carriage. The presumption on transfer of the bill to the buyer is that the bill of lading is then the contract of carriage between the buyer and the charterer.

6.4   SELLER USING SERVICES OF FREIGHT FORWARDER

Figure 6.7

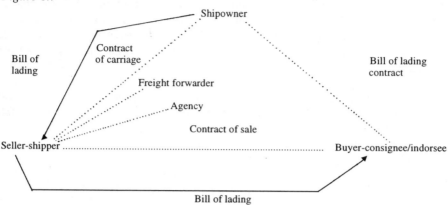

A freight forwarder may act in a number of different capacities. In the situation shown in figure 6.7, the freight forwarder acts as the seller's agent for the shipping of the consignment of goods destined for the buyer. The bill of lading would, therefore, be issued by the shipowner to the seller as principal and shipper of the goods. The bill of lading, therefore, evidences the contract of carriage between the shipper-seller and the shipowner when it is in the former's hands.

The seller then indorses and delivers the bill of lading to the buyer in performance of the contract of sale. The bill of lading should then become the contract of carriage between the buyer and the shipowner by virtue of COGSA 1992.

Figure 6.8

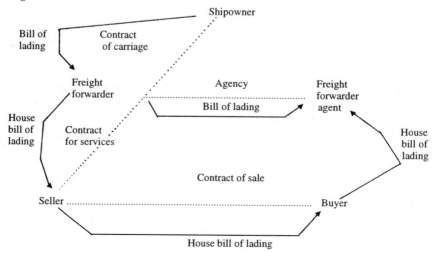

In the second situation, the freight forwarder acts as the seller's agent in the preparation of the goods for shipment, the finding of a vessel, and the fixing of the rates of freight. However, when he ships, he does so as principal. The bill of lading is issued by the shipowner to the freight forwarder who is, therefore, the legal shipper. The bill of lading is a receipt for the goods, a document of title and evidences the contract of carriage between the shipowner and the freight forwarder.

The freight forwarder then transfers the bill of lading to his own agent at the port of destination to enable the agent to take possession of the goods from the ship, and then hold the goods to his principal's order. The freight forwarder issues a 'house bill of lading' to the seller. This is not a true bill of lading, and is not a document of title at common law, as it is not issued by a sea-carrier of goods.

The seller may then attempt to perform his contract of sale by tendering the house bill of lading to the buyer. The seller would have to stipulate in his contract of sale for a house bill to be good tender, otherwise the buyer would be entitled to reject this house bill of lading.

The bill does not entitle the buyer to demand the goods from the ship. Nor does it entitle him to demand them from the freight forwarder's agent who will have obtained the goods from the ship by tendering the true bill of lading. The house bill of lading does not in itself create privity of contract between the buyer as holder and the freight forwarder or his agent, although there is scope for an implied contract once the buyer tenders the document intending to receive the goods in exchange.

Where the goods are damaged during transit, the buyer has no contractual claim against the shipowner. There is no scope for the implication of a contract on the basis of the buyer's taking delivery of the goods from the ship, as this is done by the freight forwarder as principal. As has already been seen, there would be no contractual claim against the freight forwarder.

The buyer may, however, have a claim in tort against the shipowner provided that property in the goods had passed to the buyer before the damage occurred; see *The Aliakmon* [1983] 1 Lloyd's Rep 203. If not, it seems that the buyer may ask the seller to sue the shipowner on his behalf, though in the absence of any contractual provision, the seller would not be bound to accede to the buyer's request; see *The Sanix Ace* [1985] 1 Lloyd's Rep 246. The only other alternative for the buyer is to argue that the sale was not a f.o.b. or c.i.f. contract but ex ship, requiring the seller actually to deliver goods which conform to the contract.

The difficulty in assessing the true role of the freight forwarder is illustrated by *Harlom & Jones* v *P J Walker Shipping* [1986] 2 Lloyd's Rep 141. Although the freight forwarder had agreed to act as the seller's agent, he in fact contracted with the shipowner for the carriage of the goods as principal. No bill of lading was, therefore, issued to the seller. The freight forwarder succeeded in obtaining preferential rates of freight which he refused to extend to the seller's benefit, claiming reimbursement at the normal rate. The seller claimed that he was entitled to the preferential rate. The freight forwarder succeeded before Bingham J on the issue that he had, in fact, contracted with the shipowner as principal. However, the seller succeeded in arguing that there was an implied term in the contract of agency with the freight forwarder that the latter would extend to the seller any preferential rights he might acquire when acting as freight forwarder in deals concerning the seller. Judgment was, therefore, entered for the seller.

The freight forwarder may, however, be the agent of the shipowner (the actual carrier), or the shipowner himself. Here the bill of lading issued by the freight forwarder would be a true bill of lading.

Finally one must consider the position of freight forwarder who is a combined transport operator (CTO). A CTO takes responsibility as principal for the complete transit of the goods from the seller's warehouse to the buyer's warehouse. Often the CTO will not be a sea-carrier. Indeed he will rarely be an actual carrier by any mode. He will sub-contract all the various stages to others. Although the buyer or seller need only concern themselves with the CTO if damage to the goods should occur during transit, it remains important to establish when the loss or damage occurred. Different international conventions apply to different modes of transport. The extent of a CTO's liability will be governed by the relevant convention. Further the combined transport document (CTD) issued by the CTO might not be a bill of lading. It may be bad tender under a c.i.f. and f.o.b. contract and the COGSA 1992 may not apply. The International Chamber of Commerce drew up Rules in 1975 for a CTD. These, however, do little to solve the problems in c.i.f. and f.o.b. contracts.

6.5 INCORPORATION OF THE CHARTERPARTY INTO THE BILL OF LADING: 'CHARTERPARTY BILLS OF LADING'

Whether the charterer of the ship uses the vessel to carry his own goods or as a general ship, carrying consignments from other shippers, the bill of lading may incorporate some or all of the terms of the charterparty. When the bill of lading comes into the hands of a third party who is a stranger to the charterparty, the question of the propriety and effect of such incorporation is raised. The case law requires first that the fact of incorporation must be established. Then the consistency of the *prima facie* incorporated term(s) must be tested with the provisions of the bill of lading contract.

6.5.1 Incorporation

The first task is to construe the incorporation clause in the bill of lading. This involves looking at both the terms of the incorporation clause itself and at the clauses to the charterparty. Donaldson MR in *Skips Nordheim v Syrian Petroleum Co.* [1984] 1 QB 599 stated:

> The starting point had always to be the provisions of the bill of lading contract producing initial incorporation. What had to be sought was incorporation, not notice of the existence of the terms of another contract which is not incorporated.

Incorporation clauses have received restrictive interpretation from the courts. The following clauses have received judicial consideration:

(a) *'Freight and all other conditions as per charterparty'* This clause has been held to incorporate into the bill of lading all the conditions of the charterparty which are to be performed by the consignee of the goods. Freight in the case itself was an obligation on the consignee or indorsee of the bill of lading. The following words, 'all other conditions', were to be construed *eiusdem generis* and, therefore, were to be restricted to conditions to be performed by the consignee or indorsee.

Therefore, in *Russell* v *Niemann* (1864) 34 LJCP 10 it was held that the words 'paying freight and other conditions as per charterparty' did not introduce into the bill of lading an exception of perils which was in the charterparty but not expressly in the bill of lading; see also Lord Robson in *Thomas* v *Portsea SS Co.* [1912] AC 1.

Such an incorporation clause would not, therefore, cover a clause in the charterparty which states that the captain, although paid by the shipowner, is to be the agent of the charterer when signing the bills of lading; see *Manchester Trust* v *Furness* [1895] 2 QB 539.

In *Gullischen* v *Stewart* (1882) 13 QBD 317 such a clause was held to incorporate into the bill of lading contract provisions for demurrage at the port of discharge, as this was an obligation in the charterparty on the consignee of the goods.

In *Hogarth Shipping Co.* v *Blythe* [1917] 2 KB 534 the bill of lading contained this form of incorporation clause. A steamer was chartered to carry a cargo of sugar to one of several ports of discharge and there to discharge it. A clause in the charterparty itself provided that the captain was to sign bills of lading which were deemed to be conclusive proof of cargo shipped. The captain signed a bill of lading for a specified number of bags, but stating that 'weight, measure, quality, contents, and value unknown'. At the port of discharge, there was a shortage in the number of bags of sugar. The holder of the bill of lading sued the shipowner for short delivery. He relied upon the conclusive evidence clause in the charterparty arguing that it had been included into the bill of lading by the incorporation clause. The court followed the restrictive rule of interpretation in *Russell* v *Niemann*. The conclusive evidence clause did not fall within the words 'freight and other conditions'. The conditions impliedly mentioned were limited to such as were to be performed by the consignee.

The actual decision of the case, however, went further. An incorporation clause in the bill of lading included 'exceptions as per charterparty'. The consignee argued that the conclusive evidence clause was included through this phrase. The shipowner argued that the conclusive evidence clause was not an exception and, therefore, still fell outside the scope of the incorporation clause in the bill of lading. The court found in the shipowner's favour. The conclusive evidence clause was not an exception to or qualification of the shipowner's liability. It was rather an extension of it, since he rendered himself liable for goods stated to be carried whether actually shipped or not. Since the conclusive evidence clause was not incorporated, the shipowner was not precluded from showing that not all the bags said to have been loaded were actually delivered to the ship.

(b)   'All other terms and conditions and exceptions as per charterparty, including negligence clauses'   Thomas v Portsea SS Co. [1912] AC 1.

(c)   'All other terms and exceptions contained in the charterparty are herewith incorporated'   Van Liewen v Hollis [1920] AC 239 and Hogarth Shipping Co. v Blythe [1917] 2 KB 534.

(d)   'All other terms, conditions, clauses and exceptions contained in the said charterparty, apply to the bill of lading and are deemed to be incorporated herein'   Aktieselskabet Ocean v Harding [1928] 2 KB 371.

All these clauses are wide and of similar effect. However, the courts have interpreted them narrowly.

In *Thomas v Portsea SS Co.* it was held that general words of incorporation will only include those terms of the charterparty which are directly germane to the shipment, carriage and delivery of the cargo and payment of freight. This was followed by the Court of Appeal in *The Annefield* [1971] P 168.

In *Skips Nordheim* the bill of lading contract had an incorporation clause 'all conditions and exceptions of which charterparty, including the negligence clause, are deemed to be incorporated into the bill of lading'. The consignee of the goods tried to argue that this was sufficient to include in the bill of lading the arbitration clause in the charterparty since the word 'condition' was wide enough to incorporate all provisions of the charterparty. The Court of Appeal held that 'all conditions' referred only to all conditions of the charterparty concerned with the actual performance of the obligations in the bill of lading, namely, the delivery of the goods. The arbitration clause was, therefore, irrelevant to that obligation.

In *The Merak* [1965] P 223 it was held that if there was a general incorporating clause in the bill of lading, then it was proper to look at the terms of the charterparty itself to ascertain exactly which clauses were included; see also *The Emmanuel Coloctronis* [1982] 1 All ER 823. In *The Merak* the charterparty provided for arbitration. The claimant's timber was shipped under a bill of lading which stated that the voyage was 'as per charterparty dated the 21st April' and contained a clause incorporating 'all the terms, conditions, clauses and exceptions . . . contained in the said charterparty'. In the course of the voyage, the cargo was damaged and just within 12 months of discharge of the goods the claimants, as indorsees of the bill of lading, issued a claim form claiming damages. The shipowner, relying on the arbitration clause alleged to be incorporated in the bill of lading and, therefore, on s. 4, Arbitration Act 1950, moved for a stay of proceedings. In opposition to the application one of the grounds on which the claimants relied was that there was an ineffective incorporation of the arbitration clause into the bill of lading. The Court of Appeal held that the arbitration clause was incorporated into the bill of lading contract and, therefore, that a stay should be granted. The court thought that the words of the incorporation clause in the bill of lading were adequate because, although there was no specific incorporation in the bill of lading, clause 32 of the charterparty itself expressly applied to disputes arising out of the bill of lading. The arbitration clause stated that 'any dispute arising out of this charterparty or any bill of lading issued hereunder, shall be referred to arbitration'.

The Court of Appeal distinguished the case from the decision of the House of Lords in *Thomas* v *Portsea*. In that case, there was a similarly wide incorporation clause in the bill of lading, and as in *The Merak* the clause made no specific mention of the arbitration. However, the arbitration clause in the charterparty stated: 'any dispute or claim arising out of any of the conditions of this charter shall . . . be settled by arbitration'. Since the arbitration clause only referred to disputes under the charter, the general words of incorporation in the bill of lading together with the words of the arbitration clause in the charterparty were insufficient to subject disputes arising out of the bill of lading contract to arbitration. Russell LJ in *The Merak* said:

> I think the true view of *Thomas* v *Portsea* is that it shows that clauses which are directly germane to shipment, carriage and delivery may be incorporated by general words though the fact that they are found in the charterparty, may involve a degree of verbal manipulation to fit exactly a bill of lading, but that where there is a clause whose subject matter is not thus directly germane such as an arbitration clause, it is not permissible to construe general words of incorporation as extending to a clause, which does not in terms relate to a bill of lading.

It is worth commenting that *The Merak* and *Thomas* v *Portsea* were cases dealing with arbitration clauses which by definition at least temporarily exclude the jurisdiction of the courts. Courts are jealous of their jurisdiction. The restrictive interpretation of such clauses and the rule that a clause must be germane to shipping, carriage and delivery to be included must be read in that light. A more liberal interpretation at least as to what is so germane may be given to clauses which do not affect the court's jurisdiction to hear the case.

In *The Annefield* [1971] P 168 the Court of Appeal followed Russell LJ's reasoning in *The Merak*, but to different effect on the facts. The charterparty included an arbitration clause which provided that 'all disputes arising out of this contract should be referred to arbitration'. The incorporation clause in the bill of lading issued under it provided that 'all the terms, conditions, and exceptions of the charterparty including the negligence clause are incorporated herewith'. The goods were damaged during the course of transit. The cargo owners failed to institute arbitration proceedings in time. They issued a writ five years after the discharge of the goods. The shipowner applied for a stay of proceedings. The Court of Appeal held, following *The Merak*, that since there was no specific incorporation in the bill of lading, there would only be effective incorporation of the arbitration clause into the bill of lading if the clause in the charterparty itself made provision for it to do so. Since the words 'and dispute under this contract' in the arbitration clause referred to the charterparty contract, there was no such express incorporation. Lord Denning said:

> . . . if the clause is one which is not directly germane to shipping etc., it should not be incorporated into the bill of lading contract unless it is done explicitly in clear words either in the bill of lading or in the charterparty.

The arbitration clause was, therefore, not incorporated and the cargo-owner was not barred from continuing his action.

In *Federal Bulk Carriers Inc* v *C Itoh & Co. Ltd, The Federal Bulker* [1989] 1 Lloyd's Rep 103 the Court of Appeal considered a slight variant on the clauses discussed above:

> All terms and conditions and exceptions as per charterparty dated ... and any addenda thereto to be considered as fully incorporated herein as if fully written.

The clause was held insufficient to incorporate a charterparty arbitration clause into bills of lading properly issued pursuant to it. The Court of Appeal again recognised the strict rules of interpretation with regard to incorporation by reference of arbitration clauses. The rationale expressed was commercial certainty: bills of lading might come into possession of a foreign party who had no knowledge of the terms of the charterparty. Parties should spell out the arbitration provision in the bills of lading. The additional words 'as if fully written' in the instant case had no effect. Following *Thomas* v *Portsea* the court held that the effect of general words of incorporation was limited to clauses which were germane to the bill of lading, i.e. those to be dealt with by both the shipowner and consignee relating to carriage, discharge and delivery of cargo.

6.5.2 Consistency

If the terms have been incorporated into the bill of lading contract, it must still be consistent with the express terms of the bill of lading. In *Gardner* v *Trechmann* (1885) 15 QBD 154 Brett MR said:

> ... the general reference to the charterparty ... brings in only those clauses of the charterparty which are applicable to the contract contained in the bill of lading, and those clauses of the charterparty cannot be brought in which would alter the express stipulations in the bill of lading.

Furthermore the intentions of the parties must be considered even if there is no inconsistency with the express provisions of the bill of lading.

The principle was discussed by the House of Lords in *Miramar Maritime Corpn* v *Holborn Oil Trading* [1984] 1 AC 676. There the bill of lading purported to incorporate all the terms of the charterparty except for payment and rate of freight, but including a clause which made the charterers liable for demurrage. The shipowners claimed that the demurrage clause as incorporated into the bill of lading contract had the effect of rendering the consignees of the cargo, as holders of the bill of lading, directly liable for the demurrage costs.

The House of Lords held that, on the true construction of the bill of lading, it was the intention of the parties to the bill of lading contract that the charterers alone should be liable for demurrage. Lord Diplock said:

So if the owners are right in their contention [that the bill of lading holder is liable for demurrage], every consignee to whom a bill of lading covering any part of the cargo is negotiated, is not only accepting personal liability to pay to the shipowner freight, as stated in the bill of lading, but is also accepting blindfold a potential liability to pay an unknown and wholly unpredictable sum for demurrage which may, unknown to him, already have accrued even though that sum may actually exceed the delivered value of the goods to which the bill of lading gives him title ... I venture to assert that no business man who had not taken leave of his senses would intentionally enter into a contract which exposes him to a potential liability of this kind ... and this in itself, I find to be an overwhelming reason for not indulging in verbal manipulation of the actual contractual words used in the charterparty so as to give them the effect when they are treated as incorporated into the bill of lading.

It appears, therefore, that each case must be considered on its facts. There is no general rule of construction either way requiring the consignee/indorsee to be read in the place of the charterer when terms in the charterparty which are germane to the carriage of the goods are incorporated into the bill of lading contract.

What is germane to the carriage of goods was discussed in the earlier House of Lords case, *Kish* v *Taylor* [1912] AC 604. Here a charterparty fixed the rate of freight and stated that the shipowner had a lien for dead freight. The bill of lading issued under the charterparty referred to payment of freight at a specified rate, and stated that 'all other conditions as per charterparty'. The charterers failed to load a full and complete cargo. On arrival at the port of destination, the shipowner claimed a lien on the goods for dead freight, as set out in the charterparty. The House of Lords held that dead freight is merely damages for breach of contract by the charterers in failing to load a full cargo. It is not freight as such and, therefore, the clause in the charterparty claiming a lien for dead freight was consistent with the bill of lading and could be incorporated.

A possible problem resulting from the application of the Hague-Visby Rules to bills of lading contracts but not to charterparties was discussed in *The Merak* (6.5.1). The plaintiffs argued that even though there may be *prima facie* incorporation of the arbitration clause into the bill of lading, since the Hague-Visby Rules applied after incorporation, the arbitration clause was bad since it was inconsistent with Art. III(6) which provides for the bringing of 'suit' against the carriers. The Court of Appeal held that the Hague-Visby Rules applied internationally. Since Art. III(6) did not specify any particular mode of procedure for the settlement of disputes, it must be interpreted to cover different modes of procedure in different countries. 'Suit', therefore, could not in this context be limited to an action in the English courts.

The answer might have been different if the arbitration clause was, in fact, inconsistent with the Rules by, say, barring proceedings under it after three months, sooner than the period allowed in Art. III(6). Davies LJ in *The Merak* refused to comment on the point as in that case the time period in the arbitration clause was the same as the Rules, namely, one year. It is probable that such a clause would not be incorporated as it would be inconsistent with Art. III(6) and would in any event be disapplied.

Similarly, any exception in the charterparty which if incorporated into a bill of lading would reduce the carrier's liability below that set out in the Rules would be in conflict with Art. III(8) and probably would not be incorporated. Incorporation of the terms of the charterparty into the bill of lading contract is disliked by the courts for a practical reason. If the bill of lading which purports to incorporate some or all of the terms of the charterparty under which it was issued, is delivered without a copy of the terms so incorporated, the consignee/indorsee would be unable to determine his precise legal relationship with the carrier. However, in *Finska Cellulosaforenigen* v *Westfield Paper Co.* [1940] 4 All ER 473 a c.i.f. seller tendered a bill of lading which contained the words 'all conditions and exceptions as per charterparty'. It was held that the seller was not obliged to tender the charterparty 'in the circumstances of the case', since there had been a long standing course of dealing between the parties on the terms of the standard form of charterparty, which was known to the buyer. In *SIAT di dal Ferro* v *Tradax Overseas SA* [1980] 1 Lloyd's Rep 53 a tender of bills of lading showing the destination to be 'as per charterparty' was held to be bad as it did not enable the buyer to tell from the face of the documents whether they contained or evidenced a contract of carriage to the c.i.f. destination.

The principle seems to be that the charterparty should be tendered where this is necessary to enable the buyer to tell whether the documents are in accordance with the requirements of the contract. Where this is not necessary, the charterparty need not be tendered even though it is referred to in the bill of lading.

6.6 INCONSISTENCIES BETWEEN THE BILL OF LADING AND THE CHARTERPARTY

In time and voyage charterparties, the master of the ship normally signs the bills of lading when issued to the charterers as the agent of the shipowner. A problem which may arise is the resolution of inconsistencies between the charterparty and the bill of lading. Such inconsistencies might occur as a result of the time or voyage charterer tendering a bill of lading for signature, which imposes greater liabilities on the shipowner than the charterparty itself. The problem is resolved by considering which of the charterparty or bill of lading has contractual force between the relevant parties.

In *Kruger* v *Moel Tryvan Ship Co.* (6.3.2) the master of the ship signed a bill of lading presented by the charterer which did not have the exclusion of negligence clause as set out in the charterparty. The negligence of the master during transit led to the loss of the cargo. The indorsees of the bill of lading, the buyer, recovered the value of the cargo from the shipowner, the legal carrier. The House of Lords held that the defendant charterers were entitled by their charterparty to tender a bill of lading if they thought it proper to do so, but that such bill of lading should expressly incorporate the terms of the charterparty, including the negligence clause. Failure to do so was a breach of contract which caused the loss to the shipowner in their liability to the buyer.

This is, therefore, authority for the implication of a term into the contract of carriage between the shipowner and the charterer that if the master is to sign a bill of lading at the charterer's request, the bill should not be in the form of a contract which would increase the shipowner's liability above that contained in the charterparty. Therefore, when the indorsee sued the shipowner, the legal carrier on the contract contained in and on the terms of the bill of lading, the shipowner could claim an indemnity from the charterer in so far as the latter was in breach of the contract in the charterparty.

Kruger was distinguished in *The C Joyce* [1986] 2 All ER 177. The shipowner let the vessel to the charterer who then used it to ship a cargo of milk powder to Southampton. On discharge the holder of the bill of lading claimed damages for damage to the cargo and short delivery. The shipowner settled the claim and then sought an indemnity from the charterer. Under the charterparty the shipowner was relieved from liability for loss or damage unless there was proof of a personal lack of due diligence by the shipowner. The charterparty also expressly agreed that any bill of lading issued under the charterparty should be subject to the Hague Rules, which do not permit exclusion of liability for negligence. This meant that when the shipowner was sued by the holder of the bill of lading on the contract contained in the bill, the shipowner was under a greater liability than that set out in the charterparty. The shipowner argued that the Kruger right to an indemnity should be implied into the charterparty. Bingham J distinguished *Kruger*. In that case, the charterers were in breach of the charterparty by tendering a bill of lading which conflicted with the terms of the charterparty. Here the charterers were obliged to tender a bill of lading which imposed the liability of the Hague-Visby Rules on the shipowner. There was, therefore, no breach of the charterparty. No contract of indemnity could be implied, and there was no express collateral contract by which the claim could succeed.

7 Rights of Carrier and Cargo Interests

7.1 INTRODUCTION

The problem that often arises in the context of international sales is that the buyer of goods is not the shipper of the goods and is therefore not privy to the contract of carriage with the carrier. Property in those goods may have passed to the buyer as may also risk of loss or damage to the goods. Furthermore, the buyer may have had constructive possession of the goods at the time of the loss if he had received a bill of lading in respect of those goods prior to that loss, as the bill of lading is a document of title at common law. Nevertheless the buyer would be unable to sue the carrier for breach of the contract of carriage in respect of the loss or damage to his goods. The Bills of Lading Act 1855 was passed to remedy this problem arising from the doctrine of privity of contract. The Bills of Lading Act 1855 gave rise, however, to its own particular problems and consequently the Carriage of Goods by Sea Act 1992 was enacted to simplify this area of the law.

7.2 BILLS OF LADING ACT 1855

At common law the transfer of a bill of lading did not operate as an assignment of the contract of carriage evidenced by the bill of lading. The Bills of Lading Act 1855 altered the position in favour of the consignee or indorsee of the bill of lading. Section 1 of the 1855 Act provided that:

> Every consignee of goods named in a bill of lading, and every indorsee of a bill of lading to whom the property in the goods therein mentioned shall pass, upon or by reason of such consignment or indorsement, shall have transferred to and vested in him all rights of suit, and be subject to the same liabilities in respect of such goods as if the contract contained in the bill of lading had been made with himself.

So long as s. 1 was satisfied, the consignee or indorsee of the bill of lading was able to sue the carrier who had issued the bill of lading as if that consignee or indorsee had been a party to a contract of carriage on terms contained in the bill of lading. For a subsequent holder of the bill of lading to be able to take the benefit of s. 1, three requirements had to have been satisfied: (1) the document concerned must have been a bill of lading; (2) the holder of the bill of lading must have been the consignee or indorsee of the bill of lading; and (3) property in the goods must have passed to the holder of the bill of lading upon or by reason of such consignment or indorsement. Where those three conditions were satisfied, there was an assignment of the contract contained in the bill of lading and the consignee or indorsee was then able to sue in respect of breaches of the contract of carriage contained in the bill of lading even when those breaches occurred before the bill of lading had been transferred; see *Monarch* v *Karlshamms* [1949] AC 196.

It should be noted that under the 1855 Act the contract upon which the consignee or indorsee was entitled to sue was that *contained* in the bill of lading. When the Bills of Lading Act was invoked the bill of lading no longer merely *evidenced* the contract of carriage, as in *The Ardennes* [1951] 1 KB 55, but expressed the terms of the contract of carriage upon which the consignee or indorsee could sue; see *Leduc* v *Ward* (1888) 20 QBD 475.

7.3   COMMON LAW BILL OF LADING

It was only the consignee or indorsee of a bill of lading, recognised as such by the common law, who was able to take advantage of s. 1 of the Bills of Lading Act 1855. This was because the Bills of Lading Act 1855 was passed to deal with a specific problem. By the custom of merchants a bill of lading was transferable by indorsement and the transfer could constitute a transfer of property in the goods represented by the bill of lading — the bill of lading was recognised as a document of title at common law; see *Lickbarrow* v *Mason* (1794) 5 TR 683. Nevertheless the indorsee, not being privy to the contract of carriage contained in or evidenced by the bill of lading, could not sue upon it. The 1855 Act was passed so as to allow contractual rights to pass with the property in the goods. No other document was recognised as a document of title by the common law so the 1855 Act did not encompass any other shipping document such as the seaway bill or the ship's delivery order.

Although it is clear that a bill of lading must be issued by a sea-going carrier, the question of whether a 'received for shipment' bill of lading fell within the ambit of the 1855 Act was open. In *The Marlborough Hill* [1921] 1 AC 444 the Privy Council accepted that 'received for shipment' bills of lading were documents of title and suggested that a received for shipment bill of lading might satisfy the 1855 Act. Nevertheless in *Diamond Alkali Export Corp* v *Bourgeois* [1921] 3 KB 443 McCardie J refused to accept that a 'received for shipment' bill of lading fell within the 1855 Act.

The question of whether 'through' bills of lading and combined transport bills of lading come within the terms of the 1855 Act has not been determined and opinion is divided. If such bills of lading were to fall within the ambit of the 1855 Act they would have to have been issued by a sea carrier. A house bill of lading issued by freight forwarders who pack the containers and ship the goods themselves without being the actual carriers would be outside the 1855 Act as being merely a receipt.

7.3.1 Consignee or Indorsee

The consignee of a bill of lading is the person named as consignee in the bill of lading and is the person to whom delivery of the goods is to be made. The consignment referred to in s. 1 is the consignment of the goods to the carrier; see *The Sevonia Team* [1983] 2 Lloyd's Rep 640. The indorsee is the person to whom the bill of lading has been indorsed and delivered by the consignee or by a prior indorsee.

7.3.2 Full property rights must have passed to the consignee or indorsee upon or by reason of the consignment or indorsement

It is this requirement which proved to be most unsatisfactory and led to calls for reform and the eventual introduction of COGSA 1992. Problems arose with the use of s. 1 of the 1855 Act when property either did not pass at all or passed independently of the transfer of the bill of lading. The following are some examples where s. 1 of the 1855 Act did not operate in favour of the consignee or indorsee of the bill of lading.

Section 1 of the 1855 Act did not operate in favour of an indorsee of the bill of lading who did not obtain full property in the goods but only the special property of a pledgee. In *Sewell* v *Burdick* (1883) 10 App Cas 74 the House of Lords held that an indorsee of the bill of lading who had merely taken the bill of lading as security for a loan was not within s. 1 of the 1855 Act and was not, therefore, liable on contract of carriage for unpaid freight. This means that where the pledgee wishes to realise his security and take up the goods, he cannot sue the carrier under the 1855 Act; see *The Future Express* [1992] 2 Lloyd's Rep 79.

Problems also arose under the 1855 Act when property did not pass at all although the buyer was on risk. In respect of one of the bills of lading in *The Aramis* [1989] 1 Lloyd's Rep 213 there was no delivery of the relevant goods and so no passing of property. Likewise in *The Aliakmon* [1986] AC 785 property did not pass because the seller had reserved the right of disposal. Furthermore if the consignee or indorsee is already the owner of the goods shipped under the bill of lading then he was not to be able to rely on s. 1 of the 1855 Act; see *The Kapetan Markos* [1986] 1 Lloyd's Rep 211. Property might pass after consignment or indorsement by reason of the operation of s. 16 of the Sale of Goods Act 1979 which prevents property from passing before the goods have been ascertained. Thus in respect of bulk cargoes property will not normally pass until discharge of goods from the vessel at the earliest. Property might also pass before or independently of, consignment or indorsement, as in *The Delfini* [1990] 1 Lloyd's Rep 252 where the relevant indorsements took place eleven days after the completion of delivery and did not play a part in the passing of property.

Prior to the Court of Appeal decision in *The Delfini* two interpretations of s. 1 of the 1855 Act had been put forward. The first was the narrow view according to which the phrase 'upon or by reason of' meant that property in the goods had to have passed at the same time as the consignment or indorsement; see *Scrutton on Charterparties* (20th edn, 1996). The second interpretation took a wider view, according to which it was sufficient for the purposes of s. 1 if property passed from the shipper to the indorsee under a contract in pursuance of which a bill of lading was to be indorsed to the indorsee; see *Carver's Carriage by Sea* (13th edn, 1982); *The San Nicholas* [1976] 1 Lloyd's Rep 8; *The Sevonia Team* [1983] 2 Lloyd's Rep 640. The Court of Appeal in *The Delfini* rejected the wide view but equally did not accept the narrow view. Instead the Court of Appeal preferred to interpret s. 1 as requiring the act of indorsement to play an essential causal role in the chain of events by which property is transferred. See also *The Elafi* [1982] 1 All ER 208. Purchas LJ gave as an example of a situation where there would be a sufficient connection between the indorsement of a bill of lading and the passing of property, the case of the unascertained bulk cargo which only became ascertained on discharge.

The decision in *The Delfini* does not, however, assist in cases where there has not been the sale of part of a bulk as in *The Delfini*, nor in cases where the buyer of a part of the bulk receives nothing at all, as happened to one of the plaintiffs in *The Aramis* [1987] 2 Lloyd's Rep 58. Problems are particularly acute where the goods are subject to a lengthy string of contracts but are only to be carried on a comparatively short voyage. Title to cargoes will often be transferred well ahead of the transfer of the bill of lading, the vessel reaching its destination long before the documents and discharge taking place against a letter of indemnity. The situation is made all that much worse where payment is to be made by documentary letter of credit, as the shipping documents will have to move through the various banks involved. The intention is that the shipping documents, including the bill of lading, will be passed on down the string until they reach the final buyer who will then be brought into a contractual relationship with the carrier. The Law Commission's view (see 7.5) was that 'unfortunately the law on this point no longer gives effect to reasonable commercial expectations' and that 'the decision in *The Delfini* seriously weakens the bill of lading as a commercially useful document'.

7.4 ALTERNATIVES TO THE BILLS OF LADING ACT 1855

Before turning to examine the provisions of the Carriage of Goods by Sea Act 1992, enacted to cure the defects in the Bills of Lading Act 1855, it is useful to consider the alternatives to a claim under s. 1 of the 1855 Act.

7.4.1   Agency

The first argument that may be open to the consignee or indorsee of the bill of lading is that the shipper contracted with the carrier as agent, with the consignee or indorsee as undisclosed principal. If this option is not open to the consignee or indorsee then consideration should be given to a claim in tort.

7.4.2   Tort

If a claim is made in tort the consignee or indorsee will have the burden of proving not only negligence but also that he had either legal ownership of, or a possessory title to, the goods in question at the time when the loss or damage occurred; see *The Aliakmon* [1986] AC 785. In the case of a purchaser of a bulk cargo this will often prove impossible as any loss or damage is likely to have occurred when the goods were still unascertained. In other cases it will usually be very difficult to identify the exact point in time when the goods were damaged or even when title passed to the consignee or indorsee; see *The Nea Tyhi* [1982] 1 Lloyd's Rep 606. Difficulties will also face the carrier who may wish to rely on contractual limitations or exceptions such as those contained in the Hague-Visby Rules; see *The Aliakmon* at pp. 819, 820; *The Captain Gregos* [1990] 1 Lloyd's Rep 310 at p. 318.

If the buyer did not have the necessary title at the time of the loss or damage he might ask the seller to sue on his behalf. In *The Sanix Ace* [1987] 1 Lloyd's Rep 465 it was held that the owner of the goods could sue and recover substantial damages merely by virtue of the fact that he had title to the goods at the time of the loss or damage. The fact that the owner of the goods had contracts of sale enabling him to collect the price from the purchaser, irrespective of the loss or damage, did not disentitle him from recovering damages in full assessed by reference to the sound arrived value of the goods. It is the loss to the property in, or possession of, the goods which is to be compensated, not any other financial loss.

7.4.3   Implied Contract

Where the recipient of the cargo was not able to rely on s. 1 of the 1855 Act it was, occasionally, possible to argue that a contract should be implied between the recipient and the actual carrier; see *Brandt* v *Liverpool, Brazil and River Plate SN Co. Ltd* [1924] 1 KB 575. The problem with this approach is that the courts were unwilling to imply a contract from the mere fact that the holder of a bill of lading, entitled to demand delivery, did so, and the shipowner, bound by his contract with the shipper to deliver the goods to the party presenting the bill of lading, delivered the goods; see *The Aramis* [1989] I Lloyd's Rep 213.

Whether a contract is to be implied is a question of fact and such a contract will only be implied where it is necessary to do so. In *The Elli 2* [1985] 1 Lloyd's Rep 107 May LJ said:

... no such contract should be implied on the facts of any given case unless it is necessary to do so; necessary, that is to say, in order to give business reality to a transaction and to create enforceable obligations between parties who are dealing with one another in circumstances in which one would expect that business reality and those enforceable obligations to exist.

It is, therefore, fatal to the implication of a contract on the terms of the bill of lading if the shipowner and the holder of the bill of lading who wishes to take delivery of the goods from the ship, would have acted exactly as they did in the absence of such a contract. Otherwise the implication of a contract on the terms of the bill of lading in such circumstances would have rendered s. 1 of the 1855 Act obsolete.

There will be evidence from which a contract can be implied where a shipowner, who has a lien on cargo for unpaid freight or demurrage or other charges, makes delivery of the cargo to the holder of the bill of lading. In *Brandt* v *Liverpool, Brazil and Riverplate SN Co. Ltd* bags of zinc ash were shipped on the defendant's vessel for carriage to London. Some of the bags were wet before shipment. The defendant, nevertheless, issued a clean bill of lading. The bags were discharged at an intermediate port and subsequently completed their voyage on a second vessel. As a result the goods arrived three months later and the price of zinc ash had meanwhile fallen. The bill of lading had been indorsed to the claimants as security for an advance to the shippers. When the second vessel arrived, the claimants presented the bills of lading and paid the freight which was outstanding and then attempted to sue the defendant carrier for damages for delay. The claimants, as pledgees, were not able to rely on s. 1 of the 1855 Act. Nevertheless the court held that a contract could be implied from the acts of presenting the bill of lading, payment of freight and the delivery and acceptance of the goods specified in the bill of lading. Furthermore the defendant carriers were estopped from adducing evidence contrary to the terms of the bill of lading and were therefore bound by the representation that the goods were apparently in good condition on shipment.

The same would follow if in the same situation the buyer had not presented the bill of lading but had merely given an undertaking that he would do so as soon as it came into his possession; see *The Elli 2* (above). The same would also follow where the buyer tendered a ship's delivery order incorporating the terms of the bills of lading, paid the freight and received delivery of the goods; see *Cremer* v *General Carriers SA* [1974] 1 WLR 341; see also *The Captain Gregos (No 2)* [1990] 2 Lloyd's Rep 395.

The contract that is implied between the carrier and the holder of the bill of lading only includes those rights and liabilities which concern the carriage and delivery of the goods and not, for example, a warranty by the consignee as to the fitness of the goods for carriage; see *The Athanasia Comninos* [1990] 1 Lloyd's Rep 277 at p. 281.

Given the difficulties with implied contracts where the buyer does not furnish consideration such as the payment of freight or demurrage, or where there is insufficient evidence from which to infer that the parties intended to enter into contractual relations, the Law Commission (see 7.5) concluded that 'the *Brandt* v *Liverpool* contract is clearly no substitute for legislation.'.

7.4.4 Assignment

The buyer could ask for an assignment of the benefit of the contract evidenced by the bill of lading; see the facts of *The Kelo* [1985] 1 Lloyd's Rep 85. The assignment must comply with the requirements of s. 136 of the Law of Property Act 1925, that is to say it must be in writing and notice must be given to the carrier. The mere indorsement and delivery of the bill of lading would not in itself be sufficient. Because of these requirements, and also because the buyer would only take the rights of his transferor and would not, for example, be able to rely on Art. III r. 5 of the Hague-Visby Rules (see 8.8), assignment in this manner is clearly not an appropriate solution to the problems with the 1855 Act. Moreover when the seller is the charterer of the vessel the assignment of rights will be of the rights under the charterparty which may be substantially less generous than under the Hague or Hague-Visby Rules.

7.4.5 Seller Suing on Buyer's Behalf

As mentioned in 7.4.2, the buyer could ask the seller to sue on the buyer's behalf if, at the time of the damage, property in those goods remained with the seller though risk was with the buyers; see *The Sanix Ace* [1987] 1 Lloyd's Rep 465. There is, however, another situation in which the seller may be able to sue on the buyer's behalf.

If property has passed to the buyer before loss or damage to the goods occurred (and the buyer does not wish to rely on an action in tort), he could ask the seller to sue on the contract of carriage, relying on the principle in *Dunlop* v *Lambert* (1839) 6 Cl & Fin 600 as explained in *The Albazero* [1977] AC 774. Lord Diplock in *The Albazero* explained that the decision in *Dunlop* v *Lambert* arose at a time when rights under an executory contract could not be transferred otherwise than by novation and the tort of negligence was undeveloped so that the indorsee was not in a position to sue directly, and if suit was also denied to the indorser the innocent indorsee would be without a remedy. To avoid this injustice, the indorser was permitted to sue for the full loss, but had to account to the indorsee for the damages recovered.

Normally a party to a contract can only recover in an action for damages for breach of contract the actual loss which that party had sustained. This is subject to an exception in the case of a commercial contract concerning goods where it is in the contemplation of the parties that the proprietary interest in the goods may be transferred from one owner to another after the contract has been entered into and before the breach which causes loss or damage to the goods. In these circumstances the original party to the contract of carriage is treated in law as having entered into the contract for the benefit of all persons who have or may acquire an interest in the goods before they are lost or damaged, and is entitled to recover by way of damages for breach of contract the actual loss sustained by the person for whose benefit the contract was entered into. Lord Diplock in *The Albazero* at p. 847 said that:

... in a commercial contract concerning goods where it is in the contemplation of the parties that the proprietary interests in the goods may be transferred from one owner to another after the contract has been entered into and before the breach which causes the loss or damage to the goods, an original party to the contract, if such be the intention of them both, is to be treated in law as having entered into the contract for the benefit of all persons who have or may acquire an interest in the goods before they are lost or damaged, and is entitled to recover by way of damages for breach of contract the actual loss sustained by those for whose benefit the contract is entered into.

The owner of the goods, however, has no means of compelling the consignor to bring an action for his benefit. If the consignor does bring a successful action for substantial damages the owner could, nonetheless, recover from the consignor the amount recovered from the carrier as money had and received for his benefit. The principle in *Dunlop* v *Lambert* extends to all forms of carriage by sea but is restricted to those situations where there is no contract between the carrier and the person who actually suffered the loss. But this principle does not extend to contracts of carriage which contemplate that the carrier will enter into separate contracts of carriage with whoever may become the owner of the goods, (i.e. a charterparty which provides for the issue of bills of lading). Because of these restrictions the principle in *Dunlop* v *Lambert* could not provide the solution to the problems left by s 1 of the 1855 Act.

7.5   CARRIAGE OF GOODS BY SEA ACT 1992

In 1985, the Law Commission was invited to consider the law relating to the rights of suit of those concerned with contracts for the carriage of goods by sea with the view to possible reform. Initially the Law Commission was concerned merely with the problems occasioned by the carriage of goods in bulk and in 1989 a Working Paper on *Rights to Goods in Bulk* was published. It soon became apparent that reform would have to go beyond rights in respect of goods forming part of a larger bulk and the Report of the Law Commission, *Rights of Suit in Respect of Carriage of Goods by Sea* (Law Com 196) published in 1991, dealt with rights of suit in respect of carriage by sea generally and principally with the problems created by the Bills of Lading Act 1855.

The Law Commission considered three main approaches to solving the problems created by the inadequacies of the 1855 Act. The first approach was simply to allow the lawful holder of a bill of lading to sue the carrier if at some stage the property passed to him under a contract in pursuance of which he became the lawful holder. This was the wide view of s. 1 of the 1855 Act which was discussed at 7.2 above. This solution would have, in principle, solved most bulk cargo cases and cases such as *The Delfini*, but would not have assisted the buyer who never obtained property in the goods where, for example, they were lost before being ascertained. Consequently this approach was rejected.

The second option was to permit the lawful holder of a bill of lading to sue and be sued if he was on risk in respect of the loss which occurred when it occurred. The Law Commission, however, rejected this approach for several reasons and decided to adopt the third option which had been canvassed. This last and broadest approach of the three considered allows the lawful holder of a bill of lading to sue the carrier in contract for loss or damage to the goods covered by the bill, irrespective of whether property in the goods had passed to the holder and regardless of whether the holder was on risk at the time of the loss. This approach follows the practice in the USA and a number of European countries such as France, Germany, Holland, Sweden and Greece.

As a consequence of the Law Commission's recommendations, the Carriage of Goods by Sea Act 1992 was enacted to give effect to this approach to rights of suit in respect of the carriage of goods by sea. The Act received Royal Assent on 16 July 1992 and came into force three months later on 16 September 1992 (s. 6(3)), and affects all shipping documents covered by the Act issued after that date. The Bills of Lading Act 1855 was repealed (s. 6(2)).

7.5.1   Shipping Documents

The first thing that should be noted is that the 1992 Act is not limited to bills of lading in its application. The Act applies to any bill of lading, any sea waybill and any ship's delivery order (s. 1(1)).

As with the Bills of Lading Act 1855, bill of lading is not defined but it is made clear, following the preamble to the 1855 Act, that a bill of lading must be in transferable form (s. 1(2)(a)). A 'straight' consigned bill of lading, that is to say one which is not made out 'to order' or 'to X or order', is not a document of title at common law and will, therefore, merely be a receipt for the goods upon which the terms of the contract of carriage may be found. Such a bill of lading will resemble a sea waybill, and will therefore fall within the ambit of the Act, so that the only practical consequence is that the holder of such a bill of lading will not be able to take advantage of s. 4 of the Act (see 7.5.5).

Since the term bill of lading is not defined it is still open to question which types of bill of lading fall within the scope of the Act. Nevertheless the term bill of lading includes 'received for shipment' bills of lading (s. 1(2)(b)), recognising the fact that traders and bankers deal with received for shipment bills of lading in the same way as shipped bills of lading. The question of whether 'through' bills of lading and combined transport bills of lading come within the terms of the Act has been left open, the Law Commission recognising the multiplicity of different types of multimodal documents and the difficulties in making any specific provision for such documents. As the Act is expressed to cover any bill of lading, including 'received for shipment' bills of lading, multimodal documents are, however, capable of falling within its ambit.

The Law Commission recognised that reform should not be limited to bills of lading but should extend to sea waybills given their increasing commercial importance. Modern conventions on road, rail and air transportation all give the consignee named in a waybill the right to sue the carrier, recognising that it is commercially inconvenient that such a consignee should be able to sue a carrier and the fact that the waybill is a classic example of a contract made for the benefit of a third party. The Law Commission recommended that any new legislation should extend to sea waybills and, consequently, the COGSA 1992 covers such documents.

A sea waybill is a receipt for the goods. It is defined by the Act as any document which is not a bill of lading but which is a receipt of goods which contains or evidences a contract for the carriage of goods by sea and identifies the person to whom delivery of the goods is to be made by the carrier in accordance with that contract (s. 1(3)). It is non-transferable and is not a document of title. Its main advantage is that, unlike a bill of lading it does not have to be transferred to the consignee to enable the consignee to obtain possession of the goods. The shipper retains the sea waybill and delivery is made to the named consignee upon proof of the consignee's identity. There is also the additional advantage that the shipper can vary his instructions to the carrier at any time during transit.

The Act also extends to ship's delivery orders but not merchant delivery orders (mere delivery orders). Ship's delivery orders are commonly used when the seller wishes to sell parts of a bulk cargo to different buyers. Such a bulk cargo will often be covered by a single bill of lading so the seller will be unable to tender a bill of lading to each of his buyers so, instead, he stipulates for the tender of a delivery order under the contract for sale. As mentioned at 5.3.2–5.3.4 there are two types of delivery order, the difference between the two depending on whether the carrier has given an independent undertaking to the holder of the delivery order to deliver to him or to his order. Where the carrier has given such an undertaking the delivery order is a ship's delivery order. The Law Commission considered that, in the interests of commercial expedience, a carrier should be bound by that undertaking so as not to weaken the position of a purchaser of part of a bulk cargo.

Ship's delivery orders can be of two types. They are either documents issued by or on behalf of the carrier, while the goods are in his possession or under his control and which contain some form of undertaking that they will be delivered to the holder or to the order of a named person, or documents addressed to the carrier requiring him to deliver to a named person with the carrier subsequently attorning to that person. A ship's delivery order is defined in the Act as any document which is neither a bill of lading nor a sea waybill but which contains an undertaking which is given under or for the purposes of a contract for the carriage of goods by sea to which the document relates and is an undertaking by the carrier to a person identified in the document to deliver the goods to that person (s. 1(4)).

Provision is also made for the possibility of paperless transactions in the future. The Secretary of State is empowered to make regulations for the application of the Act to such paperless transactions (s. 1(5), (6)).

7.5.2 Person Entitled to Sue the Carrier

The persons who are entitled to sue the carrier on the contract of carriage under the Act are set out in s. 2 of the Act. In short those persons are the lawful holder of a bill of lading or the person to whom delivery of the goods is to be made in the case of a sea waybill or a ship's delivery order. Those persons have transferred to and vested in them all rights of suit under the contract of carriage as if they had been a party to that contract (s. 2(1)):

> Subject to the following provisions of this section, a person who becomes—
>
> (a)   the lawful holder of a bill of lading;
>
> (b)   the person who (without being an original party to the contract of carriage) is the person to whom delivery of the goods to which a sea waybill relates is to be made by the carrier in accordance with that contract; or
>
> (c)   the person to whom delivery of the goods to which a ship's delivery order relates is to be made in accordance with the undertaking contained in the order, shall (by virtue of becoming the holder of the bill or, as the case may be, the person to whom delivery is to be made) have transferred to and vested in him all rights of suit under the contract of carriage as if he had been a party to that contract.

The lawful holder of a bill of lading is defined as the consignee named in the bill of lading or the indorsee of the bill of lading who, in either case, has possession of the bill of lading (s. 5(2)). It matters not that the consignee or indorsee comes into possession of the bill of lading after possession of the bill of lading no longer gives the holder a right to possession, as against the carrier, of the goods to which the bill of lading relates (s. 5(2)). That is to say, a person can still become a holder of the bill of lading after the carrier has, in fact, delivered the goods to which the bill of lading relates.

With regard to the last point there is, however, one limitation. When a person becomes the lawful holder of a bill of lading but possession of the bill of lading no longer gives a right, as against the carrier, to possession of the goods to which the bill relates, that person does not have any of the rights under the contract of carriage transferred to or vested in him unless he becomes the holder of the bill of lading by virtue of a transaction effected in pursuance of some contract or other arrangement made before the time when such a right to possession ceased to attach to possession of the bill (s. 2(2)(a)). This last provision is intended to prevent the emergence of a paper market in rights of suit against carriers in which traders buy and sell bills of lading, not because those bills of lading represent goods, but because those bills of lading represent valuable rights of suit against carriers. Bills of lading will have such value because the Act allows the lawful holder of a bill of lading to sue the carrier for the benefit of the person who actually sustained the loss. Take as an example a string of contracts for the sale of goods to be delivered in March. The goods are sold by A to B in January and from B to C in February, but when the goods are delivered in March they are found to be damaged. The bill of lading only reaches C in April who then sells the bill of lading to D. In such a situation C would have been able to sue the carrier on the contract of carriage contained in or evidenced by the bill of lading if in possession of the bill of lading. On the other hand, D would not be able to sue the carrier on the contract of carriage.

A person who becomes the lawful holder of a bill of lading after the bill of lading has ceased to give the holder a right of possession, as against the carrier, because of the rejection of the goods or documents delivered to that other person in pursuance of a contract or some other arrangement made before the time when this right of possession ceased to attach to possession of the bill of lading, is also protected. Utilising the example given above, if C rejects the goods on arrival and sends the bill of lading back to B in April, then B will still be entitled to sue on the contract of carriage contained in or evidenced by the bill of lading.

One consequence of giving the holder of a bill of lading rights of suit against a carrier regardless of the passage of property is that pledgees and other persons holding a bill of lading as security will be able to sue on the contract of carriage. Such persons will not, therefore, encounter the problems raised by *Sewell* v *Burdick* (1884) 10 App Cas 74 and those persons will consequently not have to rely on an implied contract as in *Brandt* v *Liverpool, Brazil & River Plate Steam Navigation Co. Ltd* [1924] 1 KB 575.

Another consequence of divorcing rights of suit from the passing of property is that there will be cases where the holder of the bill of lading will have the right to sue on the contract of carriage vested in him though he has suffered no loss himself. In such cases the holder of the bill of lading will be able to exercise the rights of suit for the benefit of the person who has actually suffered the loss (s. 2(4)) and would, therefore, recover more than mere nominal damages. It would seem that the holder of the bill of lading could not be compelled to sue the carrier but if he did and was successful the holder would have to hold the damages recovered on account for the person who actually suffered the loss.

When the document in question is a sea waybill, the person in whom all rights of suit are transferred is the person to whom delivery of the goods is to be made in accordance with the contract of carriage (s. 2(1)(b)). It should be noted that the person in whom the rights of suit are transferred is not necessarily the person in possession of the sea waybill. The shipper of goods under a contract of carriage covered by a sea waybill normally retains the right to order the carrier to deliver the goods to whomsoever he pleases and the right to take delivery of the goods is not dependent on the tender of the sea waybill.

In the case of a ship's delivery order it is the person to whom delivery of the goods is to be made in accordance with the undertaking given by the carrier (s. 2(1)(c)). It is made clear by the Act that in the case of a ship's delivery order the rights vested are subject to the terms of the delivery order and that the rights vested only relate to that part of the goods to which the order relates (s. 2(3)). For example, if the contract of carriage covers 5,000 tonnes of grain and five delivery orders are issued, each covering 1,000 tonnes, the rights of each holder of a delivery order are confined to 1,000 tonnes and not the whole of the 5,000 tonnes.

7.5.3 Rights of the Shipper and Intermediate Holders

Under the 1855 Act once s. 1 had operated in favour of the consignee or indorsee of a bill of lading the original shipper was no longer entitled to sue on the bill of lading.

This was apparent from the terminology of the 1855 Act which referred to the 'transfer' of rights; see *Sewell* v *Burdick* (1884) App Cas 74; *Short* v *Simpson* (1866) LR 1 CP 248. The intermediate holder of a bill of lading was in a similar position once he had transferred the bill of lading to another holder. This has not been changed by COGSA 1992 in so far as it relates to bills of lading.

Section 2(5) provides that where rights are transferred by virtue of the operation of s. 2(1) the transfer must extinguish any entitlement to those rights which derive from a person having been an original party to the contract. Likewise such a transfer extinguishes the rights of a holder who was not an original party to the contract of carriage contained in or evidenced by the bill of lading.

The position is, however, different where the document in question is a sea waybill and not a bill of lading. One of the merits of a sea waybill is that the shipper can, before delivery, direct the carrier to deliver the goods to a person other than the consignee named in the sea waybill. The carrier would be obliged to comply with this order as the contract of carriage would be construed as requiring the carrier to deliver to the named consignee or such other person as the shipper might direct. Thus in the case of a sea waybill the consignee's rights are without prejudice to the rights of the shipper (s. 2(5)) and the shipper's rights are not extinguished by the operation of s. 2(1).

Once the shipper has changed his orders to the carrier as to delivery of the goods, the person who was to receive the goods will no longer have any rights of suit against the carrier. This is apparent from the terms of s. 2(1)(b) which identifies the person entitled to exercise the rights of suit under the sea waybill as the person to whom delivery of the goods is to be made by the carrier in accordance with the contract. The contract of carriage will normally provide that delivery is to be made to the named consignee or such other person as the shipper might direct. Where, therefore, the shipper orders the carrier to deliver to someone other than the named consignee the named consignee will not be able to rely on s. 2(1)(b) and will lose his rights of suit. The matter is put beyond doubt by s. 2(5)(b) which provides that the transfer of rights under s. 2(1) operates to extinguish those rights which derived from the previous operation of s. 2(1).

Where the document in question is a ship's delivery order the position is the same as with a sea waybill. The operation of s. 2(1) is without prejudice to the rights of the original shipper but extinguishes the rights of persons who had previously enjoyed rights of suit under s. 2(1).

7.5.4 Separation of Rights and Liabilities

Section 1 of the 1855 Act, whilst not referring to the transfer of liabilities, did provide that the consignee/indorsee was subject to the same liabilities in respect of the goods as if the contract contained in the bill of lading had been made with himself. It was, therefore, clear that the consignee or indorsee who had rights of suit was also subject to liabilities. It was, however, not clear whether s. 1 of the 1855 Act operated to subject the consignee or indorsee to all the liabilities of the shipper, whether incurred before or at the time of shipment, or before indorsement of the bill of lading, or only those liabilities subsequent to shipment or the indorsement of the bill of lading.

The Law Commission realised that extending rights of suit to a wide class of persons might be problematic if such persons were also to be subject to liabilities of the shipper of the goods. It was pointed out that if shipper's rights and liabilities were transferred to all holders, including those holding the bill merely as security, it would mean that such people, including banks who take up shipping documents in the normal course of financing international transactions, would suddenly find themselves liable for freight, demurrage and other charges. This would have reversed the decision of the House of Lords in *Sewell* v *Burdick* (7.3.2) and would have been commercially undesirable.

It was, however, decided that there was no unfairness in making the person who either claims delivery or who takes delivery of the goods, from being subject to the terms of the contract of carriage since in both cases the person is enforcing or attempting to enforce rights under the contract of carriage. Section 3(1) therefore provides that:

Where subsection (1) of section 2 of this Act operates in relation to any document to which this Act applies and the person in whom rights are vested by virtue of that subsection

(a) takes or demands delivery from the carrier of any of the goods to which the document relates;

(b) makes a claim under the contract of carriage against the carrier in respect of any of those goods; or

(c) is a person who, at a time before those rights were vested in him took, or demanded delivery from the carrier of any of those goods,

that person shall (by virtue of taking or demanding delivery or making a claim or, in a case falling within paragraph (c) above, of having the rights vested in him) become subject to the same liabilities under that contract as if he had been a party to that contract.

It should be noted that s. 3(1) draws no distinction between pre-shipment and post-shipment liabilities. It was suggested that it would be unfair for the final holder of a bill of lading to be liable in respect of such matters as the shipper's breach of warranty in shipping dangerous goods, demurrage incurred at the port of loading and dead freight. It was pointed out that the consignee or indorsee often stands in no relation to the goods at the moment of shipment and to make him liable in respect of such pre-shipment liabilities is to make him subject to retrospective liability for acts with which he had nothing to do. The Law Commission, however, concluded that no satisfactory line could be drawn between pre-shipment and post-shipment liabilities and that no special provision should be made for liability in respect of dangerous cargo.

The liabilities of a person entitled to take delivery of goods to which a ship's delivery order relates are restricted to those liabilities which relate to the goods covered by the ship's delivery order but no more (s. 3(2)).

With regard to the original shipper the Law Commission decided that he should not be able to escape liability on the contract of carriage merely by transferring his rights and liabilities to another party. An example was given of an exporter who shipped a cargo of highly poisonous gas which escaped and caused extensive property damage and loss of life. A shipowner would be disturbed to find that the shipper had been absolved of his liabilities simply by indorsing the bill of lading to another. Section 3(3) therefore provides:

> This section, so far as it imposes liabilities under any contract on any person, shall be without prejudice to the liabilities under the contract of any person as an original party to the contract.

7.5.5   False Statements in Bills of Lading

One matter which is dealt with by COGSA 1992, but which is not directly related to rights of suit in the carriage of goods by sea, is the problem caused by the decision in *Grant* v *Norway* (1851) 10 CB 665 in which the Court of Common Pleas held that a ship's master has no authority to sign a bill of lading for goods not put on board. The carrier was, therefore, not bound by the representation made in the bill of lading that goods had been shipped on board.

The decision has been much criticised and rightly so in that the master of a ship is normally held out by the shipowner as having ostensible authority to make representations as to quantity. The courts have, on occasion, gone to extraordinary lengths to avoid the implications of this decision; see *V/O Rasnoimport* v *Gutherie & Co. Ltd* [1966] 1 Lloyd's Rep 1. Section 3 of the 1855 Act appears to have been intended to solve the *Grant* v *Norway* problem but was singularly unsuccessful in that respect. Section 3 of the 1855 Act provided that a bill of lading representing goods to have been shipped on board was conclusive evidence of such shipment against the master or other person signing the bill of lading. Unfortunately the master of a vessel rarely contracts personally and it is often not worth suing him in any event.

Consequently the Law Commission recommended that the rule in *Grant* v *Norway* be abolished. Section 4 therefore provides that:

> A bill of lading which—
> (a)   represents goods to have been shipped on board a vessel or to have been received for shipment on board a vessel; and
> (b)   has been signed by the master of the vessel or by a person who was not the master but had the express, implied or apparent authority of the carrier to sign the bills of lading, shall, in favour of a person who has become the lawful holder of the bill, be conclusive evidence against the carrier of the shipment of the goods, or, as the case may be, of their receipt for shipment.

It should be noted that s. 4 does not extend to persons who are only entitled to the delivery of goods covered by a ship's delivery order or sea waybill.

7.6   LIABILITY FOR FREIGHTS

Freight is defined as the remuneration which is paid to the carrier for getting the goods to their destination in merchantable condition and delivering them to the merchant; see *Asfar* v *Blundell* [1896] 1 QB 123. If the carrier has not fulfilled all the requirements of the definition, then he has not earned his freight; see *Dakin* v *Oxley* (1864) 10 LT 268. The definition requires the carrier to deliver the goods at their destination. If the act of the cargo-owner prevents the carrier from making delivery at the port of destination, then he will be entitled to full freight nevertheless.

In *Atkielskabet Olive Bank* v *Dansk Fabrik* [1919] 2 KB 162 a charterparty contained a clause allowing goods to be discharged at a United Kingdom or Danish port at the option of the consignees. The consignees directed the vessel to a Danish port at which the carrier could not discharge because at that time an importation ban prevented the goods from being landed. The carrier discharged at Plymouth and was, nevertheless, entitled to full freight as the consignees were obliged to give the carrier the opportunity to earn his freight in making their nomination.

If the goods are merchantable on arrival, then the carrier is entitled to freight. Therefore, even if they are damaged on arrival, if that damage does not have the effect of making them unmerchantable, then the carrier may still receive his freight; see *The Metula* [1978] 2 Lloyd's Rep 5. The cargo-owner is not entitled to put forward the damage to his goods as a defence to payment and he would need to pursue a separate Part 20 claim (formerly a counterclaim) in respect of the damage suffered.

In *Aries* v *Total Transport* [1977] 1 WLR 185 HL the Court of Appeal refused to interfere with the rule that a cargo-owner cannot set off the damage to his cargo against the freight owing from him, he must pay that freight in full.

It is an implied term of the contract of carriage between shipper and carrier that the shipper will pay the freight. This fact may also be stated in or on the bill of lading which is issued by the carrier. If the goods are sold in transit and the bill of lading is transferred to a third party purchaser, s. 3 Carriage of Goods by Sea Act 1992 has the effect of enabling the carrier to claim the freight from the indorsee of the bill and treating the indorsee as if the contract contained within the bill of lading had been made with himself. Where the goods are shipped by one person and the consignee is another person, then s. 3 of the 1992 Act affects a consignee, making him liable for freight in exactly the same way as the indorsee is made liable. In any event, it would be an implied term of the conditions upon which a holder of the bill takes delivery of the goods, that he would pay their freight if they were handed over to him; see *Bell* v *Kymer* (1814) 3 Camp 545.

The amount of freight which is to be paid may either be stated in the bill of lading or charterparty, or it will be determined in accordance with trade custom at the time of shipment.

7.7   TYPES OF FREIGHT

The parties may specifically agree to abrogate the general rule requiring freight to be paid when the goods are delivered in merchantable condition. They may choose, instead, one of the following types of freight.

(a)   lump sum freight;
(b)   advance freight;
(c)   back freight;
(d)   pro rata freight.

7.7.1   Lump Sum Freight

In order to receive lump sum freight the shipowner has only to make his vessel, or a portion of it, available for the use of the shipper. According to *Scrutton on Charterparties* it is 'a gross sum to be paid for the use of the ship, or a portion thereof. According to Carver it is 'freight which is payable if the ship completes her voyage with or without the cargo'.

The problem which, therefore, must be considered is whether a carrier is entitled to lump sum freight if he does not deliver any goods at all. According to *Atkinson* v *Ritchie* (1809) 10 East 530, a shipowner is entitled to full lump sum freight providing he delivers some of the goods, although he is not required to deliver all of them. This accords well with the notion that lump sum freight is payable for the use of the vessel and payment is not dependent upon safe delivery of the goods. There is, however, no decided case on whether a shipowner would be entitled to full lump sum freight if he did not deliver anything, although there are obiter dicta in two cases which suggest that there would be no entitlement. In *The Norway* (1865) 3 Moo PC 245 it was stated that lump sum freight was 'in the nature of a rent to be paid for the hire and use of the ship on the agreed voyage'. In *Merchant Shipping Co.* v *Armitage* (1873) LR 9 QB 99 the court stated that lump sum freight was payable 'after entire discharge and right delivery of the cargo'.

7.7.2   Advance Freight

This was defined in *Allison* v *Bristol Marine Insurance* (1875) 1 App Cas 209 as 'irrevocable payment at the risk of the shipper of the goods'. Therefore, if the parties agree to the payment of advance freight and the goods are lost, then that freight must still be paid. This principle is subject to the following important qualifications.

(a)   If the parties agree to payment of advance freight on a particular date and when that date arrives the cargo is partly destroyed, then advance freight will be reduced to accommodate the fact of that destruction.

(b)   If the cargo is lost by a peril which is not a peril for which the carrier can be exempted from liability, then the advance freight, if already paid, can be recovered. In such circumstances, it is highly likely that the party liable for the payment of advance freight would have a claim against the carrier for damages.

It is important to distinguish between an agreement to pay advance freight and a loan made by the shipper to the carrier to give the carrier financial assistance with regard to expenditure involved in the carriage of goods. If it was the parties' intention that the shipper make a loan to the carrier, then the shipper can seek repayment of his loan at any time. If the goods are delivered in merchantable condition, then the shipper has only to pay the carrier the balance between the loan and the total freight payable.

7.7.3 Back Freight

In any circumstances where the carrier has to incur expenditure in preserving the cargo, either because he cannot deliver at the port of destination or because of the consignee's failure to take delivery, the expenditure can be recovered from the carrier as back freight. Normally, back freight would involve either transhipment of the goods or landing and warehousing them.

In *Cargo ex Argos* (1873) LR 5 PC 134 a shipment of oil was required by the bill of lading to be taken off the vessel within 24 hours of arrival. This was impossible at her specified port of destination where landing was forbidden and also impossible at other nearby ports. Eventually, the oil was landed at the original port of departure but it was necessary to unload it and reload it in order to discharge other cargo at the port of destination.

It was held that the shipowner was entitled to back freight for the return journey to the port of departure, as well as freight for the outward journey.

7.7.4 Pro rata Freight

Where a shipowner loads only part of a cargo or delivers only a part of the cargo, he clearly cannot claim freight as though he had loaded or delivered the whole cargo. In the first instance, he has not carried all the cargo and, in the second, he has failed to deliver it up to the consignee. He can, therefore, claim freight on a pro rata basis, i.e. directly related to the quantity delivered and, similarly, where the goods are not delivered up at the agreed port of destination but at another port. Whilst the shipowner has carried and delivered up the goods he has not complied with the terms of the contract and, therefore, is not entitled to the contractual rate of freight. There will be no entitlement to pro rata freight, however, unless it is expressly agreed by the parties; see *St Enoch Steamship* v *Phosphate Mining Co.* [1916] 2 KB 624.

7.8 RIGHTS OF THE UNPAID SHIPOWNER

At common law, a shipowner may have a lien for his freight, and expenses necessarily incurred in preservation of the cargo. This lien exists only where freight was to be paid at the time of delivery of the goods. Therefore, there can be no lien for freight payable at any other time, e.g. advance freight. The lien for freight is only a possessory lien, therefore, whilst he can keep hold of cargo on which he has earned freight, he cannot sell it. If he elects to land and warehouse, then he also has a lien for those charges, such expenses being necessarily incurred in the preservation of the cargo.

The unpaid shipowner is, however, given a statutory right of sale under Part VII of the Merchant Shipping Act 1894 in circumstances where the owner fails to take delivery of the goods within the contract period or within 72 hours of the report of the ship. The effect of Part VII (ss. 492–501) is to permit the carrier to sell the goods 90 days after they are warehoused, or even sooner if they are perishable (s. 497). The cargo-owner can obtain the return of the goods by depositing the sum outstanding with the warehouseman (s. 495).

If the goods are sold at public auction after expiry of the necessary period, then although the carrier may have instigated the sale and, indeed, incurred all relevant expenses, the debts owed to him rank only fifth in order of merit according to s. 498 which lists the charges and the priority in which the proceeds of sale must go to satisfy them.

The House of Lords in *Bank of Boston Connecticut* v *European Grain & Shipping Ltd* [1989] 2 WLR 440 considered for the first time whether a charterer of a ship, liable for freight to the ship owner, could set off against that liability damages for a repudiatory breach of the charterparty. All previous authorities had been cases of non-repudiatory breach. A rule against deduction, i.e. no set-off, had been established. In *Bank of Boston* the charterer had agreed to pay advance freight. On a proper construction of the contract it was found that the charterer's liability had accrued prior to seizure of the ship by the owner's creditors. This amounted to a repudiatory breach of the charterparty. The charterer had not forwarded freight, and refused to do so arguing that he was entitled to set off damages for the repudiatory breach against his liability for freight. The House of Lords considered previous authorities on non-repudiatory breaches and the rule against deduction; see *Government of Newfoundland* v *Newfoundland Ry Co.* (1883) 13 App Cas 199; *The Brede* [1974] QB 233; *The Aries* [1977] 1 WLR 185. Claims for breach of the charterparty could only be brought as Part 20 claims (formerly counterclaims), separate from the claim for freight, although in the same action. In particular, in *The Aries* it had been held that there was no equity to merit set-off. Dicta suggesting that the rule against deduction might not apply to repudiatory breaches were interpreted by Lord Brandon in *Bank of Boston* to mean a repudiatory breach by way of failure to deliver the cargo when freight was earned and payable on delivery. This could, therefore, be distinguished from cases in which liability for freight had accrued *prior* to the repudiatory breach. Lord Brandon thought that the rule against deduction should apply in such cases. First, there may be cases in which the loss flowing from a non-repudiatory breach, e.g. if valuable cargo were damaged, was greater than that flowing from a repudiatory breach (non-delivery). There was, therefore, no justification based on the amount of loss to have different rules. Secondly, the only situation when the rule against deduction works to the disadvantage of the charterer is when the shipowner is insolvent. This would, of course, be the same whatever the nature of the breach. Finally, their Lordships considered the approach of the legislature in the Law Reform (Frustrated Contracts) Act 1943. Charterparties are excluded from the regime of apportionment. The legislature had, therefore, preserved the indefeasibility of an accrued right to advance freight. It was not, therefore, the place of the courts to alter that policy decision. The House of Lords also refused to use the rules of procedure (RSC O. 15, r. 2(4)) to circumvent substantive rights. That rule enables a court to amalgamate the losses under a principal action and counterclaim (now a Part 20 claim) and make a single award as to the balance. Use of this procedure in the present context would be an illegitimate exercise of the court's discretion. Clearly, therefore, when the obligation to pay advance freight has accrued, damages for a subsequent repudiatory breach cannot be set off as a defence, but must be brought as a separate Part 20 claim in the same action. The courts will not use their power to amalgamate the awards since this would be to circumvent the parties' substantive rights.

7.9 GUARANTEE OF PAYMENTS FOR FREIGHTS

It would appear that an unpaid shipowner can sue and recover for freights if it was guaranteed by the charterer or his agent at common law or under statute; see *Elpis Maritime Co. Ltd* v *Marti Chartering Co. Ltd, The Maria D* [1991] 2 Lloyd's Rep 311 HL. The owners let their vessel (*The Maria D*) for carriage of wheat from Turkey to Algeria, through their agents (Tramp) and the charterer's agents (Marti). Following negotiations by telex and telephone the charterers guaranteed, by clause 33 of the contract, that demurrage and freight at the discharge port would be paid latest within 30 days after the presentation of time sheets and statements of facts for discharging port by the owners. After presentation the charterer claimed credit for various strike periods at the discharge port and the dispute went to arbitration, High Court and Court of Appeal. The respondents contended that: (1) it was not them but their agents who signed: (2) what was signed was not the contract; and (3) the guarantee was not sufficiently evidenced to satisfy the requirements of s. 4, Statute of Frauds 1677.

It was held, allowing the owners' appeal, that it was standard practice when two brokers, acting on behalf of their respective principals, negotiated by telephone or telex or both, the terms on which a ship was to be chartered, and terms were fully agreed, for those terms to be embodied in a written charter in which they were subsumed. It was clear that both agents (Tramp and Marti) intended to follow this standard practice, not only in respect of the main contract between the owners and the charterers, but also in respect of the terms of the collateral contract of guarantee between the owners and the charters' agents.

Section 4, Statute of Frauds 1677 sets down two ways in which contract guarantees might be enforceable: (1) by written agreement signed by the party to be charged or his agent and, (2) by note or memorandum, similarly signed, or an oral agreement. In the latter case it was irrelevant with what intention, or in what capacity the party signed the note or the memorandum, the fact that the party had made the note and signed it was sufficient for the purposes of enforcing the Statute of Frauds.

8   The Hague-Visby and Hamburg Rules

8.1   COMMON LAW LIABILITY OF THE CARRIER

At common law certain duties are imposed on a carrier for reward in the absence of contractual stipulations negativing or limiting such liability. Such contractual stipulations may, themselves, be subject to statutory provisions and in particular the Carriage of Goods by Sea Act (COGSA) 1971 which gives the Hague-Visby Rules (see 8.2) force of law in the United Kingdom. In considering the liability of the carrier for loss of damage to goods in his custody one must, therefore, consider the terms of the contract, the effect of statutory provisions and the common law.

The common law imposes four basic obligations on the carrier.

(a)   The carrier must deliver the goods in the same condition as when they were shipped. This is a non-delegable duty. There are, however, four common law exceptions:

(i)   act of God, such as frost, wind, fog, etc;
(ii)   act of the Queen's enemies, covering acts of any state with which the sovereign of the carrier is at war;
(iii)   loss or damage resulting from the inherent vice of the goods. This covers the inherent quality of the goods shipped. The carrier is not responsible for loss or damage to the goods resulting from the ordinary processes of the goods during transit, e.g. their ability to combust spontaneously and the disposition of certain animals. It also covers the defective packing of the goods, e.g. if this were insufficient to withstand the ordinary incidents of the voyage;
(iv)   loss resulting from jettison. If the goods are thrown overboard to save the ship, the carrier is not liable for the whole of the loss to the particular cargo-owner. The carrier is, however, liable to make a 'general average' contribution to the owner of the cargo which was sacrificed. This means that the carrier's liability is reduced to a contribution to the value of the lost cargo along with individual contributions from all those with an interest in the safe arrival of the shipment.

In addition, it must be shown that the damage to or loss of the goods was not a result of the carrier's negligence. For example, if the cargo was damaged by water escaping from a frost-cracked pipe, the carrier could not rely on an act of God if the master had left the boiler full of water during a cold night.

(b)   The carrier has an absolute duty to provide a seaworthy ship. This duty is discharged at the time of shipment, although subsequent events may be evidence that the duty was not, in fact, properly discharged. The duty is an absolute one. Therefore, even if the defect in the ship were latent, if the ship was *de facto* unseaworthy, and that unseaworthiness was a cause of the loss or damage, the carrier remains liable despite the existence of other concurrent causes; see *Monarch* v *Karlshamms* [1949] AC 196.

(c)   The carrier undertakes to proceed on the voyage without unjustifiable deviation. If there is such deviation, the carrier is liable for any subsequent loss unless he can rely on any of the common law exclusions, and can show that the loss or damage would have occurred in the absence of the deviation; see *Morrison* v *Shaw Saville* [1916] 2 KB 783.

(d)   The carrier must complete the voyage with reasonable dispatch. If there is undue delay, the carrier is liable in damages for any loss caused by the delay, unless the loss falls within one of the excepted perils, and the carrier can show that he had not been negligent.

The Athanasia Comninos [1990] 1 Lloyd's Rep 277 considered the question of the shipper's liability for dangerous goods. Mustill J held that dangerousness was not an absolute quality. It is a question of assessing the risks expressly and impliedly accepted by the carrier in respect of the specific cargo; see *Bamfield* v *Goole* [1910] 2 KB 94. Implication will involve considering the knowledge, skill and equipment of the carrier as well as the proper construction of the contract. Mustill J was reluctant to adopt any one particular test. He thought, however, that it helped to consider what was the proper method of carriage for the cargo. If a shipowner consents to carry goods of a particular description, he thereby contracts to perform carriage in a manner appropriate to those goods, and, therefore, assumes all the risks of accident if caused by a failure to carry them in that manner. This test does not resolve cases where the nature of goods is such that even strict compliance with the accepted method of carriage would not suffice to eliminate the possibility of accident. Mustill J thought that in such a case risk should fall on the carrier since he contracted to carry goods of that description and, therefore, assented to their presence on board. The degree of acceptability of the mode of carriage was a question of fact for each type of good. The standard of care required of the carrier when carrying the goods would vary with the state of the art. Mustill J expressly avoided deciding whether the shipper's duty in respect of the nature of cargo and his contractual obligations as to the suitability of the cargo for carriage on the ship were absolute or limited to that which he ought to have known. His Lordship, nevertheless, preferred an absolute obligation; see *Effort Shipping Co. Ltd* v *Linden Management SA and Another, The Giannis NK, The Times*, 5 May 1994.

8.2   THE HAGUE-VISBY RULES

As indicated these common law duties can be modified or excluded by the terms of the contract of carriage. The shipper of goods has, however, little bargaining power as against the carrier and any subsequent holder of a bill of lading has even less influence over the terms and conditions of this contract to which he becomes a party under COGSA 1992 or the Bill of Lading Act 1855. Carriers were, therefore, able to include elaborate provisions in their standard form contracts of carriage restricting or excluding their liability for loss or damage to goods which they agreed to carry.

To remedy such abuses the Hague Rules were formulated at various diplomatic conferences in Brussels in 1922, 1923 and 1924. The Hague Rules were given effect in the United Kingdom by the Carriage of Goods by Sea Act 1924. Viscount Sumner in *Gosse Millard Ltd* v *Canadian Government Merchant Marine* [1929] AC 223, indicated that the legislative intention was to:

> ... replace a conventional contract, in which it was constantly attempted, often with much success, to relieve the carrier from every kind of liability, by a legislative bargain, under which ... his position was to be one of restricted exemption.

The Hague Rules were subsequently amended by the Brussels Protocol of 1968 and the amended rules, known as the Hague-Visby Rules, were given legislative effect in the United Kingdom by COGSA 1971.

Whereas the Hague-Visby Rules have been implemented in the United Kingdom, many states, e.g. the United States, have not yet adopted them but merely apply the Hague Rules without amendment. A list of those countries applying the Hague-Visby Rules is found at 8.14 and those applying the Hague Rules at 8.15.

A further set of rules, the Hamburg Rules, were devised in 1978 by a United Nations Convention on the Carriage of Goods by Sea. These rules may eventually replace the Hague and the Hague-Visby Rules but they do not, for the moment, have effect in the United Kingdom (see 8.17).

8.3   APPLICATION OF THE COGSA 1971 AND THE HAGUE-VISBY RULES

The Hague-Visby Rules are given force of law within the United Kingdom by s. 1(2), COGSA 1971. When the Rules apply they have statutory force of law and will modify the terms of the contract of carriage. The application of the Act and the Rules is governed by s. 1(3), (4) and (6) of the Act and Art. X of the Rules. The mechanism adopted is to consider three elements cumulatively, namely, the voyage; the documents; and the goods.

8.3.1   Voyages

The Rules will *prima facie* have statutory application in the following circumstances without express incorporation:

(a)   Any voyage where the port of shipment is a port in the United Kingdom (which includes Great Britain and Northern Ireland: see s. 1(2), The Royal and Parliamentary Titles Act 1927), even though the port of destination is also a port in the UK (s. 1(3), COGSA 1971).

(b)   Any voyage between ports in two different states where:

(i)   the bill of lading is issued in a contracting state. This covers the case where neither the port of shipment nor the port of destination are in contracting states, but, provided that they are different states, the Rules will apply if the bill is issued in a contracting state (Art. X(a)). Or,

(ii)   the carriage is from a port in a contracting state. In this case, provided that the port of shipment and the port of destination are in different states, it does not matter that the port of destination and the place where the bill was issued are in non-contracting states, so long as the port of shipment is in a contracting state (Art. X(b)).

If the port of shipment is not in the UK or any other contracting state and the bill of lading is issued in a non-contracting state, the rules will not apply unless expressly incorporated, even if the port of destination is in a contracting state.

If the port of shipment is not in the UK but is in another contracting state and the port of destination is in the same state, the Rules will *prima facie* not apply.

(c)   The Rules will *prima facie* have statutory application if there has been an express incorporation of the Rules in the contract contained in or evidenced by the bill of lading, whether the voyage is between different states (Art. X(c)) or not (s. 1(6)(a)).

(d)   The Rules will *prima facie* have statutory application if the contract of carriage contained in or evidenced by the bill of lading provides that the express choice of law is to be that of a state (contracting or not) which gives effect to the Rules (Art. X(c)).

If the express choice of law implements only some of the Rules, an English court nevertheless will apply the Rules completely.

8.3.2   Documents

Generally, the Rules will only apply if a bill of lading or similar document of title is used in conjunction with one of the voyages described in 8.3.1 (Art. I(b); Art. X and s. 1(4)). The Rules do not, therefore, apply to charterparties (Art. V). It is, however, possible for the charterparty to incorporate the Hague-Visby Rules as contractual provisions with the necessary modifications; see *Adamastos Shipping Co. Ltd* v *Anglo-Saxon Petroleum Co. Ltd* [1959] AC 133. By 'similar document of title', it is presumed that this is a reference to documents of title at common law and, therefore, is limited to those documents recognised by custom as operating as such; see *Lickbarrow* v *Mason* (1787) 2 Term Rep 63; *Kum* v *Wah Tat Bank* [1971] 1 Lloyd's Rep 439.

There is one exception which is provided for by s. 1(6)(b) and that is a non-negotiable receipt marked as such which expressly provides that the Rules are to govern the contract as if the receipt were a bill of lading. There is doubt as to whether the receipt must actually state that the Rules govern the contract 'as if the receipt were a bill of lading'; see *The Vechstroon* [1982] 1 Lloyd's Rep 301. The preferred view is that it should; see *Browner International Ltd* v *Monarch Shipping, The European Enterprise* [1989] 2 Lloyd's Rep 185.

8.3.3   Goods

The Rules apply to all types of goods except for:

(a)   Live animals.
(b)   Deck cargo, which means:

(i)   cargo which by the contract of carriage is stated categorically that it is being carried on deck; and
(ii)   which is so carried.

A clause giving the shipper an option or liberty to ship the goods on deck is outside the definition, and the cargo is not 'deck cargo' for the purposes of the application of the Rules, even if the goods are, in fact, carried on deck; see *Svenska Tractor* v *Maritime Agencies* [1953] 2 QB 295.

If the contract of carriage is one which expressly incorporates the Rules by an express provision, or by a choice of law clause which adopts the law of a state which applies the Rules, then the Rules will apply to the contract, notwithstanding that the cargo is live animals or deck cargo (s. 1(7)).

The COGSA 1971 is an 'overriding statute' meaning that there is no scope for the parties to oust the operation of the Rules, either by an express ouster or exclusion clause, or by choosing a proper law for the contract which does not apply the Rules; see *The Hollandia* [1983] 1 AC 565 and also *The Benarty* [1985] QB 325.

Browner International Ltd v *Monarch Shipping Co. Ltd* [1989] 2 Lloyd's Rep 185 shows the difference between contractual and statutory incorporation of the Hague-Visby Rules. The contract of carriage was contained in or evidenced by a sea waybill. The sea waybill expressly incorporated the Hague-Visby Rules but did not contain a statement to the effect that the Rules were to govern the contract as if the sea waybill were a bill of lading. There was a contractual provision which limited the carrier's liability to a greater extent than is permitted under Art. IV r. 5 of the Rules. The goods were damaged during transit. The carrier admitted liability under Art. III r. 2. The question was whether the carrier was entitled to rely on the contractual limitation provision, or whether the Hague-Visby Rules applied. This required construction of the contract in the light of s. 1(6)(b) COGSA 1971:

Rules shall have force of law in relation to . . .

(b)   any receipt which is a non-negotiable document marked as such if the contract contained in or evidenced by it is a contract for the carriage of goods by sea which expressly provides that the Rules are to govern the contract as if the receipt were a bill of lading.

Steyn J disagreed with the interpretation afforded in *The Vechstroon* where Lloyd J held that a receipt did not require the words 'as if a bill of lading' to give them statutory force under s. 1(6)(b). He did so on the ground that he had received fuller argument from counsel. Parliament had clearly set out two requirements for the Rules to have statutory force: a non-negotiable document marked as such and a statement that the Rules are to govern as if the receipt were a bill of lading. Without such a statement, therefore, the Rules had only contractual force and could be altered. The contractual limitation clause therefore stood.

8.4   THE STAGE WHEN THE RULES BEGIN TO APPLY

Under every contract of carriage of goods by sea the carrier, in relation to the loading, handling, stowage, carriage, custody, care and discharge to such goods is to be subject to the responsibilities and entitled to the rights and immunities set out in the Rules (Art. II). By Art. I (e), 'carriage of goods' is defined as covering the period from the time when the goods are loaded on, to the time they are discharged from the ship.

In *Pyrene Co.* v *Scindia Navigation Co. Ltd* [1954] 2 QB 403 the seller sold a fire-tender f.o.b. London and delivered it alongside the ship. The ship had been nominated by the buyer. Whilst the tender was being lifted onto the vessel by the stevedores, but before it had crossed the ship's rail, it was dropped and damaged. In the f.o.b. contract of sale, risk had not passed since the goods had not crossed the ship's rail. The seller, therefore, had to sue the carrier for the cost of repairing the tender. The carrier admitted liability, but claimed that the Hague Rules applied and that he was, therefore, entitled to limit his liability under Art. IV r. 5. The seller argued that since the bill of lading had not been issued, the Hague Rules could not have been incorporated into the contract of carriage, as the Rules only apply if there is a bill of lading being used. The court held that whenever a contract of carriage is concluded which contemplates the issue of a bill of lading in due course, the Rules are not disapplied by reason of the fact that at the time damage or loss occurs, the bill of lading had not yet been issued. Once the bill was issued this would cover the contract as from the latter's inception and, therefore, the Rules would apply as from that time. The seller argued since the tender had not crossed the rail, it had not been loaded onto the ship and, therefore, the performance of the contract had not reached the stage at which the Rules applied. The court held that the words 'loaded on' in Art. I(e) did not merely refer to the goods crossing the ship's rail. They covered the whole of the loading process. They merely identified the first process in the operation of the carriage of the goods by sea. Devlin J went on to observe that the object of the Rules is:

... to define not the scope of the contract service but the terms on which that service is to be performed ... the whole of the contract is subject to the rules but the extent to which the loading and discharging are brought within the carrier's obligations is left to the parties themselves to decide.

The Rules do not impose on the carrier the obligation to load or stow the goods on board his vessel. If, however, he does undertake to load and stow the goods then the Rules apply and he must do so properly and carefully in accordance with Art. III r. 2 (see 8.6). Devlin J's observation was approved by the Court of Appeal in *GH Renton* v *Palmyra Trading Corp of Panama* [1957] AC 149 and more recently in *The Coral*

[1993] 1 Lloyd's Rep 1.

8.5   SEAWORTHINESS: ART. III R. 1

The starting point of the obligations imposed by the scheme of COGSA 1971 and the Rules is the negative rule in s. 3, COGSA 1971:

There shall not be implied in any contract for the carriage of goods by sea to which the Rules apply by virtue of this Act any absolute undertaking by the carrier of the goods to provide a seaworthy ship.

Instead there is a duty to exercise due diligence to provide a seaworthy ship under Art. III r. 1. This, therefore, is a departure from the absolute obligation at common law. If there was in fact unseaworthiness which was latent, then under the Rules the carrier would not be in breach.

The extent of due diligence, however, is not restricted to the carrier personally. Hence evidence that the carrier has employed competent experts for the task in hand is not sufficient if the contractors were, in fact, negligent.

In *Riverstone Meat Co.* v *Lancashire Shipping Co.* [1961] AC 807 tins of meat were shipped from Sydney to London. The bill of lading expressly incorporated the Rules. When the goods were discharged, most of the cases were found to have been damaged by entry of seawater which had entered the hold through defective storm-valve covers. Before the outward journey to London, the carriers had appointed a reputable firm of ship-repairers to open the storm-valve covers for inspection. After the inspection, the fitter employed by the repairers failed to replace the covers in their proper position. It was found as a fact that no visual inspection would have detected the mistake. The seawater had entered the hold on the return journey. The damage to the cases was found to have been due to the negligence of the fitter.

The House of Lords held that the negligence of the independent contractor was also the carrier's. It was irrelevant that the carrier had been diligent in his choice of independent contractor. Similarly, it was immaterial that the work required technical or special knowledge and that the mistake was not visible. The carrier was, therefore, found liable under Art. III r. 1. The duty to exercise due diligence to provide a seaworthy ship is non-delegable and arises at the time the Rules apply to the voyage and applies until the vessel sails (Art. III r. 1).

In *Maxine Footwear* v *Canadian Government Merchant Marine* [1959] AC 589 the vessel caught fire after P's goods had been loaded. The fire was found to have been due to the negligence of the carrier's servants, who had attempted to unfreeze a pipe with a torch. The carrier sought to escape liability by arguing that the duty to exercise due diligence in the provision of a cargoworthy ship ceased once the loading process was complete. The carrier conceded that the duty to exercise due diligence to provide a seaworthy ship arose on sailing. Between those two times, the carrier argued that there was no duty. The court held that Art. III r. 1 meant the period from at least the beginning of the loading process which ran continuously until the voyage began. It was held, however, in *The Makedonia* [1962] P 190 that the duty does not extend for the duration of the voyage. It ends, and is discharged either properly or in breach, at the beginning of the contractual voyage; see also *Leesh River Tea* v *British India Steam Navigation* [1976] 2 QB 250.

The duty to exercise due diligence in the provision of a seaworthy ship applies to the particular cargo and voyage under contract. Evidence that the ship was unseaworthy before that time is strictly irrelevant. The question to be considered is whether at the time of the particular contract to carry the particular cargo, the ship was still seaworthy.

8.5.1   The Meaning of Unseaworthiness

The carrier's obligation of due diligence is set out in Art. III r. 1:

> The carrier shall be bound before and at the beginning of the voyage to exercise due diligence to:
> (1)   Make the ship seaworthy.
> (2)   Properly man, equip and supply the ship.
> (3)   Make the holds, refrigerating and cool chambers, and all other parts of the ship in which the goods are carried, fit and safe for their reception, carriage, and preservation.

The obligation, therefore, includes the following.

8.5.1.1   *The Ship must be Cargoworthy (Art. III r. 1(c))*
The ship must be fit to receive the cargo at the time the process of loading the goods begins until the start of the voyage.

In *Tattersall* v *National SS* (1884) 12 QBD 297 the vessel in question had recently carried cattle suffering from foot and mouth disease. The carrier had not properly disinfected the hold before a new cargo of cattle was loaded. The new cattle contracted the disease. The court held that the ship was unseaworthy because it was not cargoworthy.

In *Ciampa* v *British Steam Navigation Co.* [1915] 2 KB 774 a vessel was en route for Naples. It failed, however, to obtain a clean bill of health from the authorities at the previous port of call. At Naples the ship took on a cargo of lemons. The contractual voyage for the lemons was from Naples to London with Marseilles as an intermediate port. Under French law, the ship had to be fumigated because of the absence of the clean bill of health. The fumigation process damaged the lemons. The carrier sought to escape liability by relying on Art. IV r. 2(g) (restraint of princes) arguing that the fumigation process was a form of administrative action and, therefore, absolved him from liability for the resulting damage. The court held the carrier liable because the ship was unseaworthy. The fact that the ship would be fumigated at Marseilles meant that from the outset the ship was not cargoworthy.

In *The Good Friend* [1984] 2 Lloyd's Rep 586 it was held that the ship must be reasonably fit to receive, carry and be able to deliver the cargo to the destination at the time of shipping. A live insect infestation prevented the latter.

8.5.1.2   *The Ship must be Fit in its Design, Structure, Condition and in its Equipment ('equipping' includes fuelling) to Encounter the Ordinary Perils of the Voyage*

At common law the doctrine of stages means that a ship is seaworthy at the first stage if it has sufficient fuel and equipment to reach the second stage. The same obligations then apply afresh for the second stage of the voyage and so on.

Under the Rules the obligation to exercise due diligence to provide a seaworthy ship arises and ceases at the first port of shipment. The obligation does not resurrect itself at the second stage. If the Rules apply at the first port of shipment, then they apply for the whole voyage in respect of cargo loaded there. If the ship was seaworthy there, it does not matter that the ship becomes unseaworthy later. Cargo loaded at an intermediate port will not be subject to the Rules, unless it independently satisfies the conditions for their application. If by then the ship had become unseaworthy, this would only affect the second cargo.

The Rules recognise the possibility of voyages in stages in the sense that provided that the ship has sufficient fuel and provision to reach the second stage, and that adequate arrangements have been made for the ship to be refuelled and stocked at the intermediate port, the obligation to exercise due diligence will have been satisfied.

8.5.1.3   *The Ship must have Competent and Sufficient Crew, and the Master must be Aware of the Idiosyncrasies of his Ship*

In *Standard Oil* v *Clan Line* [1924] AC 100 the owner of a ship of special design had omitted to inform his master that when fully loaded the ballast tanks had to be full. In ignorance the master ordered the tanks to be emptied. The ship consequently sank. It was held that the ship was unseaworthy at the time the voyage began because the master was unaware of how to run the ship. The shipowner was found not to have exercised due diligence since he had not properly informed the master; see also *Hong Kong Fir Shipping Co. Ltd* v *Kawasaki Kisen Kaisha Ltd* [1962] 2 QB 26.

8.5.1.4   A Ship is Unseaworthy if the Cargo is Stowed so as to Endanger the Safety of the Ship

In *Elder Dempster* v *Paterson Zochonis* [1924] AC 522 the ship loaded a cargo of oil in casks at the bottom of the hold. The vessel had no 'between decks'. When a heavier cargo was loaded on top, the casks broke and the oil was lost. The bill of lading protected the carrier against loss caused by bad stowage. The House of Lords held that the loss of the oil was due to bad stowage and not unseaworthiness because the ship was structurally·fit to receive the cargo; and the manner of storage did not endanger the ship.

In *Kopitoff* v *Wilson* (1876) 1 QBD 377 the ship stowed a number of armour plates. In a storm one of the plates broke loose and penetrated the side of the ship. It was held that the storm was an ordinary peril of the sea on that voyage at that time of year and it was as a result of the bad stowage that the ship was lost. It was not fit to encounter the ordinary perils of the sea, because the stowage endangered the ship and not just other cargo, so the ship was unseaworthy.

8.5.2   The Burden of Proof in Art. III r. 1

Any cargo-owner alleging a breach of the duty of the carrier to exercise due diligence in the provision of a seaworthy ship must establish actual unseaworthiness; and a causal connection between the unseaworthiness and the loss or damage; see *Minister of Food* v *Reardon Smith Line* [1951] 2 Lloyd's Rep 265.

This is illustrated in *The Europa* [1908] P 84. A ship carrying sugar collided with the dock wall at the port of destination. This caused a water-pipe to burst. Water entered the upper decks and damaged the sugar. On the upper decks, the pipes which would have discharged the water had been unplugged before the sugar was loaded. The water as a result entered the lower holds. The carrier did not dispute his liability for the damage to the sugar in the lower holds on the grounds of unseaworthiness. It was held, however, that the unseaworthiness was not a cause of the loss of the sugar in the upper holds. The carrier escaped liability by relying on the exception of peril of the sea: the collision with the dock wall.

The cargo-owner need not show that unseaworthiness was the sole cause of the loss. It is sufficient if it is proved on the balance of probabilities to have been one of a number of competing causes.

In *Monarch* v *Karlshamns* [1949] AC 196 a British ship was chartered for a voyage from Manchuria to Karlshamms in Sweden. Due to delays resulting from the admitted unseaworthiness of the vessel, the ship failed to reach Karlshamms before the outbreak of the Second World War. The British Admiralty prevented the ship from continuing on to Karlshamms. The authorities ordered that the ship put in and discharge its cargo at Glasgow. The purchaser of the cargo incurred expenses in forwarding the cargo on neutral ships. The charterparty, however, incorporated a 'war-risks clause', exonerating the shipowner from loss resulting from his compliance with orders given by the authorities of the nation under whose flag the ship was registered. The carrier argued that the immediate cause of the change of destination was the order of the British Admiralty. Before that order had been given, the ship had been repaired. There was nothing in the physical condition of the ship preventing her from reaching Karlshamms. The sole cause of the determination of the voyage, by his reasoning, was the action of the British Government. It was held that unseaworthiness was a cause of the diversion to Glasgow, because the carrier ought to have foreseen at the time the contract was made that war might shortly break out. Any prolongation of the voyage might cause the loss or diversion of the ship. The carrier was, therefore, liable for the transshipment costs which flowed naturally and in the ordinary course of things from the initial unseaworthiness. The unseaworthiness was, therefore, a cause notwithstanding that the defect no longer existed at the time the loss was actually incurred.

In *Smith, Hogg* v *Black Sea & Baltic Insurance* [1940] AC 997 the vessel began its contractual voyage with a list on account of an overload of deck cargo. The ship was unstable and, therefore, unseaworthy. It put in at an intermediate port for refuelling. The master failed to remove the deck cargo during the fuelling process. The ship listed over too far and sank. In an action against the carrier the latter sought to rely on the exception of an ordinary peril: the acts or defaults of his servants in Art. IV(2)(a). The carrier was found liable. The master's acts could have done no harm to the ship had it been seaworthy. The unseaworthiness was, therefore, a cause. Lord Wright thought that unseaworthiness could never be the sole cause of loss. Unseaworthiness is a condition and not an operating event. There would always be connecting causes. Their Lordships drew no distinction between the negligence of the master and an innocent act as being one of the connecting causes with unseaworthiness. Hence they thought that a negligent act would not be a *novus actus interveniens*. Provided that the cargo-owner proved the causal connection between unseaworthiness and the loss or damage despite the existence of co-operating causes, the carrier would be liable unless he can show that he had exercised due diligence (Art. IV r. 1). The obligation to provide a seaworthy ship is, therefore, an 'overriding obligation'. Cargo-owners, therefore, always look for a breach of Art. III r. 1, as this then shifts the burden of proof on to the carrier.

8.5.3   Innominate Term

The contractual obligation imposed on a carrier to provide a seaworthy vessel was considered to be an innominate term by the Court of Appeal in the *Hong Kong Fir* case (8.5.1.3). There, Diplock LJ held that the express or implied obligation of seaworthiness is a contractual undertaking one breach of which may amount to a breach of condition, and another may amount merely to a breach of warranty. The distinction is in the effect of the breach on the performance of the contract.

In the case itself, a ship was chartered for 24 months. The charterparty contained an express undertaking to provide a seaworthy ship (the Rules do not apply to charterparties). The ship was unseaworthy at the beginning of the voyage. The engine room staff were insufficient in number and incompetent. As a result there was a 20-week delay during which time the freight markets fell. The charterers sought to terminate the contract on account of the carrier's repudiatory breach in failing to provide a seaworthy vessel and to proceed with due expedition. The shipowner brought an action for wrongful repudiation. The court found that the unseaworthiness did not on the facts go to the root of the contract. Also it was held that the delay was not such as to destroy the commercial purpose of the contract of carriage. The contract, therefore, remained alive, the breaches operating merely as breaches of warranty. The shipowner, therefore, succeeded in his claim for the contractual rates of freight, subject to the carrier's set-off for the loss caused by the 20-week delay.

8.6 THE SECOND OBLIGATION: ART. III R. 2

Article III r. 2 imposes on the carrier a duty to 'properly and carefully load, stow, carry, keep, care for and discharge the goods'. This does not mean that the carrier is actually under a contractual obligation to load and stow the goods. The shipper of the goods may have agreed to load and stow the goods, for example. If, however, the carrier has undertaken to load and stow the goods he must do so properly and carefully; see *The Coral* (8.4). Furthermore where the shipper actually assents or superintends the loading and stowing of the cargo, if the cargo is subsequently damaged by virtue of the loading process undertaken, or the method/place of stowage, the shipper may be estopped from denying that he approved of the loading and stowing and he cannot claim that the carrier was in breach of Art. III r. 2; see *Ismail* v *Polish Ocean Line* [1976] 1 All ER 902.

8.6.1 'Properly'

The tasks listed in Art. III r. 2 must be properly carried out. Therefore, a recognised system must be used which must be suitable having regard to everything which the carrier knows or ought to know about that particular cargo; see *Albacora* v *Westcott* [1966] 2 Lloyd's Rep 53. Therefore, the cargoes which may taint each other should not be stowed together; see *The Thorsa* [1916] P 257.

8.6.2 'Carefully'

This requires the carrier to take reasonable skill and care in using the established, suitable system referred to in 8.6.1. In the same way that the carrier cannot escape liability for lack of due diligence under Art. III r. 1 by delegating the responsibility for the task to someone else, so he cannot escape liability under Art. III r. 2 by appointing someone competent who is, in fact, negligent in his use of the recognised system. Therefore, in *International Packers* v *Ocean Steamship* [1955] 2 Lloyd's Rep the carriers were liable for loss incurred as a result of negligent advice given by surveyors.

8.6.3 The Burden of Proof in Art. III r. 2

Article III r. 2 is expressly subject to Art. IV rr. 1 and 2. The burden is initially on the cargo-owner to show that the goods had been shipped as set out in the bill of lading, and then to show that they have not been delivered or that they have been delivered damaged. The cargo-owner is, of course, helped by the estoppels in Art. III r. 3 etc., and under COGSA 1992 if applicable.

Hobhouse J in *The Torenia* [1983] 2 Lloyd's Rep 210 thought that it was only because the contract of carriage is a form of bailment that the cargo-owner claimant may set up a sustainable cause of action by proving the non-delivery of the goods. Negligence need not be proved. The legal burden instead shifts on to the carrier to show that the cause of the loss or damage falls into one of the excepted perils.

The facts of the case were as follows. A 21-year-old ship encountered rough seas when travelling from Cuba to Denmark. Water entered the ship as a result of a major failure in the vessel's port side. The ship sank five days later. The carrier relied upon the exceptions in Art. IV r. 2(c) — perils of the sea — and Art. IV r. 2(p) — loss due to a defect in the ship's structure which was latent and which could not be discovered by due diligence.

It was held that the peril of the sea, the incursion of seawater, was no more than one cause co-operating with another, the defective structure of the ship. Since the carrier had failed to discharge the legal burden of proving that the defect of the ship's structure was latent, he remained liable for the whole loss.

> Where loss is caused by the concurrent effect of an excepted and non-excepted peril, then there is only an exception of liability if the excepted peril was the only cause. If there is in addition the operation of the non-excepted peril, then mere pleading and proving of the former is not sufficient.

There was no argument in the case that there had been a breach of Art. III r. 1. The carrier had succeeded in establishing that there was no legal burden on him to show the exercise of due diligence in the provision of a seaworthy ship unless the cargo-owner had discharged the burden of showing actual unseaworthiness, which was a cause of the loss. The unseaworthiness of the vessel had not been raised by the cargo-owner.

At common law, if there is no actual unseaworthiness and the carrier is able to rely on an exclusion clause, the burden then shifts back to the cargo-owner to show that the carrier had in any event been negligent in carrying out his contractual duty; see *The Glendarroch* [1894] P 226. There is, in effect, at common law an implied duty to take all reasonable care in the carriage of the goods, which would override all other causes.

Both Scrutton and Carver, the leading textbook writers, consider that the rule is the same under the Rules as at common law. Negligence and unseaworthiness are treated as exceptions within the exceptions. In the event that the carrier has excluded all causes of the loss, the burden then falls on to the cargo-owner claimant to show negligence. The only exception to this, obviously, is when the exception in the Rules, in Art. IV r. 2(a), (p) and (q), requires the carrier to prove that he had acted with due diligence. The pattern of proof is therefore as follows:

(a)   The cargo-owner must show that the goods were shipped and did not arrive.

(b)   The carrier must show that he falls within one or more of the excepted perils.

(c)   The cargo-owner would then have to show that the carrier had been negligent, provided that the excepted peril within which the carrier falls did not require him to prove the exercise of due diligence. Alternatively, the cargo-owner would have to show that the ship was in any event actually unseaworthy which contributed to the loss.

Lloyd J held:

> The cargo owner must raise a *prima facie* case against the ship owner that the cargo was shipped in good condition and arrived damaged. The ship owner can meet that by relying on an exception. The cargo owner may then displace this by showing unseaworthiness at the start of the voyage and that the unseaworthiness was a cause of the loss. If the court finds that there was unseaworthiness, the ship owner can only succeed by showing that this was not due to lack of due diligence on their part.

8.7   THE EXEMPTIONS

The exemptions on which the carrier can rely are to be found in Art. IV r. 2(a)–(q):

> Neither the carrier nor the ship shall be responsible for loss or damage arising or resulting from:
>
> (a)   Act, neglect, or default of the master, mariner, pilot or the servants of the carrier in the navigation or in the management of the ship.
>
> (b)   Fire, unless caused by the actual fault or privity of the carrier.
>
> (c)   Perils, dangers and accidents of the sea or other navigable waters.
>
> (d)   Act of God.
>
> (e)   Act of war.
>
> (f)   Act of public enemies.
>
> (g)   Arrest or restraint of princes, rulers or people or seizure under legal process.
>
> (h)   Quarantine restrictions.
>
> (i)   Act or omission of the shipper or owner of the goods, his agent or representative.
>
> (j)   Strikes or lockouts or stoppage or restraint of labour from whatever cause, whether partial or general.
>
> (k)   Riot and civil commotions.
>
> (l)   Saving or attempting to save life or property at sea.
>
> (m)   Wastage in bulk or weight or any other loss or damage arising from inherent defect, quality or vice of the goods.
>
> (n)   Insufficiency of packing.
>
> (o)   Insufficiency or inadequacy of marks.

(p)   Latent defects not discoverable by due diligence.

(q)   Any other causes arising without the actual fault or privity of the carrier, or without the fault or neglect of the agents or servants of the carrier, but the burden of proof shall be on the person claiming the benefit of this exception to show that neither the actual fault or privity of the carrier nor the fault or neglect of the agents or servants of the carrier contributed to the loss or damage.

Some of these exemptions can now be examined in detail:

8.7.1   Act, Neglect or Default of the Master, etc.

The acts of neglect or default which are covered are those which endanger the ship, not merely those which affect the preservation of the cargo. In *Gosse Millard* v *Canadian Government Merchant Marine* [1929] AC 223 the hatches of a vessel were left open so that water entered the hold and damaged a cargo of tinplate. The cargo owners sued the carrier for breach of Art. III r. 2. The carrier failed in his attempt to rely on Art. IV r. 2(a) because his neglect of the tinplate endangered only the cargo, not the vessel.

In *The Washington* [1976] 2 Lloyd's Rep 453 whilst the master's decision to maintain his course and speed, in spite of reports of bad weather, was negligent, it was not an act of neglect or default for which exemption could be claimed under this paragraph as it did not endanger the vessel, only the cargo.

Since the carrier must show that he has exercised due diligence in discharging the obligations imposed on him by the rules, it follows that this exemption cannot be invoked by him for acts of personal negligence. See also *The Mekhanik Evgrafov and The Ivan Derbenev* [1987] 2 Lloyd's Rep 634 and the carrier's inability to rely on the exceptions in Art. IV r. 2(a).

8.7.2   Fire

Under this exception, the carrier will not be liable for loss or damage resulting from fire, even though caused by the negligence of his servants or agents. The carrier will be liable if the loss was caused by his own 'actual fault or privity' or if the fire resulted from unseaworthiness of the ship in breach of Art. III r. 1.

The requirement as to 'actual fault or privity of the carrier' requires a connection between the activities or knowledge of the legal carrier and the fire. In *Lennards* v *Asiatic Petroleum* [1915] AC 705, a decision under s. 502 of the Merchant Shipping Act 1894, fire was caused as a direct result of the failure of the managing director of the shipowning company to give instructions on defective boilers of which he had knowledge. Therefore, the carrier could not show that the fire took place without his actual fault or privity, it being the direct result of the omission of the managing director of the shipowning company.

Where the vessel is a British ship then the carrier may escape liability under s. 18, Merchant Shipping Act 1979 (see 8.16).

8.7.3 Perils, Dangers and Accidents

It is not every action of the wind and the waves which constitutes a peril of the sea within this exception. In *The Tilia Gorthorn* [1985] 1 Lloyd's Rep 552 Force 10 on the Beaufort Scale did not constitute a peril of the sea as it was within the contemplation of the parties. Therefore, the carrier was unable to rely on this exemption to exclude his liability when a deck cargo was washed overboard. He was, however, able to avoid liability altogether since the court held that he exercised due diligence in the supply of adequate equipment to lash the deck cargo, as a matter of trade practice.

The ordinary action of the wind and waves are not included. Only the unforeseen action of the sea which could not be protected against will constitute a peril of the sea. Therefore, the normal wear and tear which is expected from the journey will not be covered; see *Wilson Sons* v *Cargo ex Xantho* (1887) 12 App Cas 503. The exemption is intended to cover 'the perils of the sea, not the perils of journeying'; see *Hamilton* v *Pandorf* (1887) 12 App Cas 518. It is impossible to devise an absolute test which can be applied in order to determine what is, and what is not, a peril of the sea. Simply because the damage is caused by seawater does not make the cause a peril of the sea. In *Sassoon* v *Western Assurance* (1923) 16 Ll LR 129 damage occurred because seawater percolated through the vessel's rotten hull. The damage was not caused by a peril of the sea, but by the rotten condition of the hull.

It is clear from the decided authorities that the types of perils covered are those which are peculiar to the sea and could not have occurred on land: stranding, listing (*The Stranna* [1938] 1 All ER 458), collision, severe storms and seawater. Therefore, perils which cause damage whilst the ship is at sea but are not, in fact, peculiar to the sea, will not be covered, e.g. cockroaches and rainwater. Yet, somewhat inconsistently, the exemption will protect against damage resulting from the ship's machinery or means of navigation.

Often there will be another cause as well as the perils of the sea. The carrier will only be able to rely on the exclusion if the perils of the sea was the dominant or proximate cause of the loss or damage; see *The Torenia* [1983] 2 Lloyd's Rep 210. Thus in *The Thrunsco* [1897] P 301 the exemption covered damage to cargo due to overheating after the hatches were closed during a bout of bad weather.

8.7.4 An Act of God

The exception 'act of God' includes any accident which the shipowner can show that is due to natural causes, directly or exclusively, without human intervention, and that it could not have been prevented by any amount of foresight, pains and care, reasonably to be expected of him; see *Nugent* v *Smith* (1876) 1 CPD 423 at p. 444 *per* James LJ.

8.7.5   An Act or Omission

Act or omission of the cargo-owner or shipper is frequently relied on to exempt the carrier from loss or damage which results from instructions or information given to him by the shipper of the goods, on which he relies and which, in fact, result in damage to those goods. In *Ismail* v *Polish Ocean Line* [1976] 1 All ER 902 a cargo of potatoes arrived in a damaged condition because the master relied on information given to him by the agent of the shipper, that as the potatoes were packed in bags they needed no more packaging.

8.7.6   Inherent Vice

Inherent vice is relied on where the damage to the cargo results from the internal condition of the goods rather than their external circumstances, for example, oxidisation or rusting of metals, expansion of orange juice, spontaneous combustion of hemp, internal moisture levels of certain cargo, discoloration of foodstuffs, etc. In *Berk* v *Style* [1956] 1 QB 180 it was decided that insufficient packing was also inherent vice if it was so insufficient that it made the goods unable to withstand the ordinary incidents of transit. It makes no difference whether we treat insufficient packing as inherent vice or not, since insufficient packing is itself exempted under Art. IV r. 2(n). The decision in *Berk* v *Style* was taken at a time when, for marine insurance purposes, an insurer was exempt from liability for loss or damage caused by inherent vice but not insufficient packing.

8.7.7   Insufficiency of Packing

Whether the packing is insufficient is obviously a question of fact in every case, which may be resolved by reference to trade practice. However, if the goods have always been packed in a particular way and have not suffered damage, this may raise a presumption of fact in favour of the adequacy of the packing, and the carrier may be able to prove that the damage occurred without his fault; see *The Lucky Wave* [1985] 1 Lloyd's Rep 80.

8.7.8   Any Other Causes

As the words 'any other causes' are used and not 'any other cause whatsoever', the exceptions in r. 2(q) should be interpreted as being *ejusdem generis* with the exceptions from (a) to (p), provided there is any genus which will embrace all the exceptions. But it is difficult to imagine any genus which would embrace them all, and therefore it seems necessary to give these words the wider interpretation and thus to exclude the responsibility of the carrier in all cases where neither he nor his servants are at fault.

Agents or servants include the servants of an independent stevedore in r. 2(q). The dishonest act of the carrier's servants or agents (such as theft by a stevedore) is not a 'cause arising without the fault or neglect of the agents or servants of the carrier' unless it takes place outside the performance of the duties entrusted to the servant or agent by the carrier. Thus the carrier cannot escape liability under r. 1 (q) for the theft of goods by a servant or agent charged with the custody of the goods. But where a stevedore stole part of the ship's equipment, so rendering it vulnerable to the perils of the sea, the carrier was held to be protected by r. 2(q).

8.8 THE DUTY OF THE CARRIER TO ISSUE A BILL OF LADING: ART. III R. 3

These exclusions must be read in connection with Art. III r. 3–8 which set out the rights and duties of the carrier and shipper in respect of the bill of lading. Article III r. 3 provides:

After receiving the goods into his charge the carrier or the master or agent of the carrier shall, on demand of the shipper, issue to the shipper a bill of lading showing among other things:

(a) The loading marks necessary for the identification of the goods as the same as furnished in writing by the shipper before the loading of such goods starts provided such marks are shown or otherwise stamped clearly upon the goods if uncovered, or on the cases or coverings in which such goods are contained, in such a manner as may ordinarily remain legible until the end of the voyage.

(b) Either the number of packages or pieces, or the quantity, or weight as the case may be as furnished in writing by the shipper.

(c) The apparent order and condition of the goods.

Clearly the carrier is not obliged to issue a bill of lading, containing information which he cannot see or cannot check. Article III r. 3 additionally states:

Provided that no carrier, master or agent of the carrier shall be bound to state or show in the bill of lading, any marks, number, quantity or weight which he has reasonable ground for suspecting not accurately to represent the goods actually received, or which he has no reasonable means of checking.

Therefore, not only can the carrier refrain from issuing the bill containing unverifiable statements, but he need not issue a bill with facts which he believes to be inaccurately represented.

If the shipper so demands, then the bill of lading must also be a 'shipped bill' showing the goods to be actually on board rather than merely received for shipment. Article III r. 7 provides:

> After the goods are loaded the bill of lading to be issued by the carrier, master, or agent of the carrier to the shipper, shall, if the shipper so demands, be a 'shipped bill' of lading, provided that if the shipper shall have previously taken up any document of title to such goods, he shall surrender the same as against the issue of the shipped bill of lading, but at the option of the carrier such document of title may be noted at the port of shipment by the carrier, master, or agent with the name or names of the ship or ships upon which the goods have been shipped and the date or dates of shipment, and when so noted if it shows the particulars mentioned in paragraph 3 of Art. III, shall for the purpose of this article be deemed to constitute a 'shipped bill' of lading.

Thus, where a shipper demands a bill of lading from the carrier, the carrier need not make out a new 'shipped' bill, but he can convert any received for shipment bill already issued into a shipped bill simply by noting the progress of the goods since they were 'received for shipment', in accordance with the provisions of Art. III r. 7.

Once the carrier has issued a shipped bill of lading it is, as we have seen, *prima facie* evidence that the goods have been shipped in the condition stated in the bill of lading. As against a third party who takes the bill of lading pursuant to a contract of sale, the carrier may also be estopped from denying the truth of the representations made in the bill of lading.

Article III r. 4 recognises these effects arising from the issuance of a bill of lading. Article III r. 4 states:

> Such a bill of lading shall be *prima facie* evidence of the receipt by the carrier of the goods as therein described in accordance with paragraph 3(a), (b) and (c). However, proof to the contrary shall not be admissible when the bill of lading has been transferred to a third party acting in good faith.

It is important to note the differences between the position of the shipper of the goods and the transferee of the bill of lading. It is also important to remember that these are merely provisions relating to the evidence which may or may not be adduced in proceedings concerning the carriage under the bill of lading.

Where goods have been delivered in a defective condition, or there has been a short delivery, and the shipper brings an action against the carrier, the carrier may adduce evidence that the goods were in fact loaded on board his vessel in a defective condition or that the full quantity of goods was not in fact loaded. The carrier will, nevertheless, have to explain why he issued a bill of lading which contained false statements.

If, however, the bill of lading has been transferred to a third party, such as a buyer under a c.i.f. contract, the carrier will not be able to adduce evidence in an action brought by the third party, to show that the goods were loaded in a defective condition or that all the goods were not in fact shipped. With regard to the question of the quantity of goods shipped the third party might also be able to rely on s. 4, COGSA 1992 (see 7.5.5).

The estoppel generated by the Rules differs from that at common law, as there is no need for the transferee to show reliance on the bill. In practice this distinction is insignificant as reliance will be presumed where a third party takes delivery of the bill of lading pursuant to a contract of sale.

Where the carrier has been ordered to pay damages to a third party transferee because of inaccuracies in the marks, number, quantity or weight provided by the shipper, the carrier is entitled to seek an indemnity from the shipper in respect of those damages (Art. III r. 5). This may create problems when goods are shipped in containers and a bill of lading is issued in respect of the container. In such circumstances such representations as may have been made in the bill of lading may relate not to the goods but the container; see *Marbig Rexel Pty Ltd* v *ABC Container Line NV, The TNT Express* [1992] 2 Lloyd's Rep 636 (Supreme Court of New South Wales).

As can be seen in Art. III r. 3 above, the carrier can be asked by the shipper to issue a bill of lading which shows the leading marks on the goods necessary for the identification of the goods. The carrier cannot be compelled to issue such a bill of lading if the marks are not shown clearly on the goods themselves, nor if the marks are such as will not remain visible and legible until the end of the voyage. Also the carrier need not comply if he has no means of checking that the marks on the goods are as the shipper describes, or if he suspects that the marks on the bill do not tally with the marks on the goods.

Finally, the shipper can demand a bill of lading which states the apparent condition of the goods on receipt. This is confined to a reasonable external examination. In *Silver* v *Ocean SS Co.* [1930] 1 KB 416 the carrier issued a bill of lading stating that the goods had been shipped in apparent good condition. This representation estopped the carrier as against the transferee of the bill of lading from proving that the tins of frozen eggs were, in fact, dented on receipt. It did not estop him from saying that the cans had pin-sized punctures.

In any circumstances where goods arrive damaged or are lost and there is, therefore, inconsistency between the cargo as delivered and that as described in the bill of lading:

> ... the notice of loss or damage and the general nature of such loss or damage [is to] be given in writing to the carrier or his agent at the port of discharge before or at the time of removal of the goods into the custody of the person entitled to delivery thereof under the contract of carriage or, if the loss or damage be not apparent, within three days ... [otherwise] such removal shall be *prima facie* evidence of the delivery by the carrier of goods as described in the bill of lading. (Art. III r. 6.)

8.9 CONTRACTS OF INDEMNITY

As appears from 8.8 the carrier, when asked to sign a clean bill of lading, may find himself in a difficult position if he feels that the condition of the goods does not warrant a clean bill of lading. If he obliges, he may find himself liable to the transferee of the bill of lading, if he refuses he inconveniences his client, the shipper, who may have difficulty in dealing with a claused bill of lading. In these circumstances the shipper may offer, or the carrier may request, a contract of indemnity in return for a clean bill of lading. Two situations must be distinguished: first, where the carrier knows that the terms he is representing on the bill of lading are false; and, secondly, where he has genuine, but unproven, misgivings as to the correctness of the terms requested by the shipper.

The courts have not shown much sympathy to the first type of indemnity on the grounds that the consideration moving from the carrier is illegal, namely, deliberately misstating the position with the intention to deceive innocent third parties subsequently dealing with the bill; see *Brown Benkinson* v *Percy Dalton* [1957] 2QB 621.

This, however, does not cover the second type of indemnity. Lord Morris in *Percy Dalton* thought that if the carrier was suspicious of the quality of the goods in respect of the terms he was being asked to represent, it might be perfectly reasonable and good commercial practice to issue the bill of lading against a contract of indemnity as valid security for his unproven suspicions. If such were the case, the courts would hold the parties to their obligations.

In *Naviera Mogor* v *Société Metallurgique de Normandie* [1987] 1 Lloyd's Rep 456 charterers shipped their own consignment of steel wire. The transferees of the wire succeeded in recovering damages from the shipowner. The shipowner was unable to adduce evidence that the steel wire had been damaged prior to shipment and had issued a clean bill of lading. The shipowner was, therefore, estopped from leading evidence in contradiction of the bill of lading against the transferee. The shipowner's agents had issued the bill of lading when ignorant of the defective condition of the goods because the master of the ship who had loaded the cargo had failed to note the condition of the goods on the mate's receipt. The shipowner sought to recover the loss from the charterer by arguing:

(a)   The charterer was in breach of his contract with the shipowner by presenting for signature a bill of lading which incorrectly stated the condition of the goods.

(b)   The charterer had impliedly undertaken to indemnify the shipowner against the latter's liability under the bill of lading signed at the former's request.

The Court of Appeal held respectively:

(a)   The charterer had not breached his contract by tendering a bill of lading containing misstatements. The act of the master in not noting the condition of the goods was the cause of the shipowner's loss and not the charterer's act. In short, the master's negligence was taken as a *novus actus interveniens*.

(b)   The implication of a contract of indemnity was not automatic, but always depended upon the particular facts and the terms of the underlying contractual relationships. On the facts of *Naviera Mogor*, since there was a clean mate's receipt from the master, the Court of Appeal refused to accept that the charterer in tendering the bill of lading had undertaken to indemnify.

Hence there is, it seems, scope for an implied contract of indemnity, when there is no actual knowledge of false statements on the part of the carrier, though whether a contract of indemnity will be implied or not will depend on the facts of each case. The negligence of the master may in any event prevent such an implied contract from operating.

In the USA such letters of indemnity are contrary to s. 3(8), US Carriage of Goods by Sea Act 1936; see *Hellenic Lines Ltd* v *Chemoleum Corporation* [1972] 1 Lloyd's Rep 350. The claimants' carrier issued a clean bill of lading to the defendants in respect of a shipment of bagged fertiliser in a leaky condition, under a letter of indemnity from the defendants. The claimants sued the defendants for the cost of rebagging the goods and other expenses at the port of destination after incurring liability to the consignee.

On the defendants' motion for summary judgment, based on the clean bill of lading, the Supreme Court of New York ordered that the claimants were not estopped from proving the true conditions of the shipment. On appeal it was held by the New York Supreme Court that the letter of indemnity contravened public policy as expressed in s. 3(8), Carriage of Goods by Sea Act 1936 and should not be enforced. The court was also of the view that in any event the claimants could sue in the tort of negligence, using the letter of indemnity as an admission.

8.10 TIME LIMIT: ART. III R. 6

The carrier and the ship will be discharged from all liability whatsoever in respect of the goods unless suit is brought within one year of their delivery or the date when they should have been delivered, unless that period is extended by express agreement between the parties after the cause of action has arisen (Art. III r. 6).

In *Empressa Cubana Importadora* v *Octavia Shipping, The Kefalonia Wind* [1986] 1 Lloyd's Rep 273 a bulk cargo of maize in three parcels was damaged as a result of an incursion of seawater through the hatch covers, during a period of stormy weather. The claimants issued a claim form in respect of one parcel, nine months after the damage and within the statutory period prescribed by Art. III r. 6.

They subsequently sought to amend the claim form outside the limitation period, to claim for damage to the remainder of the cargo. The Commercial Court held that the claimants' claims for damage to the remainder were not time barred as a result of Art. III r. 6. The actions in respect of which the claimants now sought to claim were not mentioned in the original claim form, but since they arose from or included facts which gave rise to the cause of action that was claimed in the original claim form, the amendment would be permitted. This would be treated as though it was made at the date of the claim form, even though it might otherwise have been time barred. This English procedural rule regarding the amendment of a claim form normally operates in the context of statutory limitation periods the effect of which is to bar a remedy. After a certain period of time, Art. III r. 6 by comparison does not bar a remedy, rather it extinguishes a right. However, the court was of the opinion that this was no sufficient reason to exclude the normal procedural rule.

Two recent decisions of the Commercial Court indicate the importance of ensuring that the right parties are joined in an action under a contract of carriage to which Art. III, r. 6 applies.

In *Transworld Oil (USA) Inc* v *Minos Compania Naviera SA, The Leni* [1992] 2 Lloyd's Rep 48 a claim form had been issued naming four companies as claimants including Transworld Oil Ltd the parent of, and Transworld Oil (USA) Inc the subsidiary of, Transworld Oil Inc. The claim was for short delivery of two cargoes of oil made under bills of lading issued by the defendant shipowners which incorporated the Hague-Visby Rules. The claim form was subsequently amended by the deletion of three of the claimants leaving only Transworld Oil (USA) Inc and the claim form was then served. The defendant shipowners denied that Transworld Oil (USA) Inc had title to sue and, three and a half years after the expiry of the one year limitation period Transworld Oil Inc applied to be joined as a claimant. Judge Diamond QC thought that Art. III r. 6 should be construed in its international context, unconstrained by technical rules of English law, so as to give effect to the purpose which the Hague-Visby Rules were designed to achieve. Approaching the problem in this way, the judge thought that the mere fact that the action had been brought in the name of a party who had no title to sue did not mean that the action was a 'non-suit' and therefore outside the terms of Art. III r. 6. Nevertheless he found himself constrained by authority, namely *Compania Colombiana de Seguros* v *Pacific Steam Navigation Co.* [1963] 2 Lloyd's Rep 479 and *The Nordglimt* [1987] 2 Lloyd's Rep 470, and held that Art. III r. 6 provided a substantive defence to any claim by Transworld Oil Inc and that the court had no power to allow that company to be joined as a claimant.

In *Payabi* v *Armstel Shipping Corporation, The Jay Bola* [1992] 2 Lloyd's Rep 62 the action had been commenced against the wrong company. An action had been commenced by the claimants upon bills of lading, which incorporated the Hague Rules, in respect of damage to their goods by a fire on board the *Jay Bola*. The claim form issued named Oceanview Ltd as the defendant shipowner. After the time limit under Art. III r. 6 had expired, the claimants discovered that the *Jay Bola* had, prior to the voyage in question, been sold to Armstel Shipping Corporation. They therefore applied for and obtained leave to substitute Armstel Shipping Corporation as defendants in the action. Hobhouse J, in setting aside the leave granted, indicated that RSC Ord. 20 r. 5, which allowed such substitution, could not deprive a party of a substantive defence.

The absoluteness of the limitation r. in Art. III r. 6 was stressed by the Court of Appeal in *The Captain Gregos* [1990] 1 Lloyd's Rep 310. Unlike s. 33, Limitation Act 1980, there is no discretion in the court to waive the application of the limitation period. Consequently, where goods had been stolen whilst in the possession of the carrier, and a breach had been found of the carrier's duty properly to keep, care for etc., the goods in Art. III r. 2 of the Rules, the carrier will be discharged of all liability under the Rules unless the cargo owner brings his action within one year of his loss.

8.11 AVAILABILITY OF AN ACTION IN TORT

The definition of 'carrier' in Art. I(a) includes the owner or charterer who enters into a contract of carriage with a shipper. The carrier to which the Hague-Visby Rules refers is, therefore, the legal carrier.

Where the legal carrier is also the actual carrier the question arises as to whether the Hague-Visby Rules could be avoided by the cargo-owner commencing an action in tort. Where a contractual relationship exists between the parties which governs the matter with which the action is concerned, the courts are very reluctant to admit a tortious remedy; see *Tai Hing Cotton Mills* v *Kamsing Knitting* [1979] AC 91; *Greater Nottingham Co-op* v *Cementation Piling and Foundations Ltd* [1989] QB 71.

In any event the Hague-Visby Rules have a specific provision dealing with this problem. Article IV *bis* 1 provides:

The defences and limits of liability provided for in these Rules shall apply in any action against the carrier in respect of loss or damage to goods covered by a contract of carriage whether the action be founded in contract or tort.

Where the actual carrier is a different person from the legal carrier, he may be sued in tort and the problem in *Tai Hing* does not arise. Article IV *bis* 1 would not appear to apply as that provision refers to an action against the legal carrier, bearing in mind the definition of carrier found in Art. I(a). The actual carrier may, however, be able to rely on the terms of the bill of lading which may incorporate the Hague-Visby Rules, by relying on the decision of the House of Lords in *Elder Dempster* v *Paterson Zochonis* [1924] AC 522, where the master, who was employed by the shipowner, took goods on board and rendered the very services provided for in the bill of lading, and it was held that the proper inference was that the shipowner had received the goods into his possession on the terms of the bill of lading, even though, in this case, the shipowner was not a party to the bill of lading contract.

The question of third parties relying on the terms and conditions of the bill of lading is examined in more detail in **8.13**.

8.12 LIMITATION OF LIABILITY

8.12.1 Minimum Liability

If the Hague-Visby Rules apply, the effect of their application is to impose on the carrier a maximum level of liability in the event of loss or damage for which he is made liable to the shipper/consignee. The cargo owner does not recover this limit in every case. What he actually recovers is determined by the value of the goods at the place of arrival. Article IV r. 5(b) provides:

The total amount recoverable shall be calculated by reference to the value of such goods at the place and time at which the goods are discharged from the ship in accordance with the contract, or should have been so discharged.

If the goods are actually worth more than the upper limit prescribed by the rules, the shipper cannot recover more unless any of the exemptions given below apply. If they are worth less, then the shipper will recover their value in accordance with Art. IV r. 5(b). However, the carrier cannot reduce the upper limit for which he is liable. The measure of his liability is found in Art. IV r. 5(a) which states:

> ... neither the carrier nor the ship shall in any event be or become liable for any loss or damage to or in connection with the goods in an amount exceeding the equivalent of 666.67 units of account per package or unit or 2 units of account per kilo, of gross weight of the goods lost or damaged, whichever is the higher.

At 28 November 1984 the carrier's liability under this Article stood at £548.97 per package or unit and £1.65 per kilo of gross weight. The carrier cannot reduce this upper limit, for example, to £300. Such an attempt to reduce his liability will be void. He is at liberty to increase this level.

Article IV r. 5(g) provides:

> By agreement between the carrier, master or agent of the carrier, and the shipper, other maximum amounts than those mentioned in subparagraph (a) of this paragraph may be fixed, provided that no maximum amount so fixed shall be less than the appropriate maximum mentioned in that subparagraph.

Article V further provides:

> A carrier shall be at liberty to surrender in whole or in part all or any of his rights and immunities or to increase any of his responsibilities and obligations under these rules.

It is, therefore, permissible for the carrier to increase his liability above the levels set out in Art. IV r. 5(a) but he may not reduce it. Mention should be made of Art. III r. 8 which provides as follows:

> Any clause, covenant or agreement in a contract of carriage relieving the carrier or the ship from any liability for loss or damage to or in connection with goods, arising from negligence, fault or failure in the duties and obligations provided in the article or lessening such liability otherwise than as provided in these rules, shall be null and void and of no effect. A benefit of insurance in favour of the carrier or similar clause shall be deemed to be a clause relieving the carrier from liability.

An example of a case in which a clause purporting to lessen the liability below the levels set by the Hague-Visby Rules was held to be null and void is provided by the House of Lords decision in *The Hollandia* [1983] AC 565. In this case machinery was being shipped from Leith in Scotland to Bonaire in the Dutch West Indies. Carriage began on a Dutch vessel and then the machinery was transhipped on a Norwegian vessel. The bill of lading contained the following clause, selecting Dutch law as the proper law of the contract, and limiting the liability of the carrier below the level fixed by the Hague-Visby Rules:

The law of The Netherlands in which the Hague-Visby Rules as adopted by the Brussels Convention are incorporated with the exception of Art. 9 shall apply to this contract. The maximum liability per package is D.Fl. 1,250.

It also contained the following jurisdiction clause:

All actions under the present contract of carriage shall be brought before the Court of Amsterdam and no other court shall have jurisdiction with regard to any such action unless the carrier appeals to another jurisdiction or voluntarily submits himself thereto.

The machinery was damaged during unloading, and the shipper brought an action against the carrier in England which the carrier then attempted to stay on the grounds of the above clause. If he had succeeded then Dutch law would have determined his liability. Dutch law does not apply the Hague-Visby Rules, but its predecessor the Hague Rules. Whilst the carrier's liability under the former was £11,490, under the latter it was only £250. The House of Lords refused to grant a stay on the following grounds:

(a) Section 1(2), Carriage of Goods by Sea Act 1971 says that the rules have 'the force of law'. This means that they are given supremacy over every other bill of lading which is inconsistent with the rules or which derogates from the effect of them and which is, therefore, to be rejected.

(b) Article X applies 'to every bill of lading whatever'. Therefore, if the provisions of Art. X are complied with, the rules apply irrespective of the nationality of the ship, shipper, consignee, law of the flag or proper law of the contract.

(c) The choice of Dutch law as the proper law and the lessening of liability to D.Fl. 1,250, infringe Art. III r. 8. They are null and void because they are clauses by which the carrier attempts to lessen his liability below that provided by the Hague-Visby Rules.

The decision in *The Hollandia* must be compared with the decision of the Court of Appeal in *The Benarty* [1985] QB 325 in which the carrier successfully relied upon Art. VII which provides that:

The provisions of these Rules shall not affect the rights and obligations of the carrier under any statute for the time being in force, relating to the limitation of the liability of owners of sea-going vessels.

In *The Benarty* the bills of lading contained clauses applying the law of Indonesia and giving jurisdiction to the courts of Djakarta. If this clause was to be upheld, then the Hague-Visby Rules would not have applied when otherwise they would have done.

The Court of Appeal considered that a clause which submits a dispute to the court of a country in which the liability of the shipowner or charterer was less than the limit of the Hague-Visby Rules was not void and ineffective, and it could be effective to the extent that the application of the foreign law was sought to be applied, not for the purpose of limiting package liability under the Rules, but to provide a limitation in respect of tonnage. Therefore, the Indonesian Commercial Code to which the dispute was subject was 'any statute' within the meaning of Art. VIII, and whilst it lessened the liability of the charterers, that lessening of liability was permissible. Article VIII in referring to 'any statute' was not simply referring to any English statute.

Article VIII therefore allows the carrier to rely on statutes which limit his liability, such as the Merchant Shipping Act 1894 as amended by the Merchant Shipping Acts of 1958 and 1979. The ability to rely upon s. 18 of the Merchant Shipping Act 1979 is not affected by the fact that the section not only operates to reduce the liability of the carrier, but also to exempt him from liability in certain circumstances. Section 6(4), COGSA 1971 provides:

It is hereby declared that for the purposes of Article VIII of the Rules, s. 18 of the Merchant Shipping Act 1979 which entirely exempts shipowners and others in certain circumstances from liability for loss and damage to goods, is a provision relating to limitation of liability.

Thus Art. IV r. 5 provides both a minimum and maximum level of liability. It is a minimum level to the extent that it is a lower limit which cannot be reduced. It is a maximum level to the extent that save in certain specified cases, the carrier cannot be liable for more. Where goods have been containerised, then these limits will apply to each package or unit in the container rather than the container as a whole, providing that the number of packages or units in the container is specifically enumerated in the bill of lading. Article IV r. 5(e) provides:

Where a container, pallet or similar article of transport is used to consolidate goods, the number of packages or units enumerated in the bill of lading as packed in such article of transport, shall be deemed the number of packages or units for the purpose of this paragraph as far as these packages or units are concerned. Except as aforesaid such article of transport shall be considered the package or unit.

If there is no enumeration in the bill of lading, then the higher of the two limits applies to the container as a whole. For example:

1.   'One container containing fabric': the limit would apply to the container as a whole, there having been no enumeration.
2.   'One container containing 200 rolls of fabric': the limit would apply to each individual roll, the contents of the container having been sufficiently enumerated.
3.   'One container said to contain 200 rolls of fabric': this would probably also be a sufficient enumeration to apply the limit to each roll rather than the container as a whole.

The rules expressly provide that there are two situations in which the limit set down in Art. IV r. 5 will have no application.

8.12.2   Exemption 1

This is found in Art. IV r. 5(a) which expressly states that the limit set down by Art. IV r. 5 applies 'unless the nature and value of such goods have been declared by the shipper before shipment and inserted in the bill of lading'. Therefore, it is possible for the shipper to make the carrier liable for a sum exceeding that stipulated by the rules, providing he acts in accordance with Art. IV r. 5(a) and declares the value before shipment. Where such a declaration is made before shipment, then whilst it is prima facie evidence, it is not binding or conclusive on the carrier (Art. IV r. 5(f)) and the carrier will not be liable where it has been knowingly misstated (Art. IV r. 5(n)).

8.12.3   Exemption 2

This is found in Art. IV r. 5(e) which provides:

Neither the carrier nor the ship shall be entitled to the benefit of the limitation of liability provided for in this paragraph, if it is proved that the damage resulted from an act or omission of the carrier done with intent to cause damage or recklessly and with knowledge that damage would probably result.

It would seem that if either the carrier or the alter ego of the company is at fault, no reliance can be placed on Art. IV r. 5, whereas if the carrier's servants or agents are at fault, the carrier may still rely on Art. IV r. 5.

8.13   THE CONTRACT OF CARRIAGE OF THIRD PARTIES

The situation under discussion in this section is where the shipper makes a contract of carriage with the carrier and the goods are lost or damaged by a third person employed by the carrier to perform some or all of the duties involved in the transit of the goods. The case law concentrates on loss or damage to goods whilst they are being handled by stevedores. However, the principles to be discussed apply to all third parties involved in the performance of the contract of carriage. The question is whether the third party may take the benefit of the exceptions and limits of liability contained in the contract, whether by means of incorporation or application of the Hague-Visby Rules.

The decision of the House of Lords in *Elder Dempster* v *Paterson Zochonis* [1924] AC 522 illustrates the point. A ship had been time chartered. The master signed the bill of lading as agent for the charterer, and not the carrier as usual. The contract of carriage appeared, therefore, to be between the shipper and the charterer. The bill of lading excepted liability for negligent stowage. The shipowner, who was the actual though not the legal carrier, was sued in tort for damage to the cargo caused by negligent stowage. The House of Lords held that the shipowner was entitled to rely on the exception in the bill of lading.

The principles were not properly worked out and explained until the House of Lords decided *Scruttons* v *Midland Silicones* [1962] AC 446. In this case Lord Reid described the decision in *Elder Dempster* as an 'anomalous and unexplained exception to the general principle that a stranger cannot rely for his protection on provisions in a contract to which he is not a party' and the ratio of that case as 'very obscure'. A drum of chemicals was shipped from America to London. The bill of lading expressly incorporated the Hague-Visby Rules. It also limited the liability of the carrier to £179 per package shipped. Stevedores engaged by the carrier dropped the drum whilst unloading. This caused £500 damage. The consignees of the drum sued the stevedores in tort. They claimed the full amount of loss. The stevedores argued that they were entitled to the limitation of liability in the bill of lading, following *Elder Dempster*. The House of Lords distinguished *Elder Dempster* on two grounds:

(a)   The third party in *Elder Dempster* was the shipowner, and was the bailee of the goods. He was the actual carrier.

(b)   The master was employed by the shipowner. Although he contracted as agent for the charterer, he remained the servant or agent of the shipowner for the purposes of carrying the goods. The third party, the shipowner, through the master's agency, therefore rendered the very service provided for in the bill of lading contract.

In these circumstances, the proper inference was that the shipowner received the goods in his possession on the terms of the bill of lading, although he was not in fact a party to the bill.

On the facts in *Scruttons*, the stevedores did not become bailees of the goods. Bailment signifies a transfer of possession. This was found not to be the case when goods were simply being handled in transit.

Lord Reid, obiter, suggested that the stevedores or any other third party not being an actual bailee of the goods, would be able to rely on the terms of the bill of lading if four conditions were satisfied:

(a) The bill of lading makes it clear that the third party was intended to be protected by the provisions of the bill, including the limits of liability.

(b) The bill of lading makes it clear that the carrier, in addition to contracting on his own behalf, is also contracting as agent for the third party.

(c) The carrier has authority from the third party so to contract, or there is post contractual ratification.

(d) Consideration moves from the third party.

A properly drafted 'Himalaya' clause may have this effect. (This is a clause which seeks to bind the crew, together with the shipowner, as if they were party to the bill of lading: *Adler* v *Dickson* [1955] 1 QB 158.) In *New Zealand Shipping Co. Ltd* v *AM Satterthwaite, The Eurymedon* [1975] AC 154 the Privy Council decided that all four of Lord Reid's criteria were satisfied. The bill of lading incorporated a 'Himalaya' clause which incorporated provisions similar to (a) and (b) above. The contract was governed by COGSA 1924. Machinery was damaged whilst being unloaded by stevedores. The consignees sued the stevedores more than one year after the damage was done. The stevedores successfully claimed that the claim was time barred. The one year time limit after the cause of action arose in the Act applied. Lord Wilberforce representing the majority of the Council found that the stevedores had authorised the shipowner to make the contract in the bill of lading on their behalf. His Lordship also found that consideration had moved from the stevedores. He described the transaction as follows:

The bill of lading brought into existence a bargain initially unilateral but capable of becoming mutual, between the shipper and the stevedores, made through the carrier as agent. This became a full contract when the stevedores performed services by discharging the goods. The performance of these services for the benefit of the shipper was the consideration for the agreement by the shipper that the stevedores should have the benefit of the exemptions and limitations contained in the bill of lading ... An agreement to do an act which the promisor is under an existing obligation to a third party to do, may quite well amount to valid consideration and does so in the present case. The promisee obtains the benefit of a direct obligation which he can enforce. This proposition is illustrated and supported by *Scotson* v *Pegg* which their Lordships consider to be good law.

Leggatt J in *Raymond Burke Motors Ltd* v *The Mersey Docks and Harbour Co.* [1986] 1 Lloyd's Rep 155 applied Lord Wilberforce's analysis of the contract as being unilateral. The claimants had bought a consignment of motor cycles on an ex warehouse basis in England. Property, therefore, passed as soon as the bikes left the seller's warehouse. The bikes were packed into a container and taken by the seller as agent for the buyer to a container park at Liverpool docks. The seller as agent for the buyer made the contract of carriage with the carrier. No bill of lading had been issued at the relevant time. However, the seller and carrier had contracted many times before and it was found as a fact that a bill of lading containing a standard type 'Himalaya' clause covering the stevedores at the docks would have been issued in due course. The defendants were stevedores at Liverpool docks. An employee of the defendants had an accident whilst moving another container containing chemicals in the same park as the container of motorcycles. The spilt chemicals entered the claimant's container and damaged the bikes. The defendants admitted negligence, but sought to rely on the limits to liability in the standard form of bill of lading to be issued by the carrier.

Leggatt J held that the defendant stevedores could only rely on the bill of lading if they were contractually bound to the claimants. Any contract would be unilateral (*The Eurymedon*). The defendants at the time of the accident had not done anything which constituted an acceptance of the claimant's offer. Leggatt J thought that the first act which might constitute acceptance by being performance of the obligations under the contract would be the discharge of a straddle container carrier to transport the claimant's container to the ship from the container park. The storage of the container in the park was not related to the stevedores. The discharge of other containers not connected with the claimants' container was irrelevant, even if the containers in question came from the same carrier. Since the unilateral contract had not been accepted at the time of the accident, the stevedores could not rely on the limits to liability normally incorporated in that contract, and were liable to the claimant in tort for the full foreseeable loss.

The Eurymedon, of course, took the scenario one stage further. The Privy Council had to consider the case of an indorsee or consignee of the bill of lading suing the third party to the bill of lading contract. Lord Wilberforce relied upon s. 1, Bills of Lading Act 1855, and if that failed the implied contract found in *Brandt v Liverpool Steam Navigation Co.* [1924] 1 KB 575. He said:

> The consignee is entitled to the benefit of and is bound by the stipulations in the bill of lading by his acceptance of it and request for delivery up of the goods thereunder. This is shown by *Brandt* ... The Bills of Lading Act 1855, s. 1 gives parties statutory recognition of this rule, but where the statute does not apply, the previously established law remains effective.

The Eurymedon was distinguished in *The Suleyman Stalsky* [1976] 2 Lloyd's Rep 609 on the question of the third of Lord Reid's requirements, namely, authorisation or ratification by the third party of the contract of carriage. In *The Eurymedon* the stevedore had seen the bill of lading before performing the work, and was also the carrier's parent company. In *The Suleyman Stalsky* the stevedores were merely dock handling agents, and not connected with the carrier. The court found that there was not the necessary authority in the carrier from the stevedores to contract on their behalf. Lord Reid, however, recognised the possibility of implied authority or ratification when necessary for the purpose of business efficacy.

This possibility was explored and developed by the Privy Council in *The New York Star* [1981] 1 WLR 138. Their Lordships advised that there was room in each case for evidence as to the precise relationship of carrier and stevedore and the practice of the port of discharge. However, they found that it was established law that in the normal situation involving the employment of stevedores by a carrier, commercial practice required that the stevedores enjoyed the benefit of the contractual provisions in the bill of lading. Shippers, carriers and stevedores know that such immunity or limitation of suit was intended and, in principle, a search for the factual ingredients required to confer the benefit was unnecessary.

8.13.1 Art. IV *bis* 2 of the Hague-Visby Rules

Art. IV *bis* 1 and 2 provide:

(1) The defences and limits of liability provided for in these Rules shall apply in any action against the carrier in respect of loss of damage to goods covered by a contract of carriage whether the action be founded in contract or tort.

(2) If such an action is brought against a servant or agent of the carrier (such servant or agent not being an independent contractor) such servant or agent shall be entitled to avail himself of the defences and limits of liability which the carrier is entitled to invoke under these Rules.

Art. IV *bis* 2 avoids all of the uncertainty of the position at common law where a servant is being sued. Such servant can rely on the exclusions and limits of liability in the Rules. The provision only applies, however, when the Rules themselves apply. If the Rules have ceased to apply for any reason, the servant is reduced to his rights and liabilities at common law.

Servants or agents of the carrier who are independent contractors are not included within the scope of these provisions. Stevedores would, therefore, not normally be able to avail themselves of the limitations and exclusions contained in the Hague-Visby Rules by relying on Art. IV *bis* 2. Such independent contractors would have to rely on the four conditions outlined by Lord Reid in *Scruttons* v *Midland Silicones* being satisfied and the contract in question being subject to the Hague-Visby Rules. Whether a third party is acting as an independent contractor should, in each case, be a question of fact.

8.14 COUNTRIES APPLYING THE HAGUE-VISBY RULES

Belgium
Bermuda
British Antarctic Territory
British Virgin Islands
Cayman Islands
Denmark
Ecuador
Egypt
Falkland Islands
Falkland Islands Dependencies
Finland
France
German Democratic Republic
Gibraltar

Hong Kong
Lebanon
Montserrat
Netherlands, The
Norway
Poland
Singapore
Sri Lanka
Sweden
Switzerland
Syrian Arab Republic
Tonga
Turks and Caicos Islands
UK (including Isle of Man)

8.15 COUNTRIES APPLYING THE HAGUE RULES

Algeria
Angola
Antigua and Barbuda
Argentina
Ascension Island
Australia
Barbados
Belize
Bolivia
Cameroon
Cape Verde
Cuba
Cyprus
Dominican Republic
Fiji
Gambia
Germany
Ghana
Goa
Grenada
Guinea Bissau
Guyana
Hungary

Iran
Israel
Italy
Ivory Coast
Jamaica
Japan
Kenya
Kiribati
Kuwait
Madagascar
Malay States, Federated
Malaysia
Mauritius
Monaco
Mozambique
Nauru
Palestine
Papua New Guinea
Paraguay
Peru
Portugal (Macau)
Republic of Ireland
Romania

Sabah	Somalia
Saint Helena	Spain
Saint Lucia	Tanzania
Saint Vincent and the Grenadines	Timor
São Tomé and Principe	Trinidad and Tobago
Sarawak	Turkey
Senegal	Tuvalu
Seychelles	USA
Sierra Leone	Zaire (now Democratic Republic of
Solomon Islands	Congo)

8.16   THE MERCHANT SHIPPING ACTS

The law relating to the limitation of the liability of owners of British owned ships was originally contained in part in ss. 502 and 503 of the Merchant Shipping Act 1894. These sections have now been replaced by ss. 18 and 17 respectively of the Merchant Shipping Act 1979 which came into force on 1 December 1986.

Section 18 of the 1979 Act allows the owner or part owner of a ship to exclude his liability for loss or damage caused by fire. Therefore, a carrier whose shipowner expressly elects to rely on the exclusion conferred by s. 18 has two bases upon which to exclude liability for fire: s. 18 and Art. IV r. 2(b). A shipowner can rely on s. 18 to exclude his liability for loss or damage caused by fire if the following conditions are satisfied:

(a)   the ship in question is British;

(b)   the loss or damage occurred whilst the goods were on board the ship;

(c)   the loss or damage occurred by reason of the fire.

(Section 18 of the 1979 Act also excludes liability for the owner of the ship for loss or damage to valuables by reason of their theft or other dishonest conduct provided that their value had not been declared in writing to the shipowner at the time of shipment.)

The original s. 502 of the 1894 Act prevented exclusion of liability if the fire had been caused with the fault or privity of the shipowner. This provision has now been replaced by s. 18(3) of the 1979 Act. This provides that if it is proved that the loss resulted from the shipowner's personal act or omission, committed with the intent to cause such loss or recklessly and with knowledge that such loss would probably result, the shipowner remains liable.

The protection of s. 18 is extended by s. 18(2) to the master and member of the crew or servant, but does not cover an independent contractor in the *Scruttons* v *Midland Silicones* (8.13) type situation. Section 503, Merchant Shipping Act 1894 has been replaced by s. 17 of the 1979 Act. The shipowner is entitled to limit his liability to a specified amount for particular types of damage, provided that he can show that the loss or damage occurred without any fault or personal act or omission on his part which was intended to cause loss or damage, or recklessness as to whether that loss or damage would result. The types of damage covered are:

(a)   Loss of life or personal injury to persons carried on the ship.

(b)   Damage to goods, merchandise or other things on board the ship.

(c)   Loss or life or personal injury to persons not carried on the ship through the act or omission of any person in the navigation of the ship or in the loading carriage or discharge of its cargo, or in the carriage or disembarkation of its passengers or any other act or omission of any person on board the ship.

(d)   Any loss or damage or any rights infringed through the act or omission of any person in the navigation or management of the ship, etc.

The 1979 Act also gives effect to the London Convention 1976 which concerned Maritime Claims. The Convention allows shipowners and certain carriers and salvors to limit their liability in certain specified circumstances.

8.17   THE HAMBURG RULES

8.17.1   Purpose of the Rules

In March 1978, an international conference in Hamburg adopted a new set of rules (the Hamburg Rules) which radically alter the liability which shipowners have to bear for loss or damage to goods in the courts of those nations where the Hamburg Rules apply. The main differences between the new Rules and the old Hague-Visby Rules are outlined below. These are proposed uniform rules to be applied to bills of lading, intended to replace the Hague-Visby Rules. The Hamburg Rules would considerably reduce the carriers' present protection against liability.

8.17.2   Carrier's Liability

The carrier will be liable for loss, damage or delay to the goods occurring whilst in his charge unless he proves that 'he, his servants or agents took all measures that could reasonably be required to avoid the occurrence and its consequences.'. The detailed list of exceptions set out in the Hague and Hague-Visby Rules is no longer available to the carrier. In particular, the carrier is no longer exonerated from liability arising from errors in navigation, management of the ship or fire. All the case law that has built up over seventy years since the Hague Rules were introduced, and which has largely clarified and made certain the effect of those Rules, to the great benefit of both merchant and carrier alike, will be inapplicable where the Hamburg Rules are applied. They are therefore bound to lead to far more disputes. No less a person than Lord Diplock observed about the requirement that the shipowner is liable unless he proves that he 'took all measures that could reasonably be required to avoid the occurrence and its consequences' that 'speaking from many years experience as a Judge I think, given that very broad definition, I could decide almost everything as I personally like and I think other Judges may feel exactly the same!' Hardly a recipe for certainty!

The carrier is liable for delay in delivery if 'the goods have not been delivered at the port of discharge provided for under the contract of carriage within the time expressly agreed upon or, in the absence of such agreement, within the time which it could be reasonable to require of a diligent carrier having regard to the circumstances of the case'.

8.17.3   Limitation of Liability

The dual system for calculating the limit of liability, either by reference to package or weight as set out in the Hague-Visby Rules, has been readopted, but the amounts have been increased by about 25 per cent to 835 special drawing rights per package and 2.5 special drawing rights per kilo. (A special drawing right (SDR) is a unit of account for the official reserves created by the International Monetary Fund. The unit was originally expressed in terms of gold, but as from 1 July 1974 its value is calculated daily as the US dollar equivalent of specified amounts of currencies that are widely used in international trade.) The liability for delay is limited to an equivalent to two and a half times the freight payable for the goods delayed, but not exceeding the total freight payable for the whole contract under which the goods were shipped. In no case is the aggregate liability for both loss/damage and delay to exceed the limit for loss/damage.

8.17.4   Contracts Covered

The Hamburg Rules cover all contracts for the carriage by sea other than charterparties whereas the Hague/Hague-Visby Rules only apply where a bill of lading is issued. The Hamburg Rules are therefore applicable to waybills, consignment notes, etc. (one of the few advantageous provisions in the Hamburg Rules). They cover shipment of live animals and deck cargo, whereas the Hague/Hague-Visby Rules may not. They will apply to both imports and exports to/from a signatory nation (i.e. all that nation's trade) whereas the Hague/Hague-Visby Rules (if applied as intended by the drafters) apply to exports only. This will create conflict and undesirable forum shopping for litigation.

8.17.5   Contracting Parties

The Hamburg Rules became operative as an international convention one year after ratification or accession by twenty nations, with no minimum tonnage qualification. The requisite 20 nations were obtained in November 1991 with the signature of Zambia, so the Hamburg Rules came into force in November 1992. Present signatories are:

Austria	Lesotho
Barbados	Malawi
Botswana	Morocco
Burkina Faso	Nigeria
Cameroon	Romania
Chile	Senegal
Czech Republic	Sierra Leone
Egypt	Slovakia
Guinea	Tanzania
Hungary	Tunisia
Kenya	Uganda
Lebanon	Zambia

(Note that 10 of these signatories are landlocked).

Carriers and carrier nations do not wish to be burdened with these new Rules, which will add to the confusion of practitioners over the recourse to which they are entitled by destroying the uniformity currently in existence, as the Hague and Hague-Visby Rules are complementary. Hamburg Rules, as a third force, introduce conflict and threaten to be a 'lawyers' charter to print money'.

However, unless one trades with Africa, the chances of encountering the Hamburg Rules are relatively remote at present, as none of the major trading nations is, or seems likely to become, a Hamburg signatory in the near future. Furthermore, Chile considered denunciation and many of the signatories to the international convention have not, as yet, enacted the necessary national legislation to give effect to the Rules in their courts. In fact, to date, only Barbados, Chile, Egypt, Lebanon, Morocco, Senegal and Tunisia appear to have done so.

So far, apart from Austria and four Central/Eastern European nations (see above), no European nations appear likely to adopt these Rules and that will be the time when it will be necessary to take significant account of the Hamburg Rules. In this context it is interesting to note that at a colloquium in Antwerp in November 1993 entitled 'The Hamburg Rules: A choice for the EEC', at which papers were presented by leading maritime law academics (Herber, Tetley, Berlingieri, Ramberg, Remand-Gouilloud, Gaskell, Japikse, Hill and Delwaide), not a few of whom are self-confessed proponents of the Hamburg Rules, not one of them actually recommended the widespread adoption of the Hamburg Rules. Instead, it was recognised that there was considerable controversy surrounding the Rules, even amongst academics who have nothing to lose or gain from their implementation, and the talk was of a further diplomatic conference to review the Hamburg Rules to make them more acceptable to the maritime community at large. Meanwhile, the Hamburg Rules merely create an anomalous irritant.

Gard P&I Club recently conducted a survey on the Hamburg Rules and were unable to identify any instances of the Hamburg Rules being applied in a court case anywhere in the world. Clearly, the Hamburg Rules have no claim as an acceptable basis for producing conformity in carriers' liability regimes.

8.18 LIMIT OF LIABILITY FOR MARITIME CLAIMS

8.18.1 Introduction

The liability of the carrier under any of the above sea carriage conventions is, of course, always subject to the overriding application of the provisions of the 1976 International Convention on the Limitation of Liability for Maritime Claims (the London Convention) or equivalent Convention relating, amongst other things, to limitation of liability. The current UK Act is the Merchant Shipping Act 1979, which implemented the London Convention with effect from 1 December 1986.

8.18.2 The Extent of Limitation

This Convention applies a virtually unbreakable right to limit with increased levels of limitation as follows:

(a) In respect of loss of life or personal injury (other than passengers for whom a separate fund applies):

    (i) 333,000 units of accounts (SDRs) for a vessel with a tonnage not exceeding 500 tons.
    (ii) For a vessel with tonnage in excess thereof, in addition:
        For each ton from 501 to 3,000 tons: 500 SDRs
        For each ton from 3,001 to 30,000 tons: 333 SDRs
        For each ton from 30,001 to 70,000 tons: 250 SDRs
        For each ton in excess of 70,000 tons: 167 SDRs.

(b) In respect of any other claims:

    (i) 167,000 SDRs for a vessel not exceeding 500 tons.
    (ii) or a ship with a tonnage in excess thereof, in addition:
        For each ton from 501 to 30,000 tons: 167 SDRs
        For each ton from 30,001 to 70,000 tons: 125 SDRs
        For each ton in excess of 70,000 tons: 83 SDRs.

The balances of unsatisfied loss of life or personal injury claims (a) can participate equally along with the other claims (b). Accordingly, total limitation where loss of life and/or personal injury claims are involved in conjunction with other claims is found by adding the amounts produced by formulae (a) and (b) together. (A separate fund is established for passengers based on Athens Convention limits.)

8.18.3   Contracting Parties

At the present time the 1976 London Convention has been ratified or acceded to by the following nations:

Australia	Japan
Bahamas	Liberia
Barbados	Mexico
Belize	Netherlands
Belgium	New Zealand
Benin	Norway
Croatia	Poland
Denmark	Spain
Egypt	Sweden
Finland	Switzerland
France	United Kingdom
Germany	Vanuatu
Greece	Yemen

8.18.4   National Legislation

China and Korea (South) have enacted legislation broadly in line with the London Convention. Most other nations apply earlier conventions with lower levels of limitation and a 'fault and privity' approach to the right to limit, whilst others (USA being a prime example) use the basis of the value of the ship plus freight earned at the end of the voyage.

9 Carriage of Goods by Air, Land and Multimodal Transport

9.1 INTRODUCTION

9.1.1 Common Carrier and Private Carrier

A common carrier is one who holds himself out as prepared to carry for reward goods or passengers or both and who, unlike the private carrier, does not reserve a general right to accept or reject prospective customers. The common carrier is under a duty to accept goods or passengers of the types he carries on the routes he follows subject to certain exceptions. For goods these exceptions are that the vehicle is full, that the goods are inadequately packed, that they are offered at an unreasonable time, that reasonable pre-payment of charges is refused, that the goods present an extraordinary risk or that they cannot be carried, e.g. because of unwieldy size or because their value is disproportionate to precautions the carrier can take. For passengers the exceptions are that the prospective passenger is not in a fit state to be carried, that there is no accommodation and that he has not tendered the proper fare.

At common law a common carrier of goods was said to be 'an insurer', meaning that, subject to contrary agreement, he was liable for loss or damage to the goods unless it resulted from an Act of God, an act of the Queen's enemies, inherent vice in the goods or inadequate packing. These exceptions do not avail the carrier if he contributes to their operation by his negligence. 'Act of God' means some operation of natural forces so unexpected in nature or extent of operation that no human foresight could be expected to foresee or guard against it; *Bridden* v *GNR* (1858) 28 LJ Ex 51 (snow). 'Inherent vice' is some defect in the goods causing the harm, *Nugent* v *Smith* (1876) 1 CPD 423 (horse struggling during storm). The consignor must inform the carrier of any reason for special care or the carrier will not be liable for harm which otherwise might not have occurred, *Baldwin* v *L.C.D. Rly* (1882) 9 QBD 582 (wet rags spoilt in delayed journey — carrier not liable because not told of their condition). The carrier's strict liability continues during transit and for a reasonable time thereafter. Then the carrier becomes a warehouseman, liable only for negligence, *Mitchell* v *L.Y.R.* (1875) LR 10 QB 256. The carrier's liability for delay to goods is not strict but only for negligence and a common carrier of passengers is only liable in negligence in any event.

9.1.2   Liability Under The Carriers Act 1830

The Carriers Act 1830 provides that by a displayed notice a common carrier may exclude liability for loss or damage to certain types of valuable goods worth more than £10 unless they are declared and an extra charge paid. Otherwise a common carrier cannot limit his liability by a notice as distinct from a ticket or other contractual transaction. The Unfair Contract Terms Act 1977 applies to contracts of carriage and is a much more important restraint on exclusion clauses. Since the privatised rail companies and most road hauliers are now once more common carriers, the 1830 Act is of some practical importance and may apply to the carriage of goods and passengers' luggage by these companies and on buses and coaches running as public service vehicles.

The carrier should follow his ordinary route, not necessarily the shortest, but without unnecessary deviation or delay. Misdelivery is a breach of contract, or when circumstances should have aroused suspicion, will render the carrier liable not only in contract but for conversion. A consignor impliedly warrants both to a common and to a private carrier that the goods are fit to be carried with safety and if not, is liable if he is negligent in not knowing of or in not disclosing the danger; *Bamfield* v *Goole & Sheffield Co.* [1910] 2 KB 94; *G.N.R.* v *LEP Transport* [1922] 2 KB 742. At common law the common carrier has a particular lien on the goods he carries for his charges. This takes priority over an unpaid vendor's lien and stoppage *in transitu* (see 2.11). A carrier's general lien must arise from contract or binding usage.

9.2   CARRIAGE OF GOODS BY AIR

9.2.1   Air Freight

Overall some 10 per cent in value and approximately 1 per cent in volume of international trade is conveyed by air. The great majority of the merchandise is conveyed on scheduled airline services as distinct from chartered services.

The document accompanying the goods throughout transit is called an air waybill. Some 80 per cent of the goods are conveyed under consolidation/groupage arrangements initiated by the International Air Transport Association (IATA) agent who issues the (house) air waybill. The remainder is booked direct with the airline that issues the air waybill.

When cargo has arrived at a destination airport, it is the practice for the airline or air freight agent to inform the consignee. However, where the consignee has no agent specified in the air waybill and has failed to contact the airline regarding the processing of the imported goods, an (air) cargo arrival notice may be issued by the airline.

Where the consignment forms part of a groupage or consolidated international consignment, a house air waybill is issued by a consolidator (usually a freight forwarder) and is a certificate of shipment of a specified consignment for a particular flight. Information for the preparation of the air waybill by the airline or IATA agent is supplied by the shipper in a shipper's letter of instruction.

9.2.2 Conventions and Legislation

International conventions to which effect has been given by statute embody codes applicable to international air transport. The principal convention is the Warsaw Convention 1929 to which effect was given by the Carriage by Air Act 1932. The Warsaw Convention was amended at the Hague in 1955 (the Hague Protocol) and the Carriage by Air Act 1961 (which repealed the 1932 Act) enabled the UK to ratify the Hague Protocol in 1967. The Carriage by Air (Supplementary Provisions) Act 1962 gives effect to the Guadalajara Convention 1961 dealing with sub-contracted carriage. The Carriage by Air and Road Act 1979 gives effect to the Montreal Protocols which further amend the (already amended) Warsaw Convention.

The conventions were intended to provide uniform rules of law applying irrespective of the nationality of airlines, passengers and cargo, but since the conventions and their amendments bind only countries acceding to them, this has only been partially achieved. The unamended Warsaw Convention applies to flights to countries which have not accepted the Hague Protocol and the amended version applies to flights to those which have. The conventions and protocols are primarily applicable to 'international carriage' as defined (see below), but power was reserved by s. 10 of the 1961 Act to apply them to non-international carriage, i.e. internal flights or flights between the UK and countries which have not acceded to the conventions. The Carriage by Air Acts (Application of Provisions) Order 1967 brought this power into force.

These conventions apply to all international carriage of persons, baggage or cargo by aircraft for reward and also to gratuitous carriage by aircraft performed by an air transport undertaking. 'International carriage' means all carriage in which 'the place of departure and the place of destination, whether or not there be a break in the carriage or a transshipment, are situated either within the territories of two High Contracting Parties or within the territory of a single High Contracting Party if there is an agreed stopping place within the territory of another State even if that State is not a High Contracting Party'. Carriage to be performed by a series of carriers will be regarded as one undivided carriage if the parties have treated it as a single operation and will still be international even if one or more of the separate contracts have to be performed wholly within one state.

The conventions prescribe the form of a passenger ticket, baggage ticket and air waybill (air consignment note under the unamended convention) and the effect of failure to provide these or to provide them in proper form. The conventions also cover liability of the carrier, limitation of the carrier's liability, combined carriage and jurisdiction over claims.

9.2.3 The Air Waybill

All three forms of the Warsaw Convention (original, as amended at the Hague and as amended at Montreal) make provision in the international air transport of goods for the issue of a document by the consignor containing prescribed particulars. The consignor may require the carrier to accept this document. The document required by the original Warsaw Convention was an 'air consignment note'. Absence of or irregularity in such a document resulted in the carrier not being able to limit liability. The document was renamed an 'air waybill' by the amended Hague Convention (given effect to in the UK by the Carriage by Air Act 1961). The contents required were reduced. It was to be in triplicate with one part marked 'for the carrier', and another 'for the consignee' and another 'for the consignor'. This was to accompany the cargo. The waybill was to contain details of the route. The consignor was responsible for accuracy and was required to indemnify the carrier for loss arising from inaccuracy or irregularity.

Absence of or irregularity in the waybill did not affect the validity of the contract but the carrier could not limit liability. The Montreal Protocol (given effect to in the UK by the Carriage by Air and Road Act 1979) makes further changes. Any other suitable means of recording the contract may be used instead of a waybill, but the carrier must, on request, give the consignor a receipt for the goods. The impossibility of using these substituted means on the route does not entitle the carrier to refuse to accept the cargo. Non-compliance with the requirements of the waybills does not affect the contract and the carrier may limit his liability. By Article 34 of the Convention, the documentary requirements (consignment notes and waybills) do not apply to carriage in extraordinary circumstances outside the normal scope of an air carrier's business.

It appears that the air waybill is neither a document of title nor a negotiable instrument. Article 15 of the Hague version of the Convention says that nothing in it is to prevent the issue of a negotiable air waybill but this does not appear in the Montreal version. The air waybill must contain necessary information for police and customs and have attached to it any necessary documents. The carrier need not check its sufficiency and the consignor is liable to the carrier for any loss caused by such insufficiency unless it results from the carrier's fault.

9.2.4 Forum of Action

An action for damages must be brought at the option of the claimant in the territory of one of the High Contracting Parties to the Warsaw Convention before the court having jurisdiction either where the carrier is ordinarily resident or has his principal place of business or has an establishment by which the contract was made at the place of destination. The Montreal Protocol adds that for death, injury or delay of a passenger or for destruction, loss, damage or delay of luggage the action may be brought in one of the above courts or in the territory of a High Contracting Party before a court within whose jurisdiction the carrier has an establishment, if the passenger has his ordinary or permanent residence in that territory. Where carriage is performed by successive carriers, all forms of the Convention provide that each carrier who accepts passengers, baggage or cargo is subject to the Convention and is deemed to be a contracting party for his part of the carriage. A passenger can only sue the carrier performing the contract at the time when the accident or delay occurred except when the first carrier by express agreement assumes liability for the whole journey. In regard to baggage or cargo carried by successive carriers, the passenger or consignor can sue the first carrier and the passenger or consignee can sue the last carrier and each may take action against the carrier in whose part of the journey the harm or delay took place. These carriers are jointly and severally liable to the passenger, consignor and consignee.

9.2.5 Rights of Consignors and Consignees

All three forms of the Warsaw Convention make similar provision for these rights. Subject to his obligations under the contract of carriage, the consignor may dispose of the cargo either by withdrawing it at the departure or destination aerodrome or at an intermediate landing, or by calling for it to be delivered either at destination or in transit to a person other than the consignee, or by requiring it to be returned to the departure aerodrome. In this the consignor must not prejudice the carrier or other consignors and must pay expenses. If it is impossible to carry out the consignor's orders the carrier must inform him forthwith. If the carrier obeys the consignor's orders without requiring production of the air waybill delivered to the latter (or, the Montreal Protocol adds, the receipt for cargo given to him), he will be liable to any person lawfully in possession of the waybill (or receipt) but may recover against the consignor. The rights of the consignor cease when the rights of the consignee begin to operate on arrival but revive in the event of non-acceptance. On arrival, subject to contrary agreement, the carrier must give notice to the consignee. Except when the consignor has withdrawn the cargo the consignee is entitled to delivery on arrival on payment of dues and on complying with the conditions of carriage. The Hague Protocol adds that the consignee is entitled to delivery of the air waybill. If the carrier admits loss of the cargo or it is delayed more than seven days the consignee may enforce his contractual rights against the carrier.

9.2.6 Liability of the Carrier

All three forms of the Warsaw Convention (see 9.2.2) make provision for the carrier's liability for death or personal injury to passengers, loss or damage to baggage or cargo and delay. In any event, the carrier will not be liable if he can prove that he or his servants or agents took all necessary measures to avoid the harm or that it was impossible to do so. In the case of death or personal injury, the carrier is only liable if it occurred on board or in embarking or disembarking and the Montreal Protocol adds that the carrier is not liable if it resulted from the passenger's state of health. Under the Hague Protocol it was provided that if it was proved that the harm was caused or contributed to by the negligence of the injured person the court might, in accordance with its own law, exonerate the carrier wholly or in part. The Montreal Protocol does not refer to the law of the court and is more specific, mentioning passengers, baggage and cargo and allowing partial or total exoneration not only for negligence but also for any wrongful act or omission, causing or contributing to the harm, by the claimant or the person on whose behalf the claim is made. Also, under the Montreal Protocol, it is expressly provided that the carrier is not liable for damage to baggage resulting from inherent vice. Under the Montreal Protocol the liability for baggage operates when the baggage is on board or being embarked or disembarked. Under the Hague Protocol baggage liability operates during 'carriage by air', defined as for cargo in all three protocols. This 'carriage' lasts as long as the goods are in the charge of the carrier, whether in an airport, on board, or in a landing outside an airport, at any place whatever. This 'carriage' does not *prima facie* apply to carriage by land, sea or river outside an airport, but if that external carriage takes place in performing an air carriage contract any damage is presumed to have taken place during air carriage. The Montreal Protocol expressly provides that the carrier is not to be liable for cargo damage resulting from inherent vice, defective packing by some person other than the carrier, act of war or armed conflict or act of public authority relating to the entry, exit or transit of the goods.

Any provision tending to relieve the carrier of liability or to fix lower financial limits for liability is null and void but this does not entail the nullity of the whole contract. Exclusion clauses are allowed by the Hague and Montreal Protocols in respect of inherent vice in cargo.

Under the original convention and the Hague Protocol it was provided that limitation of liability did not apply in respect of any intentional or reckless act done by the carrier or his servants or agents in the course of employment, but this does not appear in the Montreal Protocol. The original convention also provided a defence in respect of cargo if the harm was caused by negligent pilotage, navigation or handling of the aircraft and in all other respects the carrier and his servants took all necessary measures to avoid the harm. This defence does not appear in either the Hague or Montreal Protocols.

9.2.7   Limitation of the Carrier's Liability

All three forms of the Warsaw Convention (see 9.2.2) make provision for the carrier's liability for injury, loss or damage to be subject to financial limits. For death or injury to a passenger in flight, embarking or disembarking liability was limited under the original convention to 125,000 gold francs. Under the Hague amendment this was increased to 250,000 gold francs. For cargo the limit has always been 250 gold francs per kilogram unless a special declaration was made and an increased charge was paid if required, and for articles in the passenger's personal charge the limit was 5,000 gold francs. The Carriage by Air and Road Act 1979, s. 4, provides for the Hague figures to be replaced by 16,600, 17 and 332 SDR respectively (see 8.17.3 for the meaning of SDR). Under Articles 22 and 22A of the Montreal Protocol the limits will be 100,000 special drawing rights for death or injury to a passenger, 4,150 for delay to a passenger, and 1,000 for each passenger's baggage. It remains 17 special drawing rights for each kilogram of cargo unless a special declaration is made and any extra charge paid. If a servant or agent of the carrier is sued he may avail himself of these limits if he proves he was acting within the scope of his employment. If the carrier and his agents and servants are sued the total recoverable in respect of each victim or unit of loss must not exceed the limit.

9.2.8 Limitation of Action

Time limits are also applicable. Any action for damages must be brought within two years of arrival. Receipt without complaint of baggage or cargo is *prima facie* evidence of correct performance. In the case of damage, complaint must be made forthwith after discovery and in any event within seven days in the case of baggage and fourteen days in the case of cargo. Partial loss of contents of baggage is 'damage' for this period of notice; see *Fothergill* v *Monarch Airlines* [1980] 3 WLR 209. For the 1961 Act and the Hague Protocol the Carriage by Air and Road Act 1979, s. 2, now expressly provides that partial loss and partial receipt are damage requiring this notice. In the case of delay, complaint must be made within twenty-one days of receipt of the goods. All complaints must be in writing. These limits may be set aside if there is fraud by the carrier.

9.2.9 Exclusion of Carrier's Liability

Any contractual provision relieving the carrier of liability or fixing limits lower than those in the appropriate version of the Convention is null, but this does not entail nullity of the entire contract. Under the original Convention and the Hague Protocol, irregularities in the passenger ticket, air consignment note or air waybill, or in the baggage check, all resulted in the carrier being deprived of financial limitation on liability, but this is not the case under the Montreal Protocol scheduled to the Carriage by Air and Road Act 1979.

9.2.10 Air and Combined Carriage

When carriage is partly by air and partly by other means, the Warsaw Convention applies only to the air carriage provided that it falls within its definition of international carriage. Terms relating to non-air carriage can be inserted in the air carriage document provided that the Convention is observed in regard to the air carriage (see 9.5 for Carriage of Goods by combined transport).

9.3 CARRIAGE OF GOODS BY ROAD

9.3.1 Carriage by Road

Some 80% of consumer goods exported to continental Europe from the United Kingdom are conveyed by international road transport, usually under a document known as the CMR Consignment Note. CMR is the international convention concerning the carriage of goods by road that came into force in the United Kingdom in 1967 (see 9.3.2). It is embodied in the Carriage of Goods by Road Act 1965 as amended by the Carriage by Air and Road Act 1979. It is aligned to the UN's ECE operating system (layout key) and can be used on aligned documentation systems. It permits the carriage of goods by road under one consignment under a common code of conditions applicable to 26 countries, primarily in Europe. The statutory provisions are embodied in the Carriage of Goods by Road Act 1965.

The world-wide transportation group, TNT Ipec, has developed an alternative consignment note, the exclusive TNT Ipec Consignment Note for the carriage of goods, which combines an air freight/sea freight leg with an overland leg to and from airports/seaports.

It is the practice for road trailer operators to instruct their drivers to complete an equipment condition report on each occasion when the trailer is used, so that the condition of the equipment can be monitored on a regular journey basis for insurance and legal purposes. It also places an onus on the driver for accountability in regard to the management of the vehicle in international transits.

The equipment handover agreement is a document which enables the operator to hand over the container from one carrier to another, such as road to rail, or road to ship, and thereby to monitor the container's condition throughout its combined transport journey. Any damage would be recorded in the document.

9.3.2 Conventions Applicable: The CMR

This is the convention governing the International Carriage of Goods by Road signed at Geneva in 1956 and enacted into the laws of the United Kingdom by the Carriage of Goods by Road Act 1965. The convention only appears to have been adopted by European nations and applies to contracts for the international carriage of goods by road in vehicles over the territories of two different countries of which at least one is a contracting party to CMR. It therefore only applies to UK imports/exports by roll-on/roll-off ferry or the Channel Tunnel where goods remain on road vehicles throughout. If the same container on the same journey was lifted off the trailer at Dover onto a vessel and carried to the Continent and there lifted onto another trailer, there would have been no crossing of a frontier on a road vehicle and therefore the convention would not apply. For this reason the CMR convention is not applicable to UK exports or imports in all container services, but it will apply in some containers shipments to or from the continent, for instance where Belgian imports or exports are fed from or to Rotterdam. It will not apply mandatorily where Dutch imports or exports are shipped via Rotterdam, since such imports and exports do not cross a frontier on a vehicle.

Under this convention the carrier is liable for loss or damage from the time he takes over until the time he delivers the goods to the consignee, unless he can prove that the loss or damage occurred because of one of the list of excepted perils. In short, these exceptions allow the carrier to escape liability if he has not been negligent. He is entitled to limit his liability to SDR 8.33 per kilo. The carrier is also liable for delay if the goods have not been delivered within the agreed time limit or, if there is no such agreement, within a reasonable time.

9.3.3 Carriage of Goods by Road Act 1965

This gives statutory effect to the Convention on the Contract for the International Carriage of Goods by Road (CMR). It applies to every contract for the carriage of goods in road vehicles for reward when the place of taking over of the goods and the place of delivery are in two different countries, of which at least one is a contracting country, irrespective of the residence and nationality of the parties. It applies to state and government carriage, but not to postal convention carriage, funerals and furniture removal, nor to carriage between the United Kingdom and the Republic of Ireland. The contracting parties agree not to vary the convention by special agreement except to make it inapplicable to frontier traffic or to authorise within their territories the use of consignment notes representing a title to goods. Where the road vehicle is carried over part of the journey by sea, rail, inland waterway or air and (except when performance becomes impossible) the goods are not unloaded, the convention applies to the whole journey. If harm occurs merely through the use of the other means of transport the liability of the carrier is regulated by the law applicable to that other means. The carrier is responsible for his servants and agents.

9.3.4 The Road Consignment Note

A consignment note must be made out in triplicate containing numerous prescribed particulars. The consignment note is not a document of title nor a negotiable instrument. The first copy is for the sender, the second accompanies the goods and the third is kept by the carrier. The sender is responsible for loss to the carrier resulting from inadequacy or inaccuracy of many of these particulars, but the carrier must check the note and the goods and packaging. The sender is responsible for loss caused by defective packing unless this was known to the carrier when he received the goods. The sender is responsible for Customs documents and other formalities. The sender may dispose of the goods whilst in transit until the second copy of the consignment note is delivered to the consignee; thereafter the consignee has the right and by special entry on the note, may have it from the time when the note is drawn up. If the journey becomes impossible the carrier must seek instructions from the person entitled to dispose of the goods. If the consignee rejects the goods they must be disposed of according to the sender's instructions, but the carrier may dispose of them without instructions if they are perishable, if their condition warrants this or the storage expenses would be disproportionately large.

9.3.5 Liability of the Carrier

The carrier is liable for total or partial loss, damage or delay but not if this is caused by the wrongful act of the claimant or by his instructions not consequent on a wrongful act or neglect of the carrier, by inherent vice, or through circumstances which the carrier could not avoid and the consequences of which he was unable to prevent. The carrier is not relieved of liability because of the defective condition of the vehicle or the neglect or wrongful act of the person from whom he hired the vehicle but, in general, he is not liable for loss or damage arising from the use of open, unsheltered vehicles when this use was agreed; lack of or defect in packing; handling, loading and unloading by the sender, the consignee and their agents; the nature of the goods rendering them vulnerable to harm; insufficiency of marks or numbers and the carriage of livestock. He must prove that refrigerated or similar vehicles were properly maintained. Non-delivery within thirty days of the agreed time limit or, if none, within sixty days of handing to the carrier is conclusive evidence of loss. The person entitled to claim may request to be notified if the goods are recovered within a year. The carrier will be liable for failure to collect 'cash on delivery'.

9.3.6 Duties of Consignor and Consignee

The sender must tell the carrier of dangerous goods, otherwise the carrier may unload, destroy or render them harmless without compensation and claim expenses from the sender. The value of goods is fixed by the commodity exchange price or market price. In the absence of special declaration and surcharge, compensation must not exceed the amount of loss or 8.33 SDR per kilogram (see Carriage by Air and Road Act 1979, s. 4). Five per cent interest is payable on compensation. Where there is an extra-contractual claim, the carrier may avail himself of time limits in the Convention. In case of wilful misconduct or its equivalent neither the carrier nor his agents may avail themselves of limits on liability or any shifting of the burden of proof provided in Chapter IV of the Convention. The consignee must notify apparent damage to the carrier on delivery and non-apparent within seven days. Delay must be notified within twenty-one days. Proceedings must be taken either in a court or tribunal of an agreed contracting country or in the country where the defendant is ordinarily resident or has his principal place of business or where the branch where the contract was made is located or where the goods were taken over by the carrier or where the place of delivery is located.

9.3.7 Limitation of Action

The period of limitation is one year or, in case of wilful default or its equivalent, three years starting from, in the case of partial loss or damage, the date of delivery, in the case of total loss from thirty days after the agreed time limit or, if none, sixty days from receipt by the carrier and in other cases from three months after the contract. If carriage is performed by successive road carriers each is responsible for the whole operation, the second and successive carriers becoming party to the contract by accepting the goods and the consignment note. Only the first or last successive carrier or the one in whose charge the goods were when lost or damaged may be sued singly, but all may be sued together. A carrier who pays compensation under this may, subject to contrary agreement, recover against the other carriers who are in whole or part responsible for the loss or damage. Except for such an agreement between successive carriers, no contracting out is allowed. Any stipulation which would directly or indirectly derogate from the Convention is null and void, but this does not involve the nullity of the rest of the contract. A benefit of insurance in favour of a carrier or any similar clause or a clause shifting the burden of proof will be null.

In *James Buchanan* v *Babco* [1978] AC 141, the House of Lords, in holding carriers liable to excise duty on stolen whisky, said that the English text was to be broadly interpreted to produce, if possible, conformity amongst contracting states but foreign decisions were not to be used; see *Thermo* v *Ferrimaster* [1981] 1 All ER 1142 for the position when a lorry is loaded on a ship.

9.4 CARRIAGE OF GOODS BY RAILWAY

9.4.1 Introduction

Carriage of goods by railway is part of carriage of goods by land (which includes road carriage) and is sometimes treated as such. It can also be part of combined carriage. However, a significant amount of exports and imports is transported solely by rail, especially in continental Europe.

9.4.2 Conventions Applicable: COTIF/CMI

The COTIF Convention Concerning International Carriage by Rail was signed in Berne in May 1980. It was given legal effect in the UK by s. 1 of the International Transport Conventions Act 1983 with effect from May 1985. COTIF abrogated the existing CMI convention which did not have force of law in the UK and an amended draft of CMI was attached to COTIF as Appendix B to govern the carriage of goods (COTIF has a wider application and covers passengers etc. as well as goods).

Like CMR (see 9.3.2), COTIF/CMI applies only to international carriage and is not applicable to domestic traffic. The opening of the Channel Tunnel extended the application of COTIF/CMI recourse. As a private company, the Channel Tunnel operates an independent contract not subject to any mandatory law in which liability for delays is excluded and a limitation of 8.33 SDR (same as CMR) is applied. The terms and conditions of COTIF/CMI are similar to CMR, but limitation is substantially higher at 17 SDR per kilo.

9.4.3 Carriage of Goods by Railway Act 1972

This gives effect to the Convention Relating to the Liability of the Railway for Death of and Personal Injury to Passengers which is scheduled to the Act. This convention is supplemental to the first of two major conventions dealing with international rail traffic — the International Convention Concerning the Carriage of Passengers and Luggage by Rail (CIV) (known in the Act as the 'Railway Passenger Convention') and the International Convention Concerning the Carriage of Goods by Rail (CIM) (known in the Act as the 'Railway Freight Convention'). The two major conventions are not scheduled to the Act, but s. 6 provides that no action of any kind relating to liability provided for in the conventions may be brought against a railway, its servants or its agents except in accordance with the conventions and s. 7 provides that where goods are carried in accordance with the Freight Convention the consignee is not to be entitled to enforce any right against the railway except in accordance with the convention. Moreover, when the consignee accepts the consignment note in respect of the goods prescribed by the convention, or purports to exercise any rights given him by the convention he is then to be treated as if he were a party to the contract of carriage from its formation, having all the rights and obligations conferred by the convention. Railway authorities in this country have used the tickets and consignment notes prescribed by the conventions for international traffic, thus incorporating the provisions of the appropriate convention into the contract of carriage. The Freight Convention requires the use of a consignment note with specified contents which must accompany the goods. It makes provision for the carrier's liability for loss, damage and delay to the goods, with certain exemptions from liability. Special provision is made for dangerous goods and certain other special consignments. Liability is limited both in respect of amount and time. The normal period of limitation is one year, but exceptionally may be two years.

9.5 CARRIAGE OF GOODS BY COMBINED TRANSPORT

9.5.1 Combined Transport Operator (CTO)

The essential feature of a combined transport operation is that the CTO assumes responsibility for the entire movement of goods from exporter to importer. In the event of any loss, damage or delay the CTO will put matters right in so far as this is possible, or will compensate the aggrieved party and will then pursue the person actually at fault to recover what he can. Naturally such an operator needs a large and sophisticated organisation staffed internationally by qualified representatives or agents. They are therefore international carriers prepared to offer all the usual forwarding services plus the willingness to assume responsibility for the conduct of the entire transit as explained above. They have thus to some extent usurped the role of the traditional freight forwarder.

9.5.2 ICC Rules for a Combined Transport Document

Some years ago, an attempt was made to draft a convention to cover loss or damage to goods carried under a combined transport document. Known variously at different stages as the 'Tokyo–Rome Rules', the 'Tokyo Rules' and the 'TCM Convention', it failed to secure general support. The International Chamber of Commerce took up the rejected draft and made several amendments to make it commercially more attractive. The final draft was published as the 'ICC Rules for a Combined Transport Document (Brochure No. 298)'. These have found wide acceptance amongst combined transport operators, and most large operators, like P&O Containers, apply terms and conditions which are based on the ICC Rules, if not precisely complying with them (see also 9.5).

9.5.3 UNCTAD MMO Convention

The United Nations Conference on Trade and Development (UNCTAD) was dissatisfied with this situation and decided to intervene with an international convention to govern combined transport. This was finally adopted at an international conference in Geneva in May 1980 as the 'United Nations Convention on International Multimodal Transport of Goods' (or 'UNCTAD MMO Convention' as it is more commonly known).

Like the Hamburg Rules (see 8.17), if introduced it seems inevitably bound to increase a carrier's insurance costs, which will probably be reflected in increased freight rates without any corresponding reduction in cargo insurance premiums.

It will come into force 12 months after the deposit of the documents of ratification, acceptance, approval or accession with the UN in New York by the thirtieth country, with no minimum tonnage qualifications. To date, it has been ratified by seven countries only: Cameroon, Chile, Malawi, Mexico, Rwanda, Senegal and Zambia. UNCTAD MMO owes much in its drafting to the Hamburg Rules and its approach to limitation of liability may be described as 'a plateau with peaks showing through'. That is to say, the Rules set a limit (about 10 per cent above the Hamburg limit and expressed in SDRs) with a dual weight/package alternative criterion, but where any unimodal conventions apply a higher limit of liability, and loss or damage occurs in their period of applicability, their limits apply in preference to the UNCTAD MMO limit.

UNCTAD MMO has few supporters, so it is to be hoped that its implementation (if ever) is some way off yet.

9.5.4 UNCTAD/ICC Rules for Multimodal Transport Documents

There has been a difference of opinion between the ICC, which is not keen on the MMO Convention, and UNCTAD, which is its architect.

As part of their continuing campaign to promote the Hamburg Rules and UNCTAD/MMO Convention, UNCTAD sought the cooperation of the ICC to review and update the ICC Rules for a combined transport document (see 9.5.2). However, the ICC Rules were not in need of revision and their general basic application world-wide attested to their acceptability to the parties concerned. Nevertheless, the ICC were persuaded to join UNCTAD in this matter, possibly on the basis that a workable compromise which would appease UNCTAD might be achieved.

The working party constituted under Professor Jan Ramberg to review these Rules was given a clear brief to base its draft on the Hague-Visby Rules. They claim to have done so, but to claim to provide Rules based on the Hague-Visby Rules without incorporating the Article 4 Rule 2 tariff of exceptions is, in this author's opinion, untenable. Merely adding back the Nautical Fault and Fire exclusions to a Rule based on the Hamburg Rules, Article 5 does not equate to the Hague-Visby Rules. Professor Ramberg claims that a bill of lading issued subject to these Rules could still list the Hague-Visby Rules, Article 4 Rule 2 exceptions without contravening the Rules. However, if the Article 4 Rule 2 tariff of exceptions is acceptable, why not retain it in the Rules and retain the wealth of case law based thereon rather than introduce the ambiguous wording of Article 5 of the Hamburg Rules? Accordingly, there will be few, if any carriers prepared to be persuaded to adopt these voluntary Rules instead of the present ICC Rules, which will most likely remain the basis for most combined transport contracts, including those of P&O Containers.

9.5.5   CSC Convention

The 1972 Convention for Safe Containers introduced a requirement for regular inspection of containers by qualified personnel, a record of which is made by punching details on a metal plate at the door end of the container so that a cursory inspection can verify that a container is 'in time'. It is rather like a container MOT test.

FURTHER READING FOR PART III

(a)   Carriage of Goods by Sea

Carver, T.G., *Carriage by Sea,* 14th edn, London: Sweet & Maxwell, 1999.

Hughes, A.D., *Casebook on Carriage of Goods by Sea*, 2nd edn, London: Blackstone, 1999.

Mankabady, S., *The Hamburg Rules on the Carriage of Goods by Sea*, London: Euromoney, 1991.

P&O Containers: The Merchant's Guide, 6th edn, P&O Containers, 1992.

Boyd, S.C., *Scrutton on Charterparties,* 20th edn, London: Sweet & Maxwell, 1996.

Sturley, M., *The Legislative History of the Carriage of Goods by Sea Act and The Travaux Préparatoires of the Hague Rules*, Littleton: Fred Rothman & Co., 1990.

Wilson, J.F., *Carriage of Goods by Sea*, 3rd edn, London: Financial Times, 1998.

(b) Carriage of Goods by Air

Giemulla *et al.*, *Warsaw Convention*, The Hague: Kluwer, 1992.
Goldhirsch, L.V., *The Warsaw Convention Annotated*, The Hague: Kluwer, 1988.
IATA, *IATA Airway Bill Handbook*, 17th edn.
Magdelenat, J-L., *Air Cargo Regulations and Claims*, Ontario: Butterworths Canada, 1983.
Mankiewicz, R.H., *The Liability Regime of the International Air Carrier*, The Hague: Kluwer, 1981.
Shawcross and Beaumont, *Air Law*, 4th edn, London: Butterworths, 1991.

(c) Carriage of Goods by Road

Clarke, M.A., *International Carriage of Goods by Road: CMR*, 3rd edn, London: Sweet & Maxwell, 1997.
Glass, D. and Messent, A.D., *CMR: Contracts for the International Carriage of Goods by Road*, 2nd edn, London: LLP, 1995.
Yates, D. and Hawkins, A.J., *Standard Business Contracts*, London: Sweet & Maxwell, 1986.

(d) Carriage of Goods by Rail

Haenni, J., *Law of Transport*, Jirbinger, 1973.
Palmer, N.E., *Bailment*, 2nd edn, London: Sweet & Maxwell, 1991.

(e) Carriage of Goods: Multimodal

Diamond, A., *The 1980 Convention on Multimodal Transport, Legal Aspects of the Convention*, 1981.
Goode and Schmitthoff, *International Carriage of Goods: Some Legal Problems and Possible Solutions*, London: Centre for Commercial Law Studies, 1988.
Harrington, S., 'Legal problems arising from containerisation and international transport', (1982) 17 ETL 3.
ICC Uniform Rules For Combined Transport Document, ICC, Brochure 298, 1975.
UNCTAD/ICC Rules For Multimodal Transport Documents, UNCTAD/ICC, Publication No. 481, 1992.

(f) Carriage of Goods: General

Brigg, R. and Whitehead, G., *Elements of Transportation and Documentation*, Cambridge: Prentice Woodhead, 1990.

Cashmore, C., *Parties to a Contract of Carriage, Who Can Sue?* London: LLP, 1990.
Glass and Cashmore, C., *Introduction to The Law of Carriage of Goods*, London: Sweet & Maxwell, 1989.
Lloyd's of London, *Contracts For Carriage of Goods*, 3 vols , London: LLP.

PART IV
PAYMENTS AND FINANCE IN INTERNATIONAL TRADE

10   Payments in International Trade

10.1   INTRODUCTION

A typical example of an international sale transaction is a seller selling goods to an overseas buyer in a f.o.b. or c.i.f. contract so that the buyer is to pay the price against the delivery of conforming documents. The buyer may not have sufficient cash flow to pay the whole of the price and is relying upon possession of the documents to effect a sub-sale of the same goods and then to use the proceeds of the sub-sale to complete his obligations under the main sale. The buyer will, therefore, have stipulated in the main contract for a period of credit from the seller, i.e. a stated period of time after he has obtained possession of the documents before he actually has to pay the price. From the seller's point of view this is unsatisfactory, since during the period of credit he has lost control of the goods without receiving the price. The question with which the financing of the international sale contract is concerned is, how can this period of credit be extended without causing either the buyer to part with his money before receiving at least the constructive possession of the goods, or the seller to lose control of the goods without receiving the price? There are a number of ways in which this question can be resolved.

PART I   DIRECT METHODS OF PAYMENT

10.2   CASH AND DIRECT MEANS OF PAYMENT

10.2.1   Direct Means of Payment

There are four major means of payment in international trade: direct means of payment; bills of exchange and promissory notes (bills of exchange); barter or countertrade (see 1.6); and letters of credit (see Chapter 11). The direct means will normally involve considerably less money and risk, whereas the letters of credit will normally involve a complex transaction with higher risks thereby drawing a bank as a third party guarantee. Otherwise the payment clause in the contract will provide for where, when, how and through whom payment is to be made.

The direct means, sometimes also known as a simple means of payment or payment on open account, can take any of the following forms.

10.2.1.1   Cash Payment

Unless otherwise indicated in the contract of sale, there is nothing to stop parties paying in, and accepting, cash in the local currency of the seller, or in any other stipulated currency. In this case, the banker arranges to draw money in the stipulated currency and pays the seller in cash. The buyer can do this in person or through an agent. Although it is a risky venture, buyers have been known to carry cash in suitcases across borders for this purpose. Safer ways of obtaining cash include use of credit cards, travellers cheques or even personal cheques where the buyer has a bank account in the seller's country. International merchants, companies and organisations have been known to maintain bank accounts overseas or locally in foreign currency for this purpose.

10.2.1.2   Cash with Order

As with cash payments, cash with order is used where the transaction is simple and the value involved is not large. It is attractive where both parties wish to reduce their costs by cutting out the middleman and avoiding bank charges. Cash with order is suitable for mail orders and payments for publications involving postage and courier services. In this case, the buyer fills out the order/application form (e.g. a catalogue), obtains a warrant from a bank or giro bank and mails it back to the seller, upon receipt of which the merchandise is shipped.

10.2.1.3   Cash against Documents

Cash against documents operates in almost the same way as cash with order, except that in this case the documents for the goods are presented to the buyer but the goods are not delivered to him until cash payment has been received. An example of this is where buyer and seller meet at a border crossing, one with goods and documents and the other with cash. Alternatively, the buyer can request his bank to transfer to the buyer's bank. At its inception, the c.i.f. contract was a cash against documents contract, and remains so in theory. This payment method is now suitable for ex-works contracts.

10.2.1.4   Cash on Delivery

Cash on delivery is a service where the Post Office undertakes to collect money due to the sender of a parcel or packet provided certain stringent conditions are met. The amount never exceeds £50 sterling and the sender has to complete a trade change form supplied by the Post Office. This form guarantees that the goods sent have been requested specifically by the addressee (buyer). The service only applies to registered packets and parcels. No more cover is given to them than to other registered post and the sender (seller) pays a trade charge and customs clearance or declaration.

The service is available to both inland and overseas postal deliveries, though where overseas deliveries are concerned, certain extra rules apply. Until the advent of letters of credit, cash on delivery was the principle on which f.o.b. was delivery. This remains so in principle, since in f.o.b. contracts physical delivery of the goods is the most important function performed by the seller. Delivery is when property passes to the buyer, i.e. upon crossing the ship's rail. Otherwise, cash on delivery is also suitable for goods transported through the CMR (see 9.3.2).

10.2.1.5   Telegraphic Transfer

Telegraphic transfer is a swift method of transferring money abroad, operated by a bank at the customer's request and risk. The bank cables the relevant instructions to its overseas agent, normally another bank or the overseas branch of (in this case) a UK bank. The agent then effects the necessary credits or debits, usually in the currency of the transferee. Needless to say, such cash transfers must conform to current exchange control regulations in both countries where they apply.

10.2.1.6   Mail Transfer

Mail transfer operates on the same basis with the exception that, as the name suggests, the money is transferred by mail which is slower but cheaper to the transferee. It should be noted that, unlike in bills of exchange and letters of credit cases, here the bank does not provide credit to the buyer; the buyer must have an account in credit with the bank to cover the transaction or must pay cash in local currency.

10.2.1.7   Banker's Drafts

Although a simple direct means of payment, both banker's drafts and mail transfers introduce the bank as liable third party, where the money is not received or is received late by the beneficiary through the fault of the bank. Otherwise, a banker's draft is an instrument by which a branch of a bank orders another branch or its head office to make payment locally or overseas. Since the bank's organisation is one corporate body and the drawer and drawee are the same person, so the holder of the draft may, by the Bills of Exchange Act 1882, s. 5(2), treat the draft either as a bill of exchange or as a promissory note. Since the banker's drafts thus embody a bank's own obligation to pay, they are treated as the equivalent of cash and purchased for use in transactions where a very reliable means of payment is required, as in the purchases of real property or payments for overseas purchase. It is for that reason that they are regarded as a direct means of payment.

10.2.1.8   Electronic Transfers

Buying and selling can be done through the Internet. Payments too can be made through websites on the WorldWideWeb (www). Thus, payments can now be made by the push of a button through Electronic Data Transmission (EDT) or Electronic Data Interchange (EDI).

10.3   NOVATION

The seller could 'novate' the contract with the buyer using one of the seller's creditors, usually his bank. Novation is the creation of a new agreement between the seller's creditor (the bank) and his debtor (the buyer). In the new agreement, the buyer agrees to pay the debt due to the seller directly to the bank, thereby extinguishing the buyer's debt to the seller and the seller's debt to the bank. The consideration for the new agreement moving from the bank is its abandonment of its claim against the seller. This procedure is cumbersome and requires the express consent of all three parties before the bank receives the right to sue the buyer.

10.4   ASSIGNMENT OF THE DEBT

The seller could assign the buyer's debt to his creditor (the bank). Notice must be given to the buyer before he ceases to be liable to the seller (the assignor) and becomes liable to the bank (the assignee).

The assignee (the bank) also takes subject to equities. Equities are different from equitable interests. An equitable interest is a real right in an asset or thing, whereas a 'mere' equity is not an interest in an asset at all. It is simply a personal right given to someone who has conferred an interest or right on another in circumstances giving the transferor the right to set aside or qualify the document or transaction by which the interest or right was conferred. Typical examples of equities are the personal rights to avoid a contract for misrepresentation, fraud, duress, mutual mistake, undue influence, or to have a document rectified when it does not properly reflect the agreement it purports to represent.

Further, the assignee (the bank) takes the debt subject to any rights of set-off which the debtor (the buyer) might have against the assignor (the seller) arising out of the right assigned. Thus the debtor (the buyer) could set up against the assignee of the debt (the bank) any liquidated claim he had against the assignor (the seller) before he received notice of the assignment.

PART 2   BILLS OF EXCHANGE

10.5   INTRODUCTION

The seller could alternatively use a bill of exchange. The seller (the drawer) would draw a bill on the buyer (the drawee) ordering the buyer to pay the price with or without interest at a specified time after the date of the bill (the period of credit). The seller would then normally present the bill to the buyer for acceptance immediately, thereby making the buyer 'the acceptor' of and liable on the bill. Then the seller would discount (sell) the bill to the bank discharging his own liability to the bank, or receiving a sum, a little less than the face value of the bill, in exchange. The bank, which is presumed to be a 'holder in due course' of the bill, would present the bill to the buyer on the expiry of the period of credit and receive the amount on the face of the bill.

The benefits of the bill of exchange are that there is no need for notice to be given to the debtor (the buyer) or for his consent before the bank can enforce the promise to pay incorporated in the bill. In addition, the bank, as the holder in due course, will take the bill of exchange free of equities and other claims. Indeed, the only defence which can be set up against the holder in due course of the bill is that the document is not a bill of exchange at all, i.e. a material element is missing in the form of the bill.

The three special features of a bill of exchange are:

(1) it can be transferred by delivery (though sometimes the transferor's indorsement is required);

(2) such transfer operates free of equities and other personal claims against the transferee; and

(3) there is no requirement to give notice to the debtor and together give the bill 'negotiability'.

A negotiable instrument, therefore, is a chose in action, the full and legal title to which is transferable by mere delivery of the instrument (possibly with the transferor's indorsement depending upon the terms as to delivery on the instrument itself) with the result that complete ownership of the instrument and all the property it represents passes free from equities to the transferee, provided that the latter takes the instrument in good faith and for value.

'Negotiation', 'assignment' and 'transfer' are three different concepts. All three represent a change of ownership of an instrument of value, but there is a difference in each as to how this is effected and the nature of the interest passed on.

'Transfer' is the passing to another of an instrument of value by delivery (and sometimes indorsement) without the need to give notice to the person liable on the instrument. It is, therefore, correct to speak of bills of exchange being 'transferred'. 'Transfer' does not, however, indicate whether the transferee takes the instrument free from equities or not; only 'negotiation' has this effect.

'Assignment' denotes a change of ownership by the completion of a separate document evidencing the transfer and giving notice to the party liable. It also tells one that the transferee takes the instrument subject to equities. It is not, therefore, correct to speak of the delivery of a bill of exchange as an assignment, or that negotiability and assignability are the same.

Although a particular class of instruments may, by usage, have become negotiable, whether the particular instrument of that class in question has been 'negotiated' depends upon the particular form of the delivery in question. If the delivery did not comply with the accepted requirements for negotiation, the instrument will still have been transferred, but the transferee does not enjoy the instrument free of equities and other personal claims the party liable had against the transferor. The accepted requirements for a negotiation of a negotiable interest are as follows:

(a) The transfer must be for value. This is self explanatory, although there are some rules peculiar to bills of exchange in the Bills of Exchange Act 1882.

(b)   The transferee must take the instrument in good faith. This is a question of fact for each case. It is a subjective concept, but the more unreasonable the particular transferee's beliefs, the more likely the courts will find that he was not, in fact, honest and was acting in bad faith.

(c)   The instrument must be complete and regular on its face. This means that the instrument must not be lacking in any material particular, for instance, if the name of the payee is missing.

(d)   The instrument must be in a deliverable state. This means that the requirements for delivery have been fulfilled. If the instrument is drawn to 'bearer', then no indorsement is required and the bill is deliverable in the state in which it was drawn. If the instrument is drawn to 'order', then delivery must be accompanied by the indorsement of the transferor.

(e)   There must be nothing on the instrument negativing the transferability of the instrument.

The law relating to bills of exchange is contained in the Bills of Exchange Act 1882 (BEA 1882). All references in this chapter are to this Act unless otherwise stated.

10.6   THE STATUTORY DEFINITION

The statutory definition of a bill of exchange is found in s. 3 which provides as follows:

(1)   A bill of exchange is an unconditional order in writing, addressed by one person to another, signed by the person giving it, requiring the person to whom it is addressed to pay on demand or at a fixed or determinable future time a sum certain in money to or to the order of a specified person, or to bearer.

(2)   An instrument which does not comply with these conditions, or which orders any act to be done in addition to the payment of money, is not a bill of exchange.

It appears from the definition that a bill of exchange is an order in writing to pay a certain sum of money at a certain time to a certain person, and that the order is independent of any other obligation. Certainty and autonomy are the essential and, to merchants and businessmen, the attractive features of a bill of exchange. The parties to a bill of exchange are as follows:

(a)   The *drawer* gives the order to pay, and is usually the seller in sale contracts.

(b)   The *drawee* is the person to whom the order is addressed. He must be someone other than the drawer and in international sales is usually the buyer, or the buyer's bank.

(c)   The *acceptor* is the person who accepts the obligation to pay which is embodied in the bill. The acceptor will usually be the drawee. Obviously, the drawer cannot be the acceptor. Acceptance of the bill is different from payment of the bill.

Acceptance will occur before the bill matures, i.e. before the time when the period of credit has expired, and involves the holder of the bill presenting the bill to another who will often be named on the bill or in the underlying contract of sale. If the person to whom it is presented accepts the bill, he then becomes liable on the bill and bound to pay its face value at the specified time. It follows, therefore, that when the bill is payable the moment it is presented (a 'sight bill'), there is no scope for acceptance. It is only when the bill is a 'time bill' that acceptance is desirable, though not usually necessary.

(d)   The *payee* is the person who is to be paid by the drawee or acceptor on the instructions of the drawer. In overseas sales the drawer and the payee are usually the seller.

(e)   The *indorser* is the holder of the bill who negotiates the bill by indorsement and delivery to a third party in exchange for a sum usually slightly less than the face value of the bill. Often the seller will be the first indorser.

(f)   The *indorsee* is the person to whom the bill is negotiated. In overseas sales he will usually be the seller's bank discounting the seller's drafts.

(g)   The *holder* is defined in s. 2 as 'the payee or indorsee of a bill or note who is in possession of it, or the bearer thereof'. His possession must be legal possession. The seller (the payee) is the first holder of the bill, though as will be seen later, the seller cannot in his own right be a holder in due course as the statutory definition requires negotiation, and a bill is 'issued' to the payee and not 'negotiated' to him. There are three types of holder which will be discussed in detail at 10.14: (1) the holder; (2) the holder for value; and (3) the holder in due course.

The various elements of the definition of a bill of exchange in s. 3 will be examined in turn.

10.6.1   Unconditional Order

There must be a definite order. A mere request to pay is not enough. 'Pay' or 'please pay' are acceptable. However, 'I should be grateful if you were to pay' is not an order and cannot constitute a bill of exchange.

The order must be unconditional. This means that the payment obligation must not be subject to any contingency. Since it is the obligation to pay which must be unconditional, it does not matter if a particular payee's entitlement to payment is subject to a contingency provided that if the contingency were to fail the drawee remains liable on the bill. In *Roberts* v *Marsh* [1915] 1 KB 42 the words 'to be retained' were held not to have made the order conditional as they were directed to the payee or indorsee, and not to the drawee. The drawee's liability obviously remained throughout the life of the bill.

If the order is conditional on some contingency, this is not cured by the occurrence of the event (s. 11). It is, however, possible for delivery of the bill to be conditional so that the recipient is not a holder of the bill unless and until the conditions upon which he received the bill are satisfied (s. 21(2)(b)); see *Clifford Chance* v *Silver, The Times*, 31 July 1992.

An order to pay out of a particular fund is conditional for the fund may be too small (s. 3(3)). Again it is irrelevant that the fund is in fact sufficient. If the reference to a fund is merely to indicate to the drawee from where he may seek reimbursement, and not a direction to pay out of the fund, the order remains unconditional (s. 3(3)(a)).

A reference to the commercial transaction which has given rise to the bill of exchange does not make the order conditional (s. 3(3)(b)). Examples of such references are 'drawn against cotton' or 'drawn against shipment on the *Sinker*'. Similarly, bills of exchange drawn under a documentary credit are not rendered conditional as a result. In *Guaranty Trust Co. of New York* v *Hannay* [1918] 2 KB 623 the court said:

> ... such expressions are used to denote the fact that the draft is drawn as part of a mercantile transaction and not to indicate that the fund produced by the transaction is the only one to be used.

10.6.2   Writing

The order must be in writing, though the medium used is irrelevant. However, the drawing of instruments in pencil is not encouraged by banks because of the ease of alteration. Addressed by one person to another, s. 6(1) provides that the drawee must be named or otherwise indicated with reasonable certainty. If the bill, therefore, did not mention the drawee's name but stated a place of residence and was accepted by a person living there, the acceptor would not be allowed to object. Similarly, if the bill were drawn on a multi-branch organisation, such as a bank, without stating a particular branch, the drawee would be indicated with reasonable certainty. Joint drawees are permitted, but alternate drawees are not (s. 6(2)).

If a man draws a bill on himself so that the drawer and the drawee are the same person, the document is *prima facie* outside the definition since it is not 'addressed by one person to another'. In *Capital & Counties Bank* v *Gordon* [1903] AC 240 the branch of a bank drew a bill on its head office. It was held that since a bank is one legal entity, the bank had drawn the bill on itself and consequently the document was not a bill of exchange.

However, s. 5(2) provides that 'where in a bill the drawer and the drawee are the same person ... the holder may treat the instrument, at his option, as a bill of exchange or as a promissory note'.

It should be noted that the drawer of a bill of exchange may often be the payee. Where, for example, a seller of goods draws a bill of exchange on the buyer for the price, the seller is both the drawer of the bill of exchange and the payee and the buyer is the drawee to whom the order is directed.

10.6.3   Signed by the Person Giving the Order

The drawer's signature is essential to the validity of the bill. Hence no action can be maintained on a bill which has not been signed by the drawer. The drawer's signature is usually written at the bottom right-hand corner of the bill, though there is no absolute rule. The forgery of a signature on a bill is not a signature at all; it is a nullity (s. 24). If the bill is signed for the drawer by someone authorised, this operates as the drawer's signature, e.g. '*per pro* Phillip, Joshua'. If the signatory did not have such authority, the signature is treated as if it were a forgery and, therefore, a nullity.

10.6.4   The Date When the Bill of Exchange is to be Paid Must be Certain

A bill will satisfy this requirement if it is payable on demand or at a fixed or determinable future date. A bill of exchange is payable on demand (s. 10) when it is:

(a)   expressed as such; or
(b)   expressed payable on sight or on presentation; or
(c)   where no time for payment is expressed at all; or
(d)   if a bill is accepted or indorsed after maturity it is deemed payable on demand as against the acceptor or indorser. A bill will have passed maturity if it were drawn for instance 30 days after the date of the bill and was accepted on the 31st day.

A determinable future time is one which is either:

(a)   payable at a fixed period after date; or
(b)   payable at a fixed period after sight (meaning after its presentment for acceptance, but not requiring that the bill actually be accepted); or
(c)   payable on or at a fixed period after the occurrence of a specified event which is certain to happen, notwithstanding that the date of its occurrence is uncertain, e.g. someone's death.

In *Korea Exchange Bank* v *Debenhams* [1979] 1 Lloyd's Rep 548 the Court of Appeal held that an instrument in the form of a bill drawn payable at a fixed period after acceptance was not a bill of exchange as acceptance is not a certain event.

In *Claydon* v *Bradley* [1987] 1 All ER 522 a promissory note promising that a loan would be repaid 'by 1 July 1983' was an instrument containing an option to pay at an earlier date. It, therefore, was not an unconditional promise to pay at a fixed or determinable future time.

10.6.5   A Sum Certain in Money

A sum of money is certain for the purposes of the BEA 1882 notwithstanding that it is required to be paid with interest, or in a particular way, e.g. by instalments, or according to a specified rate of exchange (s. 9(1)).

When a bill is payable with interest, in the absence of stipulations to the contrary, interest runs from the date of the bill. If the bill is undated, interest runs from the date of the issue of the bill (s. 9(3)). 'Issue' is defined in s. 2 as the first delivery of the bill to a person who takes as holder, i.e. the payee.

A bill can only be payable in money or legal currency. Where, therefore, part of the sum agreed to be paid is not, in fact, by the terms of the instrument, to be paid, but to be treated as set off, that will invalidate the instrument as a bill of exchange. The same applies if the payment is to be by the rendering of services.

If the amount is stated in words and figures and there is a discrepancy between the two, the sum payable is that stated in words (s. 9(2)).

10.6.6   To, or to the Order of, a Specified Person, or to Bearer

The various possibilities permitted by the definition are as follows:

(a)   a specified person, e.g. 'pay Toby'; or
(b)   the order of a specified person, e.g. 'pay the order of Nathan' or 'pay Nathan or order'; or
(c)   bearer, e.g. 'pay bearer'.

The nature of the requirements as to the payee are dealt with below. If an instrument in the form of a bill fails to comply with the definition in s. 3, this does not mean that the promisee (the seller) will not be paid. The instrument will not confer the benefits of negotiability. However, it will probably operate as an assignment of the promise represented by the instrument and entitle the assignee to the rights therein subject to equities, etc. If the instrument had been drawn under a contract of sale requiring payment by bill of exchange, the buyer would be in breach of his payment obligations, the seller could reject the instrument and call on the buyer to comply with the contract if still in time.

10.7   COMPUTATION OF TIME IN BILLS OF EXCHANGE

Section 14(1), which deals with how time is to be computed in a bill of exchange transaction, has been repealed and replaced by s. 3(2), Banking and Financial Dealings Act 1971. A bill is deemed due and payable in all cases on the last day of the time for payment as fixed by the bill, or if that is not a business day then on the succeeding business day.

Where a bill of exchange is payable on a fixed period after sight, date or the happening of a certain future event, the time for payment is determined by excluding the day from which time is due to run but by including the day of payment (s. 14(2), BEA 1882).

When a bill is due payable at a fixed period after sight, sight is deemed to run from the date of acceptance of the bill, or if the bill was not accepted, from the date of noting or protesting the bill (s. 14(3)).

10.8   THE DATE OF THE BILL

The omission of the date on a bill is not fatal (s. 3(4)). When a bill is expressed to be payable at a fixed period after date, but is issued with the date missing, or where the acceptance of a bill payable at fixed period after sight is undated, any holder may insert the true date, and if he acts in good faith the date he inserts will be taken as the true date, even if wrong, if the bill is in the hands of a holder in due course (s. 12). Dating of the bill is not, of course, necessary where the bill actually specifies the date on which it is to fall due. A bill is never invalidated by reason of the fact that it is post-dated or ante-dated (s. 13).

10.9 THE FICTITIOUS OR NON-EXISTING PAYEE

Where the payee is a fictitious or non-existing person the bill may be treated as payable to bearer (s. 7(3)). The BEA 1882 does not define 'fictitious or non-existing payee', and consequently this was left to the courts to decide. A fictitious person has been held not to be the same as a non-existing person. Hence in each case it must be determined whether the payee is (1) existing; (2) non-existing; or (3) fictitious. This is done by finding what was intended by or in the mind of the drawer when he signed the bill.

10.9.1 Existing Payee

If the drawer knew of the existence of the payee at the time he signed the bill and intended the payee to receive payment, then the payee is existing. In *North and South Wales Bank* v *Macbeth* [1908] AC 137 White fraudulently induced Macbeth to draw a cheque in favour of Kerr. Kerr was an existing person and was someone known to Macbeth, but had no knowledge himself that the cheque had been drawn in his favour. On obtaining possession of the cheque, White forged Kerr's indorsement and paid it into his (White's) own bank account with the appellant bank. The bank presented the cheque for collection from Macbeth's bank and received the stated amount. Macbeth brought an action against White's bank for the money on the basis that Kerr's indorsement was a forgery and, therefore, a nullity as neither White nor his bank had title to the bill and also that the bill was not a bearer bill but an order bill as he (Macbeth), the drawer, had intended it to be drawn on an existing and named payee, Kerr.

The House of Lords held that the explanation of the expression 'fictitious person' in s. 7(3) involves an investigation into the mind of the drawer when drawing the cheque. If the drawer intended that the existing person whom he designated as payee should receive the money, such payee is not a fictitious person within the section. It was accordingly held that Macbeth should succeed: when he drew the bill, Macbeth intended that Kerr should be paid the amount of the bill, notwithstanding that this intention had been induced by White's fraud. The bill was not payable to bearer within the subsection. The bank did not have good title to the bill as it was not a party to it — the bank was seeking to claim title through a forged and, therefore, void indorsement and negotiation. The bank was bound, therefore, to pay the value of the bill to Macbeth.

10.9.2   Non-existing Payee

If it is found that the drawer did not know of the existence of the payee when he signed, then the payee is a non-existing person notwithstanding that there was an actual living person of that name. In *Clutton* v *Attenborough* [1897] AC 90 a dishonest clerk had induced his employer to sign cheques payable to Brett by saying that he was Brett's debtor. There were, however, no such debts and the drawer had never heard of anyone called Brett. Thus, although the drawer apparently intended payment to be made to Brett, he did not know of the existence of any such person and the court held that the payee was non-existing and the cheques payable to bearer.

10.9.3   Fictitious Payee

In determining whether a payee is fictitious or not, the intention of the drawer of the bill is decisive. If he inserted the name as a mere pretence, to colour the instrument, the payee is fictitious, even if that person was known to exist. In *Bank of England* v *Vagliano Bros* [1891] AC 107 Vagliano's clerk obtained the acceptance of his employer to instruments which purported to be bills drawn by Vagliano's customers on Vagliano payable to Petridi, someone known to Vagliano and with whom Vagliano had previously done business. The bills were, in fact, forgeries by the clerk. The clerk forged Petridi's indorsement in each case to a fictitious indorsee, Moratis, and obtained payment from Vagliano's bank. The question for the court was whether the bank could debit Vagliano's account with the amount of the bill which it had paid out, thereby treating the bill as payable to bearer. The House of Lords held that the real drawer of the bills was the clerk who forged them, and he knew of the existence of the payees but did not intend them to receive payment. The payees were accordingly considered fictitious and the bills payable to bearer under s. 7(3) thus entitling the bank to obtain the amount of the bill from the acceptor, Vagliano.

The importance of finding that a payee is non-existing or fictitious and, therefore, treating the bill as payable to bearer is that this eliminates the effect of a forged indorsement on the line of title to the bill. As will be seen below, a forged signature on an order bill breaks the line of title and discharges the liability of the parties prior to the forgery. Since indorsement is not necessary to the negotiation of a bearer bill, the fact that a particular indorsement is forged does not alter the validity of the bill itself.

10.9.4   Pay 'Cash'

Section 3 requires that a bill must be payable to the order of a specified person or to bearer. Consequently, documents drawn up as bills but payable to cash or some other impersonal payee cannot be a bill of exchange within the BEA 1882. The addition of the words 'or order' is inconsistent with the apparent intention of the drawer, and is ignored in favour of the impersonal word 'cash' or 'wages'. It is doubtful whether such instruments are negotiable.

The use of such instruments is, however, confined generally to cheques intended to be cashed at the drawee-bank counter. By virtue of s. 1(2), Cheques Act 1957 and the decision in *Orbit Mining and Trading Co.* v *Westminster Bank Ltd* [1963] 1 QB 794 bankers are placed in the same position, whether paying or collecting these instruments, as though they were valid cheques; see also *North & South Insurance Co.* v *Westminster Bank Ltd* [1936] 1 KB 328.

If the instrument is drawn payable to 'wages or bearer' or to 'cash or bearer' then the words 'or bearer' are heeded and the instrument, if otherwise in the form of a bill, is treated as a bearer bill in s. 8(2).

10.9.5 The Making of a Bearer Bill

By s. 8(2) bills designed payable 'to bearer' are called 'bearer bills' and are negotiable by mere delivery. There are two ways in which a bill can become payable to bearer (s. 8(3)). First, where the bill is originally payable to bearer, and is, therefore, always a bearer bill. Even if someone other than the drawer and acceptor signs the bill, the bill does not become an order bill. Secondly, where the bill is on its face an order bill, but the last indorsement on the back of the bill is 'in blank'. An order bill can, therefore, be converted into a bearer bill by the way in which it is negotiated. It can subsequently be converted back into an order bill if the holder for the time being indorses with a special indorsement, naming the transferee. Thereafter, until the next indorsement in blank, the bill is again an order bill.

The importance of assessing the type of bill, order or bearer, lies in the class of persons who can become holders of the bill. By s. 2 the holder of a bill is any person to whom the bill has been issued (the payee) or negotiated. Anyone who is not a holder of the bill, even if in possession of it, cannot sue on it in his own name.

10.10 TRANSFER

Suppose that Matthew has drawn a bill on Mark ordering him to pay to the order of Luke six months after the date of the bill. Luke (the payee) may not want or be able to wait the six months for the bill to mature before he receives his money. He may prefer to get a little less than the face value of the bill by selling (negotiating) the bill for cash at a discount. This process is called discounting the bill. Luke would, therefore, approach his bank or a finance house or some third party who is willing to wait the six months before the maturity of the bill. The purchaser or discounter will make his profit from the difference between the purchase price and the face value of the bill. Luke would, therefore, get most of his money immediately, and the discounter will be the party who presents the bill to Matthew for payment. When a number of bills are discounted at a time to the same person, this is called 'block discounting'.

There must, however, be a proper and valid negotiation of the bill from Luke to the discounting transferee. 'A bill is negotiated when it is transferred from one person to another in such a manner as to constitute the transferee the holder of the bill' (s. 31(1)).

If a bill is payable 'to bearer' there is a valid negotiation by mere delivery (s. 31(2)). The possessor of the bill is the 'bearer' and, therefore, the holder in s. 2. He is entitled to sue on the bill in his own name (s. 38).

If the bill is an order bill there is a valid negotiation making the possessor the 'holder' if there is both an indorsement by the prior holder and delivery to the possessor (s. 31(3)). The 'indorsee' becomes the s. 2 holder.

There are two types of indorsement as defined by s. 34. First, is the 'special indorsement' in s. 34(2) which indicates the name of the new indorsee on the back of the bill: 'Pay John, Luke'. This means that only John or a person to whom he has indorsed the bill can present the bill for payment. No other person, even if in possession of the bill, qualifies as the holder. The second type is an 'indorsement in blank' where the intended transferee is not named, but the prior holder simply signs his name: 'Luke' (s. 34(1)). The bill becomes a bearer bill until converted back into an order bill by the holder specially indorsing. A bill which was drawn to bearer can never become an order bill, even if there is a purported special indorsement. The original nature of the bill can be determined by looking at the way in which it was drawn.

When an order bill is delivered to someone without indorsement, the transferee is not the holder of the bill as there has not been a proper negotiation of the bill to him. Neither can he be the bearer of the bill, as it was not a bearer bill. Section 31(4) provides that such a transfer for value gives the transferee the title that his transferor had on the bill, i.e. he takes subject to equities and can only sue on the bill through the name of the last holder. Furthermore the transferee for value can require the transferor to indorse the bill to him.

Also, to be effective in transferring title to a bill, an indorsement (if necessary) must be made by the holder. Where a stranger to the bill signs it, he becomes liable on the bill as any other indorser, though he never had title to the bill. He is commonly called a quasi-indorser or, in the terms of the Act, an 'accommodation party'. Section 28(1) defines an accommodation party to a bill as a person who has signed the bill as drawer, acceptor or indorser, without receiving value therefor, and for the purpose of lending his name to some other person. The effect of such a signature is to make the accommodation party liable on the bill to a holder for value; and it is immaterial whether, when such holder took the bill, he knew such party to be an accommodation party or not (s. 28(2)).

The reason for such accommodation parties is that they provide greater currency to the bill, rendering more parties liable on the bill in the event of dishonour and, therefore, providing security for a person purchasing the bill, particularly if there is uncertainty as to the creditworthiness of the drawee or acceptor. The use of accommodation parties can best be illustrated by an example. Suppose that Simon, being short of funds, takes a loan from his wealthy friend, Joseph, and draws a bill payable in two months time on Joseph. Joseph duly accepts the bill on presentment for acceptance. Joseph becomes liable on the bill by accepting it. However, he has given no value. As Joseph is both creditworthy and the party primarily liable on the bill by virtue of his acceptance, the bill is excellent security and Simon should have no difficulty in discounting it immediately, thereby short-circuiting his cash-flow problems. Joseph has signed the bill as acceptor to accommodate Simon and, consequently, is an accommodation party. This method of raising funds is sometimes known as 'kite flying' or 'raising the wind'.

An accommodation party need not be the acceptor, but can indorse the bill after it has been accepted simply to add currency to the bill. The accommodation party thereby assumes the liability of an indorser, but only to someone claiming as a holder in due course (s. 56). This provision has attained considerable importance when bearer bills are used.

The accommodation party is not liable on his signature to the party accommodated since the latter gives him no value for undertaking liability.

The term accommodation bill is used where the acceptor is the accommodation party. The reason for this is in s. 59(3), which states that an accommodation bill is discharged on payment by the party accommodated. This can only be the case where the acceptor is the accommodation party. If an indorser were the accommodation party, and he paid out on the bill, the bill would not be discharged and the acceptor would still be liable on the bill. A bill is only discharged when no party is liable on it.

There is one other situation in which a party may sign a bill when his signature is not essential for the validity of the bill. By s. 56 where a person signs a bill otherwise than as drawer or acceptor, he thereby incurs the liabilities of an indorser to a holder in due course. This provision enables a transferee of a bearer bill to insist on the indorsement of the transferor before he will take the bill. It provides the transferee with some commercial armoury rather than an actual legal right. The indorsement, commonly called a 'quasi-indorsement', is not necessary to make the transferee a 'holder' for s. 2. The indorsement merely adds to the currency of the bill by increasing the number of parties liable on it as guarantors. The indorser will only be liable to someone who is claiming as holder in due course: it is not enough that the claimant is a holder for value.

Section 34(3) provides that the indorsee of a special indorsement is in effect a new payee, and the provisions of the BEA 1882 relating to the payee apply to the indorsee.

10.11 ACCEPTANCE

Acceptance is defined, and the requirements for a valid acceptance are set out, in s. 17:

(1)   The acceptance of a bill is the signification by the drawee of his assent to the order of the drawer.

(2)   An acceptance is invalid unless it complies with the following conditions, namely:

(a)   It must be written on the bill and be signed by the drawee. The mere signature of the drawee without additional words is sufficient.

(b)   It must not express that the drawee will perform his promise by any other means than the payment of money.

It is clear, therefore, that acceptance of a bill is a written promise to pay the bill when due, in money and by no other means. Until this written agreement to pay has been given by the drawee, he is not liable on the bill, even though his name may appear on it. His signature is essential, and sufficient. Generally, however, the acceptor will add to his signature the word 'accepted' and perhaps the date, which is of course important in the case of bills which are payable after sight: the date on which the bill was presented for acceptance, whether accepted or not.

Acceptance is usually completed when the bill is delivered (handed back) to the person who presented for acceptance. Acceptance may, however, also be completed, and is therefore irrevocable, by the drawee giving notice to, or in accordance with the directions of, the person entitled to the bill (s. 21(1)).

After acceptance the drawee is called the 'acceptor' and is personally liable on the bill if properly presented for payment.

10.11.1   Who May Accept a Bill?

A bill can only be accepted by the drawee who, by s. 6, must be named, or otherwise indicated with reasonable certainty, on the face of the bill. A stranger cannot accept the bill except for honour. In *Bule* v *Morrell* (1840) 12 A & E 745 a bill was drawn on the directors of a company. It was accepted by a manager of the company who was not himself a director. It was held that his acceptance was not a proper acceptance of the bill as he was not a drawee of it and therefore he did not become personally liable on it. Similarly, if the drawee is a non-existing or fictitious person, the bill may be treated as dishonoured for non-acceptance.

10.11.2   Time of Acceptance

By s. 18(1) a bill may be accepted before it has been signed by the drawer, or while otherwise incomplete. Until the drawer's name is inserted, however, the instrument is not a bill of exchange, as a vital element is absent (s. 3). Further a bill may be accepted under s. 18(2) when it is overdue or after it has been dishonoured by a previous refusal to accept, or by non-payment. A bill when overdue is, by s. 10(2), payable on demand.

As regards the date of a bill of exchange which has been accepted after a previous dishonour by non-acceptance, s. 18(3) provides that the holder, in the absence of any different agreement, is entitled to have the bill accepted as of the date of first presentment to the drawee for acceptance.

Where an acceptance is undated, the presumption is that it was accepted before maturity and within a reasonable time of the date of the bill itself; see *Roberts* v *Bethell* (1852) 12 CB 778.

10.11.3 The Different Ways of Accepting a Bill

There are two types of acceptance: 'a general acceptance', which assents without qualification to the order of the drawer; and 'a qualified acceptance' which in express terms varies the effect of the bill as it has been drawn (s. 19(1) and (2)).

A general acceptance would be either a mere signature by the acceptor; or the signature of the drawee plus the word 'accepted'; or the signature of the drawee plus the date; or the signature of the drawee plus the word 'accepted' and the date; or any of the above plus words denoting where the bill is payable, with no absolute requirement (s. 19(2)(c)).

Section 19(2) lists what may constitute a qualified acceptance:

(a)   'Conditional acceptance', e.g. where the drawee agrees to pay the bill only if the underlying goods are of a certain standard.

(b)   'Partial acceptance', e.g. where the bill is drawn for £100 and the drawee accepts as to £50 only.

(c)   'Local acceptance', e.g. where the drawee agrees to pay only if the bill is presented for payment at a particular place. Without restrictive words such as 'only' the acceptance would be general.

(d)   An acceptance which is qualified as to time, e.g. a bill accepted payable at six months after date, where the bill is in fact drawn at three months after date.

(e)   Where there is acceptance by some but not all the drawees. If there is more than one drawee, they must all be jointly liable and therefore all must accept for the acceptance to be general.

By s. 44(1) the holder of a bill may refuse to take a qualified acceptance, and if he obtains a qualified acceptance he may treat the bill as having been dishonoured by non-acceptance.

If the holder agrees to accept a qualified acceptance, no prior indorser or drawer of the bill is bound by the holder's decision and is discharged from his secondary liability on the bill (s. 44(2)) provided that he indicates his rejection of the qualified acceptance within a reasonable time of being notified. His silence after being notified is deemed to be an assent once a reasonable time has passed (s. 44(3)). This, however, does not apply to partial acceptance so that no drawer or prior indorser of the bill is discharged. If the bill is a foreign bill, however, it must be protested as to the balance.

Most bills do not have to be presented for acceptance. Section 39 lists those bills for which acceptance is a prerequisite:

(a)   Where a bill is payable after sight, presentment for acceptance is necessary in order to fix the maturity of the bill.

(b)   Where a bill expressly stipulates that it shall be presented for acceptance.

(c)   Where a bill is drawn payable at a place other than at the place of business or residence of the drawee.

It is clear, therefore, that a bill which is payable after date does not have to be presented for acceptance by the holder in order to bring the bill to maturity. However, such a step is usually undertaken since an accepted bill is better currency for discounting purposes than an unaccepted one. Further, if the bill has properly been presented for acceptance, and it has been dishonoured for no good reason, the holder has an immediate right of recourse against prior parties and no presentment for payment is necessary (s. 43(2)).

Obviously in the case of bills payable after sight, the bill must be presented for acceptance to start time running to the date of maturity of the bill. If such a bill has been negotiated before being presented for acceptance, then the holder must either present it for acceptance or negotiate it within a reasonable time; failure to do so will discharge the drawer and prior indorsers (s. 40). What is a reasonable time is assessed by taking the nature of the bill, the usage of the trade, and the facts of the particular case into account.

Section 41(2) sets out the excuses for failure to present a bill for acceptance when need be, leading to the consequences that the bill can be treated as if dishonoured by non-acceptance:

(a)   Where the drawee is dead or bankrupt, or is a fictitious person or a person not having capacity to contract by bill.

(b)   Where after the exercise of reasonable diligence, presentment for acceptance cannot be effected.

(c)   Where, although the presentment has been irregular, acceptance has been refused on some other ground.

It should be noted that a mere *suspicion* that the bill will not be accepted, or cannot be effected, is not sufficient (s. 41(3)).

10.12   LIABILITIES OF THE PARTIES

No person is liable on a bill of exchange unless and until he has added his signature to the bill (s. 23). A person may be liable on the bill as drawer, indorser or acceptor. The drawee, the person to whom the order contained in the bill is addressed, is not liable on the bill unless he has accepted the bill. Furthermore any holder of a bearer bill who has negotiated it by delivery, but without indorsing it, is not liable on the bill as his signature does not appear on it.

The nature of the acceptor's liability on a bill differs from that of the drawer and indorsers of the bill. The acceptor is the party primarily liable on the bill. The bill must be presented to him when due. The drawer and indorsers of the bill bear a secondary liability on the bill and are treated as if they were sureties or guarantors for the acceptor's promise to pay. Where the bill has not been accepted they are also treated as guaranteeing that the drawee will pay or accept the bill. If, therefore, the drawee/acceptor's liability to pay is altered in any way, the other parties to the bill are discharged unless they assent to the change. This is best seen in the effect of a qualified acceptance (see 10.11.3).

Therefore if a bill is dishonoured when presented for payment, the holder of the bill will be able to exercise his right of recourse against the drawer and an indorser of the bill. If the bill was accepted he will also be able to sue the acceptor on the bill of exchange. If, however, the bill was not accepted he will not be able to sue the drawee on the bill itself as the drawee will not have signed the bill.

10.13 EXCLUSION OF LIABILITY

It is open to a drawer or indorser to insert an express stipulation excluding or limiting his own liability to the holder (s. 16(1)). A typical example would be where the indorser adds after his signature words such as 'sans recours' or 'without recourse'. This is found frequently when bills of exchange are used in letter of credit transactions.

10.14 THE HOLDER

10.14.1 Holding and Possession

The right to enforce payment of a bill is only given to the holder who, as already mentioned in 10.6, is defined by s. 2 as 'the payee or indorsee of a bill or note who is in possession of it, or the bearer thereof'.

To be the holder, a person must be in possession of the bill, and this is sufficient in the case of bearer bills. It is immaterial that his possession is unlawful. It is enough that on the face of the instrument he is entitled to be paid. This does not mean that a thief has the right to be paid, rather that if the acceptor pays the thief in good faith and without notice of the thief's unlawful possession, the bill is validly discharged.

If the bill is an order bill, then, as already seen, mere possession is not enough. The possessor must show that he is the person named on the bill as the present holder, i.e. that the last special indorsement was to him, or in blank.

Where an inchoate instrument is delivered, the transferee has *prima facie* authority to fill it up as a complete bill and thereby make himself a holder, though he cannot obtain the status of a holder in due course (s. 20(1)). An inchoate instrument is one lacking some material particular.

It seems that the material parts of the bill include the following: the identity of the payee; a signature necessary to establish the chain of title to the bill; and the amount of the bill — this is distinguished from the amount any particular indorsee of the bill has given as consideration to his transferor.

Elements which are *not* material include: the date; the place of issue of the bill; and the fact whether the bill has been accepted or not; see *National Park Bank* v *Berggren* (1914) 110 LT 907. Section 3(4) gives some guidance:

A bill is not invalid by reason:
    (a)   that it is not dated;
    (b)   that it does not specify the value given or that any value has been given therefor;

(c)   that it does not specify the place where it is drawn or the place where it is payable.

'*Prima facie* authority' means that the possessor is presumed to have the authority to complete the bill in any way he wishes, but in order to bind the prior parties he must do so within a reasonable time and strictly in accordance with the authority actually given (s. 20(2)). The section only applies if there has been proper delivery for the purpose of completing the bill. Hence if a thief steals an inchoate instrument the section does not come to his aid.

A typical example of an inchoate instrument is when a postal buyer of advertised goods sends his cheque to the mail order firm without completing the cheque as to the amount, leaving the sellers to complete the cheque by inserting the amount due. A fraudulent seller, of course, could easily fill the cheque out for an amount more than that due, and an innocent third party indorsee of the cheque could hold the drawer liable for the greater amount.

The BEA 1882 recognises three types of holder: a mere holder, a holder for value and, the best of all, the holder in due course, which includes any holder claiming title through a holder in due course and not himself a party to any fraud or illegality affecting the bill.

10.14.2   The Holder

The holder of a bill is not a holder for value, i.e. he has not given value for the bill in any of the ways recognised by the BEA 1882 but, nevertheless, has certain privileges denied to a non-holder. A non-holder cannot negotiate a bill, nor can he in his own name present a bill for acceptance or payment. The holder can retain possession of the bill and can sue on it in his own name and can give good discharge to a drawee or acceptor whose payment is in due course. The holder may, when the bill is payable after date, insert the date of issue or acceptance of the bill where this has been omitted. Any holder is entitled to convert an order bill into a bearer bill by indorsement in blank and to convert such a bill back into an order bill by special indorsement. He also has the power to call for his transferee's indorsement when the bill is a bearer bill. The holder of a bill which has been lost before it is overdue may apply to the drawer for a duplicate against a written indemnity, and the drawer may be compelled to accede to such request (s. 69).

A mere holder who has not given value is in an otherwise precarious position. Although any holder of a bill is presumed to be a holder in due course (s. 30(2)), if it is shown that the holder has not in fact given value, the contract generated by the bill is just a bare promise with no consideration.

10.14.3   The Holder for Value

A holder has given value if he has given any consideration sufficient to support a simple contract: the adequacy of the consideration is immaterial (s. 27(1)(a)). 'Value' therefore can include goods.

The ordinary rules as to consideration have, however, been modified. Valuable consideration for the purposes of the status of a holder for value may be constituted by an antecedent debt or liability (s. 27(1)(b)). In contract law, an existing indebtedness or past consideration is no consideration. The distinction is illustrated by *Mackenzie Mills* v *Buono, The Times*, 13 July 1986 in which the claimants were a firm of solicitors. They took a bill as indorsees from the payee, a client, and then sued the defendant, the drawer. The defendant argued that the claimants could not be the holder in due course since they had not given value for the bill. The Court of Appeal held: (1) that since the payee owed the claimants approximately £500 in respect of litigation costs incurred in an action against the defendants, they had taken the cheque for value, i.e. as part of existing and in anticipation of future debts. (2) The claimants were not holders in respect of £500 of the face value of the bill but for the full face value of the cheque, £3,700, thus underlining that the adequacy of consideration is irrelevant, even when value is constituted by an existing indebtedness.

The ordinary rules as to valuable consideration are modified in another way. By s. 27(2) where value has been given for the bill at any time, the holder is deemed, and not just presumed, to be a holder for value as regards the acceptor and all parties to the bill who became parties prior to the giving of value. This means simply that to be a holder for value, valuable consideration must have been given by a party between the possessor of the bill and the party he is suing on the bill, though the possessor need not himself have given consideration. A holder who has not given value himself can, therefore, be a holder for value as against some parties to the bill and a mere holder as against others. Goode sums this up:

> . . . a donor, though he cannot be sued by his donee, can be sued by the first holder to give value and by any subsequent holder, whether or not he gave value.

If a holder has a lien on the bill he is deemed to have given value to the extent of the lien (s. 27(3)): this is one of the few situations where the adequacy of consideration is material. For example, where a seller of goods gives a bill of exchange to a collecting bank for payment, although the bank is a holder of the bill in s. 2 (because it is the bearer of a bearer bill, or the indorsee of an order bill) it has not, in fact, given value. If the seller was overdrawn with the bank and had not given the bank instructions as to the use of the bill which were inconsistent with the bank exercising its right of lien over the bill, the bank by implication of law would have a lien over the bill and, therefore, has given value for it to the extent of the overdraft; see *Barclays Bank* v *Astley Industrial Trust* [1970] 2 QB 527.

The other principal situation in which the courts consider the amount of value actually given is where a trustee deals with a bill of exchange to which the beneficiaries under the trust have a claim. In *Barclays Bank* v *Aschaffenburger Zellstoffmerke AG* [1967] 1 Lloyd's Rep 387 Barclays Bank had bought under discount certain bills from Black-Clawson International Ltd, giving approximately 70 per cent of the face value and, therefore, holding the bills as to the remaining 30 per cent as trustee for Black-Clawsons. The result of this was that the bank held the bills partly as holder for value and partly as a mere holder so that, in respect of the latter holding, the party liable on the bill was able to raise against the trustee any defence or counterclaim which he might have against the beneficiary of the trust to the extent of the beneficiary's interest in the bill.

10.14.4   The Holder in Due Course

The holder in due course alone can acquire a title to the bill free from equities and defects in the title of his transferor and, therefore, take the full benefits of the negotiability of bills of exchange, operating as an exception to the *nemo dat* principle. The only limitation on the rights of the holder in due course is that where a signature on the bill has been forged or is otherwise of no legal effect, he has no rights against those who were parties to the bill prior to the ineffective signature. *Vis-à-vis* those parties the purported holder in due course is no holder at all.

Defects in the form of the bill itself prevent the particular possessor from acquiring holder in due course status. It is for this reason that the holder who completes a bill under s. 20 cannot be a holder in due course, though those succeeding him are not prevented from acquiring such title to the bill by reason that the bill was at one time inchoate. The defences which can be raised to a claim by a holder in due course on a bill are discussed below. The requirements to achieve the status of holder in due course are outlined in s. 29(1):

(1)   A holder in due course is a holder who has taken a bill, complete and regular on the face of it, under the following conditions, namely:
   (a)   that he became the holder of it before it was overdue, and without notice that it had been previously dishonoured, if such was the fact;
   (b)   that he took the bill in good faith and for value, and that at the time the bill was negotiated to him he had no notice of any defect in the title of the person who negotiated it.

The elements of the definition will be considered in turn.

10.14.4.1   *The Holder*
The possessor of the bill must qualify as the holder of it and, in addition, s. 29(1)(b) requires that the bill has been 'negotiated' to the holder. Since the payee is a person to whom the bill is 'issued' and not 'negotiated' (s. 2) he cannot be holder in due course *qua* payee; see *Jones Ltd* v *Waring and Gillom Ltd* [1926] AC 670. This does not prevent him from acquiring holder in due course status by derivation when he becomes the possessor of a bill returning to him on a right of recourse (see 10.14.5).

10.14.4.2   *The Bill*
The bill must be complete and regular on its face: in *Arab Bank* v *Ross* [1952] 2 QB 216 'face' was held to mean both the front and the back of the bill, the back being

where the indorsements, if any, are made. An example would be if there is a manifest discrepancy between the name of the payee and his purported indorsement, thus questioning the validity of the chain of title. In the *Arab Bank* case the claimant sued as the holder in due course of two promissory notes made out by the defendant to the Arab Bank Co. The indorsement of the Arab Bank Co. on the back of the bill omitted the word 'Co.'. The court held that there was an irregularity in the indorsement which negatived the claimant's holder in due course status. The claimant nevertheless recovered on the bill as the title of the transferor to which the claimant had succeeded was not in fact defective.

A 'restrictive indorsement' is one which prohibits the further negotiation of the bill or which expresses that it is a mere authority to deal with the bill as thereby directed and not a transfer of the ownership of the bill. Examples of restrictive indorsements are: 'Pay D only', or 'Pay D for the account of Y', or 'Pay D or order for collection'.

A restrictive indorsement gives the indorsee the right to receive payment of the bill. However, the indorsee only receives such title as his transferor had. Also, unless expressed as such, the bill ceases to be transferable. If there has been a restrictive indorsement permitting transfer, then all subsequent indorsees take the bill with the same rights and subject to the same liabilities as the first indorsee under the restrictive indorsement. In short, once there has been a restrictive indorsement, no one can thereafter acquire holder in due course status.

There is one qualification. In *Yeoman Credit* v *Gregory* [1963] 1 WLR 343 the Court of Appeal held that a restrictive indorsement in the form 'for collection' did not prevent a party who apparently took after the indorsement from being a holder in due course. Deciding by way of analogy from the settled principle that it is legitimate to look at the surrounding circumstances to ascertain the true order of indorsements and not taking the order in which they appear on the back of the bill as conclusive, the Court of Appeal held that they were entitled to consider the underlying facts to assess the true and intended effect of the restrictive indorsement. The court found as a fact that the restriction had been added after the bill had been indorsed to the indorsee claiming holder in due course status and, therefore, did not have any effect on his title to the bill.

10.14.4.3   Expiry of the Bill
The holder must take the bill before it is overdue (s. 36(2)). A bill is overdue if the time for payment has passed. If a bill is payable on demand, then it is deemed overdue when it appears on its face to have been in circulation for an unreasonable length of time (s. 36(3)). The onus of proving that a bill is overdue is on the party trying to avoid liability on it (s. 36(4)).

10.14.4.4   Dishonour of the Bill
The holder must take the bill without notice of previous dishonour. The meaning of notice is considered below. If the dishonour in question is non-payment, the holder could not be a holder in due course even if he were without notice, as the bill would be overdue.

10.14.4.5   Value

The holder must have given value in fact. The deeming provisions in s. 27 do not apply to holder in due course status. This is apparent from the wording of s. 29(1)(b). A holder with a lien on the bill in s. 27(3), however, has been held to have given value for the purposes of s. 29(1); see *Yeoman Credit* v *Gregory* (10.14.4.2); *Barclays Bank* v *Astley Industrial Trust* [1970] 2 QB 527.

10.14.4.6   Good Faith

The holder must have taken the bill in good faith. By s. 90 a thing is deemed to have been done in good faith if it is, in fact, done 'honestly, whether done negligently or not'. Of course, the greater the degree of carelessness, the more evidence there is to suggest that the transferee was not just being negligent. If the evidence of fraud or defect in the transferor's title is overwhelming, turning a blind eye to such suspicious circumstances will amount to a lack of good faith.

10.14.4.7   Defects in Title

At the time the bill was negotiated to the holder, the holder must have taken without notice of any defects in the title of the person who negotiated the bill. Negligence does not amount to notice of the defect, though as in the case of good faith, it is evidence of it. A wilful or fraudulent disregard of the means of knowledge after the transferee has or ought to have been put on inquiry is equated with notice. It is sufficient for the holder to have notice of some illegality or fraud affecting the transferor's title, and it is immaterial that he does not know of its actual nature; see *Jones* v *Gordon* (1877) 2 App Cas 616.

Section 29(2) provides an inexhaustive list of circumstances which amount to defects in title. The following are included:

(a)   Where the transferor himself obtained the bill of exchange or its acceptance by fraud, duress, force and fear, or other unlawful means (such as misrepresentation) or for an illegal consideration.

(b)   Where the transferor negotiated the bill to the holder in breach of faith or in circumstances amounting to a fraud.

(c)   Where a party prior to the holder's immediate transferor falls into either (1) or (2).

By s. 30(2) every holder of a bill is *prima facie* deemed to be a holder in due course. The presumption is rebutted if there is sufficient evidence of circumstances suggesting fraud, duress, force and fear, or illegality to be left to a jury; see *Tatam* v *Naslar* (1889) 23 QB 345. The holder would then have to show that subsequent to the fraud, etc., value had been given for the bill in good faith and in ignorance of the fraud.

10.14.5 The Holder in Due Course by Derivation

A holder, whether for value or not, who derives his title to a bill through a holder in due course, and who is not himself a party to any fraud or illegality affecting it, has all the rights of that holder in due course as regards the acceptor and all parties to the bill prior to that holder (s. 29(3)). The holder by derivation therefore need not give value in fact; it is irrelevant that he has notice of the fraud or illegality, provided that he was not a party to it. In *National Park Bank* v *Berggren* (10.14.1) the Court of Appeal applied s. 29(3) to a bill of exchange which had gone back into the possession of prior indorsers of the bill on a right of recourse. The section was not restricted to extensions of the chain of title. By this means, the payee could obtain holder in due course status.

In *Jade International Steel* v *Robert Nicholas* [1978] 1 QB 917 the claimant drew a bill of exchange on the defendant for a consignment of steel. The claimant discounted the bill to a bank in Germany. The German bank then negotiated the bill to the Midland Bank in England. The Midland Bank presented the bill and it was accepted by the defendant. The bill, however, was dishonoured on presentation for payment on account of a dispute in the underlying contract of sale as regards the quality of the steel delivered. Midland Bank gave the requisite notice of dishonour to prior parties and the bill went back up the chain of title on a right of recourse. The bill finally reached the claimant (the seller and drawer of the bill). The question exercising the court was whether the defendant, the buyer-cum-drawee of the bill, could set up any defence to the claimant's action on the bill. The Court of Appeal held that the seller had all the rights of a holder in due course by virtue of s. 29(3), notwithstanding that when the claimant first possessed the bill, he did so as payee and, therefore, was denied holder in due course status. When the claimant negotiated the bill he lost his capacity as the payee, and when he received the bill on the right of recourse, he did so as a new holder.

10.15 THE RIGHTS OF A HOLDER

For convenience this section will consider the rights accorded to the holder in due course of a bill of exchange and then look at how these rights are reduced in the cases of a holder for value and a mere holder respectively.

A holder in due course of a bill takes the bill free from defects in the title of prior parties and free from any personal defences which third parties could raise against those prior parties (s. 38(2)). The holder in due course by s. 38(1) can sue on the bill in his own name. Section 38(1) applies to all types of holders.

The only defences which can be raised successfully against the holder in due course are 'real defences'. These are circumstances which render the bill itself a nullity in respect of the party being sued. Examples are that the bill does not comply with the definition in s. 3, or that the signature through which the holder claims was a forgery and, therefore, a nullity. In both these cases, as regards the defendant, the possessor is not a holder of a bill at all. An important distinction must be drawn, however, between the holder in due course who acquires a valid title to the bill and can thus enforce it as owner against all prior parties, and the holder who, because of some defect in the bill or in its transfer, does not get a good title but acquires rights against a particular party by virtue of some estoppel created by the resulting from the other party's signature or delivery of the bill.

As will be seen in 10.16, a forged signature breaks the chain of title between those persons party to the bill before and those party after the forgery. The bill after the forgery is in essence a new instrument. By virtue of the provisions of the Act and the basic principle that persons are estopped from denying representations they made with the intention, or knowing, that the representee will rely on them, and the representee does so, the signatories to the bill after the forgery are liable on it to subsequent parties regardless of the forgery. Section 24, 'Forged and unauthorised signatures' together with s. 54, 'Liability of acceptor' and s. 55, 'Liability of drawer and indorser', set out the various estoppels and their effects.

As has already been shown at 10.14.1, s. 38(1) entitles all holders to sue on the bill in their own names. The BEA 1882 is otherwise silent as to the rights of the holder for value and the mere holder.

In *Fielding & Platt* v *Selim Najjar* [1969] 1 WLR 357 it was held that a bill of exchange should be treated as if it were cash; see also *All Trades Distributors Ltd* v *Kaufman* (1969) 113 SJ 995 and *Cebora SNC* v *SIP* (Industrial Products) Ltd [1976] 1 Lloyd's Rep 271. However, the analogy is not a perfect one, because the bill admits of certain defences which can defeat the claim of a holder for value which would not be available if the claimant was simply holding cash. As in the case of the holder in due course, real defences can be raised against the holder for value. In addition, the holder for value does not enjoy the benefits of negotiability. He takes the title of his transferor, subject to equities such as fraud or illegality which affect either the title of the transferor or the way in which the bill was transferred; see *Whistler* v *Forster* (1863) 14 CB (NS) 248. Personal defences and set-offs can also be raised provided that they are for liquidated amounts, i.e. claims the value of which can be assessed in figures even before they have been made. This, therefore, includes total failure of consideration as when the seller in the underlying contract of sale fails to deliver any goods, or delivers defective goods which the buyer rejects; see *Fielding & Platt* v *Selim Najjar*. This also includes a partial failure of consideration but only when the amount is ascertained. Where a buyer rejects that part of a consignment delivered to him which is of a different description from that contracted for, or rejects an instalment delivered under a severable contract, or accepts short delivery, there will be a partial failure of consideration; see *Saga Bond Street Ltd* v *Avalon Promotions* [1972] 2 QB 325.

A claim for unliquidated damages, however, cannot be raised in an action on a bill of exchange. A claim for breach of warranty by way of a Part 20 claim will not be entertained. In *Nova (Jersey) Knit Ltd* v *Kammgarn Spinnerei GmbH* [1977] 1 WLR 713 an English company (EC) and a German company (GC) set up a partnership pursuant to which EC would supply GC with machinery for their joint venture. An express clause of the partnership agreement referred all disputes arising out of the partnership to arbitration in Germany. EC supplied the machinery. EC accepted 24 bills of exchange as payment. GC, however, subsequently dishonoured the bills when they were presented for payment alleging that the partnership business had been mismanaged by EC and that the machinery supplied had been second-hand and not new. GC, therefore, claimed damages in an arbitration action in Germany pursuant to the partnership agreement in addition to its refusal to pay the price. EC, however, commenced its own proceedings on the bills claiming payment. GC applied to the English court for a stay of the proceedings before it. The Arbitration Acts compelled the English court to stay proceedings on the bill if those proceedings related to any matter agreed to be referred to arbitration unless the court was satisfied that there was, in fact, no dispute between the parties as to the matters which could be referred to arbitration. The House of Lords held that the claim on the bills of exchange was not a matter which had been agreed by the partnership agreement to be referred to arbitration. In any event there was, in fact, no dispute between the parties as to the substance of that claim. The claim for unliquidated damages could not be raised by way of defence, set-off or Part 20 claim against the action on the bills of exchange and, therefore, could not be used to create a dispute. The stay was refused; see also *Montebianco Industrie Tessile* v *Carlyle Mills* (London) [1981] 1 Lloyd's Rep 509.

It seems that misrepresentation inducing the contract can be claimed as a defence to an action on a bill by a holder for value. Although *Clovertogs Ltd* v *Jean Scenes Ltd* [1982] Com LR 88 was disapproved by May LJ in *Famous Ltd* v *Ge in Ex Italia SRL, The Times*, 3 August 1987 on evidential grounds, the decision was not criticised in so far as it stated the principle that misrepresentation can be used to avoid the contract and, therefore, to create a liquidated claim against the holder for value of the bill.

The mere holder, in addition to the above defences, could be challenged in a claim by the lack of any consideration moving from him. This is subject to the important qualification that the holder may have attained holder in due course status by derivation.

Although real defences affecting the transfer of or the bill itself can be raised against any party, it seems that personal defences to claims brought by holders and holders for value can only be raised if 'immediate parties' as opposed to 'remote parties' are involved. Generally, immediate parties comprise any particular transferor and his transferee. Hence the acceptor and the drawer; the drawer and the payee; the payee and the first indorser; the first indorser and his indorsee are all immediate parties. Remote parties are, therefore, on this analysis the acceptor and the payee or any indorsee of the bill; the drawer and any indorsee; the payee and the indorsee of the first indorser after the payee in the chain of title. In fact, if the question of immediate and remote parties is essentially a question of the defences which can be raised against any particular holder of the bill, the distinction lies in whether a party with holder in due course status has intervened between the claimant and the respondent. If not, the parties are immediate; if so then they are remote parties.

10.16   THE FORGED SIGNATURE

10.16.1   Effect of forgery

Subject to the provisions of this Act, where a signature on a bill is forged or placed thereon without the authority of the person whose signature it purports to be, the forged or unauthorised signature is wholly inoperative, and no right to retain the bill or to give a discharge therefor or to enforce payment thereof against any party thereto can be acquired through or under that signature, unless the party against whom it is sought to retain or enforce payment of the bill is precluded from setting up the forgery for want of authority.

Provided that nothing in this section shall affect the rectification of an unauthorised signature not amounting to a forgery. (s. 24, BEA 1882)

The first thing to be noted is that s. 24 is expressly subject to the provisions of the Act and, in particular, must be read in the light of the estoppels generated by ss. 54 and 55.

An unauthorised signature is one which is purported to have been made in a representative capacity. Whether a particular signature is unauthorised or not is a question of ostensible authority and is, therefore, answered by asking whether the purported signatory had been presented by the principal as having the authority to sign as he did. Such representation can be express (in which case the signatory has actual authority) or implied, as for instance where there is some form of holding out of the signatory or acquiescence therein by the principal.

The BEA 1882 makes no distinction between a forged and an unauthorised signature except that it recognises the possibility of ratifying the latter. A forged or unauthorised signature is treated by the BEA 1882 as wholly inoperative for the purposes of transferring title. It is a complete nullity as if the paper on which it is written were blank. It should be noted, of course, that it is not how convincing is the forgery, but the intentions of the actual signatory, which determines whether a document is a forgery or not.

The provisions to which s. 24 refers obliquely are s. 54 ('Liability of acceptor') and s. 55 ('Liability of drawer or indorser') which generate estoppels in favour of a holder in due course. Section 54 states:

... the acceptor of a bill, by accepting it: ...

(2)   Is precluded from denying to a holder in due course:

(a)   the existence of the drawer, the genuineness of his signature and his capacity and authority to draw the bill;

(b)   in the case of a bill payable to the drawer's order, the then capacity of the drawer to indorse, but not the genuineness or validity of his indorsement;

(c)   in the case of a bill payable to the order of a third person, the existence of the payee and his then capacity to indorse, but not the genuineness or validity of his indorsement.

Subsection (2) is the 'estoppel of the acceptor'.

Section 55(1) states:

The drawer of a bill by drawing it: . . .
    (b)   is precluded from denying to a holder in due course the existence of the payee and his then capacity to indorse.

This is known as the 'estoppel of the drawer'.

Section 55(2) states:

The indorser of a bill by indorsing it: . . .
    (b)   is precluded from denying to a holder in due course the genuineness and regularity in all respects of the drawer's signature and all previous indorsements;
    (c)   is precluded from denying to his immediate or a subsequent indorsee that the bill was at the time of his indorsement a valid and subsisting bill, and that he had then a good title thereto.

These provisions generate the 'estoppel of the indorser'.

The sections do not enable a good title to be obtained through a forgery. They merely grant the rights of a holder in due course against certain parties, covering the right to recover money paid for the bill. The estoppels do not concern parties who signed prior to the forgery. They merely concern parties who sign subsequent to the forgery, and can be viewed as an implied representation in the negotiation of the bill that at the time of the negotiation the bill was what it purports to be. The effect of the estoppels, subject to any particular party's insolvency, is that the party immediately subsequent to the forgery bears the loss occasioned by it.

The interaction of ss. 24, 54 and 55 is as follows:

10.16.2   Forgery of the Drawer's Signature

If the drawer has not signed, then the document cannot be a bill of exchange, as s. 3 requires that a bill be an unconditional order in writing signed by the person giving it. Consequently, there can be no holder, and no title to it.

If Nick steals John's cheque book, forges John's signature to a cheque for £100 to Nick's order and negotiates it to Thomas to cash it, Thomas will be the victim of the fraud. Thomas cannot sue John on the cheque since John did not sign it. His only remedy lies against Nick for what it is worth. If Thomas presented the cheque to the bank on which it is drawn and obtained payment, the bank would be unable to debit John's account with it, for the bank's only authority for debiting the account is John's genuine signature. Section 24 itself states that 'there is no right . . . to give a discharge therefor', and so the bank is precluded from paying the cheque. The bank would lose the money unless the forgery was immediately discovered after payment and Thomas was so informed before he could alter his position on the strength of receiving payment.

If the cheque was drawn payable at a future determinable date after sight, or at a place other than the bank's ordinary place of business, and the bank had accepted it on presentment despite the forgery, the estoppel of the acceptor in s. 54 would then apply. In the example above, suppose the bank accepted the cheque and Thomas was short of funds and could not wait for the cheque to mature. His best course would be to negotiate the bill by special indorsement and delivery to Timothy. Timothy might also negotiate the bill to Jonathan and so on to Andrew and finally to the holder, David. When David presents the cheque on maturity to the bank for payment, the bank is estopped by s. 54(2) from denying the genuineness and validity of John's signature. Nick, therefore, is granted the rights of a payee as against the bank, and provided that there is nothing irregular in Nick's indorsement to Thomas and so on down the chain of title, the bank is bound to pay David on due presentment for payment. The loss, therefore, stops at the bank's door, and unless it can find Nick it must bear the consequences of the forgery.

10.16.3   Forgery of an Essential Indorsement

Indorsements are essential for the negotiation of order bills.

If Timothy had lost the bill and his signature had been forged by the finder, Nick, who had then purported to negotiate the bill by special indorsement and delivery to Jonathan, Timothy's forged indorsement would be no different from a blank on the back of the bill. Jonathan would then not appear to be a holder of the bill at all, as there has been no valid negotiation of the order bill to him. Without the estoppels generated by s. 55 neither Jonathan nor Andrew have any right or power to transfer the bill, and David will be left, similarly, with a bill to which he has no title. He will be compelled to restore the bill to Timothy when he demands it, since it remains payable to him.

By virtue of the estoppels, however, a money back guarantee is offered to the indorsees who take as holders in due course subsequent to the forgery.

10.16.4   Forgery of Indorsements on Bearer Bills

Bearer bills are negotiated by delivery without the need for an indorsement. However, by virtue of the commercial pressure conferred by s. 56 (see 10.10) the transferee can compel his transferor to sign the bill, and thereby incur the liabilities of an indorser, adding currency to the bill. If such an indorsement were forged, there would be no effect on the chain of title to or validity of the bill, instead there would just be one person fewer to sue on the bill.

10.16.5   Payment of a Bill Bearing a Forgery of an Essential Indorsement

If the acceptor pays a bill before a forged indorsement has been discovered, he will have paid out to someone who was not entitled and is liable to pay again if compelled to do so by the rightful owner. The acceptor can recover from the party paid by mistake, who could recover from his immediate transferor and so on up the chain of title until the victim of the fraud who stands to bear the loss.

By virtue of s. 60, bankers, defined as including a body of persons whether incorporated or not who carry on the business of banking, who pay a bill drawn on them and do so in good faith and in the ordinary course of business, are deemed to have paid the bill in due course and, therefore, to have discharged their liability notwithstanding that an essential indorsement had been forged.

In addition to the estoppels generated by the BEA 1882, the ordinary estoppels in equity affect the way parties deal with bills of exchange. Hence if a man knows that his signature to a bill has been forged and he, by his actions or by his silence, knowingly leads others to believe that the signature is genuinely his, then he will be estopped from denying that the signature is his.

10.17 PREREQUISITES FOR ENFORCEMENT

10.17.1 Presentment for Acceptance

The cases in which a bill must be presented for acceptance have been discussed at 10.11. In all other types of bills, the bill can be presented for acceptance to add to the currency of it. If the bill is properly presented (s. 41(2)) and acceptance is refused, the bill has been dishonoured by non-acceptance, and an immediate right of recourse accrues against the other parties of the bill and the bill need not be presented for payment (s. 43).

The right of recourse is lost if the prerequisites for enforcement are not fulfilled, just as in the case of any other secondary liability. Indeed if the bill was duly presented for acceptance and was not accepted within the customary time, the person presenting it must treat it as dishonoured by non-acceptance, otherwise he will lose his right of recourse against the drawer and indorsers (s. 42).

10.17.2 Presentment for Payment

Presentment for payment of course is unnecessary where the bill has already been dishonoured by non-acceptance. Presentment for payment is also unnecessary to render the acceptor liable on the bill. The reason for this seems to be that in the case of a general acceptance it is the duty of the acceptor, like that of any ordinary debtor, to seek out his creditor wherever he may be found. This is, of course, artificial in the case of negotiable instruments, as the acceptor is unlikely to know to whom the bill may have been negotiated, rendering his duty to find his creditor, the current holder, impossible to perform.

A bill must be presented for payment when payment is due. If the bill is not so presented the drawer and indorsers will be discharged from their secondary liability on the bill (s. 45). Presentation of the bill for payment may be waived or excused in certain circumstances (s. 46).

The rules for presentment for payment are set out in s. 45. Briefly, the section means that a bill must be presented to the drawee/acceptor or his authorised agent on the due date at the proper place at a reasonable time on a business day, and that failure in any of these respects will discharge the prior parties from liability.

In *Yeoman Credit* v *Gregory* (10.14.3.2) a bill, payable at the Piccadilly branch of the National Provincial Bank, was accepted for payment. The acceptance itself was general, but the acceptor told the holder that there would be insufficient funds at the named branch and requested that the bill be presented for payment at the Golden Square branch of the Midland Bank. The holder presented the bill on the due date at the latter location. The bill was dishonoured. The next day, the holder presented the same bill for payment at the named Piccadilly branch of the NPB. It was again dishonoured. It was held that the bill had not been presented on the due date at the proper place: the Piccadilly branch of the NPB. The holder had thereby lost his rights of recourse against prior indorsers and the drawer of the bill.

A party may waive presentment for payment (s. 46(2)(e)), e.g. by writing on the face of the bill, 'presentment for payment waived'. Presentment is excused in various other cases outlined in s. 46(2), which follow the same pattern as the excuses for failure to present for acceptance.

10.17.3 Notice of Dishonour

Where a bill has been dishonoured by either non-acceptance or non-payment, a notice of dishonour must, unless excused, be given to the drawer and each indorser to preserve their liability. Any drawer or indorser to whom notice is not given within the rules of the BEA 1882 (s. 49) is discharged (s. 48). Mere knowledge of the fact of dishonour, gained otherwise than by a notice of dishonour under the BEA 1882, is insufficient. Notice for the purposes of the BEA 1882 need not be in writing or in any particular form other than identifying the bill and indicating whether dishonour is by non-acceptance or non-payment (s. 49(5)), but it must be given by the holder or an indorser liable on the bill, i.e. one to whom notice has already been duly given, and there is a strict time limit imposed. Notice must be given within a reasonable time of dishonour. In the absence of special circumstances, this means that where the person giving and the person receiving the notice reside in the same place, the notice must be given or sent off in time to reach the recipient on the day after the dishonour of the bill; where they reside in different places, then notice must be sent off on the day after dishonour of the bill, if there is a post at a convenient hour of the day, or if not by the next post thereafter (s. 49(12)).

What is meant by 'the same place' was discussed in *Hamilton Finance* v *Coverley Finance* [1969] 1 Lloyd's Rep 53 where the claimants' offices were in London W1 and the defendants' in London EC3. Mocatta J held that the determining factor was whether it would be reasonable in all the circumstances to send the notice by hand rather than rely on the general post. In view of the importance of giving notice of dishonour, and the cheapness of hand delivery in this case, he held that the two different postal districts were 'in the same place'.

By s. 49(14) where an indorser sends notice of dishonour the time period in s. 49(12) begins to run, not from dishonour of the bill, but from his receipt of a notice of dishonour.

The holder of a dishonoured bill can give notice to every prior party, and if he does so this enures for the benefit of all parties to the bill. The holder discharges his duty, however, simply by giving notice to his own immediate transferor, who would then give his own transferor notice and so on up the chain of liability until the drawer. By s. 49(4) the holder and prior parties can take the benefit of all notices properly given.

As has already been shown, notice given by a party who is not liable on the bill at the time is ineffective (s. 49(1)), and unless notice can still properly be given, the party so notified and all prior parties are discharged. Hence if the holder's transferor (T1), before receiving notice from the holder, gives notice to his own transferor (T2) of dishonour, the notice so given is effective to render T2 liable on the bill, and unless time allows and proper notice is subsequently given, T2 is discharged. Another situation would be where T1 gives T2 notice out of time. Such notice is invalid by s. 49(12) so that T2 is not rendered liable, and any notice subsequently given by T2 is itself invalid since it is given by a party who at the time is not liable on the bill (s. 49(1)). In such a case, all parties prior to T1 are discharged.

Delay in the giving of the notice is excused where the delay is caused by circumstances beyond the control of the party giving notice, and not imputable to his default, misconduct or negligence. When the cause of the delay ceases to operate, the notice must be given with reasonable diligence (s. 50(1)).

Notice of dishonour is dispensed with in various situations outlined in s. 50(2). Typical examples as against all parties are where despite the exercise of due diligence, which must be proved by the party seeking to enforce the bill, notice could not be given or reach the drawer or indorser sought to be charged. In addition, notice may be waived by any particular party.

As against the drawer there are two typical situations in which the BEA 1882 dispenses with notice of dishonour. First, where the drawee or acceptor owes him no duty to accept or pay the bill, usually where the drawer's account is not sufficiently in funds and the drawee/acceptor has not agreed to give sufficient credit to cover the bill. Secondly, where the drawer has countermanded payment.

10.17.4 Protest

In the case of foreign bills s. 51(2) requires more than notice of dishonour to render prior parties liable on the dishonour of a bill. The bill must be protested by the holder.

Protest is a means of obtaining legal proof of dishonour. The holder would first present the bill for acceptance or payment to the drawee/acceptor himself. On dishonour the holder would hand the bill to a notary public (a solicitor with special powers), who again would present the bill for acceptance or payment as the case may be in order to obtain the legal proof of dishonour. If acceptance or payment is still unobtainable, the notary public would draw up an official certificate evidencing the dishonour. This is called a 'protest'. The protest should state why the protest was made, the demand made to the drawee or acceptor and the answer he received. On the reverse of the certificate will be a copy of the bill. The notary will sign the certificate.

This form of protest is recognised the world over. Failure to obtain the protest would mean that all parties, excluding the acceptor or drawee, of course, would be released from their liability.

There are two cases in which an inland bill can be protested. The first is before any bill is accepted for honour or paid for honour, it *must* be protested. This is governed by sections 65 to 68. The usual situation is when a party liable on the bill is unable to meet his obligations, and some other person, concerned to maintain the former's reputation, may offer to discharge his liability by making the due payment. Alternatively, the acceptor for honour would do so to add currency to the bill or to release the party liable from his primary obligations. The party paying or accepting in honour used to be the rich uncle figure and, consequently, is not frequently found today. The second case is where the acceptor becomes bankrupt or insolvent before the bill matures then, although protest is not essential, it is advisable for better security. This 'better security' in the way of protest does not mean that the holder can demand actual security from prior parties, but that the bill is then in a form in which it can be accepted or paid for honour should the rich uncle figure materialise.

Protest must take place the day following the day of dishonour.

10.17.5   Noting a Bill of Exchange

The process of 'noting' a bill covers holders who are unsure whether their case is one for protest or not. Noting the bill is again done by the notary public who presents the bill again, after the holder has done so. If acceptance or payment is again refused, the notary attaches a slip of paper to the bill showing the answer he received, the date, his expenses and charges, and his initials. This is a cheaper process than formal protest, but by s. 93, it extends the time in which a protest can be made, and thereby enables the holder to obtain legal advice as to the necessity of protest.

The other occasion in which noting serves any purpose is where a bill payable after sight is dishonoured by non-acceptance. Section 14(3) provides that the maturity of such a bill is calculated from the date of noting or protest of the bill. Hence the holder of an inland bill would note it in order to obtain the maturity date of the bill.

10.18   REMEDIES FOR DISHONOUR AND THE FORM OF THE ACTION

Where a bill of exchange is dishonoured, whether by non-acceptance or non-payment, the holder can sue all the parties liable on it provided that the prerequisites for enforcement have been fulfilled.

Where the holder took the bill from his transferor in discharge of the latter's liability to him under a separate contract, the holder has the option of suing on that contract, as the dishonour of the bill restores the contractual duty of payment, which was suspended by the giving of the bill. The exercise of this option is usually not as advantageous as suing on the bill up the chain of title. The issue or negotiation of a bill generates an entirely independent contract which has already been referred to as the autonomy of the bill. The courts do not entertain any unliquidated claim against an action on the bill which might affect the holder's action on the underlying contract, e.g. if the underlying contract were a contract for the sale of goods, the action on the dishonoured bill will not be affected by an unliquidated claim for breach of warranty in the performance of the contract of sale, though the action on the breach of sale would be so affected. Nor will an arbitration clause in the underlying contract affect the action on the bill. A claim on a bill of exchange, therefore, almost always results in summary judgment for the plaintiff.

Part 24 of the Civilo Procedure Rules sets out the summary judgment procedure whereby a claimant who has served a statement of claim, to which the defendant has given notice of an intention to defend, can apply to the court for judgment on the ground that the defendant has no defence to the claim. The practice of the courts has been set out by Kerr LJ in *S L Sethta Liners Ltd* v *State Trading Corporation of India* [1985] 1 WLR 1398:

> If a point of law is raised on behalf of the defendants, which the court feels able to consider without reference to contested facts simply on the submissions of the parties, then it is now settled that in applications for summary judgment under Order 14 the court will do so in order to see whether there is any substance in the proposed defence. If it concludes that, although arguable, the point is bad, then it will give judgment for the plaintiffs. [The new rules will not change the basis of this decision.]

Consequently, in most actions on bills, all of the issues involved will be aired at the Part 24 stage.

By CPR, r. 24.2 the court may give judgment for the claimant 'if it considers that the defendant has no real prospect of successfully defending the claim and there is no other reason why the case or issue should be disposed of at a trial'.

In an action on a bill of exchange, the practice of the courts has been summarised by Lord Denning in *Fielding & Platt* v *Selim Najjay* [1969] 1 WLR 357:

> We have repeatedly said in this court that a bill of exchange or a promissory note is to be treated as cash. It is to be honoured unless there is some good reason to the contrary.

Accordingly, the general rule is that the defendant will not be allowed to set off or counter-claim damages for breach of the underlying or any other contract and the claimant will be entitled to summary judgment, unless there is a total failure of consideration or a liquidated partial failure as between the immediate parties: *per* Lord Wilberforce in *Nova (Jersey) Knit* v *Kammgarn Spinnerei GmbH* [1977] 2 All ER 463.

If fraud is sufficiently set up by the defendant on the facts, then the court will be inclined to give leave to defend. In *Bank für Gemeinmirtschaft* v *City of London Garages* [1971] 1 WLR 149 Cairns LJ said:

> In Order 14 the defendant is entitled to leave to defend if he sets up a case of fraud affecting the bill, unless the plaintiff in his turn can establish that the bill was taken in good faith for value and without notice.

Cairns LJ thought that the question to be asked was:

> ... can the facts in the plaintiff's affidavit in support of his application for summary judgment establish good faith and the giving of value with such a degree of probability that if the case went to trial, the defendant's defence of fraud would have no real chance of success?

Hence if this were established judgment should be given; if not and there is a real issue as to whether the bills were taken in good faith, etc., then unconditional leave to defend would be given. The amount of the bill is recoverable by way of debt and need not be treated as damages. This is true of any interest stipulated by the bill though not, it seems, where the interest is claimed in the action under s. 57(1) without there being any stipulation for it in the bill itself.

Non-payment of money is also a breach of contract, and since the holder may not have stipulated for interest in the bill and may have suffered other losses and expenses as a result of dishonour, s. 57 makes provision for a claim in damages. This is not necessarily disadvantageous to the holder as the damages are deemed by s. 57 to be liquidated, so that he need not prove more than the fact of the bill, the dishonour and compliance with the dishonour procedure. He is in particular under no duty to mitigate his loss.

The measure of damages is the amount of the bill, interest from the time of presentment for payment for a demand bill and from the maturity of the bill in any other case, and the expenses of noting, or where necessary, protest.

The primary liability on the bill is that of the drawee/acceptor. However, each party liable on the bill can recover from his predecessors once he can prove that he has discharged his liability, i.e. by paying when due. If the holder succeeds immediately against the acceptor, then all intermediate parties are discharged.

In practice, the holder of the bill will ensure that all parties are properly notified of dishonour and will join all parties so liable in one action. The discharge of a particular party does not necessarily result in the discharge of the bill, since this only occurs when there is no party liable on it, e.g. when the acceptor has paid the bill in due course.

Payment in due course is made by the party liable at or after the maturity of the bill to the holder in good faith and without notice that the holder's title to the bill is defective.

A bill may be discharged in a variety of other ways. For example, where, despite the bill remaining unpaid, there is no one who can sue on it, which could happen where there had been failure duly to present a bill in respect of which the acceptor had given a qualified acceptance; or where the bill is intentionally cancelled by the holder and such cancellation is apparent on the face of the bill; or where the holder at or after maturity absolutely and unconditionally renounces his rights against the acceptor either in writing or by delivery of the bill to the acceptor (s. 62(1) and (2)).

The various defences to a claim on a bill, depending on the type of bill, have been discussed above.

10.19 CHEQUES

The rules as to cheques are found principally in Part III, BEA 1882 (ss. 73 to 82) and in the Cheques Act 1957. A cheque is a bill of exchange drawn on a banker payable on demand. It is, therefore, a narrow class of bills of exchange and, therefore, the definition of a bill of exchange in s. 3, BEA 1882 must be satisfied.

Since a cheque is a demand bill, it is not accepted, and the drawee bank must pay when it is duly presented. Although a cheque is subject to the provisions of the BEA 1882, it is, in fact, a very different animal from a bill of exchange. For instance, it is primarily a payment order, rather than a credit instrument. Cheques are, therefore, not usually negotiated. Indeed the Cheques Act 1992 introduced the non-transferable cheque. Where a cheque is crossed and bears across its face the words 'account payee' or 'a/c payee', either with or without the word 'only', the cheque is no longer transferable by indorsement and delivery but is only valid between the parties thereto. Since it is an essential part of the process of banking, it is coloured by the banker-customer relationship, and the special position conferred on banks by statute. The chief protection thus afforded to a banker can be found in s. 60, BEA 1882 dealing with paying banks (drawee banks) and s. 4, Cheques Act 1957 concerned with collecting banks:

(1)　Where a banker, in good faith and without negligence:

(a)　receives payment for a customer of an instrument to which this section applies [including cheques]; or

(b)　having credited a customer's account with the amount of such an instrument, receives payment thereof for himself;

and the customer has no title, or a defective title, to the instrument, the banker does not incur any liability to the true owner of the instrument by reason only of having received payment thereof . . .

(3)　A banker is not to be treated for the purposes of this section as having been negligent by reason only of his failure to concern himself with absence of, or irregularity in, indorsement of an instrument.

11　Finance in International Trade

11.1　INTRODUCTION

Where an exporter enters into a contract of sale with an overseas buyer, he will want to be sure that having shipped the goods he will receive the contract price. The overseas buyer, on the other hand, will be unwilling to pay the contract price until he has some assurance that his seller has complied with his contractual obligations.

Obviously, the form that the contract takes will reflect the relative negotiating strengths of the parties. If the seller is unsure of his buyer's creditworthiness, and is in a sufficiently strong bargaining position, he may be able to stipulate for payment in full in advance of shipment. Alternatively, payment may be made on delivery of the documents. As another alternative, the seller may be willing or pressurised into giving the buyer credit, as for instance where the buyer requires the documents to effect a sub-sale of the goods, with the proceeds of which he will discharge the main sale.

Whether credit is given or not the parties may wish to reinforce their respective positions by exacting undertakings from third parties. The seller may reinforce the buyer's payment obligation by a documentary credit, in which the primary payment obligation becomes that of a bank. The buyer may reinforce the seller's delivery obligation by a performance bond, in which a third party, usually a bank, promises to compensate the buyer to a specified amount in the event that the goods are not delivered.

Where credit is extended to the buyer, this may take a number of forms. The two most common are the use of a time bill of exchange to be presented with the documents (the 'documentary bill') and the provision of a documentary credit.

11.1.1　The Documentary Bill

The term 'documentary bill' denotes a bill of exchange accompanied by the shipping documents and intended to be accepted or paid in exchange for those documents. The seller usually sends the bill of exchange and shipping documents to the buyer, who is then required to accept or pay the bill (depending on its type) and return it to the seller. If the buyer fails to honour the bill of exchange, he is bound by s. 19(3), SGA 1979 to return the bill of lading. If he wrongfully retains the bill of lading, the property in the goods does not pass to him, and his retention of the document constitutes a conversion. A second conversion would be committed if the buyer were to sell the goods on and either effect a transfer of title by virtue of one of the exceptions to the *nemo dat* rule, or deliver the goods to the sub-purchaser. To avoid this possibility the seller will normally arrange for the presentation of the documents by a bank which would be under instructions not to part with the documents except against payment or acceptance. It would, therefore, be this collecting bank which presents the documents to the buyer and which would receive payment, to be remitted to the seller.

11.1.2   The Documentary Credit

Although the obligation on the buyer to pay against documents rather than on the receipt of the goods themselves gives the seller a certain amount of security, he would still have incurred expense in the manufacture or acquisition of the goods before the buyer's payment is due. It is to cover this exposure that bankers' documentary or commercial credits were developed and are used.

A documentary credit is simply a banker's promise to pay against the presentation of specified documents. Article 2 of the Uniform Customs and Practice for Documentary Credits (UCP) (see 11.2) defines documentary credits in the following terms:

> For the purposes of these articles the expression 'documentary credit(s)' ... (hereinafter referred to as 'credit(s)'), mean any arrangement, however named or described, whereby a bank (the issuing bank), acting at the request and on the instructions of a customer (the applicant) or on its own behalf
>
> (i)   Is to make a payment to or to the order of a third party (the beneficiary), or is to accept and pay bills of exchange (drafts) drawn by the beneficiary; or
>
> (ii)   Authorises another bank to effect such payment, or to accept and pay bills of exchange (drafts); or
>
> (iii) Authorises another bank to negotiate against stipulated document(s) provided that the terms and conditions of the credit are complied with.

11.1.3   The Contract

The starting point in a typical transaction would be the contract of sale in which the buyer, Marco in Milan agrees to buy and the seller, Simon in London agrees to sell a quantity of flour. The contract of sale would stipulate that payment is to be made by an irrevocable confirmed letter of credit to be issued by the Milan bank and advised and confirmed by the London bank.

Marco would have to apply to his Milan bank, the 'issuing bank' (IB) to open the credit in favour of Simon. This would involve IB in issuing a letter of credit to Simon undertaking payment of the contract price, or payment, acceptance or negotiation of a bill of exchange drawn for the price. Marco would be required by IB to complete its usual application form setting out the details of the credit. Marco must avoid ambiguity when doing this. IB is not concerned with the underlying contract of sale, but is concerned only to ensure that the documents it receives from Simon correspond exactly with the terms of Marco's instructions.

IB may require Marco to put it in funds to cover IB's projected commitment to Simon or, if satisfied with Marco's creditworthiness, IB may be willing to enter the transaction and be reimbursed by Marco on performance.

Usually the application form completed by Marco would expressly incorporate the UCP and will give IB a charge over the goods to be supplied by Simon and over the shipping documents relating to them.

The credit in this case is an irrevocable one, meaning that once issued, IB has entered into a binding undertaking to Simon, independent of the contract of sale, and which IB cannot cancel. If the credit had been revocable, there is no such binding undertaking, so that IB could revoke it at any time.

If the letter of credit in question did not require confirmation, IB or its branch or another more convenient bank would advise Simon of the opening of the letter of credit in his favour. If IB chose to use another bank to advise Simon that the credit had been opened, the latter bank is called the 'advising bank' (AB). AB does not itself incur any liability to Simon. On notification, IB would become bound by the payment obligation to Simon.

The contract of sale between Simon and Marco, however, requires that a confirmed letter of credit be opened. This would require IB requesting AB, who would normally be named in the contract of sale, to add its own undertaking to honour the credit on presentation of documents. This undertaking is independent of, and in addition to, IB's undertaking to Simon and it irrevocably binds AB to Simon. This additional promise of payment is called 'confirming the credit' and the bank is called the 'confirming bank' (CB). Simon, therefore, has three separate promises of payment: Marco's, IB's and CB's. At this point the letter of credit would be issued, and Simon would be obliged to perform his obligations under the contract of sale.

After shipment, Simon must present shipping documents to CB in accordance with the terms of the letter of credit. If the documents are in order, CB will pay, accept or negotiate the bill of exchange in accordance with the letter of credit. CB will then pass the documents on to IB, who will release them to Marco, enabling him to sell the goods on or take possession of them from the ship on arrival at the port of destination. IB will hand the documents over to Marco either unconditionally, or in exchange for a trust receipt.

IB will settle its account with CB covering the payment to Simon and any charges CB may be entitled to credit to IB's account.

11.2 THE UNIFORM CUSTOMS AND PRACTICE FOR DOCUMENTARY CREDITS (UCP)

11.2.1 Definition

The Uniform Customs and Practice for Documentary Credits (UCP) is a body of articles which regulates the implementation and operation of the documentary credit. The rules are published by the International Chamber of Commerce and recognised universally in over 150 countries.

The rules were revised in 1993 and came into force on 1 January 1994, replacing the 1983 revision. All references to the articles in this chapter will be to the 1993 revision, unless otherwise stated.

The revised rules take account of new practices introduced by bankers, commercial parties, transport companies and through the development of technology. The rules are divided into six sections lettered A to F. These deal with the various stages in the operations of the credit, as follows:

A General provisions and definitions
B Form and notification of credits
C Liabilities and responsibilities
D Documents
E Miscellaneous provisions
F Transferable credits
G Assignment of proceeds.

The rules do not automatically apply under English law, but must be expressly incorporated by the parties to the credit, i.e. the buyer and the issuing bank. There will only be effective incorporation in the manner prescribed by Article 1:

The Uniform Customs and Practice for Documentary Credits, 1993 Revision, ICC Publication No 500, shall apply to all Documentary Credits ... where they are incorporated into the text of the Credit.

Even where the parties do incorporate the provisions to determine the operation of the credit they remain free to exclude individual provisions which they consider inappropriate to their particular credit. Indeed the UCP is subject to the express terms of the credit; see *Royal Bank of Scotland* v *Cassa di Risparmio Delle Provincie Lombard, Financial Times*, 21 January 1992.

Where a credit facility is opened through a London bank, then the application form which is completed by the buyer and prefaces the opening of the credit will in many cases contain a clause which specifically applies the UCP.

11.2.2   Security For The Credit

When the buyer seeks to open a credit, the bank will usually demand some form of security or collateral for that credit. Usually, the application form which is completed by the buyer in opening the credit, gives the bank a charge over the goods and their documents of title.

Where the buyer has no other form of security which he can offer, he may pledge to the bank the documents of title to goods which form the subject-matter of the sale contract. The Factors Act 1889, s. 1(5) states:

> The expression 'pledge' shall include any contract pledging or giving a lien or security on, goods, whether in consideration of an original advance or of any further or continuing advance or pecuniary liability.

Where he does this he is effectively pledging the goods themselves. Section 3, Factors Act 1889 states:

> A pledge of the documents of title to goods shall be deemed to be a pledge of the goods.

Where the buyer has pledged the documents to the bank, he may then find it impossible to reimburse the bank unless he is able to sell the goods and make a profit on them; and he cannot do this unless he is in possession of the documents of title. Therefore, the bank may choose to release the documents to the buyer under a letter of lien or trust receipt. This will enable the buyer to obtain the goods, but in doing so he holds them on trust for the bank. If he acts in breach of the powers conferred on him in the trust receipt, he may be liable both for breach of trust and in conversion.

Where the buyer acts in breach of trust and sells the goods to a third party, that third party may, nevertheless, get good title to the goods as the buyer is deemed to be a mercantile agent; see *Lloyds Bank* v *Bank of America* [1938] 2 KB 147.

Section 1(1), Factors Act 1889 defines a mercantile agent as someone having in the customary course of business as such agent, authority to sell goods or consign goods for the purpose of sale.

11.3   THE PARTIES

The main parties to the documentary credit arrangement are described in this section. There are other parties and there are alternative ways of referring to these parties, e.g. the paying bank, the negotiating bank and the reimbursing bank. However, these will be considered after methods of payment have been discussed.

11.3.1   The Applicant for the Credit

This is the buyer under the contract of sale, by whom the contractual price is owed. There is no apparent objection to the applicant being someone other than the buyer, perhaps a third party who is himself indebted to the buyer and will be discharging that debt by making payment under a credit opened in favour of the seller. The buyer and seller will have previously agreed that payment should take place by way of documentary credit. This would be a term of the original sale contract, or would supplement that agreement or, perhaps, vary it, displacing a previously agreed method of payment. In any event it will normally be a term of the contract that payment should assume this form; see *Ficom* v *Cedex* [1980] 2 Lloyd's Rep 118.

The contract of sale will often make express provision for the time for opening the credit and a failure to open the credit by the stipulated time can be treated by the seller as a breach of a condition precedent to his performance and a repudiation of the contract by the buyer; see *Etablissements Chainbaux SARL* v *Harbourmaster Ltd* [1955] 1 Lloyd's Rep 303. Where there is no express stipulation as to the time for opening the credit, the credit must be opened, at the very latest, before the first date for shipment of the goods; see *Pavia & Co. SPA* v *Thurmann-Neilsen* [1952] 2 QB 84 and *Ian Stach Ltd* v *Baker Bosley Ltd* [1958] 2 QB 130. The c.i.f. buyer should not, however, wait until the time for shipment arrives but must provide the credit within a reasonable time before the first date of shipment; see *Sinason-Teicher Inter-American Grain Corp* v *Oilcakes & Oilseeds Trading Co. Ltd* [1954] 1 WLR 1394. A credit is opened when the beneficiary is notified of its existence; see *Bunge Corp* v *Vegetable Vitamin Foods* (Private) Ltd [1985] 1 Lloyd's Rep 613.

The instructions given by the buyer to his bank will reflect the sale contract between himself and the seller. These instructions comprise the buyer's mandate. They must be strictly complied with by the bank, which must exercise reasonable skill and care to determine their compliance (Art. 13).

The bank is unlikely to open the credit on the instructions of the buyer without first having some form of collateral. Ordinarily, the application form which is completed by the buyer and prefaces the opening of the credit will give the bank a general charge over the goods and documents as security for the credit facility.

11.3.2 The Issuing Bank

When the bank of the buyer is in receipt of the buyer's instructions, it will issue notice to the seller that the credit has been opened and the conditions with which the seller must comply in order to obtain payment under that credit. It is thus referred to as the issuing bank.

The issuing bank gives an undertaking, as principal, to pay against correct documents in accordance with the mandate of the buyer. This may be revocable or irrevocable in nature according to the buyer's mandate. The issuing bank may communicate the opening of the credit to the seller direct or via the mediation of another bank which is situated in the seller's country of residence. This bank is referred to as the correspondent or advising bank. Although it is easier to effect communications through a correspondent, it clearly increases the cost of the credit mechanism, and the transmission of instructions invariably carries inherent risk of inaccuracy; see *Equitable Trust Co. of New York* v *Damson Partners Ltd* (1927) 27

Lloyd's Rep 49. However, both the cost and the risk are borne by the applicant. The bank does not assume any responsibility for the communicated credit not being followed by the correspondent, even where the correspondent was itself chosen by the issuing bank (Art. 18(b)).

11.3.3 The Correspondent Bank

The correspondent bank may assume one of two capabilities, first as adviser and, secondly, as confirmer.

11.3.3.1 The Correspondent Adviser

Where a correspondent bank is used as an adviser it does not assume any undertaking to make payment to the beneficiary on its own behalf. Its purpose is merely to advise the beneficiary of the terms with which he must comply if he is to receive payment from the issuing bank. Its involvement merely facilitates the communication of the credit terms.

Where the issuing bank uses a correspondent adviser in this way, then it is the communication of the correspondent which will operate to bind the issuing bank. Whilst the correspondent adviser has no authority to pay the seller under the buyer's mandate, there is nothing to prevent the correspondent adviser from acting as agent of the issuing bank to remit tendered documents to the issuing bank for its approval, and to make payment on its behalf if those documents are correct. In doing any of these things, the correspondent adviser would be acting only within its capacity as agent of the issuing bank.

Whenever a correspondent adviser is used in this way by an issuing bank, then the cable, telegram or telex by which it instructs the adviser will be deemed to be the operative credit instrument. Therefore, unless the issuing bank makes it perfectly clear when it sends instructions to the adviser that a 'mail confirmation will follow', or that 'full details will be sent', whatever the form of words used the credit will be operative and immediately capable of communication to the seller.

The issuing bank should not then send a mail confirmation (Art. 11(a)). Whatever the method of teletransmission utilised by the issuing bank, it should be made clear from the outset that the credit is subject to the UCP 1993 revision.

Although the correspondent adviser assumes no obligation to make payment, it is nevertheless obliged to check the authenticity of the credit before it communicates it (Art. 7(a)). This should be a relatively simple task which could be discharged by the adviser comparing the signature of the issuing bank with specimen signatures retained by it for such purposes. The obligation to check the credit in this way was new to the 1993 revision, and probably derives from the fact that many beneficiaries would wrongly assume that if a credit was communicated to them by an advising bank, then that credit must be authentic, by necessary implication, otherwise the advising bank would have declined to advise it. Article 7(a) requires only that the adviser check the apparent authenticity. There is, therefore, no conflict with Art. 15 which states that: 'Banks assume no liability or responsibility for the form, sufficiency, accuracy, genuineness, falsification or legal effect of any documents'.

If, therefore, the signature of the issuing bank had been forged to resemble the true signature, then presumably the advising bank would not be liable for communicating a forged credit. If the advising bank omitted to check the authenticity of the credit and its falsification was apparent, then it would presumably be liable in negligence or for breach of an implied warranty of genuineness.

11.3.3.2 The Correspondent Confirmer

Where the correspondent bank confirms the credit facility, not only does it communicate to the seller that the credit has been opened in his favour, but it gives him a complete, separate and additional undertaking to make payment if correct documents are tendered to it. Whilst it is acting as agent of the issuing bank to the extent that if it correctly makes payment it has a right to be reimbursed by the bank instructing it (Art. 14(a)), in giving the undertaking to make payment it acts as principal *vis-à-vis* the seller (Art. 9(b)). Thus, it could not refuse to pay the seller if the documents were correct, even though at that time it had already been intimated that the issuing bank would not be prepared to reimburse it.

It is entirely possible that a bank, which is selected by the issuing bank as the correspondent confirmer, may not wish to assume that role. It is not obliged to do so against its wishes but, in such circumstances, it must inform the issuing bank of that fact without delay. It must then go on nevertheless to act as an adviser, and at least tell the beneficiary that the credit has been opened in his favour, in which event its responsibilities regarding the notification of that credit are the same as any other adviser. The only circumstances in which a correspondent which rejects the role of confirmer should not go ahead and advise the credit, is where there is an express prohibition upon this by the issuing bank in its communication, or where, perhaps, the effect of taking such a course will be construed as an acceptance of the capacity of confirmer (Art. 9(c)).

11.3.4 The Beneficiary

The beneficiary under the documentary credit is the seller under the contract of sale. Providing that the beneficiary presents correct documents to the bank, he will be entitled to receive payment, irrespective of whether any dispute has arisen on the sale contract. This is a matter which is considered in more detail below.

11.3.5 The Contractual Relationships Involved

Buyer ------------------------ Contract of sale ------------------------ Seller

APPLICANT FOR THE CREDIT
1. Notifies bank of terms of credit to reflect contract of sale.
2. Assumes obligation to reimburse issuing bank if payment is correctly made.

ISSUING BANK
1.   Opens a credit which conforms with buyer's instructions.
2.   Communicates terms of credit to beneficiary.
Or
3.   Communicates terms of credit to correspondent bank.
4.   Makes reimbursement to such bank if payment correctly made or appoints reimbursing bank.

CORRESPONDENT BANK
Either:
1.   Notifies beneficiary of where he can obtain payment and terms with which he must comply, but does not give any undertaking to make payment (adviser).
Or
2.   Notifies beneficiary of terms of credit and confirms that it will make payment against correct documents (confirmer).

BENEFICIARY
1.   Presents correct documents to:
     (a)   Correspondent confirmer. Or
     (b)   Issuing bank. Or
     (c)   Buyer, by whom the operation of the credit operated only as conditional payment.

11.4   TYPES OF CREDIT

11.4.1   Revocable and Irrevocable Credits

Credits may be either irrevocable or revocable (Art. 6(a)) and all credits should clearly indicate whether they are revocable or irrevocable (Art. 6(b)).
     Article 8(a) explains the nature of a revocable credit in the following terms:

A revocable credit may be amended or cancelled by the issuing bank at any moment and without prior notice to the beneficiary.

However, if IB has caused a correspondent AB or some other bank to be involved in the payment, acceptance or negotiation of the credit prior to its cancellation or amendment, that other bank would be entitled to reimbursement for expenses incurred and payments made from IB, who would be entitled in turn to reimbursement from the applicant, the buyer (Art. 8(b)).
     Revocable credits are little more than a statement by a bank to the seller, the beneficiary, that the buyer will do that which he was already bound to do by entering the contract of sale. They are of little value to a seller who requires security, and are used where the parties to the contract are closely linked, e.g. parent and subsidiary company, and merely require the bank's services for the transmission of funds.

As previously mentioned all credits should clearly indicate whether they are revocable or irrevocable. In the absence of such an indication the credit is deemed to be irrevocable (Art. 6(c)).

A credit is said to be irrevocable when the issuing bank gives a binding undertaking to the beneficiary that the buyer will pay against documents, or that all bills drawn in compliance with the terms of the credit will be honoured, whether by acceptance, payment or negotiation. (Art. 9(a)). This undertaking, along with that of the confirming bank (if any), is contractual in nature; see Lord Diplock in *United City Merchants* (Investments) v *Royal Bank of Canada* [1983] 1 AC 168 at p. 182. It is, however, difficult to know exactly when an irrevocable credit becomes binding on the issuing bank and the confirmed credit on the advising bank. Although the parties may regard the credit as binding as soon as it is communicated to the beneficiary, and this is also the preferred analysis in the interests of commercial certainty, it would seem that, on a strict legal analysis, the bank makes the beneficiary a unilateral offer which must then be accepted.

An irrevocable credit once issued, that is to say when it has been communicated to the beneficiary, cannot be amended or cancelled without the agreement of the issuing bank, the confirming bank and the beneficiary (Art. 9(d)). A bank which has given such an undertaking should, therefore, refuse to accept instructions from the buyer not to pay a seller who has performed the conditions of the credit; see *Urquhart Lindsay & Co. Ltd* v *Eastern Bank Ltd* [1922] 1 KB 316.

Irrevocable credits can usually be recognised by the inclusion of a clause to the following effect:

We undertake to honour such drafts on presentation provided that they are drawn and presented in conformity with the terms of this credit.

In *Stein* v *Hambros Bank* (1921) 9 Ll LR 433 Rowlatt J said:

... the obligation of the bank (under an irrevocable credit) is absolute, and is meant to be absolute, that when the documents are presented they have to accept the bill. That is the commercial meaning of it.

Article 9(a) UCP sets out the nature of the IB's payment obligation under an irrevocable credit as being one of the following:

(a)   To pay or ensure that payment will be made.

(b)   To accept bills of exchange drawn on the bank under the letter of credit or to ensure that such bills if drawn on another bank will be accepted, and then paid on presentment for payment.

(c)   To negotiate (purchase) without recourse to the drawer and/or *bona fide* holders bills of exchange drawn by the beneficiary, or to ensure that another bank negotiates the bills without recourse.

Irrevocable credits, therefore, provide the seller who is looking for security with the assurance he wants.

11.4.2   Unconfirmed and Confirmed Credits

A confirmed credit is one under which IB's undertaking under an irrevocable credit is reinforced by a similar undertaking from another bank, the confirming bank (Art. 9(b)). A credit may be irrevocable without being confirmed, but a confirmed credit is always irrevocable.

11.4.3   Sight (or Payment) Credits and Acceptance Credits

This division refers to the time and mode of the promise to pay. Both involve the use of bills of exchange drawn on IB, AB or some other bank, the distinction resting in the form of the bill. A sight credit is one which provides for payment of a sight bill of exchange drawn on IB, AB (if the credit is confirmed) or some other bank when presented with the specified documents. This type of credit will be used when the seller gives the buyer no period of credit.

An acceptance credit requires the beneficiary to present a term bill to IB, AB, or some other bank for acceptance against documents and payment by the accepting bank at maturity. If the credit is confirmed by AB, then AB will accept the bill of exchange drawn usually on the buyer and pay it on maturity and thereupon debit IB with the face value of the bill together with AB's commission and other expenses.

11.4.4   Straight Credits and Negotiation Credits

A letter of credit is not itself a negotiable instrument, so that IB's undertaking, and that of AB in a confirmed credit, is given in favour of the beneficiary, the seller, alone.

If a bill of exchange is drawn under the credit, there is nothing preventing the beneficiary from selling the draft drawn on IB or AB. The purchaser of the bill would have no claim against the drawee bank (IB or AB) if the bank were to dishonour on presentment, as the promise in the bill is linked to the engagement in the letter of credit, and cannot be detached therefrom in the absence of express words. The purchaser of the bill was not the object of the undertaking in the credit and is, therefore, not entitled to present the bill for payment. Such a letter of credit is called a straight or specially advised credit.

If the undertaking given in the letter of credit were framed as an undertaking to those negotiating the beneficiary's drafts, and not to the beneficiary alone, the letter of credit would be a 'negotiation credit'. Its effect is that anyone who negotiates the beneficiary's drafts in accordance with and in reliance on the terms of the credit and in good faith is entitled to receive payment of the bill of exchange when duly presented to the IB (or AB if confirmed).

A negotiation credit may be open or restricted. If the credit is open, IB will, by the terms of the letter of credit, permit negotiation of the bill by anyone who wishes. If the credit is restricted, on the other hand, IB will have expressly restricted those who may negotiate the bill, usually specifying a particular bank, often being IB's own correspondent.

The effect of an open negotiation credit is that IB undertakes to any person negotiating the bill that it will be honoured on due presentment of the documents. A restricted negotiation credit does not prevent the beneficiary from negotiating the credit to someone other than one authorised by the credit (unlike a straight credit), but the indorsee of the bill negotiates at his own risk, in that he will have no claim against IB on the credit if the bill is dishonoured.

11.4.5 Transferable Credits

A distinction must be drawn between an assignment by the beneficiary of his right to claim the amount of the credit and a transfer of the credit itself. Article 49 states that:

> [The fact that] a credit is not stated to be transferable shall not affect the beneficiary's rights to assign any proceeds to which he may be, or may become, entitled under such credit, in accordance with provisions of the applicable law.

It should be noted that the Article relates only to the assignment of proceeds and not to the assignment of the right to perform under the credit itself.

A credit in favour of a beneficiary is a chose in action and may be assigned in the same manner as any other chose in action. The assignee becomes entitled to be paid the proceeds of the credit when the beneficiary's claim against IB or AB matures. The obligation to procure the requisite shipping documents remains that of the beneficiary, and does not become that of the assignee.

The transfer of the undertaking in the letter of credit itself serves a different commercial object from that served by assignment of the proceeds. When the credit is 'transferred', a 'second beneficiary' steps into the shoes of the original 'first beneficiary'. He is entitled and bound to perform the obligations of the first beneficiary, but by using his own shipping documents.

The transferable credit is usually found when the seller, the first beneficiary, is not the manufacturer or original supplier of the goods, so that in effect the logistics of the sale are performed by someone other than the seller. The transfer will be arranged in such a way that prevents any contact between the supplier and the buyer. The point is to prevent the buyer from ordering a subsequent consignment directly from the supplier and, therefore, denying the seller his middleman's cut of the profits.

Article 48(b) states that a documentary credit can be transferable only if it is expressly designated as such by IB. A transferable credit can only be transferred once. It may, however, be divided into different parts and transferred to several different parties until the whole of the value of the credit has been moved on (Art. 48(g)). The initiative for the transfer must come from the beneficiary but in any event the consent of the bank which has issued or advised a transferable credit must still be obtained. The fact that the credit is designated transferable is not sufficient; see *Bank Negera Indonesia 1946* v *Lariza (Singapore) Pte Ltd* [1988] AC 583.

By Art. 48(h), the new credit issued in favour of the second beneficiary must be on the same terms as the original credit, but frequently there are in practice three exceptions:

(a)   The amount of the credit will be reduced by the seller's profit margin in the difference between the price he is paying his supplier and the sale price to the buyer.

(b)   The expiry date of the new credit and the last day for the presentation of the documents will be earlier than that in the original credit, and the shipping period may be shorter. The object is to allow for a few days between when performance is due from the second beneficiary, and that on which the seller must tender the remaining documents to IB or AB.

(c)   The percentage for which insurance cover must be effected in the new credit will be increased so as to provide for the amount of cover required under the original credit.

The second beneficiary will perform by presenting his own documents, including his supplier's invoice, to IB or AB. Under Art. 48(i) the seller then has the right to substitute for the supplier's invoice his own invoice and, where necessary, bills of exchange for a sum not in excess of the amount stipulated in the original credit.

Article 48(j) entitles the seller to request that payment or negotiation be effected to the second beneficiary, at the place to which the credit has been transferred, up to and including the expiry date of the original credit, without prejudice to the seller's right subsequently to substitute his own invoice and bills of exchange for those of the second beneficiary and to claim any difference due to him. This provision, therefore, seems to permit the seller to tender his own invoice after the expiry date of the original credit.

The new credit opened by IB or AB in favour of the second beneficiary is similar to the original credit and, therefore, binds the banks to the same obligations. Hence if, as is usual in transferable credits, the credit is irrevocable, the transferred credit will be of the same type, and IB will be similarly bound to the second beneficiary. If the original credit were confirmed, however, AB's undertaking in favour of the original beneficiary is not transferred. If the second beneficiary requires confirmation, then he must stipulate for this in his contract with the original beneficiary, who would then be bound to procure the requisite confirmation from the second beneficiary's AB.

There are two views as to the legal effect of the transfer of a letter of credit, for the UCP gives the lawyer no guidance. The first is that the transfer operates as an assignment of the documentary credit. This, however, fails to take into account that the second beneficiary is entitled to the amount transferred to him only if he performs some of the conditions precedent to the banker's duty to pay the amount of the credit.

Usually, the second beneficiary has to tender most of the documents listed in the original credit.

The second possibility is that the transfer operates as a novation of the contract embodied in the original documentary credit. This, however, ignores that the seller remains a party to the transaction and that the balance of the documentary credit is paid to him against the tender of his own invoice. If the contract were in truth novated, the seller would drop out of the picture completely.

It seems, however, that the documentary credit is in many ways *sui generis*, a characteristic which is not unworkable owing to the comprehensive nature of the UCP, contractually incorporated into most letter of credit transactions.

Benjamin on Sale of Goods, on the other hand, considers that the transfer of a documentary credit may be described as an assignment of some of the seller's rights to the second beneficiary, who can enforce them only against the tender of certain documents. The seller, therefore, remains a party to the transaction.

'Negotiation' and 'transferable' credits must, therefore, be distinguished: a transferable credit is one in which the original beneficiary may require the credit to be replaced, wholly or in part, once only by a new credit in favour of a second beneficiary. A negotiation credit does not involve the transfer of the beneficiary's rights or a replacement of one credit by another. It is an undertaking by IB that it will honour bills of exchange drawn under and negotiated in good faith and in reliance upon the credit when duly presented for payment.

11.4.6 Back-to-Back Credits

A back-to-back credit will be used by a seller who prefers to disguise the fact that the goods are not manufactured or supplied by himself, much in the same way as transferable credits, but in circumstances when transferable credits cannot be used. This would be the case where there is a string of contracts concerned with the supply of the goods destined for the ultimate buyer. A transferable credit could not be used, since it can be transferred once only.

The back-to-back credit enables the seller to use a non-transferable credit as the basis for procuring a new credit in favour of the supplier, either from one of the original banks or from an independent bank.

The seller lodges the documentary credit opened in his favour ('the primary credit') with AB or with his own bankers (IB2), and instructs them to open a new documentary credit ('the second credit'), independent of the primary one, in favour of the supplier. The second credit will be on similar terms to the original, except that the amount will be less and the date of expiry earlier than that of the primary credit.

The main difference between a transferable credit and the back-to-back credit is that in the latter it is essential for IB2 to obtain a seller's invoice, as IB or AB of the primary credit is only entitled and bound to perform on presentation of such document.

Figure 11.1   Primary Credit

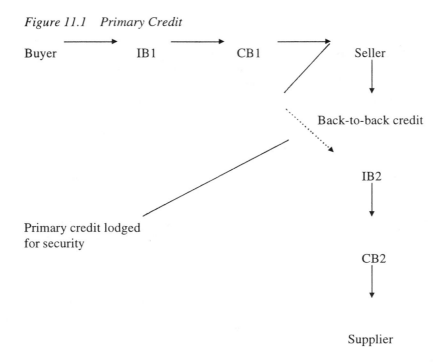

IB2 will not open the second credit in favour of the supplier until the first credit is in position. IB2 will then take possession of the first letter of credit issued to the seller and issue a countervailing credit to the supplier. Almost always IB2 will insist on the primary credit being irrevocable. It will then issue to the supplier a credit in the same terms as the first. IB2 knows that it will not be paid by the first IB or AB since there is no mandate to the first banks to pay against a supplier's invoice.

When the documents are tendered by the supplier, IB2 will pay the supplier under the back-to-back credit and will then substitute the seller's invoice for that of the supplier. IB2 will then present the documents to the first IB or AB pursuant to the primary letter of credit, acting as the seller's agent for collection. IB2 will then retain the amount needed to cover the price paid to the supplier and its charges and will then release the balance to the seller.

Back-to-back credits are not as common as transferable credits. Banks dislike them since the security afforded by possession of the letter of credit is weak, as it only holds the credit as an agent, and if the seller were to fail to perform under the terms of that credit, IB2 could not solve the problem by using the supplier's documents tendered under the back-to-back credit.

Another problem for IB2 is if the seller were to go bankrupt before IB or AB had paid out under the first credit. The proceeds would go into the bankrupt's (the seller's) estate and not to IB2 in possession of the credit itself. IB2 would, of course, be committed to the back-to-back credit, and would have no defence in his applicant's bankruptcy if he were to dishonour the credit issued in favour of the supplier.

Banks, therefore, adopt one of two courses to evade this problem. First, IB2 is the pledgee of the seller's documents before tendering them as the seller's agent under the primary credit. Consequently, IB2 is the constructive pledgee of the goods, and can, therefore, sell them to realise its losses on the seller's bankruptcy. However, this is of no use if IB2 has already relinquished the documents to the primary IB or AB and ceased to be pledgee where, for instance, the obligation under the primary credit is of deferred payment.

The alternative solution is for the seller to assign the proceeds of the primary credit to IB2. Once notice is given to the debtor, the primary IB or AB, he will not get proper discharge unless he pays to the assignee. The problem in assignment is that IB2 will take subject to the equities affecting the assignor's title, and the primary IB or AB would be entitled to refuse to pay if the documents did not conform to the terms of the primary credit.

11.4.7 Red Clause Credits

This type of letter of credit is also known as 'anticipatory credit' or 'packing credit', and originated in the South African trade in hides. The object of such a credit is to allow the seller, the beneficiary of the credit, to obtain an advance on the price before the goods are shipped. The advance will usually be conditional on the presentation of documents such as a warehouse receipt; see *Bank Melli Iran* v *Barclays Bank* (Dominion, Colonial and Overseas) [1951] 2 Lloyd's Rep 367.

In the red clause credit the buyer takes the risk in advancing money without adequate security. He is liable to reimburse IB, even if the seller disappears with the amount advanced or fails to ship the goods and becomes insolvent or bankrupt; see *South African Reserve Bank* v *M Samuel & Co. Ltd* (1931) 39 Ll LR 87.

11.4.8 Revolving Credits

Most credits are for a fixed amount and are open for a fixed period and allow for the presentation of only one set of documents. It is, however, possible to have a credit which allows the beneficiary to present documents on a regular basis drawing no more than a specified amount on each occasion. Such a credit may be used when the buyer and seller have an on-going trading relationship or when they are dealing with several shipments; see, for example, *The Future Express* [1992] 2 Lloyd's Rep 79.

11.4.9 Standby or Guarantee Credits

A standby credit is like an ordinary letter of credit in that it is activated by the tender of documents in accordance with the terms of the credit. A standby credit is intended to protect the beneficiary in case of default of the other party to the underlying contract, that is to say it is a form of guarantee. Standby credits are subject to the UCP if the parties have so agreed (Arts. 1, 2).

11.5   THE MANDATE

The instructions which are given by the buyer/applicant for the credit to his bank comprise the buyer's mandate. These instructions must be complete and precise stating those documents against which the bank is to make payment and those documents which, if tendered by the seller/beneficiary, will be unacceptable. Article 5 provides:

> Instructions for the insurance of credits, the credits themselves, instructions for any amendments thereto and the amendments themselves must be complete and precise ... In order to guard against confusion and misunderstanding, banks should discourage any attempt to include excessive detail in the credit or in any amendment thereto.

Thus, the credit should stipulate the form which such payment is to assume. It may be that the bank is to make payment by cash against documents. Alternatively, the buyer may wish to allow the seller to draw a bill of exchange on himself or the bank, for the contract price, and to present this bill together with the agreed documents so that the paying bank can negotiate the bill. Whichever form payment is to take must be clearly stated. Article 10(a) provides:

> All credits clearly indicate whether they are available by sight payment, by deferred payment, by acceptance or negotiation.

Moreover, the credit should state clearly which documents are to be tendered to obtain payment. Article 5(b) provides:

> All instructions for the issuance of credits must state precisely the document(s) against which payment, acceptance or negotiation is to be made.

Vague or imprecise terminology should not be used when describing the documents or their issuers. Terms such as 'first class', 'well known', 'qualified', 'independent', 'official' and the like should not be used to describe the issuers of documents to be presented under the credit. If such terms are incorporated in the credit terms, banks will accept the relative documents as presented, provided that they appear on their face to be in accordance with the other terms and conditions of the credit (Art. 20(b)).

It is important to note that not only the issuing bank, but also any other bank involved in the implementation of the credit, has the right to question the use of excessive detail in the credit (Art. 5.)

It is particularly important that the credit is sufficient in detail because the bank, faced with a sparse or ambiguous mandate, cannot have recourse to the contract of sale in order to clarify its instructions. This is because although it is the contract of sale and payment thereunder which requires the buyer to open the credit in the first instance, once opened, the credit is completely independent of the sale contract. It operates with complete autonomy. The reason for this is self-evident. The bank deals only in documents, it is not concerned with the sufficiency of performance under the sale contract or with the resolution of disputes which may arise thereunder; see *Home Richardson* v *Polimex Cekop* [1978] 1 Lloyd's Rep 161 CA.

The bank is concerned only with the sufficiency of the documents. If the documents tendered by the seller are correct, then the bank will make payment in accordance with the promise it has given in communicating the credit to the beneficiary. It is immaterial whether or not there has been performance on the underlying sale contract; see *Hamzeh Malas* v *British Imex* [1958] 2 QB 127. This principle is clearly stated by Art. 4:

> In credit operations all parties deal with the documents, and not in goods, services and/or other performances to which the documents may relate.

The principle is also dealt with in Art. 3(a), which requires a little more discussion:

> Credits by their nature are separate transactions from the sales or other contract(s) on which they may be based and banks are in no way concerned with or bound by such contract(s), even if any reference whatsoever to such contract(s) is included in the credit. Consequently, the undertaking of a bank to pay, accept and pay draft(s) or negotiate and/or to fulfil any other obligation under the credit is not subject to claims or defences by the applicant resulting from his relationships with the issuing bank or the beneficiary.

Art. 3(a) makes it clear that there is no connection between the credit and the sale contract, and no such connection can be made merely by virtue of the credit making an express reference to that sale contract. The second sentence in Art. 3(a) was added in the 1993 revision to counteract a growing tendency among applicants to argue that Art. 3 did not affect their right to interfere with the bank's obligation to honour the credit. The principles stated in Articles 3 and 4 are fundamental to the operation of letters of credit and are discussed in further detail at 11.7. Banks are only concerned with whether the documents presented comply strictly with the terms of the credit and are not concerned, save with one limited exception, with the underlying contract of sale.

A bank presented with an ambiguous mandate by the buyer has several possible avenues of conduct. Under Art. 12 it can, nevertheless, instruct the beneficiary that the credit has been opened on his behalf. In communicating this fact it need not thereby assume responsibility for making payment under the credit. Any obligation to make payment that may subsequently arise may be conditional upon the bank receiving clarified instructions in accordance with which it feels it can act. It appears from Art. 14 that the bank is not obliged to take this course, but if it does so it should act promptly. From the point of view of the seller, it may be advantageous for him to know that the buyer has at least attempted to open the credit, albeit that the seller will not start the carriage of his goods to the port of departure until he has prior notification of the opening of the credit. In some cases he may, therefore, elect to begin this transit, having been told that the credit does exist but the bank is not yet prepared to make payment under it.

Where the mandate is ambiguous, the common law allows the bank to place a reasonable construction upon it (*Commercial Banking Co. of Sydney* v *Jalsard Pty Ltd* [1973] AC 279), and it would not thereby exceed its mandate, having placed a reasonable construction upon it. Alternatively, the bank could simply revert to the buyer for further instruction without communicating to the seller the fact of the opening of the credit. The final course available to the bank would be to pay against the credit despite the ambiguity. This would be extremely foolish since the bank is required to comply strictly with the terms of its instructions. If it exceeds them it will lose its right to be reimbursed by the buyer.

11.6   TAKING UP THE SELLER'S DOCUMENTS

11.6.1   The Obligation to Pay

As mentioned at 11.1.2, the obligation to make payment against conforming documents can take any one of a number of forms — payment, deferred payment, acceptance or negotiation. We must now consider these options in more detail and it is appropriate to do so by considering Art. 10(a) which sets out the various obligations which the issuing bank may accept under a letter of credit. Article 9(a) provides as follows:

(a)   If the credit provides for sight payment — to pay, or that payment will be made.

(b)   If the credit provides for deferred payment — to pay, or that payment will then be made on the date(s) determinable in accordance with the stipulation of the credit.

(c)   If the credit provides for acceptance — to accept drafts drawn by the beneficiary if the credit stipulates that they are to be drawn on the issuing bank, or to be responsible for their acceptance and payment at maturity if the credit stipulates that they are to be drawn on the applicant for the credit or any other drawee stipulated in the credit.

(d)   If the credit provides for negotiation — to pay, without recourse to drawers and/or *bona fide* holders, drafts drawn by the beneficiary at sight or at a tenor, on the applicant for the credit or on any other drawee stipulated in the credit other than the issuing bank itself, or to provide for negotiation by another bank and to pay as above if such negotiation is not effected.

Whichever form payment is to take, it must be clearly indicated in the credit (Art. 10(a)). The undertakings of a confirming bank are in similar terms (Art. 9(b)). Considering each of the above alternatives:

11.6.1.1 The Bank may make Sight Payment

This means that it may pay cash, namely, the credit sum, against agreed documents. Alternatively, the seller may draw a bill of exchange for the amount of the credit on the bank, the buyer, a correspondent bank or a third party, payable on demand. If presented together with correct documents, then the bank would make payment.

11.6.1.2 The Credit provides for Deferred Payment

At one time the only way in which the bank could defer its obligation to make payment to the beneficiary was by allowing him to draw a time bill of exchange. Thus, the obligation to make payment would not arise until the bill had matured. The deferred payment credit allows the bank to agree to make payment, but only on some future date which is either specified in the credit or to be determined in accordance with a formula prescribed by the credit. Thus, the time bill of exchange is no longer the only way by which the bank can defer its obligation. This can now also be done by the deferred payment credit.

11.6.1.3 The Credit provides for Acceptance

Where the buyer draws a bill of exchange on the issuing bank, then the obligation of the bank is to accept that bill and thereby assume primary liability upon it (ss. 23 and 54, Bills of Exchange Act 1882). The issuing bank will then be required to honour the bill by making payment against it when it matures. Ordinarily, that acceptance will be conditional upon the unaccepted bill being presented together with the agreed documents. If the bill is drawn on some other drawee, perhaps the buyer or a third party, then clearly the issuing bank cannot accept such a bill, but it will be responsible for its acceptance and subsequent payment at maturity.

An interesting problem arose in *Forestal Mimosa* v *Oriental Credit Ltd* [1986] 1 Lloyd's Rep 329, perhaps the first case to be decided under the 1983 rules. The buyers agreed to payment by irrevocable credit under which the seller would present a bill of exchange drawn on the buyer, together with agreed documents. The seller drew 90-day drafts and presented them to the bank. The credit was expressly stated to be subject to the UCP 1983 revision and, therefore, Art. 10(b)(iii) (same in terms as Art. 10(a)(iii)). The relevant articles in the 1993 revision are 9(b)(iii) and 9(a)(iii) respectively. (There have been some changes made to the wording of the relevant articles in the new 1993 revision.) The bank refused to make payment because the buyer refused to accept the bill of exchange. It claimed that it had no obligation to pay the seller as it was clear from the credit that it was responsible for payment only if the buyer had accepted the bill of exchange. This, it said, was clear from the words printed in the credit which stated that it would be available 'by acceptance of . . . drafts drawn on the buyer'. It claimed that this was decisive and that no reference should be made to the UCP.

The Court of Appeal said that Art. 10(b)(iii) required the confirming bank to accept the draft and pay it on maturity. This was agreed by stating expressly that the credit was subject to the UCP. The bank could have excluded Art. 10(b)(iii), but it had not chosen to do so. The bank's own printed terms and that Article did not require such an exclusion to be implied. The bank would be responsible for acceptance and payment at maturity, irrespective of the behaviour of the buyer and it had no defence to summary judgment.

11.6.1.4 The Credit provides for Negotiation

If the credit provides for negotiation, then the bank is prepared to negotiate the bill of exchange if presented with correct documents. An open negotiation credit would allow the beneficiary to negotiate the bill, not only with the bank, but also to anyone else. A restricted negotiation credit would allow negotiation with only particular parties. The credit may require that the documents, together with the bill to be negotiated, be presented only by the named beneficiary.

However, it is usual for the undertaking to be given, not only to the seller, but also to anyone to whom he has negotiated. The essence of negotiation within the meaning of the Bills of Exchange Act 1882 is that the negotiation will result in a transfer of the bill to the recipient in such a way as to constitute him a holder of that bill (s. 31 Bills of Exchange Act 1882). The holder has rights of recourse against the prior parties and the drawee under ss. 43(2) and 47(2) in the event that he is unable to get acceptance or payment of the bill. Therefore, it is possible that the issuing bank might negotiate a bill presented to it by the seller or anyone to whom he had previously negotiated it, together with agreed documents. When the issuing bank then discovers that it is unable to obtain reimbursement from the buyer, for whatever reason, it can simply resort to the party who presented it for the amount of the bill under the right of recourse. It has long been thought that it is totally inconsistent with the rights or obligations and the undertaking which is given by an issuing bank under an irrevocable credit that it should be able to exercise rights of recourse in this way; see *Wahbe Tamari & Sons Ltd and Jaffa Trading* v *Colprogeca* [1969] 2 Lloyd's Rep 18.

It is for this reason that whenever the buyer requires a negotiation credit and the negotiation is to be effected by a bank, the issuing bank cannot undertake negotiation. In such cases, they have two choices. They can either simply pay the bills without recourse to anyone and presumably without becoming a holder of any kind, or they can nominate another bank to negotiate. In this latter respect, it is important to note that if another bank is nominated by the issuing bank in this way, the mere fact of nomination to the task will not bind the nominated negotiating bank (Art. 10(c)).

The nominated negotiating bank is free to reject its nomination in the same way as a bank chosen as confirmer could refuse to accept that capacity and simply act as an adviser. The only qualification to this is that if the bank nominated to negotiate the bill of exchange is, in fact, the issuing or confirming bank, the mere fact that it is the issuing or confirming bank will bind it to making some form of payment if the documents are correct. Therefore, only where the nominated negotiating bank is the issuing or confirming bank will there be an undertaking to negotiate (Art. 10(c)).

11.6.1.5   The forms of payment — summing-up

Whichever form payment is to take, it will be clearly stated in the credit, and whichever bank is to be responsible for effecting payment will equally be stated in the credit. The bank which is nominated to do any one of the above (11.6.1.1 to 11.6.1.4) may be referred to as the nominated bank, more specifically, the nominated paying bank (authorised to pay cash), accepting bank (authorised to accept drafts), or negotiating bank (authorised to negotiate drafts) (Art. 10(b)).

Whenever there is a need for the issuing bank to make a nomination of another bank to effect negotiation, then that selection must be made by the issuing bank. Even where a correspondent bank is involved in the implementation of the credit, it is the issuing bank that is subject to the obligation to make the nomination, even though it may be easier for that nomination to be made by the correspondent, which would no doubt be situated in the seller's country and better placed to appoint a bank to carry out the task.

11.6.2   The Doctrine of Strict Compliance

The doctrine of strict compliance is fundamental to operation of letters of credit. The documents presented under the letter of credit must comply strictly with the terms of the credit. If the documents do not comply with the terms of the credit but the bank nevertheless pays, it will not be entitled to be reimbursed by the applicant as it will have exceeded its mandate. If the documents do comply with the terms of the credit then payment must be made. Viscount Sumner in *Equitable Trust Co. of New York* v *Damson Partners Ltd* (1927) 27 Ll LR 49 indicated that documents 'which are almost the same' will not do:

> It is both common ground and common sense that in such a transaction the accepting bank can only claim indemnity if the conditions on which it is authorised to accept are in the matter of the accompanying documents strictly observed. There is no room for documents which are almost the same, or which will do just as well. Business could not proceed securely on any other lines. The bank's branch abroad, which knows nothing officially of the details of the transaction thus financed, cannot take it upon itself to decide what will do well enough and what will not. If it does as it is told, it is safe; if it declines to do anything else, it is safe; if it departs from the conditions laid down, it acts at its own risk.

When the seller tenders the documents to the bank, the bank must examine all the documents with reasonable care to ascertain whether or not they conform with the credit; see *Gian Singh & Co. Ltd* v *Banque de l'Indochine* [1974] 1 WLR 1234. The bank is, therefore, looking for the correct documents, consistency between all the documents, and that the content of each document is correct. Article 13 sets out the obligation in the following terms:

Banks must examine all documents stipulated in the credit with reasonable care, to ascertain whether or not they appear, on their face, to be in compliance with the terms and conditions of the credit. Compliance of the stipulated documents on their face with the terms and conditions of the credit, shall be determined by international standard banking practice as reflected in these Articles. Documents which appear on their face to be inconsistent with one another will be considered as not appearing on their face to be in compliance with the terms and conditions of the credit.

The bank is looking only for apparent conformity. It is not required to look beyond the face of the documents. This is consistent with the principle expressed in Art. 15:

Banks assume no liability or responsibility for the form sufficiency, accuracy, genuineness, falsification or legal effect of any document(s) or for the general and/or particular conditions stipulated in the document(s) or superimposed thereon: nor do they assume any liability or responsibility for the description, quantity, weight, quality, condition, packing, delivery, value or existence of the goods represented by any document(s).

The bank must determine on the basis of the documents alone whether or not there is compliance with the mandate (Art. 14(b)). It has a reasonable time, not to exceed seven banking days following the day of receipt of the documents, to determine whether to take up or reject the documents without regard to the sufficiency of performance under the contract of sale (Art. 13(b)); see *Banker's Trust Co.* v *State Bank of India* [1991] 2 Lloyd's Rep 443.

If the documents comply with the terms of the credit, then the bank must pay against them.

If the buyer feels that the bank has wrongly accepted the documents from the seller and failed to take reasonable skill and care, then it is for the buyer to prove that lack of care on the part of the bank; see *Bass & Selve Bank* v *Bank of Australasia* (1904) 90 LT 618.

Ordinarily, a mere visual inspection of the documents will suffice to determine that the correct documents are being tendered. The bank is under no duty, as already noted, to check their authenticity; see *Gian Singh* v *Banque de l'Indochine*.

However, this is not to be confused with the fact that the bank is obliged to accept original documents (as widely defined in Art. 20(b)). Clearly, therefore, if a document is marked as original that should suffice. The bank cannot be responsible for determining whether or not such a notation is forged. A new Art. 20(c) in the 1993 revision provides that, unless otherwise stipulated in the credit, the bank will accept as a copy, a document either labelled copy or not marked as an original.

Credits that require multiple documents, e.g. 'duplicate', will be satisfied by the beneficiary presenting an original and the remaining number in copies. This new provision is intended to bring about a uniformity of practice based on the international standard banking practices.

If the documents are correct and the bank prevaricates in making payment against them, it may find itself liable in damages to the seller. In *Ozalid Group (Export) Ltd v African Continental Bank* [1979] NLJ 295 payment was to have been made on 5 October but was not made until 12 December, even though the documents were correct. The seller/beneficiary was entitled to damages for the unjustifiable delay in making payment.

In determining whether or not to pay against the tendered documents, the bank must look for strict compliance with the terms of the mandate. The doctrine of strict compliance is rigidly applied by the bank, which will lose its right to be reimbursed by the buyer if it pays out in excess of its mandate.

In determining whether or not the documents comply, the bank will have no regard to trade custom. The bank cannot be involved in evaluating whether what was asked for in the credit has, in fact, been supplied, despite the fact that it is differently referred to in the documents. This would not only be time consuming, but would also involve the bank in going beyond the sale contract to examine the goods themselves. Therefore, in *Rayner* v *Hambros* [1943] 1 KB 37, the bank rejected documents which showed shipment of machine shelled nut kernels instead of coromandel ground nuts, as required by the credit, even though by trade custom the description in the document meant the same thing.

Under Art. 14(c) if the issuing bank determines that the documents appear on their face not to be in compliance with the terms and conditions of the credit, it may approach the applicant for a waiver of the discrepancy (or discrepancies). However, Art. 14(c) does not extend the time period of seven banking days mentioned in Art. 13(b).

There is no room for the application of the *de minimis* principle in the context of documents tendered under a credit. In *Moralice (London) Ltd* v *ED & F Man* [1954] 2 Lloyd's Rep 526 McNair J held that documents evidencing a short shipment of 0.06 per cent could be rejected as not complying with the terms of the credit. In *Soproma SpA* v *Marine & Animal By-Products Corporation* [1966] 1 Lloyd's Rep 367 McNair J again held that a bank was entitled to reject documents which only just failed to comply with the terms of the credit. The credit required documents showing shipment of Chilean fish fullmeal with minimum 70 per cent protein content. An analysis certificate tendered showed a protein content of only 69.7 per cent and a quality certificate showed only 67 per cent. The bank was entitled to reject both documents. Another objection to the documents tendered was that the credit required the bills of lading to state that the temperature on loading did not exceed 37.5 degrees centigrade whereas the bill of lading tendered showed that the actual temperature on loading did not exceed 100 degrees Fahrenheit. There is a discrepancy between the two formulae of 0.5 degrees Fahrenheit. McNair J was reluctant to allow this objection but felt constrained to do so as a matter of strict law.

The UCP does, however, allow for some margin of error in the case of the quantity of goods. Thus unless the credit stipulates that the quantity of goods specified must not be exceeded or reduced, a tolerance of five per cent more or less is permitted (i.e. '10,000 tonnes' allows 9,500 to 10,500 tonnes). This does not apply where the credit stipulates the quantity in terms of a stated number of packing units or individual items (i.e. '5,000 boxes …') (Art. 39(b)). If the words 'about', 'approximately' '*circa*' or some similar expression is used in connection with the quantity, this gives a tolerance of 10 per cent (Art. 39(a)).

Thus, the effect of the doctrine of strict compliance is that all the terms of the credit are construed strictly against the beneficiary. If there is any deviation in fact from that which the credit requires, no matter how minuscule and inconsequential it may be, then the bank will refuse the tendered documents. In *Equitable Trust* v *Damson* (above) the credit insisted upon a certificate signed by experts. Therefore, a certificate signed by one expert was insufficient.

We have dealt so far with whether or not the actual documents tendered are those requested. We must now consider the contents of each document.

It would be almost impossible for every single document to contain a description of the goods which conforms exactly with the description found in the credit. It is always available for the buyer to require this degree of conformity, but this would unduly hamper the smooth operation of the credit. It is, therefore, generally sufficient that only the invoice for the goods needs to contain a description which is exactly consistent with the description which is found in the credit. Article 37(c) provides:

> The description of the goods in the commercial invoice must correspond with the description in the credit. In all other documents, the goods may be described in general terms not inconsistent with the description of the goods in the credit.

In *Soproma SpA* v *Marine & Animal By-Products Corp.* (above) a further point taken was that whereas the credit referred to a shipment of Chilean fish fullmeal, the bill of lading tendered only referred to Chilean fishmeal. The invoice correctly referred to the goods as Chilean fish fullmeal and McNair J applying what is now Art. 37(c), held that it did not matter that the bill of lading only referred to Chilean fishmeal. The effect of this provision, that only the invoice needs to contain the detailed description, is that in many cases the bank will have to look at all the documents taken together in order to determine whether or not the seller has complied with the credit. The approach of considering all the documents together, rather than separately, has been specifically approved by the courts as a practical and sensible approach. Nevertheless, it does not affect the general rule that each single document must be correct and complete in itself; see *Midland Bank* v *Seymour* [1955] 2 Lloyd's Rep 147.

The 1993 revision states that the bank will accept the documents as presented, provided that their data content is not inconsistent with any other stipulated document presented.

11.6.3 THE DOCUMENTS

11.6.3.1 *The Invoice*
The commercial invoice for the goods must be made out in the name of the buyer/applicant for the credit (Art. 37(a)).

It should be for the amount for which the credit has been opened. If the invoice is for an amount larger than that for which the credit is available, then the bank may refuse it. However, it does appear from Art. 37(b) that the bank has a complete discretion in this respect. It is permitted to take up an invoice notwithstanding that it is for a sum in excess of that made available in the credit. If it chooses to take this course, it cannot, however, pay out more than the credit sum. In the event that such an invoice is accepted by the bank, then its decision will be binding on all parties and the buyer on the basis that the bank has not exceeded its mandate. Article 37(b) provides:

> If a bank authorised to pay ... accepts such invoices, its decision will be binding upon all parties, provided such bank has not paid ... for an amount in excess of that permitted by the credit.

Such a situation might arise where the seller ships a slightly larger quantity of bulk goods and the larger quantity falls within acceptable tolerance levels (Art. 39). The seller tenders an invoice for the larger quantity to the bank. Whilst the bank cannot pay this larger amount, they can pay the agreed sum in the credit if they decide to accept the invoice, and the seller would be obliged to seek payment of the difference between the amount actually due and the amount in the credit from the buyer direct.

The final requirement of the invoice is that it should contain a description of the goods which corresponds exactly to that found in the credit. In this respect it is quite different from other documents which need only contain a general description (Art. 37(c)) (For further details on the invoice see 5.5 and 5.6.).

11.6.3.2 The Transport Document

Transport documents are dealt with in section D of the UCP. It is in the area of documentation that the major changes between the old and the new UCP are to be found. The UCP 400 (1983 revision) dealt with transport documents in Art. 25 and that Article enabled the bank to take up any document whatever it might be called by the parties if that document satisfied certain criteria. The parties were free to stipulate expressly that the seller must present a bill of lading. In such cases, the relevant provision was Art. 26.

The UCP 500 (1993 revision) contains Articles for individual transport documents rather than one Article headed 'transport documents'. The new revision will hopefully be clearer and less likely to be misinterpreted and misapplied than the old revision.

Under Art. 23 of the new revision, if a credit calls for a bill of lading covering a port-to-port shipment, banks will accept a document which:

    (a)   indicates the name of the carrier and has been signed or authenticated by the carrier, master or agent;

    (b)   indicates that the goods have been loaded on board or shipped on a named vessel; and

    (c)   indicates the actual port of loading and the port of discharge.

Article 24 is headed 'non-negotiable sea waybill' and is a new addition to the UCP. This article provides that a non-negotiable sea waybill can be accepted by the bank if certain criteria are met. The sea waybill is not traditionally a document of title being merely a receipt and evidence of the contract of carriage. The UCP now takes account of its increased use in some parts of the world.

The charterparty bill of lading is dealt with in Art. 25. Under the old revision the bank could reject a bill of lading which referred to a charterparty contract. Under the 1993 revision, the charterparty bill of lading will be accepted by the bank. However, the bank is not required to examine the charterparty contract. If the contract is presented, the bank will forward it without incurring any responsibility (Art. 25(b)).

Article 26 deals with the multimodal transport document. If a credit calls for a transport document covering at least two different modes of transport, the bank will accept a document which covers the carrying of goods from one mode of transport to another. Even if the credit prohibits transhipment, the bank will accept a multimodal transport document which indicates that transhipment will or may take place, provided the entire carriage is covered by one and the same multimodal transport document (Art. 26(b)).

Article 30 covers transport documents issued by freight forwarders. The 1983 revision endorsed particular freight forwarders' transport documents, whereas the 1993 revision moves away from that position. A transport document issued by any freight forwarder will be accepted if it is (i) authorised in the credit, or (ii) issued and signed according to criteria laid down in the UCP.

The transport document which is presented to the bank must be 'clean'. This means that there cannot be any notation to the effect that the goods or packaging are damaged. Article 32(a) states:

> A clean transport document is one which bears no superimposed clause or notation which expressly declares a defective condition of the goods or the packaging.

At common law there is a distinction between pre- and post-shipment damage. According to *The Galatia* [1980] 1 WLR 495 a notation of damage occurring after shipment cannot have the effect of clausing the bill. It is clear from Art. 34 that it would have been extremely easy for the code to have distinguished between pre- and post-shipment clausing, but it does not do so. Surely then it can be inferred that a document presented to a bank showing that the goods are damaged will constitute a bad tender for the purpose of obtaining payment under the credit, irrespective of whether the damage occurred pre- or post-shipment. That same document would, however, be a good tender if presented to the buyer direct for the purpose of obtaining payment.

11.6.3.3   The Insurance Documents

The insurance documents, which are dealt with in section D, Arts. 34 to 36, must be stipulated in the credit and must be issued and signed by the insurance company/ underwriter or agent thereof. A broker's cover note is not acceptable (Art. 34(c)).

Unless otherwise stipulated in the credit, a bank will accept an insurance certificate or a declaration under an open cover (Art. 34(d)). Cover should be effective from, at latest, the date of loading on board, or dispatch or taking in charge, whichever is relevant (Art. 34(e)).

The credit should stipulate those risks against which the seller is to obtain cover, by using precise terms. If no such stipulations are made, then the bank will accept the insurance document which is presented by the seller without any responsibility for any risks which are not thereby covered (Art. 35). It is suggested that Art. 35 will not entitle the bank to accept an insurance document without any examination of its content. The insurance document should comply with other articles of the UCP relating to insurance and it should provide at least basic cover in respect of the relevant goods for the relevant carriage. Article 35 should be regarded more as a protection for banks who have received inadequate instructions and where particular risks have not been referred to in the credit and are not covered by the policy.

If the insurance is on all risks terms then, providing that this is clear from some clause or notation in the document, there is no need for the insurance document to bear such a heading. This is in view of the fact that insurance policies are now headed 'ICCA' for all risks cover, and it is only clear from the risks clause therein that insurance is on 'all risks' terms (Art. 36).

The goods should be insured for their contractual journey for at least their c.i.f. value plus 10 per cent. However, if the bank cannot determine from the face of the documents what is the c.i.f. value of the goods, then it will accept an insurance document which shows that the minimum amount of cover is 110 per cent of the amount for which payment, acceptance or negotiation is requested under the credit, or 110 per cent of the gross amount of the invoice, whichever is the greater (Art. 34(f)(ii)). (For further details on the insurance documents see 5.4, 12.5 and 12.8.)

11.6.3.4   Other Documents
It is usual for the buyer to insist upon presentation of an invoice, an insurance document, normally a policy, and a bill of lading or transport documents. In addition to these documents, the buyer may also wish the seller to tender a certificate of quality obtained at the port of loading or a certificate of analysis, or any other document which the buyer feels will provide him with the necessary assurance that the seller is providing the contract goods. The requirements of such documents are dealt with under Art. 21. It is perhaps helpful to refer to Art. 33 of the 1974 revision for some examples of the kind of documents which the buyer might request. Article 33 provided:

> When other documents are required such as warehouse receipts, delivery orders, consular invoices, certificates of weight, of origin, of quality or of analysis etc, and when no further definition is tendered or given, banks will accept such documents as tendered.

Article 21 of the 1993 revision does not contain a list of the documents which may be called for, lest such a list be mistakenly interpreted as definitive. However the general requirement of Art. 21 is the same. If the bank has no information as to what it should look for in any document which is tendered under the credit, and which is not a transport document, insurance document or commercial invoice then the bank can accept that document as tendered. Article 21 states:

> When documents other than transport documents, insurance documents and commercial invoices are called for, the credit should stipulate by whom such documents are to be issued and their wording or data content. If the credit does not so stipulate, banks will accept such documents as presented, provided that their data content is not inconsistent with any other stipulated document presented.

Therefore, even though there may be a complete dearth of instructions regarding other documents, nevertheless, the bank still bears a responsibility to look at least for consistency between those goods which are referred to in the additional document and those which are requested under the credit and closely described in the commercial invoice. The bank cannot simply take up the other document quite irrespective of its manifest inconsistency with the rest of the credit; see *Banque de l'Indochine et de Suez SA v JH Rayner (Mincing Lane) Ltd* [1983] QB 711. (For additional document required by the contract see 5.6.)

11.6.4 Rejection
The issuing banks, and presumably the advising or confirming bank, have a reasonable time to examine the documents for discrepancies (Art 16(b), (c)). What is a reasonable time is a question of fact taking into account all relevant factors. United Kingdom banks aim to accept or reject documents within three days.

If the documents do not strictly comply with the terms of the credit the bank will nearly always consult with the applicant (buyer) to determine whether to accept or reject the documents. The applicant may decide that the documents tendered are suitable notwithstanding their discrepancies and will then instruct the bank to accept the documents.

A 'reasonable time' includes time taken to consult the applicant but not time for the applicant to examine the documents for further discrepancies; see *Banker's Trust Co. v State Bank of India* [1991] 2 Lloyd's Rep 443.

If the bank decides to reject the documents it must give notice to that effect without delay to the bank from which it received the documents or the beneficiary. This notice must state, in accordance with Art 14(d):

(a)   the discrepancies in respect of which the bank refuses the documents; and

(b)   whether the bank is holding the documents at the disposal of, or is returning them to, the presenter.

The bank is precluded, by Art 14(e), from claiming that the documents are not in accordance with the terms and conditions of the credit if it fails to:

(a) give notice within a reasonable time (not exceeding seven banking days following the day of receipt); or

(b) give the required notice; or

(c) hold the documents at the disposal of, or return them to, the presenter.

See *Banker's Trust Co.* v *State Bank of India* (above).

Where a bank pays under a letter of credit although the documents tendered are defective, the principal (the issuing bank/buyer) may ratify the unauthorised transaction. Ratification may, in appropriate circumstances, be inferred from prolonged inaction or silence; see *Bank Melli Iran* v *Barclays Bank* (Dominion, Colonial and Overseas) [1951] 2 Lloyd's Rep 367.

11.7 THE AUTONOMY OF IRREVOCABLE CREDITS

An irrevocable credit constitutes an independent contract between IB and the beneficiary, the seller. It is not, therefore, qualified by or subject to the terms of the contract of sale between the buyer and the seller; see *Urquhart, Lindsay & Co.* v *Eastern Bank* [1922] 1 KB 316.

The letter of credit is separate from and independent of the underlying contract of sale. The bank is not concerned with the underlying contract of sale but only with the documents tendered by the beneficiary (Arts. 3, 4). If the bank makes payment against conforming documents then it is entitled to be reimbursed by the applicant. Article 14(a) provides:

When the issuing bank authorises another bank to pay ... against documents which appear on their face to be in compliance with the terms and conditions of the credit, the issuing bank and the confirming bank, if any, are bound: (i) to reimburse the nominated bank which has paid ...

This, therefore, forms the contractual basis for the autonomy of the irrevocable credit, with the effect that the applicant cannot prevent the bank from making payment, notwithstanding that it is aware of defects in the goods not manifest on the face of the documents.

This is well illustrated by *Malas (Hamazeh) & Sons* v *British Imex Industries Ltd* [1958] 2 QB 127. The claimants in Jordan agreed to purchase two shipments of steel rods from the defendants. M Bank opened two confirmed credits in favour of the defendants. The defendants made the first shipment and were paid. The claimants, alleging that the goods were defective, applied for an injunction to restrain the defendants from drawing on the second letter of credit. The Court of Appeal refused to grant the injunction. Jenkins LJ said that the confirmed credit constituted an absolute obligation of the banks to pay 'irrespective of any dispute there may be between the parties as to whether the goods are up to contract or not'. He thought that the system of financing sales of goods by irrevocable credits 'would break down completely if a dispute as between the vendor and the purchaser was to have the effect of 'freezing' . . . the sum in respect of which the letter of credit was opened'.

11.7.1   The Fraud Rule

The one established exception to the principle of the autonomy of the credit is fraud. It is an exception in the sense that the court will take into account evidence apart from the terms and conditions of the credit and the documents presented. There is no reference in the UCP to the existence of any exception to the principle of the autonomy of the credit. The exception arises as part of the common law and is founded on the maxim *ex turpi causa non oritur actio* (a right of action will not arise from a base cause).

The foundation stone of English law in this area is the American case of *Sztejin* v *J Henry Schroder Banking Corp* (1941) 31 NYS 2d 631 and the leading English authority is the House of Lords decision in *United City Merchants (Investments)* v *Royal Bank of Canada* [1983] 1 AC 168. Lord Diplock, in giving judgment for the House of Lords in the latter case, after referring to the general principle of the autonomy of the credit, said this:

> To this general statement of principle as to the contractual obligations of the confirming bank to the seller, there is one established exception: that is, where the seller, for the purpose of drawing on the credit, fraudulently presents to the confirming bank documents that contain, expressly or by implication, material representations of fact that to his knowledge are untrue . . . The exception for fraud on the part of the beneficiary seeking to avail himself of the credit is a clear application of the maxim *ex turpi causa non oritur actio* or, if plain English is to be preferred, 'fraud unravels all'. The courts will not allow their process to be used by a dishonest person to carry out a fraud.

In that case the fraud exception did not apply. The sellers were found not to have been aware that the documents they were presenting contained a material misrepresentation. The decision of the House of Lords does make one matter clear, the beneficiary must be a party to the fraud before the courts will interfere in the operation of a credit. The fraud need not, however, be limited to the presentation of the documents but may arise out of the opening of the credit by the applicant. Nevertheless the beneficiary must be a party to that fraud; see *Rafsanjan Pistachio Co-operative* v *Bank Leumi (UK) plc* [1992] 1 Lloyd's Rep 513.

Thus where there is fraud on the part of the beneficiary the bank is entitled to refuse to make payment under the credit even though the documents presented conformed in all respects with the terms and conditions of the credit. If the beneficiary is, however, innocent but tenders documents which are not accurate in that they have been fraudulently altered by a third party, the bank must still pay in accordance with the terms of the credit.

One matter which was left open by Lord Diplock in *United City Merchants* is the position in respect of documents which are forgeries. A document which has been forged is a nullity. Examples of such documents are a bill of lading made out by a person without the authority of the carrier for which the bill of lading purports to be issued, or a certificate of inspection which is required to be made by a named certification agency but was in fact made out by a third party who had no connection with that agency; see *Gian Singh & Co. Ltd* v *Banque de l'Indochine* [1974] 1 WLR 1234.

Under the UCP banks do not assume liability or responsibility for the form, sufficiency, accuracy or genuineness, falsification or legal effect of any documents presented (Art. 15). That does not mean that a bank would not be entitled to reject a forged document on the grounds that it is a nullity and it is suggested that a bank should be entitled to reject such a document even though the beneficiary was not a party to the forging of the document.

If a bank pays against documents which are fraudulent or forged but which appear on their face to accord with the terms and conditions of the credit, it is entitled to be reimbursed by the party from which its authority derives, unless the fraud of the beneficiary was clearly established to the bank at the time when the documents were presented.

In most cases, it is difficult for the bank to distinguish between a fraudulent activity and inaccuracies in the documents caused by mistake. The bank is, of course, in a difficult situation. If it refuses to pay when the inaccuracies were legitimate mistakes, the bank would be liable in damages to the beneficiary and its reputation would be severely damaged. If it pays out and the case against the beneficiary is made out, then it may not be entitled to be reimbursed. The typical course of action banks take is to insist on the applicant obtaining an injunction, either preventing the bank itself from paying out or preventing the beneficiary from drawing on the credit until the question of fraud has been tried.

To obtain an injunction the applicant must satisfy the court of a number of matters. First that he has a good arguable case against the party he is seeking to injunct which involves showing a clear case of fraud to the knowledge of the party to be injuncted. It will not normally be sufficient for the court to rely on the uncorroborated evidence of the applicant. Secondly the applicant will have to show a cause of action against the party he is seeking to injunct. In most cases this will be on the contract governing the relationship between the parties, but as between the applicant and a confirming bank a duty of care in tort will have to be shown as there is no privity of contract; see *GKN Contractors* v *Lloyds Bank* (1985) 30 BLR 48. The court must also be satisfied that it has jurisdiction over the party against whom the injunction is sought (see Chapter 15). The final matter of which the court must be satisfied is that the grant of the injunction was a correct exercise of the court's discretion after considering the balance of convenience; see *American Cyanamid* v *Ethicon Ltd* [1975] AC 396. This last matter is an almost insurmountable hurdle and it is significant that there is not one reported case in which an injunction has been granted. Indeed in *Tukan Timber Ltd* v *Barclays Bank plc* [1987] 1 Lloyd's Rep 171, Hirst J found that a clear case of fraud had been made out on the evidence but nonetheless refused to grant an injunction. The applicant would not suffer any damage which the bank would not be able to compensate, while the bank's reputation would suffer immeasurably if it was not able to make payment. In *Discount Records* v *Barclays Bank* [1975] 1 WLR 315 Megarry J refused an injunction at the instance of the applicant against the issuing bank, holding that a mere allegation of fraud is insufficient. Fraud must be 'established' or a 'sufficient case had to be made out', imposing a heavy burden on the applicant.

On the facts of *Discount Records*, Megarry J thought that no sufficient case had been made out where according to the buyer's evidence, of a consignment of 94 cartons of goods delivered to him, two were empty, five were filled with rubbish, several had had their serial numbers altered and the remainder of the boxes contained non-contractual items. Megarry J recognised the difficulty of establishing fraud where the injunction is sought against the bank, rather than against the seller, the beneficiary of the credit. In the former case, the judge would hear the buyer's side, but the bank would not be in a position to put forward the seller's arguments. Megarry J thought that the most convenient solution would be for the buyer to seek an injunction with notice to other parties against the seller, preventing the latter from drawing on the credit. In addition, Megarry J held that even if fraud were established, no injunction could be granted to prevent the holder in due course of the bills of exchange drawn and negotiated under the letter of credit from seeking to enforce the drawee/acceptor's undertaking in the draft. He thought that this promise was itself independent of the undertakings both in the letter of credit and in the underlying contract of sale.

Most of the English cases after *Discount Records* which have considered the fraud rule have involved performance bonds rather than documentary credits. As has already been seen, performance bonds are documentary credits in reverse, securing the seller's obligations to deliver the goods under the contract of sale.

In *Bolivinter Oil* v *Chase Manhattan Bank* [1984] 1 WLR 392 the Court of Appeal indicated in a practice note the factors with which the court should be concerned in an application without notice to other parties for an injunction against a bank. The first question the court should address is whether there is a challenge to the performance bond itself. If none, then no injunction should be granted, though there may be grounds for a freezing injunction. The Court of Appeal then continued in the following manner:

The wholly exceptional case where an injunction may be granted is where it is proved that the bank knows that any demand for payment already made or which may thereafter be made will clearly be fraudulent. But the evidence must be clear, both as to the fact of the fraud and as to the bank's knowledge. It would certainly not normally be sufficient that this rest upon the uncorroborated statement of the customer, for irreparable damage can be done to a bank's credit in the relatively brief time which must elapse between the granting of the injunction and an application by the bank to have it discharged.

In the case of *United Trading Corporation* v *Allied Arab Bank* [1985] 2 Lloyd's Rep 554, Ackner LJ described the evidential burden on the applicant for the injunction in the following terms:

> It is not necessary to rule out any other innocent explanation for the beneficiary's demand. But the court requires strong corroborative evidence of the allegation, usually in the form of contemporary documents from the beneficiary of the credit. For evidence of fraud to be clear, the courts expect the beneficiary to have been given an opportunity to answer the allegation and to have failed to provide any or any adequate answer in circumstances where one could have been expected. If the only realistic inference is one of fraud, then the respondent would have made out a sufficient case of fraud.

If the bank does pay out, the buyer could obtain a freezing injunction to prevent the seller from dealing with the proceeds until the question of fraud had been tried. This does not interfere with the autonomy of the credit and would attach to the action between the buyer and the seller; see *Z Ltd* v *A-Z and AA-LL* [1982] QB 558. Although a court may grant a world-wide freezing injunction it is unlikely that an injunction would be granted restraining a beneficiary from dealing with money paid to him outside the jurisdiction. There may also be a problem in finding a cause of action to which the injunction could attach, prior to the presentation of the documents and payment under the letter of credit. In the absence of a pre-existing cause of action the court does not have jurisdiction to grant a freezing injunction; see *The Veracruz* [1992] 1 Lloyd's Rep 353.

11.7.2   Payment Under Reserve and Indemnities

A bank which has doubts about the tendered documents may make payment under reserve, particularly where the beneficiary is a valued customer of good standing. Where such payment is made the beneficiary is bound to repay the money on demand if the buyer, or issuing bank if the credit is confirmed, rejects the documents. It does not matter that the reasons given by the buyer or issuing bank were not valid. That is a matter relating to the paying bank's obligations under the letter of credit but does not concern payment under reserve; see *Banque de l'Indochine et de Suez SA* v *JH Rayner (Mincing Lane) Ltd* [1983] QB 711.

Rather than making payment under reserve when the documents do not comply exactly with the terms of the credit, the paying bank may ask the beneficiary to supply an indemnity either through himself or through his bank; see *Moralice (London) Ltd* v *ED & F Man* [1954] 2 Lloyd's Rep 526.

11.8   SHORT-CIRCUITING THE CREDIT

The parties to a documentary credit may have agreed on the use of such a credit, in their original contract of sale. Alternatively, the agreement to make payment by documentary credit may have been reached at some later date, and thus vary or supplement any previous agreement. In any event, if there is an agreement to make payment under a documentary credit, then the seller does not have the right to present the documents to the buyer direct (*Soproma* v *Marine & Animal By-Products* [1966] 1 Lloyd's Rep 367).

The parties are free to agree that the opening of the credit will operate as absolute payment by the buyer. However, in the absence of such agreement, the opening of the credit operates only as conditional payment by the buyer. The buyer does not, therefore, discharge himself from liability by the very fact of the credit being opened. Therefore, in the event that the seller cannot obtain payment under the credit, he is permitted to resort to the buyer for payment. In *Alan* v *El Nasr Import and Export* [1972] 2 QB 189 Lord Denning said:

> ... if the letter of credit is conditional payment of the price the consequences are these: the seller looks in the first instance to the banker for payment but if the banker does not meet the obligations, the seller has recourse to the buyer.

In *E D and F Man* v *Nigerian Sweets* [1977] 2 Lloyd's Rep 50 an irrevocable documentary credit was opened at a Swiss bank which went into liquidation before payment was made to the seller against drafts of which the bank was drawee, payable 90 days after date. The buyers claimed that they had discharged all their liability to the seller by the very fact of opening the credit or, alternatively, since they had put the bank in funds for payment against the drafts, they had similarly discharged their liability, even though the seller had not acquired the contract price. Ackner J said that the opening of the credit was a conditional payment only. The drafts had been dishonoured and, therefore, the seller was entitled to resort to the buyer. The buyer's primary liability was merely held in suspension until such time as the seller received payment under the credit.

In *Sale Continuation* v *Austin Taylor* [1967] 2 Lloyd's Rep 403 the seller could not obtain money on a bill of exchange presented with correct documents, because the paying bank was insolvent. Therefore, the seller went directly to the buyer, who paid him the contract price. The bank argued that the seller should not be able to circumvent the credit mechanism since payment by documentary credit had been agreed to by the parties. It contended that the buyer must put the bank in funds for the amount of the credit and then the seller would have to make a claim with all other creditors in the bank's insolvency. Paull J rejected this submission. He said that the buyer did not retain any obligation to put the bank in funds, as the bank had already evinced an intention not to pay. Therefore, even though the buyer had pledged the documents to the bank, the bank lost its right to claim on the pledge once it said that it would not honour the bill of exchange presented by the seller. Therefore, the seller could resort to the buyer direct and the buyer did not have to assume the onerous burden of having both to pay the seller and put the bank in funds.

11.9 REMEDIES AND PROCEDURAL ISSUES

In *Hong Kong and Shanghai Banking Corporation* v *Kloeckner & Co. AG* [1989] 2 Lloyd's Rep 323 it was held that similar rules on remedies and procedure apply to actions based on letters of credit as to those based on bills of exchange. Both forms of payment are similar to cash. The case raised two issues. Following the Court of Appeal in *Halesowen Presswork* v *Westminster Bank* [1971] I QB 1, the claimant bank was held entitled to rely on a clause precluding the applicant for a letter of credit from establishing the bank's liabilities as a set-off defence to an action by the bank on the letter of credit. Secondly, the court considered the propriety of the set-off defence in the absence of contractual preclusion. Cases such as *Power Curber* [1981] 3 All ER 607 and *The Bhoja Trader* [1981] 2 Lloyd's Rep 256 (CA) were distinguished: they concerned liabilities arising from the sale contract underlying the letter of credit. In such cases there can be no set-off since the letter of credit is autonomous. Where the liabilities in question arose from the banker-customer relationship, however, there was no reason why such liabilities could not be set off. Obligations arising under letters of credit were no different from any other aspect of the banker-customer relationship. The customer could, therefore, set off any liquidated claims arising directly out of the same transaction giving rise to his liability to the bank.

11.10 BANKERS' GUARANTEES AND PERFORMANCE BONDS

Sometimes a beneficiary of credit may require an additional collateral from the other party. The party concerned would then have to ask his bank or other guarantor to provide the guarantee — the performance guarantee. It has been adjudicated that (by, for instance, *Edward Owen Engineering* v *Barclays Bank* [1978] QB 159) such bonds stand on similar footing to a letter of credit and that a bank giving such a guarantee must honour it according to its terms unless there is clear evidence of fraud of which the bank has notice. The Court of Appeal also held that performance bonds were similar to documentary credits in that they bear the same characteristic of autonomy from the underlying contract of sale. Lord Denning MR also observed, *per curiam*, in that case that performance guarantees are virtually promissory notes payable on demand.

Only in clear cases of fraud or other exceptional circumstances will a bank be enjoined from meeting an irrevocable obligation it assumed, provided that the forms of the bank's mandate have been complied with; see *R D Harbottle (Mercantile)* v *National Westminster Bank Ltd* [1977] 1 All ER 869, *per* Kerr J. In this case contracts for the supply of goods to Egyptian buyers, the claimants' sellers, in return for payment being guaranteed by irrevocable credit, were required to establish performance bonds whereby their bank was irrevocably authorised to pay up to five per cent of the contract price upon proof of any breach or other default of the claimants. The bonds were duly established with Egyptian banks. The claimants' bank (the defendants) was to be indemnified by the claimants in respect of all payments made under the guarantees. Disputes arose between the claimants (suppliers) and the buyers, who made demand upon the bank under the guarantee. The claimants issued proceedings against the buyers and meanwhile obtained injunctions restraining both banks from being paid or obtaining money respectively. On application by the issuing bank to discharge the injunctions, Kerr J had no hesitation in granting the application that the bank was entitled to pay under the guarantees, the terms under which it assumed an irrevocable obligation having been satisfied.

That the performance bonds are independent of the credit or sales or any other contract on which they may be based was further emphasised in *Home Richardson Scale Co. Ltd* v *Polimex-Cekop* [1978] 1 Lloyd's Rep 161, CA. A contract dated 15 January 1976 for equipment worth £500,000 to Polish buyers provided for arbitration in Zurich, and that £25,000 was payable in advance within 45 days of the contract signing on presentation of a guarantee by the seller's bank (guaranteeing, amongst other things, a refund of the advance payment in case of non-delivery of goods by 31 March 1977), and that a further £50,000 was to be paid by an irrevocable, unconfirmed letter of credit opened upon notification that the goods were ready for shipment. The guarantee was given by the seller's bank (upon taking a counter-indemnity from the seller), and the seller received the advance payment. The buyer did not open the letter of credit. The seller completed the manufacture of the goods and in due course received a sum of money on account of the final instalment. The buyer claimed repayment of the £25,000 under the guarantee on the ground that delivery had not been made by 31 March 1977. The seller applied for an injunction to restrain the buyer from claiming under the guarantee (i.e. to prevent the £25,000 from being taken out of the jurisdiction) unless and until the question of the second instalment had been arbitrated. On appeal it was held by Lord Justice Roskill that: (1) the bank was in principle in a similar position to a bank which had opened a confirmed irrevocable letter of credit; the bank's obligation under the contract did not depend on the resolution of a dispute as to the sufficiency of performance under the contract; and (2) the court would not interfere with the buyer's right under the guarantee and the balance of convenience was against the granting of an injunction, applying the principles laid down in *American Cyanamid Co.* v *Ethicon Ltd* [1975] 1 All ER 504.

When one party to a contract has arranged for a bank performance bond payable to the other party on notice to the bank of the first party's default, in the absence of fraud, no injunction will lie to prevent the giving of notice of default by the beneficiary, when the default is disputed; see *State Trading Corporation of India* v *E D & F Man (Sugar)* [1981] Com LR 235, CA.

Whether failure to provide a performance bond goes to the root of the contract depends on the surrounding circumstances. In *General Authority for Supply Commodities* v *Universal Impex SA* [1982] Com LR 210, a contract for the sale of sugar contained a clause (clause 1.10 of GOSCO General Conditions) requiring the seller to supply a performance bond by a specified date. When he failed to do so, the buyer claimed the contract was cancelled. On

the question whether the clause was a condition of the c
J, that the court had to have regard to the intention o
inferred from the contract in the light of the surrounding
from the case though that both parties recognised that c
performance bond would not affect the continued exis
obligation to provide it was no more than part of the circ
bond would be released. Accordingly, the clause was not
would be dismissed.

FURTHER READING FOR PART IV

'Letters of credit and standby letters of credit', [1982] *Arizona Law Review* (special edition) 24(2).

'Letters of credit', [1990] *Brooklyn Law Review* (special edition) 56(1).

Aster, C.E. and Patterson, C.P., *A Practical Guide to Letters of Credit*, New York: Executive Enterprises Publications, 1990.

Banking Law Institute, *Letters of Credit and Bank Guarantees*, London: Banking Law Institute, 1986.

Boyles, J., *Bills of Exchange*, 26th edn, London: Sweet & Maxwell, 1988.

Chorley (Lord), *Law of Banking*, London: Sweet & Maxwell, 1974.

Doran, J.F., *The Letters of Credit*, Boston: Warren, Garham & Lamont, 1996.

Ellinger, E.P., *Modern Banking Law*, Oxford: Clarendon Press, 1995.

Goode, R., *Payment Obligations in Commercial and Financial Transactions*, London: Sweet & Maxwell, 1983.

Gutteridge and Megrah, *Law of Bankers' Commercial Credits*, 7th edn, London: Europa, 1984.

Hapgood, M., *Paget's Law of Banking*, 11th edn, London: Butterworths, 1996.

Hillman, C.W., *Letters of Credit — Current Thinking in America*, London: Butterworths, 1987.

IBA, *Current Problems of Letters of Credit and Bankers' Guarantees*, London: IBA, 1984.

ICC, *Uniform Customs and Practice For Documenting Credits* (UCP 500), 1993.

Jack, R., *Documentary Credits*, 2nd edn, London: Butterworths, 1993.

Kingsford-Smith, D.A., *Current Developments in Banking and Finance*, London: Stevens, 1989.

Kurkela, M., *Letters of Credit Under International Trade Law (UCC, UCP and Law Merchants)*, New York: Oceana, 1984.

McCullough, B.V., *Letters of Credit,* New York: Matthew Bender, 1990.

Mooney, C.W., *Letters of Credit and Bankers' Acceptances*, New York: Practising Law Institute, 1986.

Penn, G.A. and Shea, A.M., *The Law and Practice of International Banking*, London: Sweet & Maxwell, 1998.

Pierce, A., *Demand Guarantees in International Trade*, London: Sweet & Maxwell, 1993.

D., *Guide to Negotiable Instruments*, 8th edn, London: Butterworths,

, M., *Letters of Credit*, 2nd edn, London: Euromoney, 1997.

yder, F.R., *Legal Problems of International Banking*, London: Sweet & Maxwell, 1987.

Sarna, L., *Letters of Credit*, London: Sweet & Maxwell.

Ventris, F.M., *Bankers' Documentary Credits*, 2nd edn, London: LLP, 1994.

Watson, A., *Finance of International Trade*, 4th edn, London: Chartered Institute of Bankers, 1990.

Whitehead, G., *Elements of International Trade and Payments*, Cambridge: Prentice Woodhead.

Whiting, D.P., *Finance of Foreign Trade*, 6th edn, London: Pitman, 1986.

Wood, P., *Law and Practice of International Finance*, London: Sweet & Maxwell, 1980.

Wunwickeb, D.B. and Turner, S., *Standby and Commercial Letters of Credit*, New York: Wiley, 1996.

PART V

INSURANCE IN INTERNATIONAL TRADE

12　Marine Insurance

12.1　INTRODUCTION

This chapter, together with Chapter 13, will deal with the general principles of marine insurance: indemnity, insurable interest, misrepresentation and non-disclosure, types of policy, assignment, cover available under the Institute Cargo Clauses, total and partial loss and subrogation.

Marine insurance is the oldest version of insurance. From the old Phoenician traders in the Levant to the Italian traders of Venice and Lombardy and all European merchants from the Middle Ages onwards, it was thought necessary for the traders to cover their risks when selling goods and shipping them by sea. Marine insurance developed in England from the fourteenth century: the earliest surviving English policy is dated 1555 and the first English statute dealing with marine insurance was passed in 1601. Initially marine insurance was arranged informally and was simply a matter of hawking a policy around the City of London for subscription by anyone with the private means to take a share of the risk. In the seventeenth century the marine insurance business began to centre on the London coffee houses and in particular the coffee house of one Edward Lloyd where shipowners and traders met to exchange information. The marine insurance business became increasingly sophisticated and it did not take long for the London merchants to draw up standard documents for their use in the marine insurance business, and to a surprisingly large extent these standard documents and the wording continued to be used until fairly recently.

Why do traders need marine insurance? One of the most important reasons is simply that a trader could not afford to bear frequent losses of his goods. Whether he is a rich man or not, a trader necessarily has to deal in goods that are worth far more than he is. This is usually done by borrowing money, arranging finance with other participants, or generally extending his credit to cover the deal in question. If a deal went wrong, so that goods were lost, a merchant would then have to pay his bills without the prospect of selling goods to recover his outlay and make a profit. Most merchants would be unable to survive such a loss, and would, therefore, go out of business. The fact that they had gone out of business would lead to consequent difficulties for all the people to whom they owed money, and everybody in the mercantile community would be adversely affected. Of course, nobody is going to take on the risks of merchants willingly and gratuitously, therefore, merchants developed a system whereby they would pay to somebody prepared to underwrite the risk a small premium in relation to the value of the goods. The person taking on the risk would amass all those premiums and put them in a fund so that he could use the money from that fund to pay any losses. On the law of averages, not everybody's goods would be lost in any one accounting period and, consequently, by setting the rate of premium at an appropriate amount, the person underwriting the risks would be able to make a profit after paying out any claims. It can be seen that if the premium is not set at an appropriate rate, the person who underwrites the risk is himself at risk of making a loss.

12.2   MARINE INSURANCE

Marine insurance passes the risk of loss from the owner of the goods to a professional risk underwriter. The assured is compensated for his loss, and thus he must have some risk of loss in the first place. A person cannot simply take out insurance on property that he does not own or otherwise have an interest in. This is known as having an insurable interest, and if a person does not have an insurable interest in the property that he insures, then, in fact, he is more interested in its loss than its preservation. If he does not have an interest in the property he would prefer the property to be lost so that he can claim on his insurance, and as this would lead to an unfortunate situation where people were deliberately setting out to insure goods which they then hoped would be lost, and perhaps encouraged that loss, it is a cardinal principle of marine insurance that there must be an insurable interest on the part of the assured.

  Although all countries of the world have some form of marine insurance regulations, the bulk of marine insurance is still based on the English Marine Insurance Act 1906. This Act was drafted by Sir Mackenzie Chalmers, and has remained almost unaltered since. The Marine Insurance (Gambling Policies) Act 1909 also prevents the taking out of contracts of insurance on ships where there is no insurable interest. Although this Act, which makes gambling on a marine adventure a criminal offence, is not used very much, its existence acts as a deterrent to those who might wish to take out a policy of insurance in respect of a marine adventure in which they have no interest.

  As this book is concerned with the law of international trade these chapters will look at the law relating to marine insurance through the perspective of a merchant, that is to say we will be concerned with the insurance of cargo. Although this is perhaps an obvious comment it must be considered that much of the law of marine insurance covers ships, collisions and liability for passengers and crew. None of this is required for this book, and we must consider marine insurance only from the point of view of the international trader. Nevertheless, most of the general factors will be exactly the same, and an understanding of Chapters 6, 7, 8 and 9 on the carriage of goods by sea will assist in viewing the sea elements of marine insurance in their correct context. In particular, the topics of unseaworthiness and perils of the sea are subjects that interrelate between carriage of goods and marine insurance.

Insurance is an assessable cost. A trader always knows how much it is going to cost him, and can, therefore, add it on to the price if he is responsible for arranging it. There are any number of ways that a person can insure goods and it is always up to him to take out the appropriate policy with the relevant amount of cover for a premium agreed between himself and the underwriter.

12.3 LLOYD'S OF LONDON AND THE INSURANCE MARKET

The marine insurance business centred on the coffee shop of Edward Lloyd, became increasingly sophisticated and eventually moved out of the coffee shop and into the Royal Exchange. Membership of 'Lloyd's' was regulated and in 1871 a private Act of Parliament, the Lloyd's Act, was passed establishing the corporation of Lloyd's to supervise the activities of those underwriters who were members of Lloyd's.

The corporation of Lloyd's does not carry any responsibility for individual underwriters, but provides a market place for them to work in. An individual underwriter is the only person liable on his claims, and to ensure that only underwriters who are capable of meeting claims made against them are allowed to be members of Lloyd's, the corporation exercises strict supervisory control over admissions to the Lloyd's market. Underwriters at Lloyd's are required to have a guarantee of their financial standing, and also must give a sound financial report on their background. There are many thousands of underwriting members, and for convenience they are grouped together into syndicates, with each syndicate managed by an underwriting agent who is involved in the day-to-day business. The vast majority of underwriting members of Lloyd's do not, in fact, carry on marine insurance business themselves but leave it to the syndicates of which they are members and in particular the underwriting agents of those syndicates. The public wishing to insure property at Lloyd's must, therefore, first approach a Lloyd's broker, who will take all the appropriate details and then approach an underwriting member.

Lloyd's of London does not have a monopoly on marine insurance, although it is the most well-known group of underwriters in the world, and still carries on the greatest significant proportion of insurance business in the mercantile community. In addition to Lloyd's of London, there are many other companies in England that offer insurance underwriting, and some of these are just as old and well-established as Lloyd's. The difference between an underwriting company and Lloyd's is that anybody can approach an insurance company direct, whereas they must use a Lloyd's broker for a Lloyd's underwriter.

The same basic structure exists abroad, and underwriters and companies compete for business in all financial centres of the world. There is normally no bar in obtaining marine insurance wherever the owner of the goods wishes to buy it, but it should be borne in mind that some developing countries insist that insurance on goods imported into the countries is taken out with domestic insurance firms. There is no doubt at all that the only restriction on insuring goods is the viability and financial standing of the underwriter.

The Institute of London Underwriters was set up to form a liaison between the underwriters of Lloyd's and the companies so that where necessary clauses could be drawn up to act as standard form clauses for all insurers. Since 1884 the Institute has looked after its members' interests by discussing marine insurance developments, and reporting and judging developments themselves. The most important service of the Institute has been the production of the Institute clauses and the Institute cargo clauses. These clauses were introduced on 1 January 1982 with a transitional period until 31 March 1983. A new Companies Combined Policy was also introduced by the Institute at the same time. Consequently, all references to the old Institute of London Underwriters clauses are now out of date, and strict attention must be paid to these new clauses and their meaning.

Brokers are the intermediaries between a person owning goods, the assured, and the person offering insurance, the underwriter. Although in the past brokers did not have to be qualified they are now governed by the Insurance Brokers (Registration) Act 1977, which lays down minimum professional standards and requires brokers to have professional liability insurance. Lloyd's brokers, that is to say brokers registered at Lloyd's, are entitled to be registered under the 1977 Act as of right, but all other brokers must show that they meet the minimum standards. As brokers derive their income from commission paid by the insurer, it might be imagined that they are agents of the insurer but, in fact, they are agents of the assured. The broker has a responsibility to pay the premium to the insurer, but any claim may be made directly against the insurer and does not have to go through the broker. The broker need not release the policy to the assured until he has been paid, and once paid he will pass on that premium to the underwriting insurer having deducted his commission.

A person owning goods, who will be known as the assured when the insurance is taken out, is first known as the proposer. The broker will only follow the proposer's instructions, and the broker is under a duty to carry out those instructions to the best of his ability. As the assured's agent he will be liable in the usual way if he acts negligently or fails to carry out his client's instructions. He will also be liable if he fails to arrange a policy and there is a consequent loss which would otherwise have been covered by the policy demanded by the proposer.

Protection and indemnity (P & I) clubs, must be mentioned briefly. P & I clubs are mutual insurance associations of shipowners, where shipowners form a group and pay premiums (in much the same way as they would to an outside insurer) to cover risks that are not usually underwritten by commercial insurers. Much of the work in marine insurance cases is to do with P & I clubs, but they are really outside the scope of this book and will not be dealt with further.

12.4   THE MECHANICS OF OBTAINING A POLICY

Let us take a simple example of an owner of goods who wishes to insure them. If a merchant in London wishes to export 100 cases of machine spares to South America, and wishes to insure them, he will go about it in the following manner.

First of all he will approach a broker, and the broker will ask him for certain relevant details. These details will almost certainly include the value of the goods, their condition, the name and trading name of the owner of the goods, the relationship of the owner of the goods to the proposer if they are not one and the same person, the present situation of the goods, their means of transport to South America, and their approximate relevance to any other contract, that is to say, whether they are being sold or shipped gratuitously or as part of a much larger consignment. The most important point, of course, is their value, as this will determine the maximum liability of the underwriter.

Armed with this information, the broker will approach a number of underwriters to find the cheapest and most cost effective policy. We can take the example of a Lloyd's broker and a Lloyd's underwriter for convenience, and in this situation the Lloyd's broker would go to the underwriting room at Lloyd's with the details of the policy to be underwritten on a piece of paper and would present that piece of paper to a number of underwriters who have expressed an interest in the business. These underwriters would signify their acceptance of the risk, or a proportion of the risk, by initialling on the piece of paper, known as the 'slip', together with the percentage of the risk that they take.

Once the broker has covered 100 per cent of the risk he will then go back to his office and prepare a policy on behalf of those underwriters (although in many situations this procedure differs), and he will notify the proposer that a policy has been effected. If the proposer, who is now assured, wishes to have a copy of the policy the broker will send this to him, or arrange for its dispatch, and the insurance contract is complete. The broker will request the premium from the assured, and having received this will pass on the balance, after deduction of broker's commission, to the underwriter. Where more than one underwriter is involved, the broker will pass on a relevant proportion of the premium, each underwriter taking the same percentage of the premium as the risk he has underwritten.

12.5   THE CONTRACT

12.5.1   The Role of the Broker

The broker acts as mediator between the assured and the underwriter. He is the agent of the assured and, in accordance with the instructions of the assured, arranges insurance which will hopefully provide the assured with adequate protection against loss of or damage to his goods. If a broker cannot arrange insurance in accordance with the instructions of his client he must inform him of the fact, to enable the client to seek cover elsewhere.

12.5.2 The Slip

All the main features of the adventure for which the proposer seeks insurance are noted by the broker on the slip, which is effectively a memorandum of the cover requested. This is then presented to underwriters who may agree to accept part of the risk. If an underwriter does agree to accept part of the risk he will initial the slip and indicate the proportion of the risk he has agreed to accept. This is known as writing a line.

The presentation of the slip by the broker constitutes an offer which is accepted by the insurer writing a line. This gives rise to a binding contract between the insurer and the assured; see *General Re-Insurance Corporation* v *Forsakringsaktiebolaget Fennia Patria* [1983] QB 856.

The first insurer to sign the slip is the lead underwriter and will generally be a well-established underwriter of good reputation. The broker will take the slip to other underwriters until the whole of the risk is covered. Once the slip is full the contract of insurance is final and complete between the parties and fixes the terms of contract; see *Ionides* v *Pacific Fire & Marine Insurance* (1871) LR 6 QB 674.

12.5.3 The Policy

The broker must now prepare the policy from the details on the completed slip. Once the broker has prepared the policy he will take it to the Lloyd's Policy Signing Office where it will be checked, signed and sealed on behalf of the Lloyd's syndicates concerned and is thereby executed. The terms of the policy should be identical to those on the slip.

A marine policy need not be in any particular form but ss. 23 to 26 of the Marine Insurance Act 1906 require the policy to:

(a) specify the name of the assured or some person who effects insurance on his behalf (s. 23);
(b) be signed by or on behalf of the insurer (s. 24(1));
(c) designate the subject matter insured with reasonable certainty.

12.5.4 Admissibility in Evidence

Under s. 22 of the Marine Insurance Act 1906:

A contract of marine insurance is inadmissible in evidence unless it is embodied in a marine policy in accordance with the Act.

Since the contract is in the slip then clearly the slip must be embodied in the policy. If the slip is not embodied in a policy, it will not be admissible in evidence. Once the slip is embodied in a policy, however, the slip itself is admissible in evidence. Section 89 of the Marine Insurance Act 1906 states:

Where there is a duly stamped policy, reference may be made as heretofore to the slip or covering note in any legal proceedings.

12.5.5 Conflicts Between the Slip and Policy

Since the slip is the concluded contract between the parties, if there is a conflict between the terms of the policy, as executed, and those which were agreed in the slip, then the slip prevails; see *Symington & Co.* v *Union Insurance Society of Canton Ltd (No. 2)* (1928) 34 Com Cas 233 at p. 235 *per* Scrutton LJ. The policy may then be rectified having regard to the slip in order to determine the terms of the contract; see *Eagle Star* v *Reiner* (1927) 43 TLR 259.

12.5.6 Broker's Cover Note

A cover note is normally sent by the broker to the assured after he has obtained cover on the agreed terms. It is a memorandum to the effect that insurance has been arranged. The broker should, as a matter of prudent business practice, notify the assured of the terms of the insurance which he has arranged and forward the cover note as soon as possible, but he is not under a legal duty to do so; see *United Mills Agencies Ltd* v *R E Harvey, Bray & Co.* [1952] 1 TLR 149.

Cover notes may be of two types.

12.5.6.1 Open Cover Note
This is sent to the assured in circumstances where although the broker has arranged insurance he has arranged a type of insurance where relevant details are still required from the assured, e.g. where the broker has obtained a floating policy.

12.5.6.2 Closed Cover Note
This is sent to the assured in circumstances where the broker was in full possession of all the details of the insurance and nothing remains to be clarified or communicated by the assured.

12.5.7 Payment of the Premium

The premium is the price paid by the assured for obtaining the agreed insurance cover. The payment of the premium and the duty of the insurer to issue the policy are concurrent conditions and the insurer is not bound to issue the policy until payment or tender of the premium (s. 52). It is, therefore, the duty of the assured to pay the premium when the policy is issued and in the absence of such payment the insurer need not issue the policy.

The broker is directly responsible to the insurer for the payment of the premium (s. 53(1)) and policies of marine insurance invariably contain a recital of payment, that is to say it is declared in the policy that the premium has been paid. Such a recital is conclusive as between the insurer and the assured (s. 54). The insurer, therefore, looks to the broker for payment of the premium and consequently the insurer is not able to set off against any claim made the amount of the premium outstanding; see *Power* v *Butcher* (1829) 10 B & Cr 329. The broker does, however, have a lien on the policy until the premium, commission and other charges due to him have been paid by the assured (s. 53(2)).

12.6   INSURABLE INTEREST

12.6.1   Insurance and Indemnity

A contract of marine insurance is a contract of indemnity. The object of the contract is to indemnify the assured in the event that he should suffer a loss in the course of the marine adventure insured. This is a fundamental principle of marine insurance and is set out in s. 1 of the 1906 Act:

A contract of marine insurance is a contract whereby the insurer undertakes to indemnify the assured, in a manner and to the extent agreed, against marine losses, that is to say, the losses incident to a marine adventure.

It therefore follows that in any contract of marine insurance the proposer/assured must have an interest in the subject matter of the insurance, so that when the goods are lost or damaged he can be indemnified for the effect that the loss or damage has had upon his interest. If he does not have an interest, then he will not suffer when the goods are lost or damaged and could not reasonably expect to be indemnified. The assured must, therefore, have an 'insurable interest'. The Institute cargo clauses also state the need for the assured to have an insurable interest. Clause 11.1 states:

In order to recover under this insurance the assured must have an insurable interest in the subject matter insured at the time of the loss.

According to s. 5(1) of the 1906 Act:

... every person has an insurable interest who is interested in a marine adventure.

According to s. 5(2) of the 1906 Act a person is interested in a marine adventure:

... where he stands in any legal or equitable relation to the adventure or to any insurable property at risk therein, in consequence of which he may benefit by the safety or due arrival of the insurable property or may be prejudiced by its loss, or by damage thereto, or by detention thereof, or may incur liability in respect thereof.

This section of the 1906 Act substantially incorporates the authority of *Lucena* v *Cramford* (1806) 2 Bos & P NR 269 which predated the 1906 Act by 100 years. Laurence J said:

To be interested in the preservation of a thing, is to be so circumstanced with respect to it as to have benefit from its existence, prejudice from its destruction.

12.6.2 Concept of Insurable Interest

It is therefore clear from s. 5(2) that the concept of insurable interest is fairly wide. With regard to the parties in an international contract of sale, the party in whom the property in the goods is vested clearly has an insurable interest. Likewise the party with the right to immediate possession of the goods has an insurable interest.

The party who bears the risk also has an insurable interest. Thus the c.i.f./f.o.b. buyer has an insurable interest as from shipment (s. 7(2)) and it does not matter that the goods have not been ascertained at the time of the loss (s. 8); see *Inglis* v *Stock* (1885) 10 App Cas 263. The c.i.f./f.o.b. seller will also have an insurable interest in the goods for he will have a defeasible interest as the buyer may reject the goods (s. 7). Furthermore the unpaid seller has a contingent interest because he may be able to exercise his right of stoppage in transit.

The concept of insurable interest is wider than a mere interest in the goods themselves but encompasses other aspects of the marine adventure; see *Rodocanachi* v *Elliot* (1874) LR 9 CP 518, and see s. 11 (wages of master and crew), s. 12 (advance freight), s. 13 (insurance charges).

A shareholder does not have an insurable interest in the assets of his company because the company as such is a separate legal personality and it 'owns' the assets. In *McAura* v *Northern Assurance* [1925] AC 619 the plaintiff and his nominees held all the shares in a timber company. The plaintiff took out insurance on the timber in his own name. When the timber was destroyed by fire he claimed under the insurance policy. It was held that he could not recover under the policy as he had no insurable interest in the timber. The timber was owned by the company. Lord Sumner said:

The appellant had no insurable interest in the timber described. It was not his. It belonged to the Irish Canadian Sawmill Ltd. He owned almost all the shares in the company and the company owed him a good deal of money, but neither as creditor nor as shareholder could he insure the company's assets. He stood in no 'legal or equitable relation to' the timber at all. He had no 'concern in' the subject matter insured. His relation was to the company not its goods and after the fire he was directly prejudiced by the paucity of the company's assets, not by the fire.

12.6.3 Insurable Interest at the Time of Loss

According to s. 6(1), Marine Insurane Act 1906:

The assured must be interested in the subject matter insured at the time of loss, though he need not be interested at the time when the insurance is effected.

This requirement is abrogated where the subject matter is insured on a 'lost or not lost' basis. In such cases, providing that the assured acquires an insurable interest at some time, it is irrelevant that he did not have the interest at the time of loss, unless 'at the time of effecting the insurance the assured was aware of the loss and the insurer was not'. Assuming, however, that the insurance is not on a lost or not lost basis then, according to s. 6(2):

> Where the assured has no interest at the time of loss, he cannot acquire interest by any act or election after he is aware of the loss.

12.6.4   No Existing Insurable Interest

If a person attempts to insure property in which he has no insurable interest, the contract is not one of insurance and is void as being contrary to public policy and statutory prohibition against contracts of marine insurance by way of gaming or wagering (s. 4). Where the assured believes that it may be difficult for him to demonstrate an insurable interest he may be able to get the insurer to agree that proof of interest is not necessary. Such policies are referred to as 'PPI Policies' (Policy Proof of Interest) and are not uncommon. They are regarded as legitimate but are nonetheless void (s. 4(2)(b)). Although such policies are void at law the underwriter will usually carry out his obligations to safeguard his reputation.

12.7   THE RELATIONSHIP BETWEEN INSURER AND ASSURED

The relationship between proposer/assured and insurer is one of utmost good faith. If utmost good faith is not observed by either party, then the contract may be avoided by the other party (s. 17). The obligation of good faith exists before, and continues after, conclusion of the contract; see *Black King Shipping* v *Massie, The Litsion Pride* [1985] 1 Lloyd's Rep 437.

12.7.1   Disclosure (ss. 18, 19)

One important aspect of this relationship of utmost good faith is the duty to make full disclosure of all relevant circumstances; this duty is absent in ordinary contractual situations. The assured must disclose to the insurer every material circumstance which is known to the assured and ought to be known by him in the ordinary course of business before the contract is concluded. If the assured fails to make such disclosure the insurer may avoid the contract (s. 18). A 'circumstance' includes any communication which is made to, or information received by, the assured (s. 18(5)).

There are, however, certain circumstances which the 1906 Act expressly provides need not be disclosed. These are found in s. 18(3).

(a)   Any circumstance which diminishes the risk.

(b)   Any circumstance which is known or presumed to be known to the insurer. The insurer is presumed to know matters of common notoriety or knowledge, and matters which an insurer in the ordinary course of business, as such, ought to know.

(c)   Any circumstance as to which information is waived by the insurer.

(d)   Any circumstance which it is superfluous to disclose by reason of any express or implied warranty.

Under s. 18(3)(b) an underwriter will only be deemed to know certain facts or expected to know them, if he has a specialist knowledge of that particular type of trade. In *Anglo-African Merchants Ltd* v *Bayley* [1970] 1 QB 311 the plaintiff obtained insurance on surplus clothing which the policy described only as 'new clothing'. War surplus clothing is considered a high theft risk and when the insurers discovered this fact they attempted to avoid the policy on grounds of material non-disclosure. The court held that the insurer could avoid the policy and the assured was not excused from disclosure on the grounds that the insurer ought to have known that in the clothing trade 'new' meant surplus. The insurer could not be ascribed specialist knowledge because he did not regularly deal with that type of goods.

With regard to s. 18(3)(d) if, for example, the assured knew his goods were to be shipped from port A to port B on a ship which was in an unseaworthy condition, he would not have to communicate that fact to the insurer, because under s. 39 there is an implied warranty of seaworthiness in a voyage policy. Breach of this warranty discharges the insurer as from date of breach (s. 33(3)) unless the policy otherwise provides, as clause 5.2 of the Institute cargo clauses does. Therefore, whilst the insurer would no doubt avoid the policy under s. 18 if he knew of the unseaworthiness, he will in any event be discharged under s. 33(3). Thus disclosure under s 18 is superfluous.

12.7.2   The Broker's Duty of Disclosure

The duty to make disclosure applies not only to the assured but also to his broker who is, of course, his agent. Thus the broker must disclose to the insurer every material circumstance which is known to himself or which, in the ordinary course of business, ought to have been known, or to have been communicated to him (s. 19(a)). It is important to note that it is the disclosure of the broker to the insurer which is important not that of the assured to the broker; see *Roberts* v *Plaisted* [1989] 2 Lloyd's Rep 341.

A policy of insurance effected by the broker in ignorance of a material fact known to the assured cannot, however, be avoided by the insurer if that material fact came to the knowledge of the assured too late to communicate it to the broker (s. 19(b)).

12.7.3   Representations (ss. 20, 21)

In addition to being under an obligation to disclose all material circumstances, the assured is under a duty to ensure that all material representations made by him or by his agent, to the insurer, before the conclusion of the contract, are true (s. 20(1)). If the representation is untrue the insurer may avoid the contract (s. 20(1)).

Representations fall into two categories: representations of matters of fact (s. 20(3)); and representations of matters of expectation or belief.

12.7.3.1   Representations of Matters of Fact
A representation of a matter of fact can itself be subdivided into representations of existing facts, e.g. the ship is in port today, fully loaded; and representations of future facts, e.g. the ship will be in port and fully loaded.

Both representations are positively affirming the existence of a particular state of facts and it does not matter that the state of facts exists now or will exist at some time in the future. There is, however, some controversy that a representation of a matter of fact which positively affirms a future state of facts, can ever be a representation of a matter of fact at all. It is arguable that such a representation is a promise that the future state of facts will come about, or a contract to bring them about. However, it is clear that for the purpose of marine insurance a representation concerning future facts can be a representation of a matter of fact.

> A representation relating to future events over which the assured has control, will avoid the policy if it be not (true or) substantially satisfied. (See *Edwards* v *Footner* (1808) 8 East 126.)

A representation of a matter of fact must be true (s. 20(1)), that is, it must be substantially true. Section 20(4) provides:

> A representation as to a matter of fact is true if it be substantially correct, that is to say if the difference between what is represented and what is actually correct would not be considered material by a prudent insurer.

Thus, in *Pawson* v *Watson* (1778) 2 Cowp 785, a representation was substantially true because although the ship in question did not have 12 guns and 20 men as her owner had represented, she had a sufficient complement of large and small guns, men and boys, which if anything made her a better equipped vessel.

12.7.3.2   Representations of Expectation or Belief
Simply because the assured prefaces his statements with 'I expect or I believe' does not make his representation one of expectation or belief. In order to ascertain whether or not the statement is in fact one of expectation or belief it is necessary to look at all the circumstances in which it was made, and the degree of power or control which the assured has over the subject matter of the representation. If the assured has direct control or a high degree of control over the subject matter of the statement, then whilst he is prefacing his remarks with an expression of 'expectation' or 'belief', in fact he is making a positive assertion of a matter of fact. In truth, he is really stating that a certain state of facts will or shall exist because he has the power to ensure that

they do. Unlike representations of matters of fact, representations of expectations or belief need not be true or substantially true, but they must be made in good faith (s. 20(5)). In other words, it must be a belief that any reasonable person could honestly entertain; see *Anderson* v *Pacific Fire & Marine Insurance* (1872) LR 7 CP 65.

12.7.4 Materiality of the Non-disclosure (s. 18(2)) and Representation (s. 20(2))

The insurer is not entitled to avoid the contract of insurance for any non-disclosure or misrepresentation. In order for the insurer to avoid liability he must show that the non-disclosure or misrepresentation was material, that is to say it would have influenced the prudent insurer in deciding whether to accept the risk or in fixing the premium. The test is objective and the insurer need not show that the non-disclosure would have affected his own judgment; see *Container Transport International* v *Oceanus Mutual Underwriting* [1984] 1 Lloyd's Rep 476; *Pan Atlantic Insurance Co. Ltd* v *Pine Top Insurance Co. Ltd, The Times*, 8 March 1993. In *CTI* v *Oceanus* Kerr LJ put the test in the following terms:

> To prove materiality of an undisclosed circumstance, the insurer must satisfy the court on a balance of probability — by evidence or from the nature of the undisclosed circumstance itself — that the judgment of a prudent insurer would have been influenced if the circumstance in question had been disclosed. The word 'influenced' means that the disclosure is one which would have had an impact on the formation of his opinion and on his decision-making process in relation to matters covered by s. 18(2).

It must, however, be remembered that the non-disclosure or misrepresentation need only be material; it need not relate to, or have a bearing on, the circumstances in which insured goods were lost or damaged.

12.7.5 Examples of Material Non-disclosure

Overvaluation of a cargo may be a material non-disclosure which allows the insurer to avoid the policy. In *Ionides* v *Pender* (1874) LR 9 QB 531 insuring a cargo for £2,800 when it was worth only £974 allowed the insurer to avoid the policy. Clearly the assured, being able to benefit from the destruction of the goods, may be less inclined to act for their protection.

The existence of other policies of insurance, if not disclosed, may also allow the insurer to avoid for exactly the same reasons as outlined above. It is also possible that the unsuitability or incompetence of the master if not disclosed, would be material; see *Thames & Mersey* v *Gunford* [1911] AC 529.

It is not a material fact that other insurers have already refused to accept the risk; see *Glasgow Assurance Corporation* v *Symondson* (1911) 16 Com Cas 109.

In *Alden* v *Raven, The Kylie* [1983] 2 Lloyd's Rep 444 the plaintiff took out insurance on a yacht which he had built from a kit. When he made a claim on the policy after the yacht was lost, the insurers refused to make payment on the grounds of non-disclosure of material facts. First, that the yacht had been built from a kit and, secondly, that he had at one time been convicted of handling a stolen dinghy. The court held that the facts were highly material and the underwriters were entitled to refuse to make payment.

12.7.6   Avoidance or Affirmation of the Policy

If there has been a material non-disclosure or misrepresentation then the insurer is entitled to avoid the contract. If the insurer chooses to avoid the contract it is void from the very beginning. The insurer must return the premium unless there has been fraud or illegality on the part of the assured or his agent (s. 84).

The right to avoid the contract continues until the insurer, with full knowledge (being put on inquiry is not sufficient) of the non-disclosure or misrepresentation, affirms or is deemed to have affirmed the contract. Such affirmation may be either express or implied from the insurer's conduct. The insurer will be deemed to have affirmed the contract if he has allowed so much time to elapse from the time when he had knowledge of the non-disclosure or misrepresentation that the necessary inference is one of affirmation. The insurer may also lose the right to avoid the contract if the assured has been prejudiced by the delay or the rights of third parties have intervened.

12.8   TYPES OF POLICY

There are various types of marine insurance policy which might be obtained. The marine insurance policy may be a voyage, time or mixed policy. The policy may be valued or unvalued. The assured may have taken out a floating policy or open cover. We will look first at voyage, time and mixed policies before turning to floating policies and open covers. Valued and unvalued policies will be examined in Chapter 13.

Insurance can be obtained to cover goods from one place to another, this is a voyage policy; or from one date to another, which is called a time policy. Under a mixed policy the subject matter is insured both for a particular journey and a certain time period (s. 25).

12.8.1   Voyage Policy

In a voyage policy the subject matter of the insurance is covered from its departure from the port designated in the schedule and while it is in transit to its specified destination. The cover provided by the Institute cargo clauses is that of a voyage policy, covering the goods from the seller's warehouse to the buyer's warehouse, see clause 8, the transit clause.

There is an implied condition that the adventure will be commenced within a reasonable time of the conclusion of the contract.

12.8.1.1 Deviation and Delay

The ship must sail from the designated port for the specified destination otherwise the insurance will not cover the goods. Assume there is a voyage policy expressed to cover goods from Valparaiso to Bristol. If the ship did not sail from Valparaiso but from some other South American port then the cover will not be effective (s. 43). Furthermore if, before the ship sets sail, it was decided that she will sail to Plymouth the cover will not attach to the goods (s. 44).

If the destination of the ship is voluntarily changed, the insurer is discharged from the moment that the determination to change course is manifest, whether or not the ship has actually left the course of the voyage contemplated by the policy (s. 45). Thus if the ship sets sail from Valparaiso to Bristol as required by the policy and it was decided after two days at sea that she will head for Plymouth instead, the insurer will be discharged from liability on the policy thereafter, even though the ship will not have departed from her original route, the route for Plymouth being substantially the same as that for Bristol.

Where the Institute cargo clauses are used the position is modified by clause 10, the Change of Voyage Clause, which is a 'held covered' clause. In the event of a change of destination the assured can be sure that his goods will remain covered so long as he gives prompt notice to the insurer and pays such additional premium as is agreed. Clause 10 is in the following terms:

> Where, after attachment of this insurance, the destination is changed by the Assured, held covered at a premium and on conditions to be arranged subject to prompt notice being given to the underwriters.

The ship must proceed on the voyage with reasonable dispatch and without deviation. If the ship deviates without lawful excuse the insurer is discharged from liability as from the time of deviation. There is a deviation where the ship departs, in fact, from the specified course or the usual and customary course (s. 46). The insurer is also discharged from liability under the policy once there has been unreasonable delay without lawful excuse (s. 48).

There are several circumstances in which deviation or delay is excused, but once the cause excusing the deviation or delay ceases to operate the ship must resume her course with reasonable dispatch. The circumstances excusing delay or deviation are to be found in s. 49 and the list is as follows:

(a) Where authorised by any special term in the policy, or

(b) Where caused by circumstances beyond the control of the master and his employer, or

(c) Where reasonably necessary in order to comply with an express or implied warranty, or

(d)   Where reasonably necessary for the safety of the ship or subject matter insured, or

(e)   For the purpose of saving human life, or aiding a ship in distress where human life may be in danger, or

(f)   Where reasonably necessary for the purpose of obtaining medical or surgical aid for any person on board the ship, or

(g)   Where caused by the barratrous conduct of the master or crew, if barratry be one of the perils insured against.

Where the Institute cargo clauses are used the position is, once again, rather different. Clause 8.3, part of the Transit Clause, provides that the insurance provided under the Institute cargo clauses:

> ... shall remain in force (subject to termination as provided for above and to the provisions of Clause 9 below) during delay beyond the control of the Assured, any deviation, forced discharge, reshipment or transhipment and during any variation of the adventure arising from the exercise of liberty granted to shipowners or charterers under the contract of affreightment.

Delay or deviation will, therefore, not normally deprive the assured of his cover under the Institute cargo clauses. There is, however, one qualification and that is found in clause 4, the General Exclusion Clause, which states that:

> In no case shall this insurance cover:
>
> ...
>
> 4.5   loss damage or expense proximately caused by delay, even though delay be caused by a risk insured against ...

12.8.1.2   Seaworthiness

In a voyage policy there is an implied warranty that at the commencement of the voyage the ship is to be seaworthy for the purpose of the particular adventure insured (s. 39(1)). This warranty applies not merely at the beginning of the voyage but also to each stage of the voyage (s. 39(3)); see *Greenock SS Co.* v *Maritime Insurance Co.* [1902] 1 KB 367. A ship is seaworthy if it is reasonably fit in all respects to encounter the ordinary perils of the seas of the adventure insured (s. 39(4)). Furthermore there is an implied warranty that at the commencement of the voyage the ship is reasonably fit to carry the goods to the destination contemplated by the policy (s. 40(2)).

As these are warranties, unless they are exactly complied with the insurer will be discharged from liability as from the date of breach (s. 33(3)). It is important to note that the insurer's liability up to the date of breach is not affected so that the insurer remains liable for any loss or damage caused by a peril insured against before the breach of warranty.

It should also be noted that a breach of warranty may be waived by the insurer (s. 34(4)) and the Institute cargo clauses provide for a waiver of the warranty as to seaworthiness in certain circumstances (clause 5.2). This matter will be discussed in more detail when the Institute clauses are examined in Chapter 13.

12.8.2 Time Policy

A time policy provides insurance cover for a specified period of time and is more commonly used for the insurance of vessels rather than goods. Although a time policy is a policy which provides cover for the subject matter 'for a definite period of time' (s. 25), a policy does not cease to be a time policy merely because the period of cover can be extended or determined; see *Compania Maritima San Basilio SA* v *Oceanus Mutual Underwriting Association (Bermuda) Ltd* [1977] QB 49.

There is no implied warranty as to seaworthiness in a time policy. The insurer is not, however, liable for any loss attributable to unseaworthiness if the ship is sent to sea in an unseaworthy state with the privity of the assured (s. 39(5)). Thus if the damage to the goods insured arises from some other insured peril the insurer will be liable on the policy.

12.8.3 Floating Policies and Open Covers

Floating policies and open covers are used by exporters who ship goods on a regular basis. Indeed the open cover, combined with the issue of insurance certificates, has become the most common and popular form of insurance used in the export trade.

A floating policy is intended to cover a number of consignments of goods to be shipped by the exporter. Such a policy sets out the general conditions of the insurance but not the particulars of the individual consignments to be covered. These particulars are provided by the assured by way of a 'declaration' to the insurer (s. 29(1)). These declarations may be made by endorsement on the policy or in some other customary manner (s. 29(2)).

The floating policy will cover consignments up to a certain aggregate value. As each consignment is declared the balance of the available cover under the floating policy is reduced by the value of the consignment. Consignments are declared until there is no more available cover under the policy at which point it is written off.

All consignments within the terms of the policy must be declared and the value of the goods must be honestly stated (s. 29(3)). Declarations should be made at the time of dispatch or shipment for, unless the policy otherwise provides, where a declaration is not made until after notice of loss or arrival the policy must be treated as an unvalued policy as regards those goods (s. 29(4)). This may have the effect of reducing the amount recoverable by the assured under the policy and is intended to encourage prompt declarations.

An open cover is similar to a floating policy in that the insurance is on general terms leaving the assured to declare individual consignments. Where, however, an insurer provides open cover he does not issue a policy but merely *undertakes to issue a policy* within the terms of the policy. The open cover may be limited to a period of time to cover, for example, consignments made over a 12 month period. But the open cover may also be 'always open', that is to say, perpetually subject to the right of both parties to cancel on due notice. Certificates of insurance are issued in respect of each consignment and will contain a recital of the main terms of the cover provided.

12.9   ASSIGNMENT OF THE POLICY

A marine policy is assignable unless the policy contains terms which expressly prohibit transfer. The assignment is achieved by endorsement and delivery of the policy or in any other customary manner (s. 50(3)). This may mean that in certain circumstances mere delivery of the policy will suffice to assign a policy on goods; see *Safadi* v *Western Assurance Co.* (1933) 46 Ll R 140.

An assignment is, however, only valid if there is an express or implied agreement to assign the policy concluded before the assured parts with or loses his interest in the goods (ss. 15, 51). Subject to that qualification the policy may be assigned either before or after loss (s. 50(1)); see *Mambre Saccharine Co. Ltd* v *Corn Products Co.* [1919] 1 KB 198. Difficulties do not normally arise with international sales contracts. In c.i.f. contracts, for example, there would clearly be an implied agreement for the assignment of the policy. There may, however, be problems with ex-ship contracts or contracts in which the seller undertakes to deliver the goods to the buyer; see *Yangtze Insurance Association Ltd* v *Lukmanjee* [1918] AC 585.

Once the policy has been assigned to pass the beneficial interest in the policy, the assignee may then sue on the policy in his own name (s. 50(2)). The assignee takes the policy subject to all the defences which the insurer could have raised against the original assured (s. 50(2)). In *Pickersgill* v *London & Provincial Marine Insurance Co.* [1912] 3 KB 614 A requested B to build a ship and as security for payment A obtained a policy of insurance which he assigned to B. When B tried to claim on the policy the insurers resisted on the grounds that A had failed to disclose material facts. It was held that the insurers were entitled to do so even though B, the shipbuilder, had no knowledge of those facts.

13 Institute Cargo Clauses, Loss and Indemnity

Reference has already been made in Chapter 12 to the Institute cargo clauses and certain clauses have already been considered. In this chapter the Institute cargo clauses and the cover they provide will be examined in more detail before turning to the various types of losses and the question of how those losses are calculated. This chapter is, therefore, essentially concerned with whether and to what extent an assured may recover his losses from his insurer. One final matter is also dealt with which arises after the insurer has met the assured's claim on the policy and that is the insurer's right of subrogation.

13.1 THE INSTITUTE CARGO CLAUSES: INTRODUCTION

The Institute cargo clauses were introduced on 1 January 1982, with a transitional period to 31 March 1983. They provide standard terms upon which insurance cover may be obtained for the transportation of cargo. There are three sets of cargo clauses (A, B and C) which define the risks covered and the losses which are excluded. The difference between these sets of clauses is in the extent of the cover provided.

Institute cargo clauses A provide the most extensive type of cover, that is to say, it is 'all risks' cover, while cargo clauses B and C provide more limited cover.

The Institute cargo clauses replaced the standard Lloyd's SG Policy which is found in schedules to the Marine Insurance Act 1906 along with Rules for the Construction of the Policy. The Lloyd's SG Policy was settled in the form found in that schedule in 1779 and was described as 'an absurd and incoherent instrument' as early as 1791; see *Brough* v *Whitmore* (1791) 4 Term Rep 206. Yet while the Lloyd's SG Policy has been considered by the courts on many occasions the new Institute cargo clauses have received little judicial interpretation.

13.2 INSTITUTE CARGO CLAUSES: DURATION OF THE COVER

Before turning to examine the extent of the cover provided by the Institute cargo clauses it is first worth noting the duration of the cover. As can be seen from the

'Transit Clause', that is to say clause 8 which is common to all three sets of cargo clauses, the Institute cargo clauses are intended to provide insurance cover on a 'warehouse to warehouse' basis. Clause 8.1 is in the following terms:

> This insurance attaches from the time the goods leave the warehouse or place of storage at the place named herein for the commencement of the transit, continues during the ordinary course of transit, and terminates either
>
> 8.1.1   on delivery to the Consignees or other final warehouse or place of storage at the destination named herein,
>
> 8.1.2   on delivery to any other warehouse or place of storage, whether prior to or at the destination named herein which the Assured elect to use either for storage other than in the ordinary course of transit, or for allocation or distribution, or
>
> 8.1.3   on the expiry of 60 days after completion of discharge overside of the goods hereby insured from the oversea vessel at the final port of discharge whichever shall first occur.

Thus the insurance cover should commence, that is to say the insurance cover attaches, from the moment the goods commence their voyage from the warehouse in which they are situated, unless the policy was taken out at a later date; see *Silver Dolphin Products* v *Parcels & General Assurance* [1984] 2 Lloyd's Rep 404. The insurance cover, in the normal course of events, should then continue until the goods reach the consignees or the relevant warehouse at the place of destination. If, however, the goods are instead delivered to another warehouse chosen by the assured and the insured transit has effectively come to an end, then the insurance cover will terminate in accordance with clause 8.1.2. Furthermore if the goods have been delayed once they have left the vessel in which they were transported on the ocean stage of their voyage the insurance will also terminate, under clause 8.1.3, after the expiry of 60 days from their discharge from that vessel.

In any event if the goods are to be re-routed to another destination once they have been discharged from their ocean going vessel the insurance will terminate once the goods have started their journey to their new destination. This is the effect of clause 8.2 which is in the following terms:

> If, after discharge overside from the oversea vessel at the final port of discharge, but prior to the termination of this insurance, the goods are to be forwarded to a destination other than that to which they are insured hereunder, this insurance, whilst remaining subject to termination as provided for above, shall not extend beyond the commencement of transit to such other destination.

The insurance will also remain in force, in certain circumstances, in the event of delay or deviation by virtue of clause 8.3. This is a matter which is examined in more detail when considering the General Exclusions Clause (see 13.5.1). If the contract of carriage under which the goods are being shipped is terminated the position is then rather different. The insurance cover is then terminated unless prompt notice is given to the insurers of the problem and an additional premium, if required, is paid by the assured. This is the effect of clause 9, the 'Termination of Contract of Carriage Clause' which provides as follows:

> If owing to circumstances beyond the control of the Assured either the contract of carriage is terminated at a port or place other than the destination named therein or the transit is otherwise terminated before delivery of the goods as provided for in Clause 8 above, then this insurance shall also terminate unless prompt notice is given to the Underwriters and continuation of cover is requested when the insurance shall remain in force, subject to an additional premium if required by the Underwriters, either
>
> 9.1   until the goods are sold and delivered at such a port or place, or, unless otherwise specifically agreed, until the expiry of 60 days after arrival of the goods hereby insured at such port or place, whichever shall first occur, or
>
> 9.2   if the goods are forwarded within the said period of 60 days (or any agreed extension thereof) to the destination named herein or to any other destination, until terminated in accordance with the provisions of Clause 8 above.

Finally it should be noted that if the assured changes the destination of the insured goods the insurance will once again terminate (s. 45, Marine Insurance Act 1906). This is a matter which was discussed in Chapter 12 in connection with voyage policies (see 12.8.1). If the assured wishes the insurance cover to continue he will be able to rely on clause 10, the 'Change of Voyage Clause', provided he gives the insurer prompt notice and pays any additional premium that might be required. Clause 10 provides:

> Where, after attachment of this insurance, the destination is changed by the Assured, held covered at a premium and on conditions to be arranged subject to prompt notice being given to the Underwriters.

13.3   INSTITUTE CARGO CLAUSES: THE RISKS

The fundamental distinction between Institute cargo clauses A, B and C lies in the risks covered. The risks which are covered by the insurance are set out in clause 1, the 'Risks Clause'.

13.3.1   Institute Cargo Clauses A

Insurance under Institute cargo clauses A covers the assured for all risks of loss or damage to the subject matter insured. This is an 'all risks' policy, subject to the various exclusion clauses. Clause 1 states:

> This insurance covers all risks of loss of or damage to the subject matter insured except as provided in Clauses 4, 5, 6 and 7 below.

Clauses 4, 5, 6 and 7 are the various exclusion clauses which will be examined in more detail below (see 13.5). Although the insurance is expressed to cover 'all risks' it does not follow that every single thing which causes loss or damage to the subject matter insured and does not fall within the exclusions is, therefore, a 'risk' in respect of which the assured is covered. The cover provided is for 'risks' only and not for things which are certain to happen. The assured must, therefore, show that the loss in respect of which he is claiming under the insurance was due to a 'fortuitous event' and was not inevitable; see *British & Foreign Marine Insurance Co.* v *Gaunt* [1921] 2 AC 41; *F W Berk* v *Style* [1956] 1 QB 180.

Lord Sumner in *British & Foreign Marine Insurance Co.* v *Gaunt* indicated the limits to 'all risks' cover:

> There are, of course, limits to 'all risks'. There are risks and risks insured against. Accordingly the expression does not cover inherent vice or mere wear and tear or British capture. It covers a risk not a certainty; it is something which happens to the subject-matter from without, not the natural behaviour of that subject-matter, being what it is, in the circumstances under which it is carried. Nor is it a loss which the assured brings about by his own act, for then he has not merely exposed the goods to the chance of injury, he has injured them himself. Finally the description 'all risks' does not alter the general law; only risks which it is lawful to cover, and the onus of proof remains where it would have been on a policy against ordinary sea perils.

13.3.2 Institute Cargo Clauses B and C

Institute cargo clauses B and C offer less protection to the assured for loss or damage to the subject matter insured, than Institute cargo clauses A. The risks covered are, in each case, to be found in clause 1, the Risks Clause. The risks covered by Institute cargo clauses B are the same as those covered by Institute cargo clauses C but with a few additional risks. The Risks Clause in Institute cargo clauses C is in the following terms:

> This insurance covers, except as provided in Clauses 4, 5, 6 and 7 below,
> 1.1   loss of or damage to the subject matter reasonably attributable to
>   1.1.1   fire or explosion
>   1.1.2   vessel or craft being stranded grounded sunk or capsized
>   1.1.3   overturning or derailment of land conveyance
>   1.1.4   collision or contact of vessel craft or conveyance with any external object other than water
>   1.1.5   discharge of cargo at port of distress
> 1.2   loss of or damage to the subject matter caused by
>   1.2.1   general average sacrifice
>   1.2.2   jettison

The Risks Clause in Institute cargo clauses B is more comprehensive than that found in Institute cargo clauses C and includes the following additional risks to those listed above:

1.1.6   earthquake, volcanic eruption or lightning

1.2.2   jettison or washing overboard

1.2.3   entry of sea lake or river water into vessel craft hold conveyance container liftvan or place of storage

1.3   total loss of any package lost overboard or dropped whilst loading on to, or unloading from, vessel or craft

The risks listed are for the most part self explanatory, though with regard to 'explosion' see *Commonwealth Smelting* v *Guardian Royal Exchange Assurance* [1986] 1 Lloyd's Rep 121.

In *National Justice Compania Naviera SA* v *Prudential Assurance Co. Ltd, The Ikarian Reefer* [1993] 2 Lloyd's Rep 68, it was held that the peril of fire includes fire started deliberately by a third party. Once the assured has proved fire damage the insurer can only escape liability by showing that the assured was implicated in starting the fire.

The burden is initially on the assured to show that the loss or damage falls within one of the risks covered by the insurance. This is well illustrated by *Rhesa Shipping Co. SA* v *Edmunds, The Popi M* [1985] 1 WLR 948, a case dealing with insurance on a vessel which had sunk because of the incursion of seawater through a hole in her side. The insurers claimed that the loss was due to the unseaworthy condition of the vessel, while the assured claimed that the loss was caused by collision with a submarine which was never seen and never surfaced. Both explanations were rejected and it was held that the assured had failed to discharge the burden of proof upon them; see also *Lamb Head Shipping Co. Ltd* v *Jennings, The Marel* [1992] 1 Lloyd's Rep 402.

The assured must also prove that the goods were undamaged when the insurance cover attached to them; see *Fuerst Day Lamson Ltd* v *Orion Insurance Ltd* [1980] 1 Lloyd's Rep 656.

13.4   CAUSATION

The question of causation is particularly important and the assured, unless the policy otherwise provides, must prove that the loss was proximately caused by a peril insured against (s. 55(1)). The test of proximity was discussed by the Privy Council in *Canada Rice Mills* v *Union Marine* [1941] AC 55. A cargo of rice was being shipped from one port to another. During the course of its transit there was extremely bad weather and so the hatches to the hold were closed. The cargo was then damaged by heat due to lack of ventilation following the closing of the hatches.

The Privy Council held that the proximate cause of the loss was not the closing of the hatches but the perils of the sea and that the assured could recover on the policy. In delivering the judgment of the Privy Council Lord Wright stated that:

... where the weather conditions so require, the closing of the ventilators is not to be regarded as a separate or independent cause, interposed between the peril of the sea and the damage, but as being such a matter of routine steamship necessitated by the peril that the damage can be regarded as the direct result of the peril.

The proximate cause would, therefore, appear to be no more than the real or effective or dominant cause; see also *The Yorkshire Dale SS Co. v Minister of War Transport, The Coxwold* [1942] AC 691; *Leyland Shipping Co. Ltd v Norwich Union Fire Insurance Society Ltd* [1918] AC 350. It is, however, not always easy to apply the test of proximity, especially in circumstances where it appears that several causes have cooperated to produce the loss or damage in question. Where the loss or damage is the result of two or more equally effective dominant causes, it should be enough that the loss be partly caused by a risk insured against. On the other hand if the other dominant cause is not merely a risk which is not insured against but a risk which is excluded, it is thought that the insured will not be able to recover; see *Wayne Tank & Pump Co. Ltd v Employers Liability Assurance Corp Ltd* [1974] QB 57 at pp. 67, 69, 75.

Where the loss is proximately caused by a peril insured against but the misconduct or negligence of the master or crew contributed to the loss, then the assured should still be able to recover under the policy. The misconduct must not, however, be 'wilful', that is to say done with intent (s. 55(2)(a)).

The test of proximity will clearly apply to those risks listed in clauses 1.2 to 1.3 of Institute cargo clauses B and C. In respect of clause 1.1 of those clauses the assured need only show that the loss or damage was 'reasonably attributable' to one of the perils listed. In these circumstances the policy 'otherwise provides' and the less stringent test of 'reasonably attributable' applies.

13.5 INSTITUTE CARGO CLAUSES: THE EXCLUSIONS

Once the assured has been able to demonstrate that the loss or damage in respect of which he is claiming under the policy falls within one of the risks covered by the policy it is then open to the insurer to rely on any exclusion clause in the policy which might apply. The burden shifts to the insurer to show that the loss or damage falls within one of the exclusion clauses.

Before turning to the particular exclusion clauses contained in Institute cargo clauses it must be noted that s. 55(2) of the Marine Insurance Act 1906 lists certain matters for which the insurer will not be liable unless the policy otherwise provides. In most cases the matters set out in s. 55(2) are duplicated in the exclusion clauses found in the Institute cargo clauses. Section 55(2) provides that:

(a)   The insurer is not liable for any loss attributable to the wilful misconduct of the assured, but, unless the policy otherwise provides, he is liable for any loss proximately caused by a peril insured against, even though the loss would not have happened but for the misconduct or negligence of the master or crew;

(b) Unless the policy otherwise provides, the insurer of ship or goods is not liable for any loss proximately caused by delay, although the delay be caused by a peril insured against;

(c) Unless the policy otherwise provides, the insurer is not liable for ordinary wear and tear, ordinary leakage and breakage, inherent vice or nature of the subject matter insured, or for any loss proximately caused by rats or vermin, or for any injury to machinery not caused by maritime perils.

Whether or not the policy otherwise provides is simply a question of the construction of the policy. This is illustrated by the House of Lords decision in *Soya GmbH Mainz Kommanditgesellschaft* v *White* [1983] 1 Lloyd's Rep 122. A cargo of soya beans was insured on an HSSC basis, that is to say for damage due to heat, sweat and spontaneous combustion. Soya beans have a natural tendency to display all these features when their moisture content rises above certain levels. When the beans arrived they were found to be damaged due to their heated condition. The insurers argued that they were not liable for the damage since it was a result of inherent vice for which their liability was excluded by s. 55(2)(c) and that an insurer could only be liable for loss or damage due to inherent vice if he had expressly agreed. It was held that the question of whether particular kinds of inherent vice were covered was one of the construction of the policy. The words used in this particular policy referred to something which could only take place inside the goods and, given their ordinary and natural meaning, appeared to be descriptive of particular kinds of inherent vice.

Where the policy is an 'all risks' policy, as is Institute cargo clause A, the policy will 'otherwise provide' within the terms of s. 55(2). In practice this matters little as the General Exclusions clause (Clause 4) contains almost the same exclusions as are found in s. 55(2). One matter which is, however, not covered by the General Exclusions clause but which is found in s. 55(2) is the exclusion for loss proximately caused by rats or vermin (s. 55(2)(c)). Thus where Institute cargo clauses A are used loss proximately caused by rats or vermin is a loss which is covered by the insurance, but if Institute cargo clauses B or C are used such a loss is an excluded loss although not listed in any of the Institute exclusion clauses.

13.5.1 General Exclusions Clause (Clause 4)

The General Exclusions clause, clause 4, is largely identical in all three sets of the Institute cargo clauses. Clause 4 of Institute cargo clauses A is in the following terms:

4   In no case shall this insurance cover:

4.1   loss damage or expense attributable to wilful misconduct of the Assured

4.2   ordinary leakage ordinary loss in weight or volume or ordinary wear and tear of the subject matter insured

4.3   loss damage or expense caused by insufficiency or unsuitability of packing or preparation of the subject matter insured (for the purpose of this Clause 4.3

'packing' shall be deemed to include stowage in a container or liftvan but only when such stowage is carried out prior to attachment of this insurance or by the assured or their servants)

4.4   loss damage or expense caused by inherent vice or nature of the subject matter insured

4.5   loss damage or expense proximately caused by delay, even though delay be caused by a risk insured against (except expenses payable under Clause 2 above)

4.6   loss damage or expense arising from insolvency or default of the owners managers charterers or operators of the vessel

4.7   loss damage or expense arising from the use of any weapon of war employing atomic or nuclear fission and/or fusion or other like reaction or radioactive force or matter.

Where Institute cargo clauses B or C are used, there is an additional exclusion listed in their respective General Exclusions clause at 4.7 (clause 4.7 in Institute cargo clauses A becomes 4.8 in Institute cargo clauses B and C) which provides that in no case shall the insurance cover:

4.7   deliberate damage to or deliberate destruction of the subject matter insured or any part thereof by the wrongful act of any person or persons.

Should the assured wish to be covered in the event of deliberate damage or destruction of the subject matter, he may request that the Institute Malicious Damage Clause be inserted in the policy for an additional premium. The Institute Malicious Damage Clause provides as follows:

In consideration of an additional premium, it is hereby agreed that the exclusion 'deliberate damage to or deliberate destruction of the subject matter insured or any part thereof by the wrongful act of any person or persons', is deemed to be deleted and further that this insurance covers loss of or damage to the subject matter caused by malicious acts, vandalism, or sabotage, subject always to the other exclusions contained in this insurance.

Turning to deal with the more common exclusions contained in the General Exclusions clause, the first excludes loss, damage or expense attributable to the wilful misconduct of the assured which reflects the exclusion in s. 55(2)(a). For misconduct to be wilful it must be done with intent and negligence will not suffice; see *Horabin* v *British Overseas Airways Corp* [1952] 2 All ER 1016. Thus if the insured subject matter was lost due to a peril insured against, e.g. washing overboard, the assured would not be able to recover if the loss was in any way attributable to his wilful misconduct.

The second exclusion relates to the ordinary leakage, ordinary loss in weight or volume, or ordinary wear and tear of the subject matter insured. It should be noted that the clause refers to ordinary leakage etc. of the subject matter insured. Thus where the ordinary leakage of cargo X damages cargo Y the assured in respect of cargo Y would be able to recover his losses under Institute cargo clauses A, which covers all risks (but not under Institute cargo clauses B or C for that is not a risk covered). The assured in respect of cargo X would not, however, be able to recover his loss even if his insurance cover is on the terms of Institute cargo clauses A; see *Wadsworth Lighterage & Coal* v *Sea Insurance* (1929) 35 Com Cas 1.

The third exclusion is of loss, damage or expense caused by insufficiency or unsuitability of packing or preparation of the subject matter. Thus if the insured goods were not properly packed for the journey and were consequently damaged, the insurer would not be liable. The clause covers both insufficient and unsuitable packing in containers in addition to non-container packing. It would, however, seem from the qualification in this clause that where goods are packed in a container after the attachment of the insurance and this packing was unsuitable or insufficient, the insurer would still be liable if the loss or damage arose from an insured risk.

Clause 4.4 excludes liability for loss, damage or expense caused by inherent vice reflecting s. 55(2)(c). In order for the insurer to be able to rely on the exclusion for inherent vice, he must show that the loss or damage was the result of the internal condition of the subject matter insured. If, therefore, a cargo of hemp spontaneously combusts and is destroyed, the insurer would escape liability. If the fire spread to another cargo and damaged that cargo, the insurer of that cargo would not be able to rely on this exclusion clause for it was not a result of any inherent vice of the cargo he insured. Lord Diplock in *Soya* v *White* (13.5.1) defined the term 'inherent vice' in the following manner:

This phrase (generally shortened to 'inherent vice') where it is used in s. 55(2)(c) refers to a peril by which a loss is proximately caused; it is not descriptive of the loss itself. It means the risk of deterioration of the goods shipped as a result of their natural behaviour in the ordinary course of the contemplated voyage without the intervention of any fortuitous external accident or casualty.

In *Noten (TM) BV* v *Harding* [1989] 2 Lloyd's Rep 527 a consignment of leather gloves was covered on a warehouse to warehouse basis. The gloves left the warehouse but before they were placed inside containers at a later time it was found that they had got wet. The gloves arrived in a damaged condition in Rotterdam. It was held that the packing in containers was part of the insured transit and that the gloves when they commenced this journey, that is to say when they left the warehouse, had no inherent defect which might have caused the damage. The time for considering whether goods have an inherent defect is at the commencement of the insured transit; the assured were therefore able to recover on the policy.

Clause 4.5 excludes liability for loss, damage or expense proximately caused by delay even though the delay was caused by a risk insured against. It will be remembered that in the case of a voyage policy (see 12.8.1), the adventure insured must be prosecuted with reasonable diligence and if, without lawful excuse it is not so prosecuted the insurer is discharged from liability as from the time when the delay becomes unreasonable (s. 48). The insurer is likewise discharged from liability under a voyage policy if the ship deviates, without lawful excuse, from the voyage contemplated by the policy (s. 46). There are a number of lawful excuses (s. 49) but if these do not apply then the insurer is discharged from liability under the policy if the loss suffered by the assured arose from some cause other than the delay or deviation.

The position is, however, modified, when the Institute cargo clauses are employed, for these clauses recognise the fact that in most cases the assured will have little or no control over the prosecution of the voyage. The assured is, therefore, only required to prosecute the voyage with reasonable dispatch in so far as this is in his control. Clause 18 of the Institute cargo clauses provides that:

> It is a condition of this insurance that the Assured shall act with reasonable dispatch in all circumstances within their control.

Furthermore the insurer is not discharged from liability under the policy in the event of delay or deviation if that delay or deviation is beyond the control of the assured. Clause 8.3 in the 'Transit Clause' of the Institute cargo clauses provides:

> This insurance shall remain in force (subject to termination as provided for above and to the provisions of Clause 9 below) during any delay beyond the control of the Assured, any deviation, forced discharge, reshipment or transhipment and during any variation of the adventure arising from the exercise of liberty granted to shipowners or charterers under the contract of affreightment.

Thus if there has been a deviation or unreasonable delay beyond the control of the assured then the insurance will remain in force notwithstanding ss. 46 and 48 and if the goods are lost or damaged by an insured risk such as fire after the deviation or delay then the insurer will be liable. The insurer will only be able to escape liability if he is able to show that the loss or damage was proximately caused by the delay.

13.5.2   Unseaworthiness and Unfitness Exclusion Clause (Clause 5)

The next exclusion clause after the General Exclusions clause is clause 5, the 'Unseaworthiness and Unfitness Exclusion Clause' which is common to Institute cargo clauses A, B and C. Clause 5 has already been mentioned in Chapter 12 in connection with the implied warranty as to seaworthiness found in a voyage policy (see 12.8.1.2). In recognition of the fact that the assured may have little control over the seaworthiness of the vessel in which his goods are shipped, indeed a c.i.f. buyer may have no control over the choice of vessel, any breach of this warranty to which the assured or his servants are not privy is waived by the insurer. Clause 5.2 provides that:

The Underwriters waive any breach of the implied warranties of seaworthiness of the ship and the fitness of the ship to carry the subject matter insured to destination, unless the Assured or their servants are privy to such unseaworthiness.

Thus if the vessel in which the assured's goods are shipped is put to sea in an unseaworthy condition and the assured or his servants are not privy to the unseaworthiness and the goods are damaged by a peril insured against such as, for example, the collision of the vessel with an external object, the insurer will not be able to avoid liability on the policy by reason of the breach of the implied warranty as to seaworthiness.

The insurer is only excused from liability under the policy if the loss or damage arose from the unseaworthiness of the vessel and the assured or their agents were privy to that unseaworthiness. Clause 5.1 states that:

In no case shall this insurance cover loss, damage or expense arising from unseaworthiness of vessel or craft, unfitness of vessel, craft, conveyance, container or liftvan for the safe carriage of the subject matter insured where the assured or their servants are privy to such unseaworthiness or unfitness at the time the subject matter insured is loaded therein.

Using the example above, if the vessel collided with the external object because the vessel was unseaworthy and the assured was privy to this unseaworthiness when his goods were loaded onto the vessel, the insurer would be able to rely on this exclusion clause. In this context the assured will only be privy to the unseaworthiness or unfitness if he had knowledge of, or concurred in, that unseaworthiness or unfitness; see *Compania Maritima San Basilio SA* v *Oceanus Mutual Underwriting Association (Bermuda) Ltd, The Eurysthenes* [1977] 1 QB 49.

13.5.3 War Exclusion Clause (Clause 6)

Also common to Institute cargo clauses A, B and C is clause 6, the 'War Exclusion Clause'. If the assured would like to have these war risks covered that cover can be provided through the Institute War Clauses (Cargo). Clause 6 is in the following terms:

In no case shall this insurance cover loss, damage or expense caused by
6.1 war, civil war, revolution, rebellion, insurrection or civil strife arising therefrom, or any hostile act by or against a belligerent power
6.2 capture, seizure, arrest, restraint or detainment, and the consequences thereof or any attempt thereat
6.3 derelict mines, torpedoes, bombs or other derelict weapons of war.

13.5.4   Strikes Exclusion Clause (Clause 7)

The final exclusion clause is the 'Strikes Exclusion Clause' in clause 7 of the Institute cargo clauses A, B and C. As with war risks, if the assured would like to have strikes risks covered than the Institute Strikes Clauses (Cargo) can be incorporated in the policy. Clause 7 provides that:

> In no case shall this insurance cover loss, damage or expense
> 7.1   caused by strikers, locked out workmen, or persons taking part in labour disturbances, riots or civil commotions
> 7.2   resulting from strikes, lock-outs, labour disturbances, riots or civil commotions
> 7.3   caused by any terrorist or any person acting from a political motive.

13.6   INSTITUTE CARGO CLAUSES: DUTY TO MINIMISE LOSS

Mention must also be made of the duty imposed by the Institute cargo clauses on the assured to minimise his losses. Clause 16, the 'Duty of the Assured Clause', replaces the 'sue and labour' clause which was found in the old Lloyd's SG Policy. It allows the assured to recover any expenses reasonably incurred in pursuance of his duty to minimise his losses. Clause 16 is in the following terms:

> It is the duty of the Assured and their servants and agents in respect of losses recoverable hereunder
> 16.1   to take such measures as may be reasonable for the purpose of averting or minimising such loss, and
> 16.2   to ensure that all rights against carriers, bailees or other third parties are properly preserved and exercised
> and the Underwriters will, in addition to any loss recoverable hereunder, reimburse the Assured for any charges properly and reasonably incurred in pursuance of these duties.

Under clause 16 the assured is not required to undertake any step other than that which could reasonably be expected to result in the avoidance or reduction of loss; see *Noble Resources Ltd and Unirise Development Ltd v George Albert Greenwood, The Irasso* [1993] 2 Lloyd's Rep 309, where it was held that the failure to apply for a freezing injunction to prevent the shipowners from removing the proceeds of a hull claim from England did not amount to a breach of clause 16.

13.7   TOTAL OR PARTIAL LOSS

A marine insurance policy provides the assured or his assigns with an indemnity for total and partial loss of the subject matter insured. In this respect it does not matter whether the subject matter is insured under Institute cargo clauses A, B or C. There are essentially three types of losses which the assured may suffer, i.e. an actual total loss, a constructive total loss or a partial loss. Any loss which is not a total loss, of either type, is a partial loss (s. 56(1)). There is also the possibility that the assured has suffered a general average loss, a matter which is examined below (see 13.8), but this appears to be classified as a partial loss by the Act.

The essential distinction between an actual total loss and a constructive total loss is that in the former case the goods have been irretrievably lost while in the latter case they are merely a commercial write-off. A further difference between an actual total loss and a constructive total loss is that in the former case no notice of abandonment need be given by the assured (s. 57(2)).

13.7.1   Actual Total Loss (s. 57)

An actual total loss occurs in three situations:

(a)   the subject matter of the insurance is destroyed;
(b)   the subject matter of the insurance is so damaged that it ceases to be a thing of the kind insured;
(c)   the assured is irretrievably deprived of the subject matter.

The first of these three situations requires no discussion. If the subject matter is destroyed then there is a total loss.

The second of these situations does, however, require some examination. The goods must no longer be of the nature of the goods insured. They must have lost their essential nature. The test to be applied in this situation is a commercial test as illustrated by the decision reached in *Asfar & Co.* v *Blundell* [1896] 1 QB 123, in which a vessel with a cargo of dates had sunk but had been subsequently raised after two days. In the course of his judgment Lord Esher MR dealt in the following manner with the question of whether the dates were an actual total loss:

... it is contended that although these dates were under water for two days and when brought up were simply a mass of pulpy matter impregnated with sewage and in a state of fermentation, there had been no change in their nature and they were still dates. There is a well known test which has for many years been applied in cases such as the present — that test is whether, as a matter of business, the nature of the thing has been altered. The nature of the thing is not necessarily altered because the thing itself has been damaged; wheat or rice may be damaged, but may still remain the thing dealt with as wheat or rice in business. But if the nature of the thing is altered and it becomes for business purposes something else, so that it is not dealt with by business people as the thing which it originally was, the question for determination is whether the thing insured ... has become a total loss. If it is so changed in its nature by the perils of the sea as to become an unmerchantable thing which no buyer would buy, and no honest seller would sell, then there is a total loss.

The third situation is where the assured is irretrievably deprived of subject matter insured. This means that there must be no means available either to the assured or to the underwriter by which the subject matter insured could be restored to the assured. This section is not concerned with the reasonableness of those means or the prohibitive expenditure which such means might entail. The assured is required to show a complete absence of control in bringing about the arrival of the subject matter insured.

There is one additional provision which ought to be mentioned, though in the age of modern electronic communication it would appear to have little relevance. Where the ship concerned in the adventure is missing and after a reasonable lapse of time no news of her has been received then, by virtue of s. 58, an actual loss may be presumed.

13.7.2   Constructive Total Loss (s. 60)

The lengthy provisions concerning constructive total loss are found in s. 60 and s. 60(1) states the general rule in respect of constructive total loss:

> Subject to any express provision in the policy, there is a constructive total loss where the subject matter insured is reasonably abandoned on account of its actual total loss appearing to be unavoidable, or because it could not be preserved from actual total loss without an expenditure which would exceed its value when the expenditure had been incurred.

In essence a constructive total loss occurs when the goods are a commercial write-off. The cost of recovering or repairing the insured goods makes it uneconomical to carry out such an exercise and the goods are abandoned to the insurer.

In particular, with regard to damaged goods, there is a constructive total loss when the cost of repairing the damage and forwarding the goods to their destination would exceed the value of the goods on their arrival (s. 60(2)(iii)). Furthermore there will be a constructive total loss where the assured is deprived of possession of his goods and it is unlikely that he will recover the goods (s. 60(2)(i)(a)) or where the cost of recovering the goods would exceed their value on arrival. This should be contrasted with the requirement that the goods be irretrievably lost to the assured when one is considering whether there has been an actual total loss. These provisions are mirrored in clause 13 of the Institute cargo clauses, the 'Constructive Total Loss Clause', which provides as follows:

> No claim for Constructive Total Loss shall be recoverable hereunder unless the subject matter insured is reasonably abandoned either on account of its total loss becoming unavoidable or because the cost of recovering, reconditioning and forwarding the subject matter to the destination to which it is insured would exceed its value on arrival.

In deciding whether there has been a constructive total loss the value declared in a valued policy is not conclusive (s. 27(4)).

When there has been a constructive total loss the assured has a choice. He may elect to abandon the goods to the insurer and treat the loss as a constructive total loss or he may decide to treat the loss merely as a partial loss and retain what is left of the goods and claim under the policy (s. 61). If the assured decides to declare a constructive total loss he must give notice of abandonment to his insurer. This notice of abandonment need not be in any particular form but must be clear and should indicate to the insurer that the assured unconditionally abandons the insured goods to the insurer and claims a total loss under the policy (s. 62(2)). The notice of abandonment should be given within a reasonable time after the assured has received reliable information of the loss. If the information is, however, of a doubtful character the assured is then entitled to a reasonable time to make the necessary inquiries either to verify or discount the information he has received (s. 62(3)). If the assured fails to give a notice of abandonment the loss can only be treated as a partial loss (s. 62(1)). Notice of abandonment may be waived by the insurer (s. 62(8)) and in certain circumstances it may be unnecessary (s. 62(7)). Where, however, the insurer accepts the notice of abandonment this acceptance is irrevocable (s. 62(6)) and the insurer must pay the insured value of the goods.

Once the insured goods have been validly abandoned the insurer is entitled to take over the interest of the assured in whatever may remain of the goods and may exercise all proprietary rights thereto (s. 63(1)). That is to say the insurer is entitled to whatever is left of the goods. This right of the insurer should be distinguished from the insurer's right of subrogation which is examined below (see 13.10).

13.7.3   Partial Loss

Any loss which is not a total loss is a partial loss (s. 56(1)). A partial loss of goods therefore includes both damage to the goods as well as a total loss of part of the goods. There is one specific statutory partial loss. Where goods reach their destination in kind, but by reason of obliteration of marks, or otherwise, they are incapable of identification, the loss if any is partial and not total (s. 56(5)).

13.8   GENERAL AVERAGE LOSS

There is a further type of loss which may affect the goods insured but only indirectly. This is a general average loss arising out of a general average act and includes both a general average expenditure as well as a general average sacrifice (s. 66(1)). Section 66(2) provides that:

> There is a general average act where any extraordinary sacrifice or expenditure is voluntarily and reasonably made or incurred in time of peril for the purpose of preserving the property imperilled in the common adventure.

The carriage of goods by sea is a common adventure made up of three interests which are exposed to the same risks; those interests being the ship, the cargo and the freight. In the course of this adventure a common peril may be encountered, such as a storm, and action may need to be taken to save the adventure. That action may involve the ship entering a port of refuge or part of the cargo being jettisoned, but in any event it must be deliberate; see *Ralli* v *Troop* (1894) 157 US 386.

This action will involve a loss falling on one of the interests, such as the cargo owner whose goods have been jettisoned to save the ship. In these circumstances it is only just and fair that all the other interests in the common adventure should contribute towards his loss or expense. This is known as a general average contribution and the amount of this contribution is usually determined in accordance with the York-Antwerp Rules (a shipping code formulated in 1877 setting out the rules of general average, which is generally incorporated in contracts of affreightment).

Where the assured has suffered a general average loss he may, unless the policy otherwise provides, recover his loss from the insurer and is entitled to recover the whole of his loss without having enforced his right of contribution from the other interests in the adventure (s. 66(4)). The insurer, on meeting the assured's claim, is then subrogated to the rights of the assured and is thus able to pursue the assured's claim for a contribution.

If the assured is only liable for a general average contribution he may recover this from the insurer unless the policy otherwise provides (s. 66(5)). In any event the insurer is, in the absence of an express stipulation in the policy, not liable for any general average loss or contribution where the loss was not incurred for the purpose of avoiding, or in connection with the avoidance of, a peril insured against (s. 66(6)). This is reiterated in clause 2 of the Institute cargo clauses, the 'General Average Clause', which is in the following terms:

> This insurance covers general average and salvage charges, adjusted or determined according to the contract of affreightment and/or the governing law and practice incurred to avoid or in connection with the avoidance of loss from any cause except those excluded in Clauses 4, 5, 6 and 7 or elsewhere in this insurance.

13.9   MEASURE OF INDEMNITY

The extent to which an assured can expect to recover from his insurers in respect of his loss is known as his 'measure of indemnity' (s. 67(1)). The measure of indemnity in any particular situation depends, in part, on whether the policy is valued or unvalued. A marine insurance policy may be valued or unvalued (s. 27(1)).

13.9.1   Valued Policy

A valued policy is one which specifies the agreed value of the subject matter insured (s. 27(2)). This does not mean that the assured will always recover the value stated in the policy whether the loss be total or partial. It simply means that in the event of loss, it is not open to the insurer to contend that the goods were not worth the value stated in the policy save where there has been fraud (s. 27(3)); see *Loders & Nucolene* v *Bank of New Zealand* (1929) 33 Ll LR 70.

The advantage of having a valued policy, as opposed to an unvalued policy, is that it is permissible to include as part of the declared value of the goods a percentage mark-up for the expected profits from the adventure. This may explain why unvalued policies are rarely used. ·

13.9.2 Unvalued Policy

An unvalued policy does not specify the value of the goods insured but, subject to the limit of the sum insured, leaves the value to be determined in accordance with s. 16(3). An unvalued policy merely states the maximum amount which the assured would be able to recover but, subject to that limit, what he actual recovers is determined later.

In the case of an unvalued policy, the insurable value of the goods is the prime cost of the goods, plus expenses of and incidental to shipping and the charges of insurance upon the whole (s. 16(3)). This insurable value, as with the value declared in a valued policy, is the starting point in calculating the indemnity due to the assured under the policy. In calculating the insurable interest under s. 16(3) the invoice value of the goods is *prima facie* the 'prime cost' of the goods. By the time the goods have been shipped their value may, however, have changed as the market for those goods may have moved. Thus evidence is admissible as to the value of the goods at the time of shipment so that their 'prime cost' may be ascertained; see *Williams* v *Atlantic Assurance* [1933] 1 KB 81.

13.9.3 Total Loss

Where there has been a total loss of the goods the assured can recover the full value of the insured goods. If the policy was a valued policy the assured can recover from his insurers the value fixed by the policy. Section 68(1) provides:

Where there is a total loss of the subject matter insured, if the policy be a valued policy, the measure of indemnity is the sum fixed by the policy.

This measure of indemnity is conclusive and the assured is not entitled to claim for any further additional losses he may have suffered. In *Apostolos Konstantine Ventouris* v *Trevor Rex Mountain, The Italia Express* (No 2) [1992] 2 Lloyd's Rep 281 the assured claimed in respect of the total loss of his vessel. The vessel had been sunk by explosives attached to the hull while undergoing repairs. The sole defence of the insurers was that the loss was caused by the wilful misconduct of the assured but they had to abandon this defence on the 37th day of the trial. The assured claimed, in addition to the value of the vessel as fixed in the policy, damages from the insurers for breach of contract in failing to pay the amount due under the policy immediately and for the hardship, inconvenience and mental stress caused by this failure. Hirst J held that the value fixed in the policy was definitive of the extent of the liability of the insurers for the loss of the vessel and that the claim for damages must therefore fail.

Where the policy is unvalued and the goods insured are a total loss, the measure of indemnity is the insurable value of the goods as determined by s. 16(3). Section 68(2) provides:

> Where there is a total loss of the subject matter insured, if the policy be an unvalued policy the measure of indemnity is the insurable value of the subject matter insured.

13.9.4   Partial Loss

Where there is a partial loss of goods, merchandise or other moveables the measure of indemnity is as follows:

In a valued policy it is the proportion of the sum fixed by the policy as the insurable value of the part lost bears to the insurable value of the whole, ascertained as in the case of an unvalued policy (s. 71(1)).

In an unvalued policy on the goods, the insurable value is ascertained in accordance with s. 16(3) which states:

> In insurance on goods or merchandise, the insurable value is the part lost of the property insured, plus the expenses of and incidental to shipping, and the charges of insurance on the whole.

Thus the following equation must be used:

$$\frac{\text{s. 16 insurable value of part lost}}{\text{s. 16 insurable value of whole}} \times \text{value fixed by policy}$$

Let us illustrate this with an example: A ships a consignment of bicycles to B, and takes out a marine insurance policy on the bicycles on B's behalf, which states their value to be £10,000. During the course of the voyage 220 bicycles are lost overboard. The f.o.b. price to B of each bicycle is £105. The insurance premium payable on each bicycle was 50p and freight and shipping charges £2.50. Applying s. 16(3) to these figures in order to ascertain the measure of indemnity for the 220 bicycles lost:

Prime cost of bicycle (invoice price)	£105.00
Shipping expenses	£2.50
Insurance charges	£0.50
	———
	£108.00
	———

Therefore £108 x 220 bicycles = insurable value of part lost
£108 × total number of bicycles shipped = insurable value of whole (*per* s. 16(3)).

The resulting fraction is applied to the sum in the policy, i.e. £10,000, and this is B's measure of indemnity.

In an unvalued policy, where part of the goods, merchandise or other moveables insured is totally lost, the measure of indemnity is the insurable value of the part lost ascertained as in the case of total loss (s. 71(2)). In cases of total loss the measure of indemnity is ascertained by calculating the insurable value of the subject matter insured in accordance with s. 16 or any alternative formulation which is set out in the policy. Therefore, the measure of indemnity on the unvalued policy, using the example set out above, would be:

s. 16 insurable value of 220 bicycles, i.e. £108 (£105 + £2.50 + £0.50) × 220 bicycles lost.

13.9.5 Damaged Goods

Where the goods are neither totally lost nor partially lost but only damaged, the measure of indemnity which the assured can recover is to be computed in accordance with s. 71. Once again the Act distinguishes between a valued and an unvalued policy, but the formula for both is substantially the same. Section 71(3) states:

Where the whole or any part of the merchandise has been damaged at its destination then the measure of indemnity is such proportion of the sum fixed by the policy in the case of a valued policy, or of the insurable value in the case of an unvalued policy, as the difference between the gross sound and damaged values at the place of arrival bears to the gross sound value.

According to s. 71(4):

'Gross value' means the wholesale price, if there be no such price the estimated value, with, in either case, freight, landing charges, and duty paid beforehand.

Therefore, the following formula must be used to calculate the measure of indemnity for damaged goods:

$$\frac{\text{Gross sound value} - \text{gross damaged value (at place of arrival)}}{\text{Gross sound value}}$$

To illustrate with an example. Goods have an insurable value of £20,000 or alternatively £20,000 is the value fixed by the policy. Their gross sound value is £18,000. Their gross damaged value is £9,000. Applying the above formula:

$$\frac{£18,000 - £9,000}{£18,000} \times £20,000 \text{ (sum fixed by policy/insurable value)}$$

$$= \frac{1}{2} \times £20,000 = £10,000 \text{ measure of indemnity.}$$

13.10   SUBROGATION

Subrogation is defined as:

> The substitution of one person or thing for another so that the same rights and
> duties which attached to the original person or thing attach to the substituted one.
> If one person is subrogated to another he is said to stand in the other's shoes, i.e.
> an insurer is subrogated to the rights of the insured on paying his claim. (*Osborn's
> Law Dictionary*)

Another intelligible definition was offered in *Burnard* v *Rodocanachi* (1881) 6 QBD
633:

> Where there is a contract of indemnity and a loss happens, anything which reduces
> or diminishes that loss, reduces or diminishes the amount which the indemnifier
> has to pay and, if they have already paid it, then if anything which diminishes the
> loss comes into the hands of the person to whom he has paid it, it becomes an
> equity that the person who has already paid the full indemnity is entitled to be
> recouped by having that amount back.

To illustrate the right of subrogation with an example. A is the consignor of
perishable goods shipped from Southampton to Chile and he has a marine insurance
policy on those goods. When the goods arrive they have been damaged due to the
maintenance of a high temperature in the hold when the refrigeration system broke
down mid-voyage. *Prima facie* he has two possible avenues of claim. The first is
under his marine insurance policy. The second is against the carrier for breach of his
duty under Art. III r. 2 Hague-Visby Rules.

If A chooses to recover under his marine insurance policy he cannot then also sue
the carrier and retain the proceeds. Otherwise, he would be recovering more than
once for his loss. Therefore, having been paid by the insurer, it is the insurer who is
entitled to proceed against the carrier in an effort to reduce the level of indemnity for
which the assured has made him liable; see *Dufourcet* v *Bishop* (1886) 18 QBD 373.
Moreover, in the absence of a valid assignment allowing the insurer to sue in his own
name, he is entitled to bring proceedings against the carrier in the name of the
assured; see *Simpson* v *Thomson* (1877) 2 App Cas 279; *Compania Colombiana de
Seguros* v *Pacific Steam Navigation Co.* [1965] 1 QB 101.

The doctrine of subrogation developed both at common law, which analysed the
doctrine in terms of implied contractual terms (see *Yorkshire Insurance Co. Ltd* v
Nisbet Shipping Co. Ltd [1962] 2 QB 330) and in equity (see *White* v *Dobson* 14 Sim
273) concurrently. The Act also declares the right of the insurer to be subrogated to
the rights and remedies of the assured. Section 79(1) provides:

> Where the insurer pays for a total loss either of the whole, or in the case of goods
> of any apportionable part, of the subject matter insured, he thereupon becomes

entitled to take over the interest of the assured in whatever may remain of the subject matter so paid for and he is thereby subrogated to all the rights and remedies of the assured in and in respect of that subject matter as from the time of the casualty causing the loss.

At first sight s. 79(1) may seem to be a contradiction in terms. It talks about the insurer paying for a total loss and yet taking over the assured's interest in whatever remains. Clearly where the goods are actually totally lost by reason of their total destruction there will be nothing remaining in which the assured could have an interest, whereas if the goods have merely lost their specie, the insurer may, nevertheless, be able to make a sale of those goods for some other purpose. When the Act talks about total loss it obviously also includes constructive total loss. Following payment the insurer himself may then decide to forward, repair or recover the goods which were constructively totally lost.

The insurer's right of subrogation is more limited in circumstances where he pays only for a partial loss, i.e. all those losses which are not total including constructive total losses which the assured has elected not to abandon. Section 79(2) sets out his right of subrogation in those circumstances:

> Subject to the foregoing provisions, where the insurer pays for a partial loss, he acquires no title to the subject matter insured or such part of it as may remain, but he is thereupon subrogated to all rights and remedies of the assured in and in respect of the subject matter insured as from the time of the casualty causing the loss, in so far as the assured has been indemnified according to this Act, by payment for the loss.

The fundamental difference then between a right of subrogation which arises under s. 79(1) and one which arises under s. 79(2) is that in the former case, in addition to a right of subrogation, the insurer actually takes over the interest of the assured in what remains of the subject matter insured, whereas in the latter he merely has the right to pursue claims against third parties without a coexisting interest in the goods.

In any event, whichever line of authority is relied upon and whether there has been a total loss or merely a partial loss, the insurer is only able to recover that which he has paid to the assured; see *Yorkshire Insurance* v *Nisbet Shipping* [1962] 2 QB 330; *Lord Napier* v *Hunter* [1993] 2 WLR 42.

The right of subrogation is not to be confused with the rights which accrue to an insurer when the goods have been abandoned. Abandonment of the subject matter insured is something which may or may not happen, according to whether the assured elects to treat his constructive total loss as a total loss or a partial loss. Even where the assured makes this election the insurer need not accept it. The insurer is entitled to take over the assured's interest in the abandoned subject matter, but he is not obliged to do so. Subrogation, on the other hand, arises automatically where the assured has been paid in respect of a loss, and its occurrence and effects are completely beyond the control of the assured.

14   Export Credit Guarantees and Finance

14.1   INTRODUCTION

Because of the unique nature of and enormous risks involved in international trade, there are certain undertakings that are not insurable through the normal private or commercial insurance market. The political and other non-commercial risks are insurable through the export credit insurance market. Until recently, the funding for this type of insurance came entirely from public funds through the public sector. The public monopoly has, however, been broken, culminating in private companies now providing a limited amount of export credit insurance. The bulk of it is still provided from the public purse. All the major and emerging economies now provide one type or another of export credit insurance.

14.2   CREDIT GUARANTEES

Export credit insurance is only part of a wide guarantee system operated by various trading nations in support of their exports. One of these mechanisms is credit guarantee. Credit guarantee is a type of insurance against default provided by a credit guarantee association or other institution to a lending institution. Credit guarantees enable otherwise 'sound' borrowers who lack collateral security, or are unable to obtain loans for other reasons, to obtain the credit they require through banks in the normal way. A government loan guarantee scheme insuring loans to small firms by the commercial banks was introduced in the UK in 1980.

14.3   CREDIT INSURANCE

This is a form of insurance which covers losses from bad debts. The ordinary insurance company does not normally offer this service but leaves it to specialist companies. These buy up a list of debtors from a client business at an agreed discount which will cover the costs of collection, the risk assessed, interest on slow payers and a profit margin. The business employing the collecting service loses part of its trading profit, represented by debts due, but often gains considerably by obtaining immediate cash and thus improving its cash flow position. The whole operation is usually referred to as factoring and the operatives as factors. It is very similar to the service offered by hire purchase finance companies.

14.4 EXPORT CREDIT INSURANCE

This is insurance against the additional risks attendant on foreign trade. Commercial credit insurance companies provide normal cover, but the Export Credits Guarantee Department (ECGD), attached to the Department of Trade, is available for giving normal cover against bad debts and the very valuable extra cover against political and exchange risks. One important point to remember is that the ECGD offers a complete service covering all overseas dealings. It is not available for protecting the occasional individual contract which seems to carry especial risks, except for large capital goods contracts. This is only reasonable if one considers that the ECGD, although non-profit-making, is run on commercial lines. Comprehensive policies are available for continuous contracts. Exporters with problems are invited to consult the ECGD without obligation at any time, and it will usually arrange for an inspector to call, in order to discuss the situation and the available aids.

14.4.1 Export Credits Guarantee Department

The Export Credits Guarantee Department (ECGD) is a UK government department set up in 1930 as an independent department, although it had operated in another form from 1919. It is responsible to the Secretary of State for Trade and Industry, and has the authority, under Treasury control, to issue insurance policies to cover risks met by exporters. The risks are, broadly, insolvency or default of debtor, refusal of goods on delivery and risks of a political nature such as the imposition of import licensing and exchange controls. The policies may be either 'comprehensive' or 'specific', the former being in respect of short-term cover up to six months and the latter of longer-term cover up to ten years or more. The Department generally limits the extent of its cover to about 90 per cent of the potential loss. The Department has been induced to grant better terms in the past to bring its rates into line with those of similar institutions in other countries who have used this type of insurance as a vehicle for concealed export subsidies. In 1976, the ECGD was enabled to extend its cover to include losses incurred on the forward exchange market on the default of a buyer. Before this, the guarantees were sterling based. The ECGD may also cover exporters against increases in costs within specified limits. The ECGD has, since 1972, given an interest rate subsidy to other financial institutions, such as the commercial banks, by offering export credits. Expenditure for this purpose is about £500 million per annum. There has been increasing international concern about the use of export credit subsidies to capture export markets in the developing countries.

As a consequence, twenty-two developed countries within the OECD have concluded an 'Arrangement on Guidelines for Officially Supported Export Credits', which fixes minimum interest rates and maximum repayment periods for specified categories of borrowers. These guidelines are revised as market conditions change. The Export Credit and Investment Act 1991 ended the ECGD's monopoly and liberated the market.

14.4.2   Insurance Facilities Offered by the ECGD

Insurance facilities offered by the ECGD are of four principal types, namely:

   (a)   Short-term credits

       (i)   Extended terms
       (ii)   The Constructional Short Term (CST) Guarantee
       (iii)   Re-exports
       (iv)   Stocks held overseas
       (v)   Constructional and engineering works and services policies.

   (b)   Medium and long-term credits

       (i)   Specific guarantees
       (ii)   Buyer credit guarantees

   (c)   ECGD and the provision of finance

       (i)   Hypothecation of insurance sum
       (ii)   Direct guarantees to banks
       (iii)   Buyer credit guarantees
       (iv)   Foreign currency specific bank guarantee
       (v)   Cover for lines of credit
       (vi)   Finance contracts (overseas banks) and associated borrower endorsements
       (vii) Insurance for overseas investments
       (viii) Performance guarantees
       (ix)   Cover against unfair calling of demand bonds.

   (d)   Project insurance

       (i)   Project financing cover
       (ii)   Project participants
       (iii)   Joint and several cover.

14.5   ECGD POLICIES

Under the basic terms and conditions of insurance policies between the exporter and the ECGD, the Department covers the exporter to the tune of 90 per cent of the contract price. The idea is presumably that the exporter should obtain cover for the remaining 10 per cent from the private market or be self-insured to that extent. One of the founding principles of the ECGD is based on the fact that it is not supposed to compete with the private sector since its terms are comparatively generous.

The ECGD policy is a contract of insurance to which all insurance principles apply (see 12.6 and 12.7). The policy should stipulate such terms and conditions (*Re Miller, Gibb and Co. Ltd* [1975 1 WLR 703). Because they are contracts of insurance, the principle of subrogation applies. Thus, when the Department has settled and the exporter later recovers from the buyer, the Department is entitled to 90 per cent of the proceeds. Although not considering an ECGD policy, the court in *Yorkshire Insurance Co.* v *Nisbet Shipping Co.* [1962] 2 QB 330 followed *Re Miller, Gibb & Co. Ltd* on this point.

In the course of providing cover and other services to the exporter, the ECGD owes a duty of care to the insured on the basis of the principles laid down in *Hedley Byrne* v *Heller and Partners* [1964] AC 465. In a case where a UK exporter was a sub-contractor to a German Company covered by Hermis (the German equivalent of the ECGD) on a contract to build two stadia in Saudi Arabia, the ECGD negligently advised the UK sub-contractor that there was no need for the company to obtain additional cover from the ECGD. It turned out that the UK Company, as a sub-contractor, was not covered by the main contractor's Hermis policy. The UK Company successfully sued the ECGD for negligent advice (*Culford MetalIndustries Ltd* v *Exporter Credit Guarantee Department* (1981) *The Times*, 25 March).

However, where the ECGD provides direct bank guarantees on behalf of the UK exporter, the ECGD has a right of recourse against the exporter. The ECGD retains the right, where a payment made against a bank guarantee would not have been made under its normal insurance cover, to take recourse against the exporter for the recovery of such a payment. Such a provision in a recourse agreement obliging the exporter to pay back is not in the nature of a penalty clause (*Export Credit Guarantee Department* v *Universal Oil Products Co.* [1983] 2 Lloyd's Rep. 152).

14.6   PRIVATE CREDIT INSURANCE

In the London market, credit insurance is now obtainable from private insurance and indemnity companies, the major ones being Trade Indemnity, The Export Finance Co. Ltd. (EXFINCO) and NCM (the Dutch Group). Apart from Trade Indemnity, which offers a limited cover for political risks, the others concentrate on commercial risks.

14.7   EXPORT INCENTIVES AND SUBSIDIES

In addition to export credit guarantees and insurance, some countries also offer export incentives and subsidies in the form of insurances, guarantees, finance and taxation. These incentives are preferential treatment for firms who sell their products abroad, compared with firms who sell to the home market. They may take the form of direct subsidies, special credit facilities, grants, concessions in the field of direct taxation, benefits arising from the administration of indirect taxation, and export credit insurance on exceptionally favourable terms. Various international associations discourage the practice of artificially stimulating exports by any of these methods. The 'General Agreement on Tariffs and Trade' lays down special provisions relating to export subsidies, direct and indirect, in an attempt to limit them. The Stockholm Convention, in setting up the European Free Trade Association, lists various forms of aid to exporters which member countries are required to avoid. The Treaty of Rome, which established the European Economic Community, although less specific than the Stockholm Convention, nevertheless discourages the granting of privileged aid to any economic sectors.

14.8   FORFEITING

Forfeiting is another method for obtaining finance for international trade, which is linked to guarantees of payments for bills of exchange and promissory notes. It is based on discounting bills drawn without recourse. The risk for payment is borne by the forfeiter, but at a cost to the beneficiary, as in any other discounting.

14.9   DISCOUNTING AND FINANCE HOUSES

A bill of exchange may be discounted. This means that it is purchased by a third party for a sum lower than that party will receive when the bill matures. The person discounting the bill gains by receiving money at an earlier date. The amount of discount will vary according to the risk the purchaser takes. A good bill is one which is backed or countersigned by a well-known finance house or bank. Bills are normally discounted with banks or on a larger scale with institutions known as discount houses.

Finance houses are organisations situated in the City of London whose business is discounting bills of exchange — trade bills, bank bills and treasury bills. Business is done on a large scale and funds are obtained principally from the clearing banks. To keep the interest rate as low as possible and to be able to vary the amount borrowed at short intervals, a great deal of money is borrowed overnight. This suits both bank and discount house; to the bank it is money at short notice, also earning interest. It is lent on the security of bills of exchange that have not yet matured.

14.10   FINANCIAL LEASING

14.10.1   The General Law on Leases

Leasing is one of the sources of finance in international trade. A lease is an agreement whereby the legal owner of real property gives another person the possession of that property with freedom to use it as he wishes, though possibly under certain conditions, in return for a regular specified payment referred to as rent. Although personal, as opposed to real property, can also be lent to another, that type of transaction is normally referred to as an agreement to hire. The real property is usually land and/or buildings and is normally accompanied by such rights of way as are necessary for free access. The person obtaining possession, i.e. the holder of the lease, is said to be the owner of leasehold property which can, unless the original agreement forbids, be sub-let to another person, who in turn may sub-let the property. Generally, sub-leases arise where the land contained in the first, or head, lease can be an absolute sale and lease-back is an increasingly common commercial phenomenon whereby a company, or other business organisation, which needs the cash tied up in its land and buildings to fund everyday activities, makes a contract with a property investor, usually an insurance company, to sell the relevant land and buildings thereon to that investor on condition that the sale is accompanied by a document leasing the same property back to the business for an agreed term. Sale and lease-back agreements feature prominently in e.g. airlines and computer businesses.

14.10.2 International Convention on Financial Leasing 1988

The Convention provides a uniform structure for the lease of 'plant, goods or other equipment' as a means of long-term financing, recognising that the triangular arrangement necessary when a lease is so used differs in its requirements from the traditional contract of hire. The Convention applies to transactions in which one party (the lessor) enters into an agreement (the supply agreement) for the supply of goods from the supplier at the specification of a third party (the lessee to whom the goods are then leased under a leasing agreement). It is irrelevant whether or not in the leasing agreement the lessee is given an option to buy.

The Convention is limited in its scope in that it applies only where the places of business of lessor and lessee are in different contracting states and the supplier's place of business is in a contracting state or the supply agreement and the leasing agreement are governed by the law of a contracting state. When the transaction falls within it, the Convention may be excluded or, in respect of most provisions, varied with the consent of all three parties to the transaction.

Contracting states may exclude the Convention when their laws on matters governed by the Convention are closely related. A contracting state may similarly exclude the Convention if the law of a non-contracting state is applicable and closely related and all three parties to the transaction have places of business in the two states.

The Convention sets out rights of the three parties in respect of the supply and leasing agreements and, in particular, the rights between lessor and lessee and the rights of the lessee in respect of the supply agreement. The lessor's rights in the goods are protected against the lessee's creditors and a trustee in bankruptcy and, save for any intervention by the lessor in selection of the equipment, against the lessee incurring any liability in respect of the equipment.

14.11   FINANCIAL FACTORING

14.11.1   The General Law on Factoring

Apart from leasing, factoring is another source of finance for international trade. A factor is legally a general mercantile agent dealing with a specific category or categories of goods. As an agent he is distinguished by the fact that, provided he has possession of the goods coming into these categories with the consent of the owner, he can sell and give a good title to an innocent purchaser for value, whether or not the true owner has given his permission to sell. An art dealer, for instance, could sell pictures lent to him for display, provided the buyer was not aware of this fact.

Factoring comes from a factor but has commercial, in addition to the purely legal, contexts. A factor in the financial world is different from a factor in the law of contract. Factoring is similar to invoice discounting except that a factor will normally accept responsibility for credit control, debt collection and credit risk, and of course will charge more correspondingly. There are two principal types of factoring: (1) with service, and (2) with service plus finance. The service is the collection of debts and the assumption of credit risk (invoices are handed to the factor, who pays money to the customer at stated intervals). When finance is offered as well, the customer receives up to 90 per cent of the invoice value at once from the factor, rather than 100 per cent, as it were in arrears, from the debtor. The debts are in fact purchased for cash; there is no question of repayment (provided of course that the goods are delivered and up to standard). The charge for this financing service might be 1.5 per cent over bank rate. Naturally, the factor chooses his debtors and customers carefully, and normally only deals with customers whose annual turnover is well over £100,000.

Factoring is, therefore, the business activity in which a company takes over the responsibility for collecting the debts of another. It is a service primarily intended to meet the needs of small and medium sized firms. It developed comparatively slowly in the UK compared with the USA, despite the fact that the banks took important interests in the leading factoring companies. Typically, the client debits all his sales to the factor and can draw cash up to 80 per cent of their value, thus increasing his cash flow considerably. The factor takes over the entire responsibility for retrieving the debts due from the client's customers and protects the client from bad debts. The factor, however, has some control over the sales, either by imposing a maximum credit limit which he is willing to meet or by vetting specific prospective clients. Through international factoring companies the factor can offer a service to exporters by protecting his customers from bad debts overseas and by giving, for instance, expert advice on foreign exchange transactions. In 1981, the nine members of the Association of British Factors serviced over 2,500 client companies with a total turnover of £2 billion.

14.11.2   International Convention on Factoring 1988

The Convention provides a uniform structure for transactions in which one party (the factor) performs at least one of a specified number of functions for a supplier of goods in respect of a contract of sale entered into by the supplier with another party (the debtor). The functions are: finance for the supplier, maintenance of accounts, collection of 'receivables' under the sale contract and protection against the default of the debtor.

14.11.3 General Provisions of the Convention

As with the Convention on International Financial Leasing, the Convention is limited in its scope to transactions directly connected with contracting states. The Convention applies only where the contract of sale is concluded between parties having places of business in different contracting states and the factor has its place of business in a contracting state, or both the contract of sale and the factoring contract are governed by the law of a contracting state.

The Convention may be excluded as a whole by the parties to the factoring contract or the parties to the contract of sale as from notice given to the factor. Contracting states may exclude the Convention where their laws relevant to matters governed by the Convention are closely related. A contracting state may exclude the Convention if its laws and those of a non-contracting state, on matters governed by the Convention, are closely related and the supplier, factor and debtor all have their places of business in those states.

FURTHER READING FOR PART V

Ademuni-Odeke, 'The insurance elements in Incoterms c.i.f. and c.i.p. contracts', *Tolley's Insurance Law and Practice*, 1995, 4(4), 86–94.
Arnould's Law of Maritime Insurance and Average, 16th edn, London: Sweet & Maxwell, 1981.
Badger, D. and Whitehead, G., *Elements of Cargo Insurance*, Cambridge: Woodhead-Faulkner, 1983.
Brown, R.H., *Marine Insurance*, 5th edn, London: Witherby, 1998.
Brown, R.H., *Analysis of Marine Insurance Clauses*, London: Witherby, 1983.
Clarke, M.A., *The Law of Insurance Contracts*, 3rd edn, London: LLP, 1997.
De Leon, H.S., *The Law of Insurance and Sales*, Quezan: Rex Books, 1984.
Denny, M.E.V., *Freight Insurance: A Commentary*, London: Witherby, 1986.
Dover, V. and Brown, R.H., *A Handbook of Marine Insurance*, 8th edn, London: Witherby, 1975.
Goodacre, J.K., *Marine Insurance Claims*, 3rd edn, London: Witherby, 1996.
Goodacre, J.K., *Goodbye to the Memorandum*, London: Witherby, 1988.
Hudson, N.G. and Allen, J.C., *Institute Clauses*, 2nd edn, London: LLP, 1999.
Hudson, N.G. and Allen, J.C., *Marine Claims Handbook*, 5th edn, London: LLP, 1996.
IBC, *Insuring Export Trade Credit and Political Risks*, London: IBC, 1992.
Ivamy, E.R. Hardy, *Chalmers: Marine Insurance Act 1906*, 10th edn, London: Butterworths, 1993.
Ivamy, E.R. Hardy, *General Principles of Insurance Law*, 6th edn, London: Butterworths, 1993.

Ivamy, E.R. Hardy, *Marine Insurance*, London: Butterworths, 1990.

LLP, *Marine Cargo Surveys*, London: LLP, 1979.

LLP, *Marine Insurance '79* (Cargo Conference), London: LLP, 1979.

Lowndes and Rudolf, *The Law of General Average*, 11th edn, London: Sweet & Maxwell, 1990.

Meron, T., *Investment Insurance in International Law*, Leiden: Sijthoff, 1976.

OECD, *OECD: Export Credit Systems in the OECD*, Paris: OECD.

Tetley, W., *Marine Cargo Claims*, 3rd edn, London: Butterworths, 1988.

PART VI

CONFLICT RESOLUTION IN INTERNATIONAL TRADE

15   Conflict of Laws and Procedures

15.1   JURISDICTION

When a court has jurisdiction it means that it is competent to hear a case. The basic rule for jurisdiction of an English court over actions *in personam* e.g. actions in which one person attempts to cause another to refrain from doing something or to pay damages, is the defendant's presence in England. The rule in actions *in rem*, e.g. an action brought against a ship, is the ship's presence in England.

15.1.1   Presence

Subject to the effect of the Civil Jurisdiction and Judgments Act (CJJA) 1982 which has enacted the EC Convention on Jurisdiction and Enforcement of Judgments in Civil and Commercial Matters 1968 (the Brussels Convention) which has created a special regime for the jurisdiction of civil and commercial matters concerning the domiciliaries of EU member states, the English courts have jurisdiction over any defendant where a claim form has been served on him while he was in England. The Civil Procedure Rules (CPR) 1998, r. 6.2, refers to the service of a claim form:

(1)   A document may be served by any of the following methods—

    (a)   personal service, in accordance with rule 6.4;
    (b)   first class post;
    (c)   leaving the document at a place specified in rule 6.5;
    (d)   through a document exchange in accordance with the relevant practice direction;
    (e)   by a fax or other means of electronic communication in accordance with the relevant practice direction.

In the case of a partnership, a document is served personally on a partnership where partners are being sued in the name of their firm by leaving it with a partner or a person who, at the time of service, has the control or management of the partnership business at its principal place of business (CPR, r. 6.4(5)).

A claim form may be served on a defendant who is present in England no matter how short the time he remains here (*Maharanee of Baroda* v *Wildenstein* [1972] 2 QB 283), unless he was fraudulently or deliberately induced into the jurisdiction for the very purpose of serving the claim form (*Watkins* v *North American Land & Timber Co.* (1904) 20 TLR 534).

Individuals can be served if they are present in England and the same principle applies to companies. In *La Bourgogne* [1899] AC 431 Lord Halsbury said: 'They are here, and if they are here they may be served'. A company is 'here' if it registered in England. Therefore, service may be made to its registered office (s. 725, Companies Act 1985). Where a foreign company carries on business in England it may be served at its established place of business. An address will have been registered by the company with the Registrar of Companies under s. 691, Companies Act 1985.

In *South India Shipping Corp* v *The Import Export Bank of Korea* [1985] 1 Lloyd's Rep 413, CA the defendant bank was incorporated in Korea but it maintained premises in the City of London. These were not used for financial transactions with the public, but to give publicity to the Korean bank and encourage trade between the UK and Korea. The Court of Appeal held that the claim form had been properly served by the claimants and that the defendants had established a place of business in Great Britain for the purpose of service.

In all of the above cases the defendant may be served in England and providing there is due service then English courts will assume jurisdiction over him.

### 15.1.2	Submission

An absent defendant may confer jurisdiction on the English court in any of four ways:

(a)	If the defendant accepts service of an English claim form he is taken to have submitted to the jurisdiction. This might occur when he instructs his English solicitor to go on the court record and accept service on his behalf or when he unconditionally acknowledges service.

(b)	If the defendant pleads to the merits of the case he submits to the jurisdiction. This includes requesting the court to stay its proceedings, as implicit in a stay is acknowledgement that the court has jurisdiction; see *The Messianiki Tolmi* [1984] 1 Lloyd's Rep 266. Pleading to the merits is distinguished from challenging the court's jurisdiction over him; see *Re Dulles' Settlement (No. 2)* [1951] Ch 842. If the defendant combines the two and, whilst requesting the court to stay its proceedings, contests its jurisdiction, he does not submit; see *Williams & Glyn's Bank* v *Astro Dinamico* [1984] 1 WLR 438. Finally, if a defendant challenges an interim order such as a freezing injunction, he does not submit to the court's jurisdiction over the substantive case; see *Obikoya* v *Silvernorth, The Times*, 6 July 1983.

(c)   If the defendant has contracted with the claimant to submit disputes to the jurisdiction of the English court and agrees that the claim form may be deemed served on him at a place in the jurisdiction, he submits to the jurisdiction. If no place for service in the jurisdiction is identified, service out of the jurisdiction is in the court's discretion (RSC, O. 11, r. 1(d)(iv), reenacted in CPR, Sched. 1). A jurisdiction clause is different from a choice of law clause. It is only in the former that the defendant submits to the jurisdiction. In the latter, the court has a discretion to serve outside the jurisdiction (RSC, O. 11, r. 1(d)(iii), reenacted in CPR, Sched. 1).

(d)   Where a person abroad sues a person within the jurisdiction in the English courts, the claimant submits to any Part 20 claim related to the claimant's claim; see *United Bank of the Middle East* v *Clapham, The Times*, 20 July 1981.

15.2   SERVICE OUTSIDE THE JURISDICTION

The rules of RSC, O. 11, as reenacted in CPR, Sched. 1, give the court a discretion in certain specified circumstances to allow service of an English claim form on a defendant who is abroad. The court only has this discretion, first, if the claimant can show that the case falls within one of the classes of action listed in O. 11; and then only if the claimant can show that the case is a proper one for service abroad (O. 11, r. 4(2)). This requires the claimant to show that the English court is the appropriate forum to hear the action and that he has a good arguable case against the defendant.

The courts have outlined five factors which they consider important before exercising this 'exorbitant jurisdiction', as it was described in *Mackender* v *Feldia* [1967] 2 QB 590. Principles of international comity require that its exercise is not abused. The five factors are as follows:

(a)   The court should be 'exceedingly careful' before it allows the claim form to be served abroad; see *Mackender* v *Feldia AG*.

(b)   Any doubt as to the construction of the rule should be resolved in the defendant's favour.

(c)   The claimant should make full and fair disclosure in the affidavit supporting the application which is made without notice to other parties.

(d)   Leave should be refused if the case is not within the spirit of the rule, though within the letter; see *Amin Rasheed* v *Kuwait Insurance Co.* [1984] 1 AC 50.

(e)   The court should consider whether it is or is not a convenient forum; see *Spiliada Maritime Corporation* v *Cansulex Ltd* [1987] AC 460.

The court will be reluctant to allow service out of the jurisdiction where the defendant has already submitted to the jurisdiction of a foreign tribunal, for instance, by an exclusive jurisdiction clause in the contract in question; see *Mackender* v *Feldia*.

This is not an absolute rule for the court may, in exceptional circumstances, grant leave to serve out of the jurisdiction despite an agreement between the parties to refer their disputes to a foreign court. In *Evans Marshall* v *Bertola SA* [1973] 1 WLR 349 an agreement for the shipment of sherry from Spain to England gave the Spanish courts jurisdiction to determine any disputes arising out of the contract. The claimants were the sole English agents for the sale of that particular sherry when the Spanish defendants broke the agreement. The claimants issued a claim form and sought leave to serve it outside the jurisdiction. Leave was granted despite the jurisdiction clause because many of the factors were connected with England, including the fact that all the witnesses were English, the claim was based substantially in England, and the Spanish procedure was slow in comparison.

Whether or not leave should be granted is essentially a matter for the discretion of the trial judge, and the appellate court will be slow to interfere with it; see *Amin Rasheed* v *Kuwait Insurance*.

A few of the more important heads of action in RSC, O. 11, r. 1(1), as reenacted in CPR Sched. 1, are set out below, though any particular case may fall under a number of different heads.

15.2.1   Domicile: r. 1(1)(a)

The court has jurisdiction when relief is sought against a person domiciled within the jurisdiction even though he is in fact abroad. Domicile is to be determined in accordance with the provisions of sections 41 to 46 of the Civil Jurisdiction and Judgments Act 1982 (O. 11, r. 1(4)).

In order to decide whether a party is domiciled in the United Kingdom, an English court must apply English law. If he is not so domiciled, to find if he is domiciled in another member state of the EU, the court must apply that state's law. Obviously, the defendant would suggest the state in which he considers himself domiciled, and the English court would consider the question as if sitting as a court of the state in question. So if the defendant suggests that he is domiciled in Germany, the English court will apply the German law as to domicile to the defendant. If he is domiciled in Germany according to German law, then the English court should *prima facie* relinquish jurisdiction to the German court and refuse to grant leave to serve outside the jurisdiction if O. 11, r. 1(a) were the only basis upon which jurisdiction could be founded. If he is not domiciled in that state, or is alleged to be domiciled in a non-member state, the court must apply English law to determine his domicile.

An individual is domiciled in the United Kingdom if he is both resident in and has a substantial connection with it. In the absence of proof to the contrary, residence for three months is presumed to be a substantial connection (s. 41(2), (3), (4), CJJA 1982). According, to English law a person is only resident in a non-member state if he is both resident there and has a substantial connection with the state. There is no presumption in favour of a substantial connection arising from a specified period of residence (s. 41(7)). A company, corporation or association's domicile is at its seat. Section 42(3), CJJA 1982 provides that its seat is in the United Kingdom if either (1) it was incorporated or formed under the law of a part of the UK and has its registered office or some other official address there; or (2) its central management or control is exercised in the UK. If the company, etc, does not have its seat in the UK, then the same rules are applied to determine where its seat is. However, it does not have its seat in a contracting state if the law of that state determines that it does not have its seat there.

15.2.2 Injunctions: r. 1(1)(b)

Where an injunction is sought ordering the defendant to do or refrain from doing anything within the jurisdiction, regardless of whether damages are also sought in respect of the act or omission, the English court has power to grant leave for service outside the jurisdiction. The injunction must be the genuine relief sought and not just a means of enabling the English court to assume jurisdiction; see *Rosler* v *Hilbery* [1925] Ch 250.

A claim for an interim injunction, such as a freezing injunction to restrain the defendant from dealing with his assets in the jurisdiction, is not sufficient ground for the court to assume jurisdiction under this head when the defendant is domiciled in a non-contracting state to the Brussels Convention; see *The Siskina* [1979] AC 213. Sections 24 and 25, CJJA 1982 have modified this rule in respect of the domiciliaries of contracting states, giving the court power to grant this type of interim relief even though the jurisdiction of the case is in another contracting state; see *X* v *Y and Y Establishment* [1990] 1 QB 220 in which a freezing injunction was ordered in respect of assets within the jurisdiction against a defendant to an action in the French courts.

15.2.3 Necessary and Proper Party: r. 1(1)(c)

The English courts may grant leave for service outside the jurisdiction where the claim is brought against a person duly served within or out of the jurisdiction and a person out of the jurisdiction is a necessary or proper party to the action. A typical case would be where the claimant wishes to sue joint tortfeasors, or where he has different claims against two defendants arising out of the same transaction, one of whom has been validly served and the other not.

If the claim against the party served is bound to fail, leave will be refused; see *Witted* v *Calbraith* [1893] 1 QB 577.

If the defendant properly served could be liable to the claimant, then his probable inability to satisfy any judgment against him is no reason to refuse granting leave against a necessary or proper party; see *Multinational Gas* v *Multinational Gas Services* [1983] Ch 258. However, if it is clear that the claimant's only motive for serving the defendant in the jurisdiction or under O. 11 is to gain leave to serve the party otherwise outside, O. 11 leave will be refused. If there is no purpose in suing the defendant outside the jurisdiction since full recovery is possible from the defendant already served, leave may be refused; see *Rosler* v *Hilbery* [1925] Ch 250.

The defendant outside the jurisdiction is neither a necessary nor a proper party to the action against the defendant served if he has a clear defence to the claim; see *Multinational Gas*.

15.2.4   Contract: r. 1(1)(d) and (e)

There are five different and alternative heads relating to an action on a contract between the parties in question. The court may grant leave to serve a defendant outside the jurisdiction if the claim is brought to enforce, rescind, dissolve, annul or otherwise affect a contract, or to recover damages or obtain other relief in respect of a breach of contract:

(a)   being a contract which was made within the jurisdiction (r. 1(1)(d)(i)). The English court will apply English law to determine where the contract was made, which is, therefore, governed by the well-established rules as to offer and acceptance. The posting rule in relation to the communication of the acceptance of an offer has recently been discussed in relation to modern forms of information transfer, to the effect that the immediacy of such communication abrogates the need for the posting rule.

In *Entores* v *Miles* [1955] 2 QB 327 the claimant made an offer from England to The Netherlands by telex. The defendants in The Netherlands replied by a telex which was received in England. The posting rule was not applied, which would have meant that the contract was made in The Netherlands, where the acceptance was posted, and the court held that the contract was made in England.

In *Brinkibon* v *Stalag Stahl* [1983] 2 AC 34 the buyer was in England and the seller in Austria. The buyer made an offer to the seller by telex which the seller accepted subject to certain modifications. The seller asked the buyer to open a letter of credit confirmed by an Austrian bank. The buyer opened the credit through his London bank, and sent an advising telex to the seller. The seller then purported to withdraw from the contract. The House of Lords held that the seller's telex was not an acceptance of the buyer's offer but a counteroffer. The counteroffer was accepted by the buyer's advising telex which was received in Austria, so that the contract was made in Austria. Leave was, therefore, refused to serve the seller.

(b)   being a contract which was made by or through an agent trading or residing within the jurisdiction on behalf of a principal trading or residing out of the jurisdiction (r. 1(1)(d)(ii)).

(c)   being a contract which by its terms or by implication is governed by English law. This is a reference to the proper law of the contract (r. 1(1)(d)(iii)).

(d)   being a contract which contains a term to the effect that the High Court is to have jurisdiction to hear and determine any action in respect of the contract (r. 1(1)(d)(iv)). This is an example of submission to the jurisdiction, and if the case falls under this head, the court need not be so circumspect when granting leave; see *The Chaparral* [1968] 2 Lloyd's Rep 158.

The court may grant leave to serve out of the jurisdiction where:

(e) the claim is brought in respect of a breach committed within the jurisdiction of a contract made within or out of the jurisdiction and irrespective of the fact, if such be the case, that the breach was preceded or accompanied by a breach committed out of the jurisdiction that rendered impossible the performance of so much of the contract as ought to have been performed within the jurisdiction (r. 1(1)(e)).

The claimant seeking leave must prove a *prima facie* or good arguable case of such breach. For example, since it is the rule at law that where no place of payment is provided by the terms of the contract, it is the duty of the debtor to seek out his creditor at his residence or place of business, the failure to pay money due under the contract to a claimant residing within the jurisdiction falls within the discretion; see *Thompson* v *Palmer* [1893] 2 QB 80. On the other hand if there is no obligation which had to be performed within the jurisdiction, no breach can be committed within the jurisdiction; see *Cuban Atlantic Sugar Sales* v *Compania de Vapores* [1960] 1 QB 187. Where a contract is made by a defendant in country A to employ the claimant as his representative in country B and the defendant wrongfully dismisses the claimant by a letter posted in country A, the breach takes place there; see *Holland* v *Bennett* [1902] 1 KB 867.

The words 'irrespective ... of a breach was preceded ... by a breach committed out of the jurisdiction' etc. were added in view of *Johnson* v *Taylor* [1920] AC 144 where it was decided by the House of Lords that the previous form of the sub-paragraph did not apply to breaches in the jurisdiction which were subsidiary to the substantial breach abroad, rendering the breach within the jurisdiction inevitable.

15.2.5 Tort: r. 1(1)(f)

The court has power to grant leave to serve abroad where the claim is founded on a tort and the damage was sustained, or resulted from an act committed within the jurisdiction.

In *Metall & Rohstoff AG* v *Donaldson Lufkin & Jenrette Inc* [1990] 1 QB 391 the Court of Appeal considered a number of procedural and substantive issues in an application for leave to serve a claim form out of the jurisdiction in an action based on tort. The simplified facts were that M & R, a Swiss company, traded on the London Metal Exchange through brokers, AML, a subsidiary of the US defendants, DLJ. An employee of M & R traded fraudulently with M & R's property for his own behalf. AML and DLJ, the defendants, knew of this. They, however, charged the losses made by the employee to M & R's accounts, closed those accounts and seized property belonging to M & R. M & R obtained judgment against AML but this remained largely unsatisfied. M & R, therefore, began the present proceedings against DLJ, AML's parent, to recover their losses. Several causes of action were pleaded: conspiracy, inducing breach of contract, abuse of the process of the court, accounting as constructive trustees and procuring breaches of trust. Since DLJ was in the US, leave to serve the claim form outside the jurisdiction under O. 11, r. 1(1)(f) had to be obtained. The first issue was procedural. The general rule as to statements of cases laid down by Lord Denning MR in *Re Vandervell's Trusts (No. 2)* [1974] Ch

269 at p. 321 that parties need only plead material facts from which legal results can be deduced, does not apply in O. 11 proceedings. The pleader is limited to the specific legal basis stated. The court must be clear that there is a good arguable case before giving leave. This can only be assessed on the statements of case. Parties should not thereafter be at liberty to alter the nature of their case. This would circumvent the strict procedure and intention of Parliament. Secondly, the Court of Appeal considered the situations in which English courts would have jurisdiction in actions in tort. This would be in two situations: (1) when damage was sustained within the jurisdiction or (2) the act causing damage was committed in England. These two rules had to be expanded to cover more complicated situations: (i) where damage occurred in more than one jurisdiction, English courts would assume jurisdiction if significant damage had been suffered here or (ii) where the tort consisted of acts done in more than one jurisdiction where substantial acts had been committed in England. In all four situations, English courts had first to consider whether torts had been committed according to English law. If so, and the case were one in which acts had been committed in England ((2) and (ii)), the court would assume jurisdiction; however, where the tort was in substance committed abroad but damage suffered in the jurisdiction ((1) and (i)) the court had to go on to test whether the acts were actionable as a tort in the foreign jurisdiction — the double actionability rule in *Boys* v *Chaplin* [1971] AC 356. Thirdly, under the head of inducing breach of contract, the court found that this had been committed in substance in England, where the damage was suffered. The acts inducing breach were committed in the USA, but the actual breaches of contract were committed in England. It was the latter which caused loss to M & R. The double actionability rule did not apply. The claim fell within O. 11, r. 1(1)(f). As to the claim based on conspiracy, it was held to be inadequately pleaded, following *Lonrho Ltd* v *Shell Petroleum Co. Ltd (No 2)* [1982] AC 173. Conspiracy alone was not actionable. The conspirators' sole or predominant purpose to injure the claimants had to be pleaded (and proved at the substantive trial). M & R had omitted this element from their statements of case. Tortious abuse of the process of the court requires proof that the defendants' predominant purpose in bringing an action was for some other purpose than that for which the action was designed. Mere use of false evidence and presenting a false case was insufficient. This head was, therefore, not available to M & R. English law does not recognise claims founded on a constructive trust or procuring breach of trust as tortious for the purposes of O. 11, r. 1(1)(f). Leave to serve DLJ outside the jurisdiction under O. 11, r. 1(1)(f) was, therefore, given on the basis of procuring breach of contract.

15.3 STAY OF ACTIONS AND RESTRAINT OF FOREIGN PROCEEDINGS

The court has a power both inherent in its jurisdiction and contained in s. 49(3), Supreme Court Act 1981 to stay an action which is frivolous, vexatious or an abuse of the process of the court.

The court also has the power to restrain by injunction persons subject to its jurisdiction from instituting or continuing proceedings in foreign courts.

15.3.1 The Staying of English Proceedings

After much uncertainty and intransigence, the House of Lords has expressly applied the principle of *forum non conveniens*, always the doctrine applied under O. 11, to applications by defendants to stay English proceedings in the light of existing or contemplated proceedings abroad.

In *Spiliada Maritime* v *Cansulex Ltd* [1987] AC 460 Lord Goff, with whom the House agreed, laid down strictly in obiter dicta (the case was an O. 11 application for service abroad) that the principle of *forum non conveniens* applies in the same way to applications to serve out of the jurisdiction and to stay English proceedings brought as of right, other than the distinction in the incidence of the burden of proof in the respective applications. Lord Goff set out the guidelines courts should follow, and thereby defined the doctrine of *forum non conveniens*. The guidelines are:

(a)   The court will only grant a stay if it is satisfied that there is another court having competent jurisdiction, which is the appropriate forum for the trial of the action, i.e. in which the case may be tried more suitably for the interests of all the parties and the ends of justice.

(b)   The burden of proof rests on the defendant to persuade the court to exercise its discretion to grant a stay. However, any particular matter raised by any party must be proved by that party.

(c)   The defendant must show not merely that the English courts are not an appropriate forum in which the case can be tried, but he must satisfy the court that there is another forum which is clearly more appropriate. Otherwise, if the claimant has founded jurisdiction in the English court as of right, this must not be disturbed simply because the defendant may be caused difficulties.

(d)   When considering the question whether there is another natural forum for the dispute, the court will look for connecting factors which indicate that the action has its most real and substantial connection with another forum. Such factors include the convenience or expense of the case (such as the availability of witnesses), which law governs the transaction in question, and the place where the parties respectively reside or carry on business.

(e)   If the court concludes at this stage that there is no other available forum which is clearly more appropriate for the trial of the action, it will ordinarily refuse a stay.

(f)   If, however, the court concludes at that stage that there is some other available forum which prima facie is clearly more appropriate for the trial of the action, it will ordinarily grant a stay unless there are circumstances by reason of which justice requires that a stay should not be granted. In this inquiry the court will consider all the circumstances of the case, including circumstances which go beyond those taken into account when considering connecting factors with other jurisdictions, for example, if the claimant can establish by objective and cogent evidence that he will not obtain justice in the foreign jurisdiction. On this inquiry the burden clearly shifts to the claimant.

Spiliada has been considered, slightly reformulated, but in essence applied in two later cases coming from Commonwealth Courts of Appeal.

In *The Waylink* [1988] 1 Lloyd's Rep 475 there had been a collision between two ships in a West German river. At first instance in the Gibraltarian courts a stay had been refused because it was found that there was no more than a balance of convenience in favour of Germany and this was outweighed by the disadvantage which would be suffered by the claimants by the loss of the Gibraltarian disclosure procedures.

The Gibraltarian Court of Appeal overruled this on two counts. First, they found that Germany was clearly the more appropriate forum. The only connection with Gibraltar was that one ship was owned and managed by Gibraltarian companies, who were defendants in the action. On the other hand, all the evidence relating to the collision was in Germany where surveys were carried out and one ship was repaired. Also there was a *lis alibi pendens* in Germany. Secondly, the Court of Appeal held that the loss of the Gibraltarian disclosure procedures would not cause injustice to the claimants.

In *The Adhiguna Meranti* [1988] I Lloyd's Rep 384 the defendants' ship had run aground while carrying the claimants' cargo. The first instance judge in Hong Kong found that the case could most appropriately be heard in Indonesia. *Inter alia*, the vessel, the defendants and some of the claimants were Indonesian; the crew were resident there, and most of the witnesses and documents were there. He granted a stay. The claimants appealed to the Hong Kong Court of Appeal. They claimed a number of advantages in Hong Kong. The most important was that the limit of liability was likely to be significantly lower in Indonesia. This was found to be a substantial and legitimate advantage as a result of which it would be 'unjust to confine the claimants' to their remedies in Indonesia. The stay was refused. The Court of Appeal in Hong Kong thought that although the connection with Hong Kong was tenuous, the limit under Hong Kong law reflected international public policy whereas under Indonesian law the limit was, at best, uncertain and, at worst, derisory.

Both cases followed *Spiliada*. However, they formulated the principles slightly differently. The Gibraltarian court formulated *Spiliada* as laying down a structured two-part test as follows:

A stay will be granted where:
(a)   the defendants can show that there is another forum which is the appropriate forum for the trial of the action, i.e. in which the case may be tried more suitably for the interests of all parties and the ends of justice, unless;
(b)   the plaintiff [claimant] can show that he will not obtain justice in the foreign jurisdiction.

The Hong Kong court formulated a three-part test which emphasised the general thrust behind *Spiliada* that the deprivation of an advantage becomes relevant if it can be shown that, bearing in mind that there is a more appropriate foreign forum, this deprivation will result in injustice being done as between the parties. In *The Waylink*

the loss of Gibraltarian disclosure procedures would not result in such injustice. In *The Adhiguna Meranti* the loss of the higher limit under Hong Kong law would cause injustice.

It would seem that where the two fora in question both comply with what are perceived as international standards of justice, there should be no comparison of the particular idiosyncrasies of each, and the more appropriate forum should hear the case.

The effect of *Spiliada* is, then, expressly to introduce the doctrine of *forum non conveniens* as the guiding rule in such cases and to attach less weight to the deprivation of an advantage to one or the other party. This will only affect the case if the deprivation is such as to deny justice between the parties, rather than merely to make things a little less certain for one or the other.

It does not seem that the enquiry is any different when there is already litigation between the same parties abroad when the English court is seised of the dispute; see the observations of the House of Lords in *The Abidin Daver* [1984] AC 398 which applied the doctrine of *forum non conveniens* in all but name to such a situation. Such a '*lis alibi pendens*' can take two forms: (1) where the claimant sues the defendant both abroad and in England; and (2) where the claimant sues the defendant here, and the defendant is suing the claimant abroad in a related action.

Where, however, proceedings have also been commenced in another jurisdiction special considerations apply; see *The Hagen* [1908] P 189. If those proceedings are well advanced and the parties have already incurred substantial costs then the court will normally grant a stay of the English proceedings; see *Cleveland Museum of Art v Capricorn Art International SA* (1989) 5 BCC 860. The courts will generally attempt to avoid a duplicity of proceedings with the attendant increase in costs and a claimant who commences proceedings in another jurisdiction in respect of the same subject matter will be required to elect which proceedings he wishes to proceed with; see *Australian Commercial Research & Development Ltd v ANZ McCaughan Merchant Bank Ltd* [1989] 3 All ER 65.

In *Ionian Bank v Couvreur* [1969] 1 WLR 781 the claimant succeeded before the French courts in obtaining security over the defendant's assets in France on the defendant's guarantee of a loan by the claimant to the defendant's French company. The claimant then sued the defendant again in England on the same guarantee. The defendant applied for the English court to stay its proceedings. He failed. The court's reasoning was based on the findings that the claimant could obtain judgment more quickly in England and that there were more assets here upon which he could levy execution.

In *The Abidin Daver* [1984] AC 398 a Cuban vessel was in collision with a Turkish vessel in the Bosporus within Turkish waters. An action was started by the Turkish owners in the Turkish courts. The Cuban owners began an action *in rem* in the English Admiralty Court. The Turkish owners applied for a stay of the English action. The House of Lords reversed the decision of the Court of Appeal, and restored the decision of the judge at first instance that a stay should be granted. The Turkish court was clearly established by the Turkish defendants as the natural and more appropriate forum. The Cuban claimant failed to adduce cogent evidence that he might not be accorded justice in the Turkish court or that he could, if a stay were granted, be deprived of a personal or juridical advantage such that it would be unjust to grant the stay.

Special considerations also apply where the parties have agreed to refer their disputes to the courts of a foreign jurisdiction. In such a case the English court will normally enforce the agreement if requested; see *Mackender* v *Feldia AG* [1967] 2 QB 590. The claimant in such a case therefore bears the burden of showing why the case should continue in the English courts in breach of his contractual arrangements.

Brandon J in *The Eleftheria* [1970] P 94 explained the principles to be applied and the factors to be considered. The action involved the carriage of goods by sea from Romania to Hull. A clause of the contract referred disputes to the courts of the state where the carrier carried on business. The carrier was Greek and carried on business in Greece. The vessel was arrested at Hull. The defendant applied for a stay of the English proceedings. Brandon J said that although all the circumstances should be taken into consideration, those of importance were:

(a) In what country the evidence may be most conveniently and cheaply collected.

(b) Whether the foreign law applies and, if so, whether it differs from English law in any significant respect.

(c) The closeness of the connection of either party to the foreign jurisdiction.

(d) Whether the defendants genuinely desire to proceed abroad or are doing so merely to gain procedural advantages there.

(e) Whether the claimants would be prejudiced by the proceedings abroad because they would be deprived of security for claims; or be unable to enforce a judgment obtained there; or be faced with a time-bar not applicable in England; or be unable to get a fair trial for political, racial, religious or other reasons.

Brandon J applied the above tests and held that the English action should be stayed; most of the evidence was in England, but more importantly Greek law differed from English law in material respects. Other cases to consider are: *The Kislovodsk* [1980] 1 Lloyd's Rep 565; *The Biskra* [1983] 2 Lloyd's Rep 59 and *Trendtex Trading Corporation* v *Credit Suisse* [1982] AC 679.

The rules set down by the House of Lords in *Spiliada* were applied by Sheen J in *The Irishva Ajay* [1989] 2 Lloyd's Rep 558. The foreign forum in question was India. Sheen J found that each party would bear a large part of his costs under Indian procedure. It was, therefore, advantageous to both parties that the action be tried in England: it would be unfair to deprive the claimant of the benefit of any award, that award likely to be lost in costs; the defendant might be deterred from pursuing the action if afraid of the High Court costs, and this might lead him to accept a disadvantageous out-of-court settlement.

Where a claimant starts an action in the English courts pursuant to a clause of contract submitting to the courts here, the court will not accede to the defendant's request to stay the action.

15.3.2   Restraining Foreign Proceedings

The Privy Council considered the question of when the English courts will exercise their discretion to restrain a party in the jurisdiction from commencing or continuing proceedings abroad in *SNI Aerospatial* v *Lee Kui Jak* [1987] AC 87. The court's advice was again given by Lord Goff. The Privy Council held that the principle of *forum non conveniens* did not apply on the grounds of comity between nations. Hence the original rule before *The Abidin Daver* and *Spiliada* (see 15.3.1) as explained in *Mackshannon* v *Rockware Glass* [1977] 1 WLR 376 was held to apply to such cases. An injunction of the foreign proceedings would only be ordered if their pursuit was vexatious or oppressive. The exorbitance of this exercise of discretion means that the English courts use it only in the most meritorious cases.

Applications in effect to stay the foreign proceedings by restraining a party within the jurisdiction from continuing the foreign action may occur in either of the two types of *lis alibi pendens* described in 15.3.1. *SNI Aerospatial* was *lis alibi pendens* as was the earlier decision of *Castanho* v *Brown and Root* [1981] AC 557. The claimant was a Portuguese employed on the second defendants' Panamanian ship. He suffered injuries on board when the ship was in English waters. He started an action in England against the first defendants, a UK company, and the second defendants for damages. He was then advised to commence a second action in the USA since his advisers had discovered that both defendants were members of a group of Texan companies. Higher damages could be obtained in the US courts where they were decided by juries. The second defendants had already admitted liability and made an interim payment. An injunction to restrain continuance of the Texas proceedings was refused by both the Court of Appeal and the House of Lords. Lord Scarman stated the principle as outlined above and that the Texas court was as much a natural forum as the English court. In addition, the claimant had the legitimate personal advantage that damages might be higher in the US proceedings.

The English courts prefer to hold parties to their contractual obligations and, therefore, would not restrain an action abroad if brought pursuant to a jurisdiction clause properly effected. On the other hand, where the foreign proceedings are commenced in the face of a clause of the contract submitting to the jurisdiction of the English courts, the court will be more likely to stay the foreign proceedings than it will be if no such clause exists. However, examples are rare. In *Tracomin SA* v *Sudan Oil Seeds Ltd* (No. 2) [1983] 1 WLR 1026 the Court of Appeal granted an injunction to restrain further Swiss proceedings between Swiss buyers and Sudanese sellers when the buyers had sued the sellers to judgment in the Swiss courts in violation of an English arbitration clause. However, the Court of Appeal led by Lord Denning MR in *The Lisboa* [1980] 2 Lloyd's Rep 546 adopted a different course.

Where no action has been brought in the English courts and the parties have not submitted to their jurisdiction, there is little reason for the English courts to restrain the foreign proceedings. This is even more the case when the action in the foreign court proceeds on a cause of action not known to the English courts. In *British Airways Board* v *Laker Airways* [1985] AC 58 Laker Airways had collapsed and gone into liquidation in 1982. The British liquidator commenced proceedings in the US under the US Anti-Trust laws, alleging that two British airlines had conspired with other airlines and aircraft manufacturers to bring about the collapse of Laker. If the British liquidator won he would be entitled to treble damages. The two airlines applied to the English court to restrain the liquidator from the US action, arguing that it would be unjust to them and contrary to public policy for it to continue. In 1980 the Secretary of State made an Order and general directions under the Protection of Trading Interests Act 1980 prohibiting the UK airlines from complying with any requirement or prohibition under the US Anti-Trust Acts. Parker J at first instance had decided before the Secretary of State's Order that no injunction should be granted as the anti-trust action was only available in the US, and, therefore, it would be unjust to the claimant to restrain him from proceeding in that action. The Court of Appeal considered the case after the Order had been given, and thought that it made all the difference by rendering a proper trial in the US impossible. The House of Lords reversed this decision on the ground that since the airlines were seeking an injunction they had to show some pre-existing cause of action for which an injunction would be a realistic remedy, or some legal or equitable right arising out of a contract, e.g. an English jurisdiction clause, or from the other party's unconscionable conduct, not to be sued in the foreign court on the foreign cause of action. There was no such cause of action or right.

The *SNI Aerospatial* test was used by the Court of Appeal in a *lis alibi pendens* case; see *Sohio Supply Co.* v *Gatoil* (USA) Inc [1989] 1 Lloyd's Rep 588. Under an f.o.b. contract for Brent crude oil, the buyer was required to open a letter of credit in favour of the seller by a certain date. The buyer failed to do so. The seller treated this as repudiatory and refused to load the goods. The buyer brought an action in Texas. At the same time, the seller brought an action in the English courts — the contract was expressed to be governed by English law. The seller applied to the English courts for leave to serve out of the jurisdiction under RSC O. 11 (preserved in CPR Sched. 1). The Court of Appeal found that there was an arguable case on construction of the contract that the letter of credit had been opened by the buyer out of time. This was sufficient to grant leave. The court also issued an injunction preventing the buyer from pursuing the Texan action. Although there had been delay on the part of the seller in bringing his action, this had not prejudiced the buyer or the justice of the case. The Texan action was declaratory only, clearly brought by buyers when apprehensive of an action in the English courts. Following statements by the House of Lords in *Spiliada*, such actions are to be discouraged. It was also undesirable that there should be two actions on the same issue.

The exceptional nature of injunctive relief with extraterritorial effect was stressed once again by Steyn J in *E D & F Man (Sugar) Ltd* v *Haryanto (No. 2)* [1991] 1 Lloyd's Rep 161. Haryanto had disputed in the English courts the validity of a contract, the express proper law of which was English law, and under which he had allegedly purchased sugar from Man for despatch to Indonesia. He had not raised the question of the legality of the contract under public policy considerations. His action had been rejected at first instance and on appeal in *Man* v *Haryanto (No. 1)*. Subsequently, Haryanto had brought proceedings in the Indonesian courts on the contracts where he had raised a public policy issue and succeeded. In the instant case, he sought declaratory relief that the disputed contracts were unenforceable and/or void, being illegal or contrary to English public policy. On the main issue, the public policy point, Steyn J held that the issue was *res judicata* since it could have been raised in the earlier English proceedings on the same contract between the same parties. The fact that an Indonesian court ruling had intervened in the meantime to the contrary was irrelevant.

Man brought a Part 20 claim for injunctive relief to prevent Haryanto from bringing similar proceedings to enforce the Indonesian judgment in any other jurisdiction world-wide. Steyn J rejected this claim since:

> Injunctive relief with extraterritorial effect ... must be an exceptional remedy. It ought only to be granted in exceptional circumstances. It is, after all, inconsistent with normal relations between friendly sovereign states, and it is subversive of the best interests of the international trade system ... it would be an affront to the Indonesian courts and an illegitimate interference ... with the processes of courts world-wide to grant an injunction.

Steyn J thought it better to leave it to each jurisdiction to consider for itself whether to enforce the Indonesian judgment.

15.4 JURISDICTION IN THE EUROPEAN UNION

The Civil Jurisdiction and Judgments Act 1982, enacting the Brussels Convention 1968, has imposed a new statutory regime for jurisdiction in civil and commercial disputes between persons domiciled within the EU member states. Furthermore the provisions of the CJJA 1982 have recently been adopted with regard to countries who are members of the European Free Trade Association (EFTA). The Lugano Convention was signed by the United Kingdom in September 1989 and applies the same system for establishing jurisdiction with regard to members of EFTA as is applied to members of the EU. The Civil Jurisdiction and Judgments Act 1991 made the necessary amendments to the CJJA 1982 and the Lugano Convention came into force in May 1992. The Lugano Convention is found in Schedule 3C to the CJJA 1982 and the Brussels Convention in Schedule I. The provisions are, however, largely identical and references in this chapter are to the Brussels Convention.

Articles 2 to 23 of the Brussels Convention set out the regime for jurisdiction. It should be noted that matters relating to arbitration do not fall within the ambit of the Brussels Convention (Art. 1(4)); see *Marc Rich & Co. AG* v *Societa Italiana Impianti PA, The Atlantic Emperor* [1992] 1 Lloyd's Rep 342. The basic principle is that persons domiciled in a contracting state, whatever their nationality, must be sued in the courts of that state alone. The domicile and nationality of the claimant is irrelevant (Art. 2).

There are two exceptions to the general rule. It is excluded where some other court has exclusive jurisdiction as defined by Art. 16, and also where the defendant is a party to a contractual agreement to submit to another jurisdiction (Art. 17). The principle whereby English courts assume jurisdiction on the basis of casual presence is expressly suppressed as against persons domiciled in other EU states.

The meaning of domicile for the purposes of the Convention has been explained above at 15.2.1. Briefly the test the English court should adopt is as follows:

(a)   Applying English law, is the defendant domiciled in the UK? This requires in the case of an individual both residence and a substantial connection (presumed by residence for three months) and in the case of a corporation or association the place of its seat.

(b)   If not, then the court must test whether the defendant is a domiciliary of a contracting state by applying the laws of that state. In deciding which states to consider, the court will be guided by the representations of counsel.

(c)   If the defendant proves not to be a domiciliary of a contracting state, the court will then apply English law to ascertain his domicile.

15.4.1   Special Jurisdiction under Arts. 5 and 6

In addition to being liable to be sued in the country in which he is domiciled, a person domiciled in a member state may also be sued in another state in certain specified cases. If the claimant sues the defendant in that other state, the jurisdiction of the courts of the defendant's domicile is ousted. There are eleven cases of such special or concurrent jurisdiction. The ones relevant for present purposes are as follows:

(a)   *Contract, the place of performance of the obligation* (Art. 5(1)). Art. 5(1) was recently considered by the House of Lords in *Union Transport Group plc* v *Continental Lines SA* [1992] 1 Lloyd's Rep 229 which concerned a breach of a nomination clause in a charterparty where the principal and subsidiary obligations were to be performed in different countries. The respondent charterers agreed a fixture with the appellant shipowners, domiciled in Belgium, in London by telex, fax and telephone exchanges for the charter of a vessel of suitable tonnage to be nominated by the appellants for the carriage of a cargo of telegraph poles from Florida to Bangladesh. The appellants subsequently intimated that, because of a dispute between the parties, they were no longer interested in lifting the cargo. The respondents commenced arbitration proceedings but the appellants denied the existence of a valid contract between the parties. The respondents therefore decided to bring proceedings against the appellants in the Commercial Court and served a writ out of the jurisdiction, claiming damages for breach of the charterparty by the appellants in failing to nominate or provide a vessel at the loading port in Florida as agreed. The respondents contended that the place for performance of the obligation to nominate a vessel was London and that, therefore, the appellants could be sued in England by virtue of Art. 5(1) of the Brussels Convention which provided that persons domiciled in a contracting state could be sued in the courts of another contracting state in matters relating to a contract if that was the place of performance of the obligation in question. The appellants applied to set aside the writ and service on the grounds that the court lacked jurisdiction, contending that the respondents could not found jurisdiction in England under Art. 5(1) because the obligation to provide a vessel was to be performed in Florida and not England. The judge dismissed the application to set aside, on the ground that the principal obligation of the contract was the nomination of the vessel which was to be performed in London and, accordingly, the English courts had jurisdiction under Art. 5(1). On appeal by the appellants the Court of Appeal affirmed the judge's decision. The appellants appealed to the House of Lords.

It was held by Lord Justice Goff applying the principle of European law that where there was a dispute concerned with a number of obligations arising under the same contract and forming the basis of the proceedings commenced by the claimant, jurisdiction under Art. 5(1) of the 1968 Convention was to be determined by the principal obligation under the contract. Under a tonnage to be nominated, it was the charterer's obligation to nominate a vessel of suitable tonnage, not to proceed to the loading port, since nomination of a vessel was not a mere naming of a vessel but was necessary to identify the subject matter of the contract and was an essential prerequisite to the performance of other obligations under the contract. The effect of nomination of the vessel was that the name of the vessel then became written into the contract. Since the obligation to nominate was to be performed in London the respondents had established jurisdiction in England. Accordingly, the writ and its service were valid and the appeal was, therefore, dismissed.

(b) *Tort, the place where the harmful event occurred* (Art. 5(3)). This has been interpreted as giving the claimant the option of proceeding either in the courts where the wrongful act or omission occurred or where the damage was suffered; see *Bier BV* v *Mines de Potasse d'Alsace SA* [1976] EUR 1735.

(c) *A claim arising out of the running of a branch or agency* or other establishment, the place where that is situated (Art. 5(5)).

(d) *Trust*, where the trust is domiciled (Art. 5(6)).

(e) *Salvage claims*, where the cargo or freight is arrested (Art. 5(7)).

(f) *Over co-defendants*, the court of the domicile of one of the defendants (Art. 6(1)).

(g) *Where a third party is sued* in an action on a warranty or guarantee or other third party proceedings, the court which is seised of the original proceedings (Art. 6(2)).

(h)   *Part 20 claims*, the court where the original claim was brought (Art. 6(3)).

(i)   *Limitation of liability actions* in the case of ships, the court having jurisdiction in an action relating to liability arising from the use or operation of the ship (Art. 6(A)).

There are also special provisions in the case of *insurance contracts* (Arts. 7–12) and *consumer contracts* (Arts. 13–15).

15.4.2   Exclusive Jurisdiction under Art. 16

When courts have exclusive jurisdiction under Art. 16 of the Brussels Convention, such jurisdiction cannot be ousted by agreement or submission or the courts of another state. There are five types of dispute in which the courts have exclusive jurisdiction:

(a)   Proceedings which have as their object rights *in rem* or tenancies of immovable property: the courts of the *situs* of the property.

(b)   A company: in proceedings concerning the validity of its constitution, its nullity, or dissolution or decisions concerning its organs: the courts of the state where it has its seat.

(c)   Proceedings in relation to entries in a register: the courts of the place where the register is kept.

(d)   Industrial property, the registration or validity of patents, trade marks, or designs, or other such interests: the courts of the place where their deposit or registration has been applied for or has taken place.

(e)   Enforcement of judgments: the courts of the state where the judgment is to be or has been enforced.

15.4.3   Submission under Arts. 17 and 18

There are two forms of submission considered by the Convention: (1) contractual submission, called 'prorogated submission'; and (2) submission by appearance.

15.4.3.1   Contractual Submission

By Art. 17 a contractual agreement to submit disputes to the jurisdiction of a particular court or courts will oust the jurisdiction of all other courts except in cases of exclusive jurisdiction under Art. 16. The agreement must either be in or be evidenced in writing or, in international trade or commerce, in a form which accords with practices in that trade or commerce of which the parties are or ought to have been aware. If the agreement was entered into for the benefit of one party, the other may invoke the jurisdiction of any other competent court. However, national law cannot invalidate an agreement which is otherwise effective by virtue of Art. 17.

15.4.3.2   Submission by Appearance

A defendant who enters an appearance before a court of a member state which is not otherwise entitled to exercise jurisdiction thereby confers jurisdiction on it, unless another state's courts have exclusive jurisdiction under Art. 16. An appearance merely to contest the jurisdiction is not a submission.

15.4.4   Refusal of Jurisdiction and Staying of Proceedings

If the courts of one member state have exclusive jurisdiction, those of other states must decline it of their own motion (Art. 19). Similarly, courts other than those of the defendant's domicile must decline jurisdiction unless the defendant submits or they have exclusive or special jurisdiction.

If proceedings between the same parties which arise from the same cause of action are brought in the courts of more than one state, the court first seised has jurisdiction to the exclusion of all others, but if the jurisdiction of the first court is disputed, other courts need only stay proceedings before them pending the resolution of the dispute (Art. 21). If several courts have exclusive jurisdiction, the courts other than the court first seised must decline it (Art. 23). If related actions as defined by the Convention are brought in different courts, the courts other than the court first seised may stay the actions before them pending the outcome of the first action (Art. 22).

As will be seen at 15.6 below, the courts of any member state may be asked to grant interim protective or provisional measures such as freezing injunctions and disclosure orders even if the courts of another jurisdiction have been properly seised of the case (Art. 24). The action in the member state is sufficient cause of action for the grant of injunctions; see *X* v *Y Establishment* [1990] 1 QB 220.

The Po [1990] 1 Lloyd's Rep 418 involved an application of the rules on stay of action under the 1968 Brussels Convention and the CJJA 1982. There was a collision in Brazilian waters between *The Po*, an Italian merchant ship, and *The Bowater*, a US owned vessel. Neither ship was being navigated by a local pilot. *The Bowater* brought an action *in rem* against *The Po*. The writ was served on *The Po* whilst in Southampton. *The Po* applied for a stay of the English action on two grounds: (1) Brazil was the more convenient forum; (2) the UK court had no jurisdiction under the CJJA 1982 and the 1968 Brussels Convention. It was argued for *The Po* that the case should be sent to Italy, the country of the defendant's domicile. In answer to (2) it was argued for *The Bowater* that the Convention did not apply to collisions and also that *The Po* could not rely on the International Convention for Unification of Certain Rules in matters of Collision (the Collision Convention) since the rules had not been fully incorporated into English law by English legislation. Sheen J held, first, that the Collision Convention did not need total incorporation by statute for effect in English law since the Administration of Justice Act 1956 had recognised that some of the rules were already part of English law. Secondly he held that the Brussels Convention did not apply since that Convention expressly provided that other conventions would have precedence. Both Italy and UK were signatories of the Collision Convention. The latter, therefore, would apply. Finally, following *The*

Deichland [1990] 1 QB 361 he held that the English courts had jurisdiction under the Collision Convention rule of the place of arrest of the ship. He refused to grant a stay of the English action, applying the rules in *Spiliada* (**15.3.1**). The action was to be between US and Italian shipowners; the collision had occurred in Brazil; the majority of the documents, including the charts, were in English; the only addition to a normal English action was the presence of an Italian interpreter. The case could, therefore, be tried in the UK. There was no other available forum clearly more appropriate.

The court does not have jurisdiction to stay proceedings on the ground of *forum non conveniens* where proceedings have been raised by the claimant in one of the jurisdictions in the UK; see *Foxen v Scotsman Publications Ltd and Another, The Times*, 17 February 1994, where proceedings had been started in Scotland. Drake J was of the view that as the Convention applied uniformity of rules as between different contracting states, it was inconsistent not to apply the rules as between different parts of the UK.

15.5   PROPER LAW OF THE CONTRACT

English commercial law has been radically altered as a result of the incorporation of the Rome Convention on Law Applicable to Contracts, effected more or less wholesale by the Contracts (Applicable Law) Act 1990. The Act came into force on 1 April 1991. This section will consider, first, the existing common law, and then review the changes affected by the Convention and 1990 Act.

The proper law of the contract is the system of law by which the contract is worked out. Generally, the proper law of the contract will govern the formation of the contract and the reality of the agreement; the effect of any misrepresentation, mistake or duress alleged to affect it; its interpretation; its essential validity (meaning whether the contract or its terms are valid and effective); the discharge of the obligations of the parties under the contract; and to some extent the legality of the contract.

The question where a contract was concluded is determined for the purposes of jurisdiction by the law of the court seised; see *Entores v Miles* and *Brinkibon v Stalag Stahl* (15.2.4).

The formal validity of the contract (whether it has complied with requirements regarding the form of the contract) should in principle be governed by the proper law of the contract, particularly in commercial transactions where the place where the contract was made is often more an accident than by design. However, the governing rule is that formal validity is governed by the law of the place where the contract was made.

Capacity to contract is thought to be governed by the proper law of the contract, although there is no authoritative statement for or against this proposition. Such proper law should be ascertained by looking for the system of law with which the transaction has its closest and most real connection, ignoring any express choice of law if chosen for the purpose of giving a party capacity when otherwise this would not exist. Such a proper law is often called the putative proper law, and is generally used when attempting to ascertain whether a contract exists or not. If a contract or its performance are illegal at its inception by its (putative) proper law, it will not be enforced in England; see *Kahler* v *Midland Bank* [1950] AC 24.

Even if a contract is not illegal by its proper law, it may still be unenforceable in England by reason of its contravening some other system of law. Illegality of the contract under the law of the place of contracting is, at least in the commercial context, generally regarded as irrelevant. English courts will, however, refuse to enforce a contract which is contrary to English public policy, even though it is governed by a foreign law under which it is lawful. This includes contracts the enforcement of which is regarded as likely to imperil the relations of the Crown with a foreign friendly power, meaning any state with which the Crown is not at war. Hence a contract requiring the commission of an offence by the law of the place of performance will not be enforced; see *De Wutz* v *Hendricks* (1824) 2 Bing 314; *Foster* v *Driscoll* [1929] 1 KB 470; *Regazzoni* v *Sethia* [1958] AC 301.

If a contract, whatever the proper law, conflicts with an English statute when the English courts are the forum, it will not be enforced to the extent of the conflict; see *The Hollandia* [1983] 1 AC 565.

The mere fact that a contract is illegal by the law of the place of its performance, which is a system different from the proper law and not English law, does not alone render the contract unenforceable. However, such a situation will usually render the enforcement of the contract against English public policy and, therefore, ineffective.

The effect of supervening illegality in the form of a change in the proper law of the contract or English law will operate as a frustrating event if an English court is seised of the action. When such supervening illegality takes the form of a change in the law of the place of performance, then it will only have a frustrating effect on the contract if it is such as to render the enforcement of the contract thereafter contrary to English public policy. The case law is, however, scarce and confused. The leading case is *Ralli Bros* v *Compania Naviera Sota y Aznar* [1920] 2 KB 287. Spanish shippers contracted with English charterers to carry goods from Calcutta to Barcelona. Freight was stated to be £50 per ton of goods delivered at Barcelona. After the voyage had begun, but before the ship reached Spain, a Spanish law was passed that freight must not exceed £10 per ton. The charterers agreed to pay the £10 but no more. The carriers brought an action in the English courts for the balance without success. The Court of Appeal seems to have treated the passing of the Spanish law as a frustrating event. Since English law was the proper law of the contract, the court had to apply the principle that supervening illegality frustrated the contract.

It seems, therefore, that if the proper law was that of a system which did not treat the passing of legislation making the performance of the contract a frustrating event, the English court would have awarded the carriers damages for the short payment. The fact that the performance of the contract is illegal by the law of the defendant's domicile is irrelevant provided that it is not the proper law of the contract or English law.

15.5.1   Ascertaining the Proper Law

The general approach of the courts to ascertaining the proper law of a contract has been stated by Lord Diplock in *Amin Rasheed* v *Kumiai Insurance Co.* [1984] 1 AC 50:

> English conflict rules accord to the parties to a contract a wide liberty to choose the law by which their contract is to be governed. So the first step is to examine the policy in order to see whether the parties have, by its express terms, or by necessary implication from the language used, evinced a common intention as to the system of law by reference to which their mutual rights and obligations under it are to be ascertained.

The parties are, therefore, free to select the law which should govern their contract, and if they do so by means of an express choice of law clause, the courts will uphold and keep the parties to their choice provided that it was made *bona fide* and is not illegal. The paucity of cases concerned with express choice of law cases shows that they are only rarely challenged, and such challenges rarely succeed.

The most authoritative case in which an express choice of law clause was upheld is an advice of the Privy Council; see *Vita Food Products* v *Unus Shipping* [1939] AC 277. A contract of carriage was concluded in Newfoundland by a bill of lading covering a shipment of a cargo of herrings from Newfoundland to New York. The Newfoundland Carriage of Goods by Sea Act 1932 provided that:

> ... every outward bill of lading must contain a statement that it is to have effect subject to the provisions of the Hague Rules as expressed in this Act.

The bills used did not contain the express statement required by the Act. They provided that the contracts were to be governed by English law. Since this was the case, the Rules did not apply because Newfoundland law was not the proper law and the shipment was not out of the UK — the requirement for the application of the Rules under English law. The carriers were exempted from liability both under the Newfoundland Act and the bills of lading.

It was argued that since the Newfoundland Act had not been complied with, the carriers could not take the benefit of the exceptions in that Act and in the Rules when, due to negligent navigation, the ship ran aground in Nova Scotia and the cargo was lost. The Privy Council heard the appeal from the courts of Nova Scotia. It held that the carriers obtained immunity from suit, not under the Newfoundland Act, but from the exemption in the bill of lading which was valid under English law. The decision is, therefore, a clear statement that the parties' choice is in general conclusive. Lord Wright said that, in such a case, there is no need for a connection between the transaction and the system of law chosen. He added, however, that the choice had to be *bona fide*, legal and not contrary to public policy.

How much scope there is for upsetting the choice of law clause for these reasons has been hotly debated but to little conclusive effect. One example where the express choice will be violated by the courts is where the Hague-Visby Rules are given statutory force. Lord Denning MR in *The Hollandia* [1983] 1 AC 565 said that:

> ... public policy demanded that in international trade all goods carried by sea should be subject to uniform Rules — they should not vary according to the country or place in which the dispute is tried out — therefore the Rules would apply whatever be the proper law of the contract.

This idea of party autonomy extends to the choosing of different proper laws for different elements of the contract, such as the creation on the one hand and performance of the contract on the other. However, in the absence of 'compelling and unusual circumstances' the courts are unwilling to uphold a choice applying different laws to different elements; see *Kahler* v *Midland Bank* [1950] AC 24.

If the express choice of law does not for some reason take effect, it does not follow that it serves no purpose. This is illustrated by *Compagnie Tunisienne* v *Compagnie d'Armement Maritime* [1971] AC 572. The charterparty in question had an English arbitration clause, but a choice of law clause in terms that the contract should be 'governed by the law of the flag of the vessel carrying the goods'. It contained another clause, which stated that the ship was to be 'governed or controlled or chartered by French ship-owners'. It seems, therefore, that the parties envisaged that ships flying French flags should be employed. In fact, shipments were made on a number of ships flying differing flags. The majority of the House of Lords held that the two clauses together pointed to a choice of French law.

The House of Lords considered what their decision would have been if the contract had not pointed to any particular law. Lords Morris and Diplock thought that if the express choice of law clause failed in its intended effect, it could be relied upon to show a negative intention that the parties did not intend the law of the place of arbitration — English law — to govern. Lords Dilhorne and Wilberforce thought that if the clause had failed it should be ignored. It would seem that the former view is more acceptable as it does less violence to the intentions of the parties as expressed in the contract.

Where there is no express choice of law, Lord Diplock stated in *Amin Rasheed*:

> ... if it is apparent from the terms of the contract itself that the parties intend it to be interpreted by a particular system of law their intention will prevail and the latter question as to the system of law with which, in the view of the court, the transaction to which the contract relates would, but for such intention of the parties, have had the closest and most real connection, does not arise.

Hence there is a distinction between a proper law which is inferred from the terms of the contract and one which is not. In the latter case, the proper law is taken as the system of law with which the transaction has its closest and most real connection. This distinction and the test in the latter part are not easy to apply in practice.

The inference of the choice of law in the absence of an express clause is made from the circumstances surrounding the contract itself — and not its working out. The following are some of the factors which have exercised the courts and are drawn from the case law:

(a)   If the parties have provided for an express jurisdiction or arbitration clause, there is a strong inference that they intended the law of the *situs* of the court or arbitrator to govern.

(b)   The language of the contract is generally treated as neutral, especially as English is the recognised language of commerce, and many contracts are in standard printed form. However, if the contract contains specialised legal terminology referable to a particular system of law, this might be persuasive; see *Whitworth Street Estates* v *James Miller* [1970] AC 583.

(c)   In *Whitworth Street Estates* the use of an English standard form document in the contract was used as an inference of English as the proper law. With the world-wide use of certain English standard form contracts, such as Lloyd's insurance policies, the propriety of such an inference must be in doubt (see *Compagnie Tunisienne* (above)).

Amin Rasheed (above) concerned a Liberian company resident in Dubai which had insured a vessel with Kuwaiti insurers. The policy used was a standard Lloyd's form, setting out part of the British Marine Insurance Act 1906. The policy was issued in Kuwait and provided for claims to be made and paid there. The currency used, however, was sterling. The Saudi authorities seized the ship on an allegation of smuggling. The insurers claimed on the policy. This was rejected so the assured issued proceedings in England. They sought to serve a writ on the insurers in Kuwait on the basis that the policy was by implication governed by English law. The majority of the Court of Appeal (Goff LJ dissenting) and the House of Lords unanimously held that the policy was so governed by English law. Lord Diplock, with whom the rest of their Lordships appear to have agreed, expressly said that this was not because the policy was in English. That was an irrelevancy. Such policies are used the world over. The crucial factor was that when the policy was issued, Kuwait had no indigenous law of marine insurance. The contract could only be worked out under the British Act as interpreted by the English courts.

(d)   The currency of payment is not usually crucial, though when in combination with the place of payment it may be an inference that the contract is to be governed by that system of law; see *The Assunzione* [1954] P 150.

(e)   Where one of the parties to the contract is a state or government the inference is that it intended to be governed by its own system of law; see *Bonython* v *Commonwealth of Australia* [1951] AC 201. However, this may be rebutted as in *R* v *International Trustee for the Protection of Bondholders AG* [1937] AC 500.

(f)   Where a particular term or clause in a contract is valid in the law of one country but not in another, and both are otherwise equally well connected with the contract, the courts may infer that the law in which the clause is effective was that intended by the parties to govern the contract; see *P & O* v *Shand* (1865) 3 Moo PC (NS) 272; *Sayers* v *International Drilling* [1971] 1 WLR 1176.

If at the end of this process described by Lord Diplock in *Amin Rasheed* no particular law stands out as that intended by the parties, the courts must impute the choice of law. The courts adopt a number of presumptions in relation to certain types of contracts, for instance, in contracts of insurance the law of the insurer's place of business will be imputed; in contracts concerning the running of a ship, the law of its flag will govern; contracts of agency will usually be governed by the law of the country where the principal carries on business, though any contracts made by the agent in that capacity will be governed by their own proper law. It must be stressed that these presumptions are the last resort, after the test running through express to implied to inferred choice of law has failed.

The parties' intention, or the system of law with which the contract has its closest and most real connection, must be determined at the time the contract is made, and subsequent events should be ignored. Similarly, the intention of the parties is to be ascertained at the time the contract is concluded and factors arising before and after should again be ignored.

15.5.2 The Rome Convention

The Rome Convention, incorporated more or less wholesale by the Contracts (Applicable Law) Act 1990, replaces English rules on the proper law of contract, affecting domestic and international contracts alike. It is subject to the authoritative interpretation of the Court of Justice of the European Communities. UK courts will now have to observe the convention when deciding conflicts between the laws of all foreign countries and between UK and foreign laws.

The primary rule is that the express choice of the parties to the contract, written into the contract, is to govern the contract. This continues the existing rule at common law (Article 3(1) Rome Convention).

If there is no choice of law made by the parties, the applicable law is that of the country with which the contract is most closely connected, which is presumed by Art. 4(2) Rome Convention as the law of the country of the party making the 'characteristic performance'. In a contract of sale, this will typically be the seller's country. This rule is more certain than the existing rules at common law, but rather surprisingly gives the manufacturer the upper hand over the consumer. However, where the contract is to be performed by a branch office, the law is to be that of the country in which the branch office is situated. This could cause considerable uncertainty where subsidiaries carry out the distribution of products manufactured by the principal company.

Article 4(4) provides that where the contract of carriage of goods contains no express choice of law, the general presumption in Art. 4(2) that the country with which a contract is most closely connected is that of the country of the party carrying out the characteristic performance does not apply. Instead, the contract is to be governed by the law of the country in which the carrier has its principal place of business provided that the goods are either loaded or discharged in that same country. Where this is not the case, existing conflicts of law rules on the issue of close connection will apply.

Where there is no characteristic performance, or where it cannot be determined, the presumptions in Art. 4 are not to be used if there is another country with which the contract is more closely connected. How this notion is to be applied in the absence of the presumptions is not explained.

Even where the parties have chosen a particular law to govern the contract, this will fail to disapply 'mandatory rules' of the country with which 'all the elements relevant to the situation at the time of the choice (of law) are connected' (Article 3(3) Rome Convention). Such mandatory rules would include any provisions from which contracts cannot derogate. An example of how this complicated provision works may be: an agreement made by a Japanese manufacturer for distribution in an EU member state will be subject to the EU competition rules, even if the parties have agreed that it should be governed by the law of a country which is not a member of the EU. In addition, Art. 7(2) Rome Convention safeguards application of mandatory rules of the country where the court is situated, irrespective of the law applicable to the contract.

The 1990 Act has disapplied Art. 7(1) of the Convention to cases being tried by the English courts. The parties to the contract must, nevertheless, be aware of the provision since disputes involving their contract may be tried in countries which *have* incorporated the article into their law. Article 7(1) permits the court seised to enforce the contract to apply mandatory rules of any state with which the contract has 'a close connection' if, under the law of that state, those laws must be applied to the contract in question. The court has a discretion which is to be exercised having regard to the nature and purpose of the particular laws in the other country, and to the consequences of the application or non-application of the laws. Again the Article is complicated.

Article 16 of the Convention provides that a rule of the law of any country otherwise applicable may be refused by the court seised to enforce the contract if it is manifestly incompatible with the court's public policy. The overriding force of public interest is nothing new. EU member state laws are bound to include the competition rules of the Treaty of Rome in their public policy. Consequently, where a member state is required to enforce a contract of which the chosen law is US law, the parties may find that any provisions of the contract which have the effect of dividing the common market along national boundaries are unenforceable. Other areas where this provision will be effective include penal and revenue laws.

The Convention has a number of articles dealing with particular types of contracts. Pertinent to issues of international trade is Art. 5 which protects consumers by ensuring that the mandatory rules of their country of residence apply in respect of purchases made at home from a foreign supplier's agent or on the strength of his local advertisement or direct offer, regardless of the chosen law, and even in respect of purchases made abroad where the shopping visit abroad was made at the invitation of the seller.

As has been mentioned above, the Convention applies special rules to contracts for the carriage of goods, different from those applying to other forms of commercial agreements. In addition, the Convention does not apply to all types of contracts in the commercial field. It excludes obligations which arise from the negotiable character of negotiable instruments which would include bills of exchange, cheques and promissory notes. Also excluded are arbitration agreements and agreements on the choice of court.

The Convention contains provisions relating to procedure and evidence. These, like much else in the Convention, are complicated. Article 1(2)(h) provides that the rules of the Convention do not apply to evidence and procedure except as provided for in Art. 14. Article 14 provides that the law governing the contract, as assessed under the rules of the Convention, is to determine the burden of proof in any contractual issues, where such law contains such rules. Consequently, where the contract contains no choice of law clause, but under the rule and presumption in Art. 4(1) and (2) the contract has its closest connection with UK law, a French court seised of the case would have to apply UK law on the presumptions and burden of proof. Nevertheless, the question whether any particular Act has legal effect or not is to be determined by the rules of evidence and proof provided for by the law of the court seised to try the case; see Art. 14(2). So, in this example, although UK law will determine which party must prove a particular issue, French law will determine what it is that that party must do to satisfy the court of the fact.

15.6 FREEZING (FORMERLY MAREVA) INJUNCTIONS

A freezing injunction is a form of interim relief designed to prevent the defendant to an existing action from defeating justice by transferring assets within the jurisdiction abroad or by concealing or dealing with them in this country.

In *Mareva Compania Naviera SA* v *International Bulk Carriers* [1975] 2 Lloyd's Rep 509 the Court of Appeal approved of the making of an injunction restraining the defendants from removing, or disposing out of the jurisdiction, money standing to the credit of the defendants at a London bank until trial or further order. The claimants were shipowners and the defendants were voyage charterers. The latter had received payment for the freight into the London account, but had not paid the hire due to the claimants.

Section 37, Supreme Court Act 1981 provides:

(1)   The High Court may by order (whether interlocutory or final) grant an injunction or a receiver in all cases in which it appears to the court to be just and convenient to do so.

(2)   Any such order may be made either unconditionally or on such terms as the court thinks just.

(3)   The power of the High Court under subsection (1) to grant an interlocutory injunction restraining a party to any proceedings from removing from the jurisdiction of the High Court, or otherwise dealing with assets located within the jurisdiction, shall be exercisable in cases where that party is, as well as in cases where he is not, domiciled resident or present within the jurisdiction.

Several points arise from the section. First, as with all injunctions, there must be an existing action between the parties to which the freezing injunction can attach and for which injunctive relief is available; see *The Siskina* [1979] AC 210; *The Veracruz* [1992] 1 Lloyd's Rep 353. The proceedings must be within the jurisdiction of the High Court either by virtue of the High Court being seised of the action or by virtue of the Civil Jurisdiction and Judgments Act 1982, ss. 24 and 25 extending to actions afoot in the courts of other EU member states; see *X* v *Y* [1990] 1 QB 220.

Secondly, the words 'otherwise dealing with' have been given a wide meaning and are not construed *eiusdem generis* with 'removing from the jurisdiction'. The freezing injunction, therefore, extends to cases where there is a danger that the assets will be dissipated *within* the jurisdiction as well as removed *out of* the jurisdiction; see *Z* v *A-Z and AA-LL* [1982] 2 QB 558.

The freezing injunction does not attach to the property as if it were a real right. It is a personal claim and, therefore, does not affect third parties who deal with the defendant's property in breach of the order. Third parties with notice and who deal with the assets in breach may do so in contempt of court.

Since the jurisdiction of the court is limited to those persons amenable to it, the freezing injunction cannot affect third parties outside the jurisdiction from dealing with the assets. This obviously reduces the effect of the protection. The courts have developed a form of order, which includes what is known as the 'Babanaft' proviso after the case in which it originated, which leaves scope for extra-jurisdictional effect without actually attempting to grant it. The proviso essentially restricts the relief to preventing the defendant and third parties who are within the jurisdiction and have notice of the order, or who are in another jurisdiction the courts of which have given effect to the English order from dealing with the assets in breach of its terms; see *Babanaft International* v *Bassatne* [1990] Ch 13; *Derby* v *Weldon* [1990] Ch 48. Of course, the order will affect the defendant personally whether he stays within or goes outside the jurisdiction.

A development has been the recognition by the English courts of jurisdiction to grant freezing injunctions relating to assets outside England and Wales; see *Derby* v *Weldon* [1990] Ch 48. In order to obtain a world-wide freezing injunction, the claimant must show that:

(a)   he has a good arguable case;

(b)   the English assets are insufficient to meet any likely judgment and there are assets abroad;

(c)   there is a real risk that those assets will be dissipated or secreted so as to render nugatory any judgment which the claimant might obtain.

Even if these criteria are met, a world-wide freezing injunction will only be granted in an exceptional case where the situation cries out as a matter of justice to the claimants for such an order; see *Babanaft*.

As already stated, the freezing injunction would not affect third parties outside the jurisdiction unless the courts of the state in which they are give effect to the order. All the *Babanaft* proviso does is to recognise that this may be the case.

15.6.1 The Guidelines For an Application For a Freezing Injunction

In *Third Chandris Corporation* v *Unimarine* [1979] QB 645 the Court of Appeal laid down guidelines for the courts to follow when an application for a freezing injunction is made. These have been modified as the practice has developed:

(a) First, the claimant must make full and frank disclosure of all matters in his knowledge which are material for the judge to know.

(b) The claimant should give the court particulars of his claim against the defendant. He should state the grounds for the claim and the amounts involved. This should be done in such a way as to give the judge some idea of the relative strengths and weaknesses of the case.

(c) The claimant should give some grounds for believing that the defendant has assets within the jurisdiction. If he is seeking a world-wide order, he must identify the assets in question.

(d) The claimant should give some grounds for believing that the defendant is about to deal with the assets in such a way as would defeat the ends of justice.

(e) The claimant should give an undertaking in damages in case he fails in his substantive claim or the injunction turns out to be unjustified. This undertaking need not always be supported by assets. A legally aided claimant may be granted an injunction even though his undertaking may be of little value; see *Allen* v *Jumbo Holdings* [1980] 1 WLR 1522. In an appropriate case, the undertaking in damages may be supported by security.

15.6.2 The Principles Governing the Freezing Injunction

The injunction takes effect immediately on its pronouncement and affects all the assets it is expressed to cover. The receipt by a bank of notice of a freezing injunction affecting a customer's account may override the customer's instructions and make it unlawful for the bank to honour the customer's cheques. The injunction over a bank account does not prevent the payment into that account of money due to the defendant, even where this results from state benefit to which the defendant is entitled; see *Bank Mellat* v *Kazmi* [1989] QB 541.

As a term of the injunction the claimant may be required to undertake to indemnify any third party against expenses incurred as a result of complying with the order. The injunction may extend to cover money held in a joint account if this is necessary for the protection of the claimant.

The Court of Appeal held that an English court can order the defendant to an action within the jurisdiction not to move assets held outside the jurisdiction. In *Derby* v *Weldon (No. 6)* [1990] 1 WLR 1139 the court heard an appeal from an interim hearing at which an order had been made requiring the defendants to the main trial, yet to be heard, not to transfer or cause to be transferred assets held outside the foreign jurisdiction in which they were presently being held. A further application, that the assets in question be transferred to the sole order of the receiver appointed to supervise the retention of the assets, was refused.

The Court of Appeal upheld the first order preventing removal of the assets outside the jurisdiction in which they were being held. The ability of the English court to make such an order stemmed from the personal nature of the freezing injunction. The order did not affect the assets themselves and, in that sense, could not affect third parties who had no notice of the order and were not amenable to the jurisdiction of the English courts. Instead, the order was personal to the defendant, and any other person who was a proper party to the final trial of the action. It was in this sense that the English court could control the disposition and retention of assets outside the jurisdiction.

The Court of Appeal further reversed the refusal of the lower court to order transfer of assets held abroad into the possession or control of the receiver, who was himself situated abroad. Since the person in control of the assets was the defendant, the court had power to require particular dispositions of the assets regardless of their situation. Similarly, the receiver was subject to the jurisdiction of the English courts and could, therefore, be required to take custody or control of the assets in question.

The case is a good example of the operation of the personal nature of the freezing injunction. It is important to note, however, that both Taylor LJ and Staughton LJ prefaced their ruling by emphasising that notwithstanding the personal nature of such orders, where the effect of the order is to control the disposition of assets outside the jurisdiction, such order should be made only with extreme caution — more so than that which normally obtains to the grant of freezing injunctions.

15.6.3   Dispute as to Ownership

The Court of Appeal has laid down guidelines on the effect of disputes about the ownership of assets within the scope of the injunction, in *SCF Finance* v *Masri* [1985] 1 WLR 876:

(a)   If the assets appear to belong to a third party they should be excluded from the order without evidence that they are the defendant's assets.

(b)   The mere assertion by the defendant that the assets belong to a third party need not be accepted without inquiry.

(c)   The court must attempt to do what is just and convenient between all concerned.

(d)   In a proper case the court may order that an issue be tried either before or after the main action concerning the ownership of assets.

15.6.4 Extent of freezing Injunctions and Limitations

The extent of each particular freezing injunction in question depends upon the facts of the case. In a proper case, the freezing injunction may be granted in extremely wide terms restraining the defendant from dealing in any way with any of his assets and may require him to disclose where those assets are; see the terms of the injunction in *PCW (Underwriting Agency)* v *Dixon* [1983] 2 All ER 158.

In *A* v *C* [1980] QB 965 it was held that the court has power to order the disclosure of documents and to seek further information as may seem appropriate for the purposes of ensuring that the freezing injunction is effective.

Within the context of the Civil Jurisdiction and Judgments Act 1982 and the Brussels Convention, an English court will assist another member state seised of an action to which the Convention applies, to order the disclosure of assets within the jurisdiction; see *The Republic of Haiti* v *Duvalier* [1990] 1 QB 202. However, the court will decline to make orders for such disclosure which would have far-reaching and undesirable consequences and which would be unnecessary for the operation of the freezing injunction. The term 'assets' has no specific limits and covers land, personal chattels and choses in action; see *CBS* v *Lambert* [1983] Ch 37. A freezing injunction may be granted both before and after judgment; see *Babanaft* (15.6). Some limitations on the scope of freezing injunctions are as follows:

(a)   A freezing injunction is not granted to improve the position of the claimants as against other creditors of the defendant by giving them priority over the assets subject to the order, nor to prevent him from paying debts as they fall due; see *PCW* v *Dixon*;

(b)   The freezing injunction should allow for drawings relating to the defendant's reasonable living expenses not exceeding a certain sum, which should take account of his particular circumstances. The defendant is at liberty to apply on notice for the injunction to be varied. Similarly, the defendant will be allowed to apply his assets for proper business expenses and in meeting the cost of the proceedings provided that such application is not in conflict with the underlying policy of the freezing injunction; see *Iraqi Ministry of Defence* v *Arcepey* [1981] 1 QB 65.

(c)   An innocent party may intervene to have the injunction varied as against the claimant, and if he succeeds the claimant will be bound to pay the third party's costs of the application; see *Project Development* v *KNK Securities* [1982] I WLR 1470.

A bank holding funds which become subject to a freezing injunction is entitled to a variation of the order to enable it to exercise any right of set-off it has in connection with facilities granted to the customer's account before it received notice of the injunction; see *The Theotokos* [1983] 1 WLR 1302.

The court will decline to grant a freezing injunction which will have the effect of substantially interfering with the business rights of a third party in order to secure the ultimate recovery of debts or damages from the defendant with which the third party is in no way concerned; see *Galaxia Maritime* v *Mineral Import-Export* [1982] 1 WLR 359.

16   Arbitration and Dispute Settlement

16.1 INTRODUCTION

As an alternative to litigation in court, businessmen and merchants often prefer to refer disputes to arbitration. Arbitration offers advantages to international concerns. The parties can choose their judge. The arbitrator can be chosen for his specialist knowledge in the field in question and, therefore, speed up the process. Arbitration need not be fitted into the strait-jacket of legal precedent and form. Finality is preferred to legal accuracy. It is easier to conduct arbitration in private than it is to hold court in private. Most jurisdictions recognise the decisions of properly conducted and formulated arbitrations. The enforcement of arbitral awards is, therefore, not at a significant disadvantage to judicial judgments.

There are disadvantages to the arbitration process too. The arbitrator has little power to make interim awards. The possibility of obtaining freezing injunctions or search orders is an incentive to move the court, particularly when fraud is suspected. Summary judgment under the Rules of Court is particularly useful in clear-cut cases.

16.2 TYPES OF ARBITRATION

There are essentially two distinctions to be made. The first looks at the forum of the arbitration and the dispute. The second looks at how the proceedings are to be governed.

16.2.1 Domestic and Non-domestic Arbitrations

This is a distinction created by statute. A domestic arbitration is defined by s. 85(2), Arbitration Act 1996 as follows:

> . . . an arbitration agreement . . . which does not provide expressly or by implication for arbitration in a State other than the United Kingdom and to which neither:

(a)   an individual who is a national of or habitually resident in any State other than the United Kingdom; nor

(b)   a body corporate which is incorporated in or whose central management and control is exercised in any State other than the United Kingdom;

is a party at the time the arbitration agreement is entered into.

All other arbitrations are non-domestic.

The distinction is important for two reasons. The power of the court to break an arbitration clause is wider in the case of a domestic arbitration. Secondly, the possibility for the parties to exclude judicial review of the arbitration is greater in non-domestic arbitrations.

16.2.2   Ad hoc and Institutional Arbitrations

The form which the arbitration takes depends upon the intentions of the parties as expressed in their arbitration agreement.

16.2.2.1   Ad hoc Arbitration

The parties themselves prescribe the mode of the appointment of the arbitrator. The arbitrator will control the proceedings himself, restricted only by the limits of the law.

16.2.2.2   Institutional Arbitration

The mode of the appointment of the arbitrator and the procedural rules will be governed by the form laid down by the particular trade or association in question. The institutional arbitration has advantages over the *ad hoc* form. The institution in question usually offers administrative assistance and there are fewer problems caused by technical hiccups. Among the most common international organisations concerned with commercial international arbitration are the International Chamber of Commerce and the United Nations Commission on International Trade.

16.3   THE LAW GOVERNING THE ARBITRATION

English law requires that the arbitration is conducted and makes its decision subject to the law of the forum and/or the law where the decision is to be enforced.

An arbitration agreement contained in a contract is regarded as a separate agreement capable of surviving the contract itself; see *Harbour Assurance Co. (UK) Ltd* v *Kansa General International Insurance Co. Ltd, The Times,* 1 March 1993. It is, therefore, possible for the arbitration to be governed by a law which is different from the proper law of the contract.

Without the support of the law, an arbitration agreement would be no agreement at all. There would be no legal relations between the parties, since they had no intention to contract in any way recognised by the judiciary. The award could not be enforced as it would not be recognised by the courts. Without enforcement the decision is irrelevant; see Megaw J in *Orion Compania Espanola de Seguros* v *Belford Maatschappij voor Algemene Verzekgringeen* [1962] 2 Lloyd's Rep 257.

The principle that the jurisdiction of the court cannot be ousted by agreement or otherwise applies to arbitrations as to any other contract.

16.4   THE JURISDICTION OF THE ARBITRATOR

The arbitrator must confine his inquiry and decision to the matters expressly referred to him by the parties. If one of the parties challenges the arbitrator's jurisdiction, then the court has the last word, as it would in the construction of any contractual document. The court may, therefore, be asked to consider what it is that the arbitrator had to decide, and alternatively, whether the dispute is one covered by the arbitration clause. It is doubtful whether the arbitrator can review his own jurisdiction and make a binding decision on the question.

16.5   HISTORY OF ARBITRATION LEGISLATION

16.5.1   Earlier Legislation: pre–1950

English legislation relating to arbitration dates back to the seventeenth century with the Arbitration Act 1698. Modern English arbitration law was created in the nineteenth century with the Civil Procedure Act 1833, the Common Law Procedure Act 1854 and the Arbitration Act 1889 (by which the courts were given power to enforce arbitration agreements and additional powers to support the arbitral process). The 1889 Act was amended by the Arbitration Act 1934 which enacted many of the recommendations contained in the Report of the MacKinnon Committee on the Law of Arbitration (1927 Cmnd. 2817). Mention should also be made of the Arbitration Act (Northern Ireland) 1937.

16.5.2   Era of Consolidation: 1950 onwards

The earlier legislation was consolidated in the Arbitration Act 1950 and that remained the principal arbitration statute prior to this Act. There was, in addition: the Arbitration Act 1975 which gave effect to the 1958 New York Convention on the Recognition of Foreign Arbitral Awards; the Arbitration (International Investment Disputes) Act 1966 which enacted the 1965 Washington Convention on the Settlement of Investment Disputes between Contracting States and Nationals of Other States; and the Arbitration Act 1979 which abolished the special case procedure and reduced the supervisory power of the English courts over commercial arbitrations (and enacted many of the recommendations contained in the Commercial Court Committee's Report on Arbitration, 1978, Cmnd 7284).

16.5.3   Weaknesses of Arbitration Acts 1950 to 1979

The Arbitration Acts of 1950, 1975 and 1979 were not, however, a comprehensive and exhaustive code of arbitration law and practice. For example, there were only a few statutory provisions on the powers of arbitrators and none whatsoever on the way in which a reference should be conducted. Therefore, it was necessary to refer to English case law not only for the interpretation of the Arbitration Acts but also for guidance on the numerous matters not governed by the legislation. It was generally considered that English arbitration law was not sufficiently accessible or comprehensible and did not meet the needs of modern users, especially those who were not lawyers or were lawyers from other jurisdictions.

16.5.4   Other Relevant Arbitration Acts

Before the Arbitration Act 1996, there were two further statutes of interest to commercial law and international trade. First is the Multilateral Investment Guarantee Agency Act 1988. Second is the Consumer Arbitration Agreements Act 1988. The Arbitration Act 1996 was to have a bearing on both of these Acts.

16.6   THE ARBITRATION ACT 1996

16.6.1   The Act and the Model Law

The Act restates in clearer terms the previous legislation on arbitration, codifies principles established by recent case law and improves the law, in order to increase the attractiveness and efficacy of arbitration as a method of dispute resolution and the attractiveness of London as a venue for international arbitration. The Act seeks 'to provide for the fair, speedy and cost effective resolution of disputes by an impartial tribunal' (Explanatory Memorandum, Arbitration Bill, House of Lords). The Act implements most of the recommendations of the Departmental Advisory Committee chaired by Savill LJ and reflects as far as possible the format and language of the UNCITRAL Model Law. The Act applies in England, Wales and Northern Ireland (but not in Scotland).

16.6.2   Philosophy of the Act

The Act is intended to be a comprehensive statute (but not an exhaustive code) which will more easily enable the lay arbitrator or foreign lawyer to find out how an arbitration under English law should be conducted. It contains a number of statements of general principle and should be read accordingly (s. 1). The object of arbitration under the Act is to obtain fair resolution of disputes by an impartial tribunal without delay or expense, to preserve party autonomy, and to minimise court interference in arbitration process. The general duty of the tribunal (s. 33) and the parties (s. 40) is aimed at ensuring that arbitrations are conducted fairly, economically and expeditiously. Thus, the Act defines the arbitrator's powers in common situations that might arise, reinforces the supremacy of the arbitration agreement and the notion of party autonomy, redefines the relationship between the courts and the arbitration process in favour of arbitration(s), and limits the role of the courts to those occasions when it is obvious that either the arbitral process needs assistance or that there has been or is likely to be a clear denial of justice. Finally, unlike in some jurisdictions (e.g. France), provisions for domestic and international arbitrations are contained in this one Act.

16.6.3   Confidentiality and Privacy

Subject to some exceptions, the Act contains the basic tenets of English arbitration law, i.e. confidentiality and privacy, which are often cited as two of the main advantages of arbitration over court proceedings. These principles are based on an implied contractual term which has been upheld; see *Esso/BHP* v *Plowman* (1955) 28 ALR 391 (a decision of the Arbitration Court); see also [1995] *Arbitration International* 2.34.

16.6.4   Consolidation

The Act provides that the parties may agree that five or more arbitral proceedings are to be consolidated or that current hearings must be held (s. 35).

16.6.5   Applicable Laws

Finally, when reading the Act, it is necessary to bear in mind that a number of different laws may apply or be relevant to any arbitration, namely:

(a)   the governing (or proper) law of the underlying agreement;
(b)   the governing (or proper) law of the arbitration agreement;
(c)   the procedural (or curial or adjectival) law(s) of the arbitration; and
(d)   the laws in jurisdictions other than the seat of the arbitration which give certain powers to the courts to support foreign arbitrations (e.g. to order injunctive relief or to enforce an award).

The provisions of this Act fall within categories (c) and (d) but some sections refer to (a) and (b).

The parties are free to agree the procedural law of the arbitration (category (c)) which may include the rules of one of the arbitral institutions (e.g. LCIA) or *ad hoc* rules (e.g. UNCITRAL Rules) or even the procedural law of another jurisdiction, but such agreement of the parties is always subject to the mandatory arbitration law of the seat of the arbitration (which is set out in this Act in s. 4(1) and Schedule 1).

16.6.6 Repeals

The Act repeals the following arbitration legislation to the extent indicated:

(a) the whole of the Arbitration Act (Northern Ireland) 1937;

(b) the whole of Part I and s. 42(3) of the Arbitration Act 1950;

(c) the whole of the Arbitration Act 1975;

(d) the whole of the Arbitration Act 1979;

(e) section 8(3) of the Multilateral Investment Guarantee Agency Act 1988; and

(f) the whole of the Consumer Arbitration Agreement Act 1988.

16.6.7 Amendments

The Arbitration Act 1996 effects the following amendments:

(a) For section 6 of the Multilateral Guarantee Agency Act 1988 (application of Arbitration Act) the 1996 Act substitutes:

Application of Arbitration Act

6. (1) The Lord Chancellor may by order made by statutory instrument direct that any of the provisions of sections 36 and 38 to 44 of the Arbitration Act 1996 (provisions in relation to the conduct of the arbitral proceedings, &c.) apply, with such modifications or exceptions as are specified in the order, to such arbitration proceedings pursuant to Annex II to the Convention as are specified in the order.

(2) Except as provided by an order under subsection (1) above, no provision of Part I of the Arbitration Act 1996 other than section 9 (stay of legal proceedings) applies to any such proceedings.

(b) In the Arbitration (International Investment Disputes) Act 1996, for section 3 (application to Arbitration Act 1950 and other enactments) the 1996 Act substitutes:

Application of provisions of Arbitration Act 1996

3. (1) The Lord Chancellor may by order direct that any of the provisions contained in sections 36 and 38 to 44 of the Arbitration Act 1996 (provisions concerning the conduct of arbitral proceedings, &c.) shall apply to such proceedings pursuant to the Convention as are specified in the order with or without any modifications or exceptions specified in the order.

(2) Subject to subsection (1), the Arbitration Act 1996 shall not apply to proceedings pursuant to the Convention, but this subsection shall not be taken as affecting section 9 of the Act (stay of legal proceedings in respect of matter subject to arbitration).

(3) An order made under this section—

(a) may be varied or revoked by a subsequent order so made, and

(b) shall be contained in a statutory instrument.

16.6.8   Some details of the Act

The Arbitration Act 1996 restates most of the previous legislation but also adds to it by, for example, giving the arbitrator the power to limit the amount of costs recoverable. Also, for the first time, the legislation provides for the immunity of the arbitrator. An arbitrator will not be liable for anything done or omitted in the discharge of his/her functions as an arbitrator unless he or she acted in bad faith: s. 29.

The Act applies to all written agreements to submit a dispute to arbitration and to actual submission after the dispute has been referred provided that this is evidenced in writing.

In the absence of express provision, the Acts imply a number of requirements into the arbitration agreement. These include that the parties should submit themselves to examination on oath by the arbitrator; that the witnesses to be called should give their testimony on oath; that the award made by the arbitrator should be binding and final; that the arbitrator should have the same power as the court to award specific performance of a contract; that the arbitrator should have the power to make an interim award; that the arbitrator should have the discretion as to the award of costs. With regard to costs, the Act allows the arbitrator to direct that costs recoverable are to be limited to a certain amount: s. 65.

The Act requires the arbitrator to give his/her reasons unless the parties have agreed otherwise: s. 52(4). If the reasons given are insufficient for a court to make a ruling under law, the court may order the arbitrator to supply sufficient reasons: s. 70(4). The content of the 'reasoned award' should include the arbitrator's view on the evidence of what did or did not happen; it should explain in the light of what happened how he or she reached the decision and what the decision was. The arbitrator is not expected to analyse the law or any authorities; see Donaldson LJ in *Westzucker GmbH* v *Bunge GmbH* [1981] Com LR 179; Lord Diplock in *Antaios Companie Naviera* v *Salen Referierna AB* [1984] 3 WLR 592.

If the arbitration is within the EU and, therefore, subject to the Treaty of Rome, the possibility of a reference to the European Court of Justice may arise. The arbitrator does not have *locus standi* to make such a reference under Art. 177 of the Treaty of Rome. He is not a national 'court or tribunal' deriving its authority from a member state. Where such a reference is necessary, an appeal has to be brought under the 1996 Act from the award to the High Court and the judge may then make the reference to the European Court.

16.7   STAY OF PROCEEDINGS

Despite the presence of an arbitration agreement in a contract, sometimes one of the parties to a contract will commence proceedings in court. The party who wishes to go to arbitration will then apply for a stay of proceedings. If the arbitration agreement is a domestic agreement, s. 86 of the 1996 Act provides that:

the court shall grant a stay unless satisfied—

(a)   that the arbitration agreement is null and void, inoperative, or incapable of being performed, or

(b)   that there are other sufficient grounds for not requiring the parties to abide by the arbitration agreement.

'Other sufficient grounds' may include the fact that the applicant '. . . is or was at any material time not ready and willing to do all things necessary for the proper conduct of the arbitration': s. 86(3).

If the arbitration agreement is a non-domestic agreement, s. 9(4) provides that the court must grant a stay 'unless satisfied that the arbitration is null and void, inoperative or incapable of being performed'. The 1996 Act does not, therefore, provide for the court to take account of 'other sufficient grounds' if the arbitration agreement is non-domestic.

16.8   ENFORCEMENT OF THE AWARD

Under s. 66 of the 1996 Act, and by leave of the court, an award under an arbitration agreement may be enforced in the same manner as a judgment or order of court.

If the arbitration agreement falls outside the Act, for instance, if it was not reduced to or evidenced in writing, an award does not merge with the original cause of action and is not, therefore, capable of being made a judgment or order of court. Fresh proceedings would have to be commenced to enforce the agreement comprising the award.

'Convention awards', i.e. those made in a contracting state to the New York Convention, may be enforced in the same manner as domestic awards. The issue as to what amounts to a 'Convention Award' was the subject of a ruling of the House of Lords in the case of *Hiscox* v *Outhwaite* [1992] 2 Lloyd's Rep 435. Briefly, a dispute arose on the reinsurance contract issued by a Lloyd's syndicate. An arbitration clause provided for its settlement in London and that English law would apply. The arbitration took place in stages leading to an award which, for some reason, was signed in Paris. The issue arose (1) as to whether there was an 'award' within the New York Arbitration Convention 1958; and (2) whether it was subject to English or French law. It was held (by Lord Oliver at pp. 439, 441 and 442) that an arbitration award is perfected in that place where the arbitrator signs it, irrespective of where the arbitration took place. If the award is signed in a country party to the New York Arbitration Convention 1958, thus being enforceable as a Convention award under ss. 3, 5 and 7, Arbitration Act 1975, the English court can, nevertheless, exercise its supervisory jurisdiction to hear an appeal from the award if it was made under English law.

However, the 1996 Act provides that where the start of arbitration is in England and Wales or Northern Ireland, any award is to be treated as made there, regardless of where it was signed: s. 53. If, on the other hand, the award is in fact a Convention award, it is enforceable under s. 101 of the 1996 Act.

16.8.1 Challenging the Award

A party to the arbitral proceedings may apply to the court to challenge the award because the tribunal did not have substantive jurisdiction (s. 67), or there has been some serious irregularity in the proceedings (s. 68). The serious irregularity in the proceedings must cause substantial injustice to the applicant.

16.8.2 On Leave to Appeal against an Arbitration Award

Although an arbitration award is intended to be final and binding, an appeal lies to the court on a point of law. An appeal may be made with the agreement of all the parties to the proceedings or with the leave of the court: s. 69(2), Arbitration Act 1996. Under s. 69(3) the court will only grant leave of appeal if satisfied:

(a)   that the determination of the question will substantively affect the rights of one or more of the parties,
(b)   that the question is one which the tribunal was asked to determine,
(c)   that, on the basis of the findings of fact in the award—
   (i)   the decision of the tribunal on the question is obviously wrong, or
   (ii)   the question is one of general public importance and the decision of the tribunal is at least open to serious doubt, and
(d)   that, despite the agreement of the parties to resolve the matter by arbitration, it is just and proper in all the circumstances for the court to determine the question.

On appeal the court may confirm the award, vary the award, set aside the award or send the award back to the tribunal for reconsideration: s. 69(7). A further appeal may lie, with leave of the court, to the Court of Appeal. In this case, the question must be one of general importance or one which 'for some other special reason should be considered by the Court of Appeal': s. 69(8).

16.8.3 On Exercise of Discretion by Arbitrator

An arbitrator's decision not to exercise his discretion to allow a claim to proceed notwithstanding the failure to observe time limits, constituted an 'arbitration award' and was, therefore, appealable; see *Cargill Srl v P Kadinopoulos SA* [1992] 1 Lloyd's Rep 1 concerning a contract for the sale of wheat f.o.b. which incorporated the GAFTA arbitration rules.

Under s. 12(2) the court will make an order for an extension of the time limit if any available arbitral process for obtaining an extension of time has been exhausted and the court is satisfied:

(a)   that the circumstances are such as were outside the reasonable contempla-tion of the parties when they agreed the provision in question, and that it would be just to extend the time, or (b)　that the conduct of one party makes it unjust to hold the other party to the strict term of the provision in question.

FURTHER READING FOR PART VI

Ademuni-Odeke, 'The EC Conflict of Laws Regime for Insurance Contracts', *Tolley's Professional Negligence*, 1996, 12(1), 7–14.

Cato, D.M., *Arbitration Practice and Procedure*, 2nd edn, Colchester: LLP, 1997.

Cheshire and North: Private International Law, 13th edn, London: Butterworths, 1999.

Dicey and Morris, *Conflict of Laws,* 13th edn, London: Sweet & Maxwell, 1999.

Gaja, G., *International Commercial Arbitration*, 6 vols, New York: Oceana, 1994.

Giuliano and Lagande, 'Report on the Rome Convention', *Official Journal of the European Communities*, 31 October 1990.

Harris, B., Planterose, R. and Tecks, J., *Arbitration Act 1996*, Oxford: Blackwell, 1996.

Hunter, M., Marriott, A. and Veeder, V.V. (eds.) *The Internationalisation of International Arbitration*, The LCIA Centenary Conference, London: Graham & Trotman/Martinus Nijhoff, 1995.

Johnson, D.K., *International Commodity Arbitration*, London: LLP, 1991.

Kavaas, I.I. and Liivak, A., *UNCITRAL Model Law of Commercial International Arbitration*, 1985.

Lee, E., *Encyclopaedia of Arbitration Law*, London: LLP, 1991.

Merkin, R., *Arbitration Act 1996*, London: LLP, 1996.

Sanders, P., *International Handbook of Commercial Arbitration*, 4 vols, The Hague: Kluwer, 1990.

Sornarajah, M., *International Commercial Arbitration*, London: Financial Times, 1983.

Tweeddale, A. and Tweeddale, K., *A Practical Approach to Arbitration Law*, London: Blackstone Press, 1999.

Index